Iridescent Kuwait

Laura Hindelang

IRIDESCENT KUWAIT

Petro-Modernity and Urban Visual Culture since the Mid-Twentieth Century

DE GRUYTER

The open access publication of this book has been published with the support of the Swiss National Science Foundation.

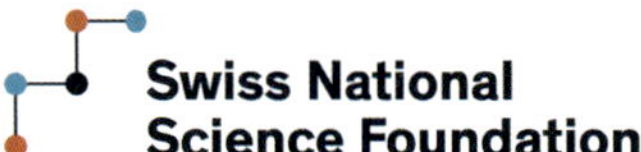

Library of Congress Control Number: 2021949433

Bibliographic information published by the Deutsche Nationalbibliothek
The Deutsche Nationalbibliothek lists this publication in the Deutsche Nationalbibliografie; detailed bibliographic data are available on the Internet at http://dnb.dnb.de.

ISBN 978-3-11-071466-1
e-ISBN (PDF) 978-3-11-071473-9
DOI https://doi.org/10.1515/9783110714739

ORCID Laura Hindelang: https://orcid.org/0000-0002-9195-9190

Copyediting: Markus Fiebig, Aaron Bogart
Coverillustration: Image from the *al-ʻArabī* magazine image archive, Kuwait.
Cover: Kerstin Protz, De Gruyter
Typesetting: Rüdiger Kern, Berlin
Printing and binding: Beltz Grafische Betriebe GmbH, Bad Langensalza

www.degruyter.com

TABLE OF CONTENTS

ACKNOWLEDGMENTS

Realizing that this book, like most books, will not be written in one day, but that it is the daily endurance in writing that will enable me to complete it, turned the world around. Realizing and cherishing that I am not alone on this research and writing journey, continues to make all the difference to me.

Writing a book takes time, for which my journey has entailed several phases and institutions that have made this endeavor possible and that have generously supported my work. I have been blessed with supervisors and research environments that have not restricted me in my choice of topics, even if working on petro-cultures and petro-aesthetics, ecological questions in post-oil environments, and on mid-twentieth century visual culture in the Middle East and North Africa (MENA) region, more specifically in the Gulf region, have not been classical themes in history of art and architecture departments in Germany and Switzerland.

I am thankful for the generous funding of the Swiss National Science Foundation (SNSF) to publish this book simultaneously in open access and print. Unrestricted access to the results of academic research is crucial in my opinion.

I would like to thank Bernd Nicolai for his ongoing trust and support in my choice of topics as well as for the freedom to focus on completing this book project during my employment at the University of Bern (2019–21).

I am immensely indebted to the Berlin Graduate School Muslim Cultures and Societies (BGSMCS) at Freie Universität Berlin that granted me a doctoral fellowship (2016–19). The generous institutional and financial support allowed me to conceptualize this research project, conduct archival research and fieldwork, and write much of the first draft. I particularly thank Bettina Gräf, Jutta Schmidbauer, and Lars Ostermeier for open doors, quick responses, and continuous encouragement. Eye-opening to me were several workshops on academic writing and positive mindfulness conducted by Katja Günther and Ingrid Scherübl—thank you for your energy! The graduate school's transdisciplinary academic culture and one of mutual support and encouragement within my 2016 cohort and among many wonderful colleagues made it exciting, fun, and so much easier to grasp what becoming an academic could possibly mean. I am especially grateful for the respectful, inspirational, and open-minded guidance I received from my two supervisors Wendy Shaw and Ulrike Freitag. Wendy, your openness for unusual objects of study, your remarkable theoretical repertoire and conceptual mindset, and your encouragement to develop a confident writing voice have proven invaluable to me. Ulrike, I have profited

https://doi.org/10.1515/9783110714739-002

immensely from your steady dedication to this project and your seasoned experience with the Arabian Peninsula and its archival sources, for which I am truly grateful.

Initially, the first step of this research project was laid during my membership in the Holy Spaces in Modernity (2014–16) research project, directed by Anna Minta at the University of Zurich and funded by the Swiss National Science Foundation. I greatly benefitted from the scientific, institutional, and financial support I received during my time there, for which I am thankful.

I am also indebted to the organizers and participants of the conferences and workshops I participated in throughout the years and that have shaped my understanding of petroleum, Kuwait and the region, visual studies, architectural history, and many more fields. Two of these events had a lasting impact on my research: "The Global Petroleumscape" at the Technical University Delft, May 2017, organized by Carola Hein, and "The Life Worlds of Middle Eastern Oil" at NYU Abu Dhabi, March 2019, organized by Nelida Fuccaro and Mandana Limbert.

Two extensive field trips to Kuwait in early 2016 and early 2018 helped to form my comprehension of the vibrant city-state on-site, by exploring highways, abandoned plots, small alleyways, main avenues, and the desert on foot and by car. The staff at the National Library of Kuwait, Abdullah al-Ghunaim and the team at the Center for Research and Studies on Kuwait, and Jussif Al-Khanderi at the Kuwait Oil Company Documentation Center in Ahmadi were extremely helpful and generously granted me access to historical sources on Kuwait. Due to Kuwait's status as a former British quasi-protectorate, several British archives host important collections of historical sources and images and I thank the following people and institutions, who kindly assisted me: Nicola Davies, librarian at the Royal Philatelic Society London; Joanne Burman at the BP Archive, University of Warwick; Debbie Usher, archivist at the Middle East Centre Archive at St Antony's College, Oxford; Rachel Chambers, assistant curator at the Victoria and Albert Museum London; the knowledgeable staff at the British Library, at the library and archives of the Royal Society of British Architects, and at the National Archives, Kew Gardens. Moreover, I would like to thank Ulrike Hammes in Cologne, who generously opened the family archive.

I am deeply grateful to the following people in Kuwait who were very generous with their time to respond to my questions and share their memories and viewpoints with me: Ziad Rajab of the Tareq Rajab Museum; the photographers Gustavo Ferrari, Sulayman Haydar, Stephanie McGehee, and Uwe Wruck; photo studio owner Mohammad J. J. Boushahri; Khaled A. Al Najdi, Asseel Al-Ragam and Rosalie McCrea from the University of Kuwait; Farah Al-Nakib, then at the American University of Kuwait; collector and researcher Hasan Ashkanani; Phoebe Al-Salem, Sharifa Alshalfan, Sabah Al-Rayes, Ricardo Camacho, and Roberto Fabbri, architects and urban planners that shape(d) the past and present of Kuwait's built environment; Zahra Ali Baba from the Kuwait National Council of Culture, Arts and Letters; Ahmad M. Alazemi and Noura Al-Deffeeri from the Ministry of Electricity and Water; Mark Makhoul, author of the legendary blog *248am*;

and Sulaiman Al-Askari as well as Ibrahim Farghali and the staff at *al-ʿArabī* magazine and archives.

I am particularly indebted to Sulayman Haydar and Uwe Wruck for sharing their photographic collections and knowledge of the history of photography in Kuwait with me. I thank the visual artists Mohammed Al Kouh, Monira Al Qadiri, Aseel AlYaqoub, Alia Farid, and Mohammad Sharaf for sitting down and discussing their artistic work and thoughts on Kuwait's past and present visual culture with me. A big thank-you goes to the team of Madeenah for their fantastic work and research-based walking tours, especially to Deema Alghunaim for eye-opening site visits and thought-provoking conversations. I am greatly indebted to the Kuwait Philatelic & Numismatic Society, in particular Adel H. Abdulrazzaq, Mohammad Abdul Hadi Jamal, Farjam Khajehee, and Khaled Alabdulmughni, for sharing their knowledge and opening their stamp collections to me. Thank you, Jana Duman and Michael Holland, for kindly hosting me during my second field trip. Most importantly, thank you to Haya Alissa for making me feel at home and among friends when I first came to Kuwait. Thank you for your friendship, the delicious food, and your wonderful sense of humor. Thank you also to Maryam (Mimi) Al Nusif, Dalal Al Tawheed, Eve, and many other wonderful people for your hospitality, your kindness, and the fun times we have shared together.

This beautiful and carefully crafted publication would not have been possible without the dedicated team at De Gruyter, especially Katja Richter and Luzie Diekmann.

Finally, my deep gratitude goes to: Markus Fiebig for his excellent proofreading of an earlier draft of this book; Florian Abe, Galina Behn, Philip Geisler, and Theresa Jeroch for the informal, highly informed, and truly inspirational colloquium sessions I have had the pleasure to participate in with you; for reading earlier chapter drafts, fruitful discussions and feedback on the concept at different stages in the project I thank Amelie Buchinger, Francine Giese, Bettina Gräf, Florin Gstöhl, Sarah Jurkiewicz, Katharina Lange, Birte Kleine-Benne, Alina Kokoschka, Birgit Krawietz, and Ismene Wyss; my parents and of course Lukas, for being there, near and far, reminding me of life beyond the desk.

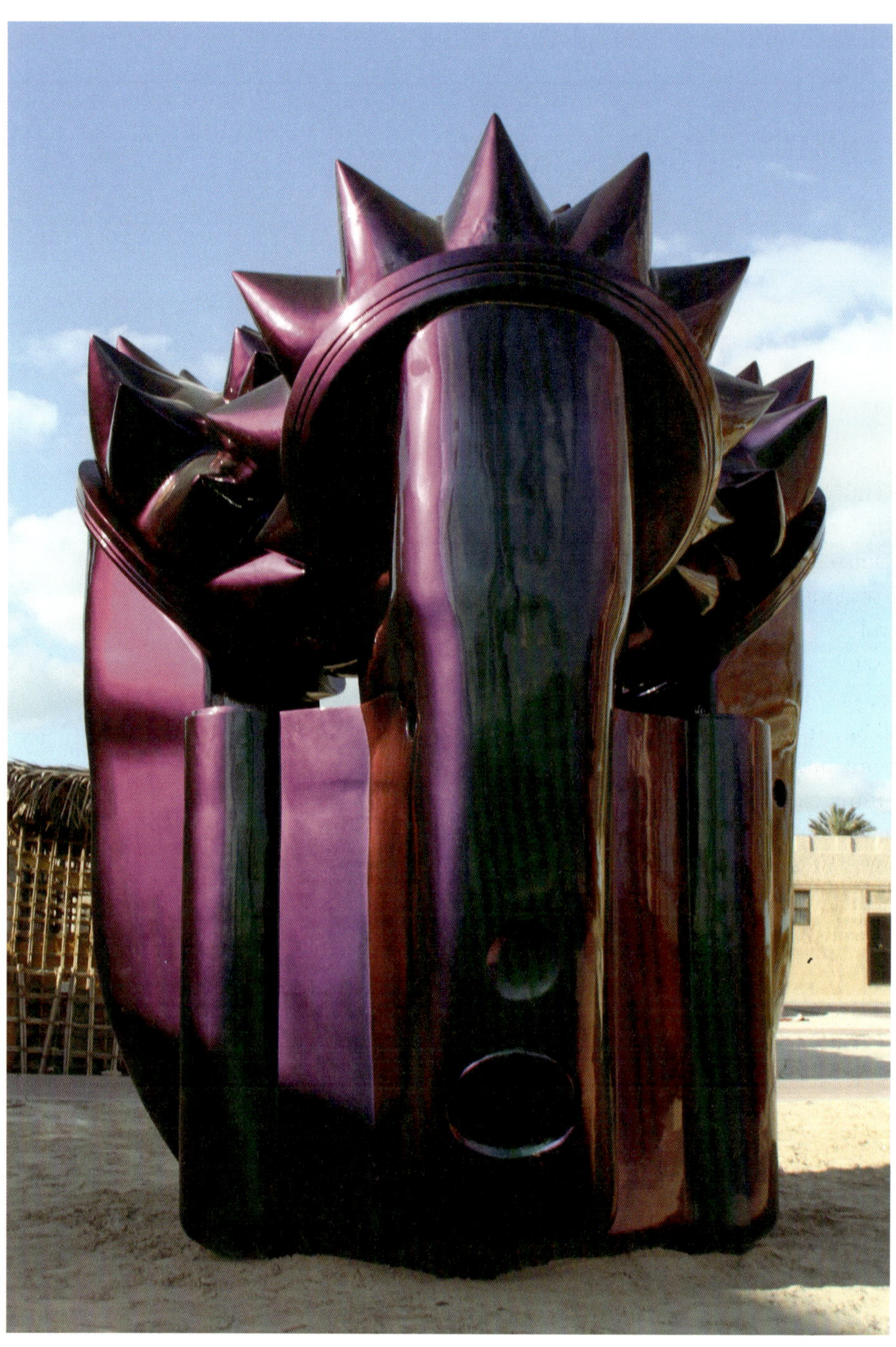

1.1 Monira Al Qadiri, *Alien Technology*, 2014–19. Fiberglass sculpture, automotive paint, 3 × 2.5 meters. Installation view at Shindagha Heritage Village, Dubai, 2014.

1. AN IRIDESCENT APPROACH TO PETROLEUM AND MODERNITY

> It isn't the oil that makes us happy, but the comfortable automobile. In other words, it's a little like food: we love the roast beef but don't want to think about the slaughter house.[1]

A giant sculpture by Kuwaiti artist Monira Al Qadiri lies stranded on the sandy shores of the Gulf like a meteorite from an unknown future in the photograph (fig. 1.1). It has the form of a blown-up drill bit and sits within the premises of the Shindagha Heritage Village in Dubai. Made of fiberglass and then carefully coated with layers of iridescent varnish, the sculpture's smooth surface shimmers mysteriously, oscillating between orange and petrol-blue depending on the angle of the light and the spectator's position in relation to the sculpture. From the rounded body reclining on the sand, the voluminous sculpture's three narrowly connected arms stretch into the air. Each arm ends in a revolving, spiky drill bit. The tri-cone drill bit displays its flower heads to the sky like a thistle. From the ground, however, only the sharply pointed crowns are visible.

Immersed in an alienating interplay of blowing-up, decontextualization, and color change, Al Qadiri's sculpture *Alien Technology* alludes to the strange shapes of some of the most vital technical components of oil production. Despite the crucial importance of drill bits, which are used to bore holes (wellbores) into the Earth's crust for the extraction of petroleum, such technical objects remain unfamiliar and often hidden from view due to the fact that oil companies carefully control access to their operations. The title of the artwork also refers to the fact that, until their nationalization, the extractive industries in the Gulf were initiated and run by foreign companies and governments. The artwork's futuristic aesthetic is suggestive of the alien(ating) nature of the built environment of the Gulf cities (and elsewhere) as a consequence of petro-capitalism and the accelerated building booms it spawned. Most importantly, the artwork reflects the acknowledged challenges of petroleum's (in)visibility, its fluctuating aesthetic that facilitates but also disguises its material omnipresence. In this way, the sculpture investigates the visual and material complexity of petro-modernity through the phenomenon of iridescence.

[1] André Küttel, "50'300'000'000'000'000'000 Joule," in *Luca Zanier: Power Book*. ed. Luca Zanier (Bern: Benteli, 2012), 7.

https://doi.org/10.1515/9783110714739-003

Iridescence is the visual effect of a lustrous rainbowlike color play caused by light being reflected at different angles depending on the (changing) angle of view and of illumination. The effect is achieved by light waves reflecting from two or more semi-transparent surfaces and can be seen in soap bubbles, mother-of-pearl, and oil dispersed in water. Iridescence is not a color but a condition, a condition that is intrinsic to petroleum and pearls, two elements that have played a crucial role in the history of the Gulf. In many ways, pearling is the iridescent forerunner of petroleum extraction, as its economy thrived on cycles of boom and bust and on the luring attractiveness of the pearlescent export product. Pearling too is serendipitous. The average ratio of finding pearls was "one pearl to a thousand oysters" and yet many hoped for the one big pearl that would make the boat crew rich.[2] Characteristic of the pearls claimed in the Persian Gulf was their spectrum of colors, to be "of all colors—white, black, gray, green, yellow, gold, and pink."[3] And luster, their iridescent sheen, was an important criterion for establishing the Gulf pearls' quality and value, besides their shape, size, and weight.[4] Obviously, iridescence is not just a color spectrum but conditional to becoming a pearl.

Iridescence is reflective of the way in which petro-modernity can enchant, seduce, and haunt us. Iridescence is a fleeting sensation that charms affectionately while it lasts and brings melancholic darkness once it vanishes. It appears as overwhelmingly beautiful, attractive, and alluring; humans go to great lengths (or rather depths) to find and extract it. Yet, iridescence is a fluctuating phenomenon that cannot be made permanent. Because it depends on the angle of the light and the position of the viewer, it is in a way as short-lived as oil. As *Alien Technology* demonstrates, the viewer is not simply a bystander but an intrinsic part of the experience, because the object's perfectly polished surface presents a mirror image of the approaching viewer back to them against the background of the surrounding environment. The sculpture's glossy sheen can thereby provoke self-reflection about one's own understanding and affectedness from petro-modernity's impact as both cure and poison, one's own position within the aesthetics, consumptive habits, and ecological liminalities of petro-modernity.

Scientific estimations of global oil and natural gas deposits project various deadlines for peak oil (the final climax of oil production before its rapid demise) and the subsequent *grande finale* of fossil fuels.[5] As petroleum is not renewable, petroleum extraction will inevitably lead to an unimaginable yet total end point that leaves us with destroyed

[2] Harold R. P. Dickson, *The Arab of the Desert: A Glimpse into Badawin Life in Kuwait and Saudi Arabia*, 4th ed. (London: George Allen & Unwin, [1949] 1967), 491. A decade later, Bowen states that "less than one-third of the oysters yield pearls and these are mostly 'seed pearls,' those very small irregularly-shaped pearls which might well be called 'pearl dust.'" Richard L. Bowen, "The Pearl Fisheries of the Persian Gulf," *Middle East Journal* 5, no. 2 (1951): 175.

[3] Bowen, "The Pearl Fisheries of the Persian Gulf," 162.

[4] See ibid., 161–62.

[5] Scholars have emphasized that the inaccurate predictions and statistics of peak oil, of oil production rates, and of worldwide oil reserves is both startling and characteristic of the oil industry. See Hannah Appel,

landscapes and unsatisfiable habits of consumption and will most likely herald the end of the world as we know it today. Petroleum has been the single most important material of the Anthropocene. It is currently a prime source of energy used by humans and the most versatile raw material: in its various permutations it is found in almost every consumer good, in every trash heap, and, increasingly, as implants and microplastics, in our bodies, too.[6] Therefore, as many scholars argue, it is almost impossible to imagine what a world "after oil" could possibly look like.

For the Gulf states, this uncertain future perspective also stimulates haunting scenarios of the region without oil *revenues*. Because current standards of living are not sustainable without oil as energy, income, and raw material, extreme future imaginaries sometimes depict the currently sky-rocketing and sky-rising Gulf capitals as re-sinking, disappearing into the sand, following petroleum's path of extraction in reverse.[7] In addition, as energy humanist Andreas Malm argues, the Persian Gulf will at some point have some of the most unbearable climatic conditions on the planet.[8] A tragic irony lies in the prediction that "fossil fuels from the Gulf are poured on fires across the globe and then return, via the concentration of CO_2 in the atmosphere, to haunt the area with a particularly stark form of the general predicament [global warming]."[9] In light of this dystopian boomerang effect, at a time when oil prices are dropping and people are rethinking fossil fuel industries and energy consumption due to increasingly rapid climate change, it is not surprising that academics and artists from the Gulf and elsewhere are reassessing the region's recent past, a past that has been both swimming and drowning in petroleum.

The almost unimaginable variety of petroleum-derived products and the almost total petro-infiltration of not just the Gulf but of our world in general make it very challenging to re-extract—as a cultural analysis—petroleum from our common and often comfortable ways of living. Petroleum gives way to a complex regime of (in)visibility because it is somehow everywhere and in everything, but its synthetization redirects our experience and knowledge of petroleum via other materials, forms of energy, infrastructure, and images. It becomes especially challenging to analyze petroleum's visuality and aesthetics,

Arthur Mason, and Michael Watts, "Oil Talk: Introduction," in *Subterranean Estates: Life Worlds of Oil and Gas*, ed. Hannah Appel, Arthur Mason, and Michael Watts (Ithaca: Cornell University Press, 2015), 5–9.

[6] Damian Carrington, "Microplastics Revealed in the Placentas of Unborn Babies," *The Guardian*, December 22, 2020, accessed January 27, 2021, https://www.theguardian.com/environment/2020/dec/22/microplastics-revealed-in-placentas-unborn-babies.

[7] This also echoes the fate of oil towns such as Pithole, Pennsylvania, an oil boomtown in the mid-1860s that was abandoned as early as 1868. Today it is a ghost town.

[8] Andreas Malm, "'This Is the Hell That I Have Heard of': Some Dialectical Images in Fossil Fuel Fiction," *Forum for Modern Language Studies* 53, no. 2 (2017): 123. Malm bases his prediction on two climate research results: Jeremy S. Pal and Elfatih A. B. Eltahir, "Future Temperature in Southwest Asia Projected to Exceed a Threshold for Human Adaptability," *Nature Climate Change* 6, no. 2 (2016) and J. Lelieveld et al., "Strongly Increasing Heat Extremes in the Middle East and North Africa (MENA) in the 21st Century," *Climatic Change* 137, no. 1/2 (2016).

[9] Ibid., 123.

its visual culture and the ways in which this has shaped how we experience the world through images and media that are fossil energy-based or materially constituted from petroleum. When we see plastic (or the visual representation of a plastic object), for example, we do not see petroleum as crude oil—we see plastic. Yet plastic has a complex history of its own. It is also a composite, extremely versatile material that has been pivotal for the development of visual technologies such as film and photography; it has even given way to a new plastic-like aesthetic of the world. But despite its omnipresence, the fact that plastic originates from petroleum is acknowledged and experienced only peripherally, if at all.

Over the recent years, studies on the social and cultural implications of oil have established a certain range of representative phenomena of oil through which to read or analytically assess how the substance has infiltrated ways of living and ways of constructing and experiencing the world. Given that certain materials, objects, and lifestyles cannot exist and work the way they do without petroleum, they can be considered emblematic of petro-modernity. Such phenomena have been, for example: infrastructure supporting the production of petroleum, such as oil derricks, offshore platforms, pipelines, and oil tankers; means of transportation that run on fuel oils, such as automobiles, trains, airplanes, and ships; and all forms of plastics that synthesize our world, including Bakelite, polyethylene (bottles, plastic film), nylon (toothbrushes), polyester (fabrics), and silicone (sealant, also in industrial paints). However, the proliferation of petroleum imagery and its petroleum-based visual technologies has not yet been comprehensively examined as emblematic of petro-modernity.

This book investigates the visual culture of petro-modernity, that is, the images that petroleum has brought about and the ways in which petroleum and petroleum-derived products shape how we experience the world aesthetically and visually. In this context, iridescence is conceptualized as the aesthetic staging of the broader normalization of the Anthropocene, as petro-modernity, in which Kuwait provides for a historic microcosm of this Anthropocenic macrocosm. The investigation is carried out using the case of the mid-twentieth-century urban transformation of Kuwait, a city-state that quickly became a prime oil producer. Although the oil industry in Kuwait was run outside of Kuwait City by the Anglo-American Kuwait Oil Company, the rapidly expanding city became the representational stage on which petro-modernity unfolded in multiple iridescent ways. The urban visual culture that developed alongside negotiated this oil-fueled transformation that coincided with Kuwait's nation-building. For this book, *Alien Technology* serves as a figure of thought that reenacts what can be called the *iridescent effect*—petroleum's ability to not only have a powerful material presence in other materials, in other textures, and objects, but, most importantly, to have a powerful aesthetic, material, and visual presence or resonance in images, in media, in the built environment, and in space in general. Finding and dissecting the iridescent effect in the visual media that emerged in connection with the mid-twentieth-century urban transformation of Kuwait City provides an analytical lens with which to detect those aesthetics and tactics of visual seduction that have created the affective relationship with petroleum, but more broadly with global petro-modernity with which we continue to deal with today.

The focus on the visual is based on the understanding that the imagery of Kuwait City's "modernization" from the mid-1940s onward not only documented and displayed but visually constructed the ways in which the petro-fueled urban transformation was perceived and the ways in which petro-modernity was negotiated. The extended 1950s—the period between 1946 and 1961, from the first shipment of oil to the independence of the Kuwaiti nation-state from Great Britain—were not just a key period of urban transformation and oil production, but a period infused with ideas of nation-building and modernization. In this period, Kuwait experienced the development of a welfare and bureaucratic state apparatus and the transmutation into a fullfledged nation-state, most of it under the reign of Shaykh Abdullah al-Salem Al Sabah.[10] Kuwait's nation-building was deeply entangled in oil revenues and the adoption of an oil-based material way of being in the world. Inherent to the logic of both modernization (theory) and nation-building is the question of how to develop from the present into the future. In these early days of the Kuwaiti nation-state, but in fact until the present day, the answer to this question has always involved petroleum. With this logic came the *petroleum promise*, which is the affective visual and/or textual framing of petroleum as a harbinger of future change and prosperity in speculative anticipation of its production or of its continuation.[11] In a way, there is always a future-making involved and this affective potentiality has attracted visualization, or rather visual representation. In the mid-twentieth century, aerial photographs, maps, architectural plans, political symbols, photography, architecture, stamps, travel guides, and even visual arts were not mere reflections or by-products of the processes of petro-modernity, nation-building, and modernization. They were, rather, active components that enabled and shaped these processes and imbued them with meaning.

Recontextualizing the images of mid-twentieth-century Kuwait City in the emerging urban visual culture of the time is an attempt to "re-carbonize" modernity in order to disclose the otherwise blurry or even invisible complicity of petroleum in it. To re-walk all the little alleyways and big highways that petroleum has tinted is a method of giving oil visibility through which it can be analyzed as a crucial factor or medium in the modern history of the Persian Gulf and in capitalist globalization at large. Indeed, as it is often difficult to see the forest for the trees, the somewhat pointed emphasis on oil within the present study is essential for leaving the current state of petroleum-blindness behind.

[10] Shaykh ʿAbdullāh al-Salim al-Mubārak Āl Ṣabāḥ (January 1, 1895–November 24, 1965) ruled Kuwait from January 29, 1950 to his sudden death in November 1965. His predecessor was Shaykh Aḥmad Jābir Āl Ṣabāḥ (born 1885), who ruled from March 29, 1921, until his death on January 29, 1950.

[11] Slightly differently, Mona Damluji defines "petroleum's promise" as "the promise of nation building and modernization of oil-producing states" that was linked to "the neo-colonial practice of oil extraction." Mona Damluji, "Petroleum's Promise: The Neo-Colonial Imaginary of Oil Cities in the Modern Arabian Gulf" (PhD diss., University of California, Berkeley, 2013), accessed January 27, 2021, https://escholarship.org/uc/item/7qk5c7kj, 2.

Petroleum's ubiquity is not exclusive to Kuwait's specific geopolitical and historical conditions, but the extreme concentration of oil in Kuwait's history makes the city-state a thought-provoking prism through which to detail and exemplify larger discourses, developments, conditions, and consequences of the global petro-modernity we all live in today.

The case study of Kuwait is emblematic of the global collective disillusionment with modernity (which has been a carbon modernity, involving first coal, then oil), with petroleum as the source of planetary destruction, and the ideologies (progress, nationalism, modernization, etc.) around it. Petroleum was dealt as *the* promise of modernity to fuel both center and periphery, but living with and in petroleum has proven to be a temporary cure and a lasting curse that are not accidentally but programmatically worked into the construction of our global modern history and the construction of Kuwait's history. Therefore, I see the regional response to the legacies of the "petroleum promise" in contemporary visual culture as a sounding board to which extent these ideologies, narratives, and imaginaries have persisted and convinced, or disenchanted and fallen apart. A younger generation is answering back through contemporary artworks which become acceptable forms of visual expression that respond in the (semi-)public arena. Circulating around notions of memory, nostalgia, collective identity, and futurism, these artworks on the one hand prove the lasting effect of the iridescent effect, and on the other hand, they demonstrate the growing resistance to such narratives. The apparent political, economic, and social stability that petroleum promised to establish has transformed into a planetary realization of how instable petro-modernity has made the past, present, and future, and its imagery.

The book *Iridescent Kuwait* seeks to do two things. At the base, it maps, describes, analyzes, and compares urban images of Kuwait using a media-historical and iconographic approach in order to understand which cultural artefacts, tropes, motifs, images, and aesthetic practices have come to (not) represent the negotiation of petro-modernity in Kuwait. Here, the focus lies on representations of architecture and the Gulf city in urban visual culture rather than on the actual built environment. At a second level, this book traces the ways in which petroleum has constituted modernity as iridescent. To do so, I investigate (1) how petro-urbanism dictated the transformation of urban space, (2) how the rise of new modes and technologies of viewing and image-making was enabled by petroleum in one way or another, and (3) how the aesthetic complexity and seductive attraction of petro-modernity is tangled up in a myriad of promotional strategies that hide petroleum's toxicity from view. Ultimately, thinking through petro-modernity allows us to view the development of our modern world not as a piecemeal combination of "avant-garde" and "belated" modernities, but as one modernity that is drenched in petroleum and from which no one can escape.

This introductory chapter (Chapter One) explores the methodological and theoretical prerequisites surrounding the core themes of urban visual culture, petro-modernity, modernization (theory), and urban transformation. Chapter Two provides a historical overview of Kuwait's socioeconomic and cultural formation as well as its spatial configuration until the mid-twentieth century. It offers a particular focus on the pre-oil urban morphology and architecture that would later become the site of major oil-fueled overhauls and considers the early stages of visual arts, their production, and display in Kuwait. Together, the theoretical opening and the historical background provide the basis for the subsequent three main chapters.

Chapter Three deals with how Kuwait (City) was visualized and envisioned in aerial photography, Kuwait City's first master plan, and cartography. The view from above triggered lasting representational ambiguities of seeing and understanding the pre-oil town of Kuwait as well as the "oil city" Kuwait. This top-down view resulted in a top-down approach in urban planning that Arab and Kuwaiti architects and urban planners critically reexamined in the following decades. Chapter Four focuses on the Kuwait Oil Company's seminal publication *The Story of Kuwait* and the company's use of professional (color) photography to present Kuwait City as a success story of petro-fueled modernization with lasting effect. By comparing these images with photographs by Kuwaiti photographer Tareq Sayid Rajab and urban images of Kuwait in the magazine *al-ʿArabī*, the prerequisite destruction of the existing town of Kuwait that occurred side by side with its colorful modernization provides for a more complex picture of the city's transformation and highlights varying, at times contrasting agendas by different actors. Chapter Five addresses the ways in which the Kuwaiti government used the first set of Kuwaiti postage stamps to promote the country as a self-confident and modernizing petro-state and how the accompanying process initiated the country's independence in 1961. Oil stamps, or petro-philately, became an important medium in the Arab world to show a nation-state's participation in petro-modernity.

As a short parenthesis, Chapter Six recalls the falling apart of Kuwait's petroleum promise by shedding light on the visuality and mediality of Kuwait's biggest petroleum calamity surrounding the Iraqi invasion, Operation Desert Storm, and the oil spills in 1990–91. This rupture in Kuwait's oil history reveals the full spectrum of petro-modernity, shifting from cure to curse and coming full circle in iridescence. Chapter Seven, the final chapter, reintroduces the sculpture *Alien Technology* along with a selection of other works of contemporary art from the Gulf that deal with petro-modernity's past and present in the region, and the corresponding theoretical discourse. By combining these contemporary perspectives with the findings of the previous chapters I discuss the ways in which the twentieth-century urban visual culture of petro-modernity is questioned today and how to come to terms with its ever-seductive aesthetics as well as the role the Gulf plays in sketching future global scenarios of with and without oil in the visual arts.

1.1 Urban Visual Culture

Today, historical images of the Gulf region feverishly circulate within the region itself. Apart from self-published photobooks and memoirs, websites, blogs, and social media accounts also bring to light a multitude of historical photos, films, and video snippets. Photographs of a wide range of paraphernalia like old posters, stamps, and even tableware of Kuwait Airways are being unearthed in a collective, transgenerational effort.[12] Clearly, a large interest in seeing, sharing, and thereby revisiting the Gulf's, a country's, and ultimately one's own past beyond established national forms of memory, history, and heritage exists. Given current technological means of publishing and sharing visual material, provenience is often impossible to establish. Yet these images keep moving, keep attracting attention, and keep posing questions to scholars of urban visual culture.

When I first visited the Gulf in 2016, I was intrigued by the plethora of historical visual material; this included historical photographs, city maps, stamps, paper money, company brochures, and government-issued coffee-table books. I wanted to move beyond a mere fascination with these objects. To this end, I developed a material-driven approach, working with material readily available instead of rejecting it in favor of other sources that might be considered more worthy of study by some. In art history it is often considered legitimate to engage with particular material when an artifact is in an archive, museum, or renown private collection (showing that it is considered worth preserving), when it has authorship (meaning that its originality, influences, and mastery can be studied), or when it speaks to established (fine) art categories and traditions (that make it compatible with classifications and canon). Much of the imagery analyzed in this book holds no artistic authorship, was not intended to be art, and has not necessarily been viewed as such. It has often become integrated into everyday popular culture and has thereby easily transcended elite circles—even if members of these circles were usually involved in its creation and dissemination—and for which it is often difficult to find historical evidence detailing its reception. Rather than the cityscape in watercolor, most historical images discussed in this study have been produced, circulated, and consumed within the logic of mass culture and mechanical or industrial reproduction, where authenticity or originality are not the most important criteria. How can we engage with this material in art history if it is not art as we know it?

From the 1990s, debates within visual culture studies, which often spilled into art history departments, campaigned to broaden the object of study to encompass all possible

[12] Among others there is *Māḍī al-Kuwayt* (mostly in Arabic with some sub-pages translated into English), although a part of the images has been recently taken down; accessed January 27, 2021, https://www.kuwaitpast.com/arabic.html. On this phenomenon in the Arab world, see Lucie Ryzova, "Nostalgia for the Modern: Archive Fever in Egypt in the Age of Post-Photography," in *Photo Archives and the Idea of Nation*, ed. Costanza Caraffa and Tiziana Serena (Berlin: De Gruyter, 2015).

expressions of the visual, irrespective of intention and reception.[13] Accordingly, in this study, visual culture is understood as all expressions of imagery with no restrictions as to their form, typology, medium, or the type of material. Despite continuing discussions about the relationship between visual studies and art history, visual culture does not work in opposition to art but rather as its enlargement, as its umbrella term. Both art itself and the academic discipline history of art are part of (the study of) visual culture. As Christine Gruber and Sune Haugbolle suggest in *Visual Culture in the Modern Middle East*, visual culture studies and art history enhance each other as two fields of expertise and knowledge production.[14] Visual studies are strong in the theoretical analysis of, for example, representations of race, gender, and power. Yet, as Gruber and Haugbolle emphasize, many studies do not pay close attention to the formal composition of the image, (political) iconography, the historical modes of image production, reception processes, and especially notions of "aesthetics."[15] Art-historical methods are notably strong in the analytical description of images as well as in their comparative and historical image-to-image analysis. Consequently, the imagery discussed in this book is approached using the methodological and theoretical apparatus of art history, despite it being material that many art historians might ignore. In addition, close attention is paid to inherent power relations, to questions of (political) representation, and ecology.

Of central importance to the question of how the imagery that is discussed in the following chapters acquires meaning is the relationship between the built environment—as physical, multisensorial, and also strong visual experience—and the image. This relationship is conceptualized as visual representation. Images of Kuwait City (as visual representations) can be understood to lastingly influence the city's *image* (as appearance and reputation). Analyzing such images serves not only to illustrate urban history; rather, visual representations form an object of study in their own right that can help us better understand the ways in which meaning is acquired. The pervasiveness of images lies in their apparent structural and visual consistency, yet images are highly ambivalent and open to changes in meaning and readings. Images of Kuwait City are understood to hold power to affect the material realities of urban space in return; visual representations therefore construct that which they represent, ultimately constituting our understanding of the world.[16]

[13] For a pertinent summary and historical examples of this discussion see William I. Homer, "Visual Culture: A New Paradigm," *American Art* 12, no. 1 (1998); Johanna Drucker, "Who's Afraid of Visual Culture?," *Art Journal* 58, no. 4 (1999).

[14] Christiane J. Gruber and Sune Haugbolle, "Introduction: Visual Culture in the Modern Middle East," in *Visual Culture in the Modern Middle East: Rhetoric of the Image*, ed. Christiane J. Gruber and Sune Haugbolle (Bloomington: Indiana University Press, 2013), xvii–xix.

[15] Ibid., xvii.

[16] See Susan Sontag, "The Image-World," in *On Photography*, ed. Susan Sontag, repr. ed. (New York: Rosetta Books, [1977] 2005).

This study is dedicated to the visual culture of the Gulf city, the mutual constitutive relationship between images and the city, and the ways in which they reenforce, inform, shape, and negotiate each other, for which I conceptualize as "urban visual culture." In a seemingly similar approach provided with the special issue "Urban Images and Imaginaries: Cities of the Arabian Peninsula through their Representations" in the journal *Arabian Humanities* (2019), Laure Assaf and Clémence Montagne consider images "both as object and method, seeking to explore what urban images do to contemporary Gulf cities," which implies focusing on "who produces these images" with its political and social implications as well as "the way urban images shape the city itself."[17] Part of the "urban visual culture" as I understand it, is of course the city's "architectural culture," as Sibel Bozdoğan has described it in *Modernism and Nation Building: Turkish Architectural Culture in the Early Republic*: "The idea behind the study of architectural culture is not to explain the work through what was said and written about it but to see the ways in which what was said, written, and built *collectively* confirm, interpret, contest, or negotiate the political and ideological agendas of the time."[18] Still, this book is predominantly concerned with the visuality, the aesthetics, the modes of representation, and the discursive elements that arise in relation to Kuwait's modern architectural culture, which has been surveyed in the two volumes of *Modern Architecture Kuwait* (2016; 2018) by its authors and editors Roberto Fabbri, Sara Saragoça, and Ricardo Camacho, and in relation to its urban history as examined by Farah Al-Nakib in *Kuwait Transformed: A History of Oil and Urban Life* (2016).[19]

Conceptualized as part of Kuwait's urban visual culture, the images examined here allow us to analyze the ways in which the urban experience of petro-modernity was negotiated. To this end, methodologically, the present analysis focuses on the way in which the visual material speaks to other images and viewers in terms of content, formal structure, iconography, time of origin, political implications, media, context, and the historicity of themes and topics. Subsequently, their meaning is investigated in relation to other larger histories, debates, and themes relevant for mid-twentieth century Kuwait and the Gulf.

[17] Laure Assaf and Clémence Montagne, "Urban Images and Imaginaries: Gulf Cities through their Representations," *Arabian Humanities*, no. 11 (2019): 2, https://doi.org/10.4000/cy.4137.

[18] Sibel Bozdoğan, *Modernism and Nation Building: Turkish Architectural Culture in the Early Republic* (Seattle: University of Washington Press, 2001), 12 (italics in the original).

[19] Roberto Fabbri, Sara Saragoça, and Ricardo Camacho, *Modern Architecture Kuwait: 1949–1989* (Zurich: Niggli, 2016); Roberto Fabbri, Sara Saragoça, and Ricardo Camacho, eds., *Essays, Arguments & Interviews on Modern Architecture Kuwait* (Zurich: Niggli, 2018); Farah Al-Nakib, *Kuwait Transformed: A History of Oil and Urban Life* (Stanford: Stanford University Press, 2016).

Representation and modernity share a complex historical relationship. Timothy Mitchell, for example, argues that modernity can be defined by "the way in which the modern is staged as representation."[20] He details:

> Representation does not refer here simply to the making of images or meanings. It refers to forms of social practice that set up in the social architecture and lived experience of the world what seems an absolute distinction between image (or meaning, or structure) and reality, and thus a distinctive imagination of the real.[21]

Mitchell subsequently implies that one way to think of modernity is as an experience negotiated through representations, which is a way of communicating between "world-as-picture" and "reality."[22] The case of Kuwait suggests that, as early as the 1950s, modernity worked effectively as a system of visual regimes, whereby the visual meaning or success of meaning-making was somewhat independent of the performative functionality that modernity is usually associated with. Large infrastructure projects, for instance, gained importance as active visual signposts quite independently of their technological function. Therefore, in Kuwait and in many decolonizing and nation-building contexts, modern architecture and modern urban space were more effective, virulent, and powerful as *visual representations* of modernity in the form of images than as physical harbingers of change.[23]

Images also have the power to profoundly shape our understanding of cities and their urban history from a transnational perspective. Pictures are significant agents of knowledge, of imaginaries, and of cultural exchange. They can become traveling vehicles of meaning in their ability to transgress natural, political, linguistic, cultural, and temporal borders. So, they can effectively overcome the otherwise geographical, spatial, and physical fixation of urban space and architecture. Given this mobility, historical visual material is best examined "as belonging in a continuing process of meaning, production, exchange, and usage," a focus that photography historian Elizabeth Edwards calls "the social biography" of images.[24] This involves resituating images in their complex sociocultural, geopolitical, and historical context as best as possible by working extensively with archival material as well as concepts, knowledge, and theories produced in other disciplines such as anthropology, Gulf and Middle Eastern studies, political science, sociology, and energy humanities.

The proliferation of visual media during the era of petro-modernity has often served to regulate, and thereby soften, its potentially controversial aspects—what I understand

[20] Timothy Mitchell, "The Stage of Modernity," in *Questions of Modernity*, ed. Timothy Mitchell, Contradictions of Modernity (Minneapolis: University of Minnesota Press, 2000), 16.

[21] Ibid., 17.

[22] Ibid., 18.

[23] For similar arguments in favor of the "visible politics" of architecture see Bozdoğan, *Modernism and Nation Building*, 9.

[24] Elizabeth Edwards, "Material Beings: Objecthood and Ethnographic Photographs," *Visual Studies* 17, no. 1 (2002): 68.

as the *iridescent effect*. Rendered visible through promotional materials, radiant color palettes, or impressive advances in technological modes of seeing, its environmental and social rapaciousness has been effectively hidden from view. Energy humanists Sheena Wilson and Andrew Pendakis emphasize that "in the age of oil it is the image, at this time more than in any other era, that proliferates as a medium of communication."[25] However, the visual symbolic practices that carefully curate petroleum's (in)visibility not only communicate, but also construct the experience of petro-modernity. While most of the discussion of the relevant literature is woven into each chapter when and where it is needed, the theoretical framework around petro-modernity that supports this study as a whole deserves its own discussion.

1.2 Petro-Modernity

Petroleum, or simply oil (the two terms are used interchangeably throughout), is a composite substance consisting of many different hydrocarbons that can be liquid, gaseous, or solid. The terms denote both unprocessed and naturally found crude oil as well as industrially refined petroleum products. As raw material it is formed from dead organisms under extreme heat and pressure, an "*ur*-commodity," as cultural theorist Imre Szeman suggests.[26] Petroleum has many useful characteristics: it is flammable (producing light, heat, fire, energy), viscous (sealing and lubricating surfaces and materials), heterogeneous (separable into different products with specific characteristics), and odorous (many consider it malodorous). Some cultures have also ascribed healing abilities to it, and advocate rubbing one's skin with crude oil or consuming small amounts of treated oil. In natural deposits, petroleum often occurs as a black, very sticky, and highly viscous liquid or semi-solid heterogeneous substance referred to as asphalt, bitumen, or tar. Petroleum's material complexity has been known to humankind for more than four thousand years, but it only gained unprecedented momentum once it began fueling modernity, once it became iridescent.

In order to make use of (and create value from) petroleum, it needs to be extracted, transported, catalyzed, refined, and synthesized.[27] Since the mid-nineteenth century, various refining processes have been invented, most involving some form of fractional distillation that separates the heterogeneous hydrocarbon-complex into homogenous

[25] Andrew Pendakis and Sheena Wilson, "Sight, Site, Cite: Oil in the Field of Vision," *Imaginations: Journal of Cross-Cultural Image Studies* 3, no. 2 (2012): 4.

[26] Imre Szeman, "Introduction to Focus: Petrofictions," *American Book Review* 33, no. 3 (2012): 3 (italics in the original).

[27] For a sharp analysis of the refinery as "a form of heart chamber that pumps fossil raw materials into the present" by means of the pipeline and the cultural technology of catalysis, see Benjamin Steininger, "Refinery and Catalysis," in *Textures of the Anthropocene: Grain, Vapor, Ray*, ed. Katrin Klingan et al. (Cambridge, MA/Berlin: MIT Press; Revolver, 2015).

products and that thereby ultimately changes petroleum's consistency, smell, shape, color, energy level, and usability. Primary petroleum-based products are the different types of energy-rich fuel oils—petrol, gasoline, propane, naphtha, kerosene, diesel, and liquefied petroleum gas—that comprise the world's most important energy sources. Other components produced during the refining process are used as a raw material or as reagents for a diverse range of chemically synthesized products.

Oil has given birth to plastics, cosmetics, pesticides, and all kinds of textiles, from maritime ropes to wedding dresses. It is a fertilizer component used for our industrialized mass agriculture. As asphalt it aids mobility around the globe. It lubricates tools and machinery. Prior to the digital age, it led to the celluloid and inks necessary to produce film, photography, and printed materials, and through this enabled most of the material and visual culture of the twentieth century. In the mid-twentieth century petro-modernity began manifesting itself rapidly everywhere around the world. Following the end of World War II, oil explorations were started or resumed across the globe and myriads of new uses for petroleum and its derivatives were promoted as part of local everyday culture. Petroleum-derived commodities were now developed into personalized forms of mobility and lifestyle that eventually affected all social strata. Kuwait City's urban development and the city-state's nation-building thus coincided with the global expansion of petro-modernity during the extended 1950s.

Viewed from this perspective, modernity since the 1850s—but particularly since the mid-twentieth century—to this day has been a petro-modernity drenched in and dependent on the same resurrected organic matter. Consequently, modernity, postmodernity, and "multiple modernities" depend on the same material condition. This invites a reconsideration of epochal delineations and their attributed characteristics.[28] Prominent scholars such as Zygmunt Bauman and Bruno Latour have already questioned and opposed the distinction between modernity and postmodernity.[29] Looking through the lens of petroleum, however, one can detect a fossil continuum spanning from the classical industrial revolution (fired by coal, another fossil carbon) to the digital age.[30] Even the digital age continues to be highly dependent on oil in order to satisfy the large energy demand of the smart lifestyle we have come to take for granted.[31] This also resonates with Nicolas Mirzoeff's reading of Dipesh Chakrabarty's essay "The Climate of

[28] As our dependency on petroleum has not declined in importance and as we cannot yet imagine a life "after oil" (meaning a life without any or at least one with substantially less petroleum), general differentiations between modernity and postmodernity cannot be upheld from the perspective of oil, as they *de facto* run on the same material conditions.

[29] Zygmunt Bauman, *Liquid Modernity*, repr. ed. (Cambridge: Polity, [2000] 2006); Bruno Latour, *We Have Never Been Modern* (Cambridge, MA: Harvard University Press, 1993).

[30] Frederick Buell, "A Short History of Oil Cultures: Or, the Marriage of Catastrophe and Exuberance," *Journal of American Sudies* 46, no. (2012).

[31] The digital economy, which is often considered to be fossil-free, was already consuming ten percent of the world's total energy (mostly produced from fossil fuels) by 2015. This represents the same amount that was

History". The visual culture theorist concludes pointedly: "In the Anthropocene [the era brought forth by humans, especially by burning fossil fuels], all past human history in the industrial era is the contemporary. No location is outside the Anthropocene, although some are affected far more than others."[32] Focusing on petroleum invites us to rethink our global history and its material conditions as fundamentally common and interconnected. Center and periphery as well as avant-garde and "rear guard" have shared similar material conditions of being in this modern world, even if to very different degrees.

Everything we do, feel, and see is touched by oil, infused with petroleum; yet, analytically, we have long blanked out the crude conditions of producing, living, and experiencing our modern world. The question looms large why the humanities and social sciences have ignored energy and petroleum for so long. For one, there is the almost unimaginable size of the industry as well as the incalculability and often inaccuracy of numbers and timelines (peak oil, production outputs, oil prices, etc.), which scholars in the field attest to causing "intellectual vertigo."[33] Most importantly, to be hidden in plain sight is an acknowledged characteristic of petroleum (and other forms of energy).

Questions of aesthetics, visual representation, and (in)visibility in particular have posed challenges for researchers across all fields.[34] Andreas Malm and others explain this as a "crisis of the imagination," caused among other things by the material fugitiveness and infrastructural disguise of petroleum.[35] Artist Ursula Biemann, who was one of the first to systematically approach the politics of petroleum through artistic research, sees "this level of abstraction in the representation of oil as yet another way to keeping it firmly in the hands of market dynamics."[36] Literature scholars Andrew Pendakis and Sheena Wilson also point to petro-capitalism and argue that "the problem of visualization … is not specific to oil, but one politically structural to a system that is at once spectacularly consumerist and fully globalized on the level of production."[37] In order to begin to imagine alternatives to oil, we first have to dissect how petroleum has come to shape how

used to light the entire planet in 1985. See Shumon Basar, Douglas Coupland, and Hans Ulrich Obrist, *The Age of Earthquakes*: A Guide to the Extreme Present (New York: Blue Rider, 2015), n.p.

32 Mirzoeff explains the Anthropocene as "the name given by scientists to the new era in geology caused by human intervention, primarily the burning of fossil fuels." Nicholas Mirzoeff, "Visualizing the Anthropocene," *Public Culture* 26, no. 2 (2014): 213, 215; Dipesh Chakrabarty, "The Climate of History: Four Theses," *Critical Inquiry* 35, no. 2 (2009).

33 Appel, Mason, and Watts, "Oil Talk," 5–9.

34 Scholars have emphasized "the surprising limits of aesthetics and representation in relation to energy". Sheena Wilson, Imre Szeman, and Adam Carlson, "On Petrocultures: Or, Why We Need to Understand Oil to Understand Everything Else," in Wilson, Carlson, and Szeman, *Petrocultures*, 5; see also Ross Barrett and Daniel Worden, "Oil Culture: Guest Editors' Introduction," *Journal of American Studies* 46, no. 2 (2012): 269; Appel, Mason, and Watts, "Oil Talk," 4–5.

35 Malm, "This Is the Hell That I Have Heard of," 126.

36 Ursula Biemann and Andrew Pendakis, "This Is Not a Pipeline: Thoughts on the Politico-Aesthetics of Oil," *Imaginations: Journal of Cross-Cultural Image Studies* 3, no. 2 (2012): 8.

37 Pendakis and Wilson, "Sight, Site, Cite," 4.

we see our modern world. Consequently, scholars have started revisiting works considered "canonic" as well as introducing formerly marginalized material within their respective fields to understand where, why, and how petroleum has slipped the critical viewer's or reader's eye.

For a long time, chemists and engineers, as well as economists and political scientists, have dominated the study of petroleum. However, in asking what petroleum does in social and cultural contexts, recent studies have argued that oil (and energy) are pivotal in shaping habits, ways of living, modes of transportation, and even our epistemologies.[38] Lately, a large part of the knowledge production on petroleum has developed from a social and cultural perspective and especially in the field of energy humanities, an interdisciplinary field across the arts, humanities, and social sciences.

Energy humanities works to "position oil and energy as the fulcrum around which many of today's most pressing social, economic, and political issues must be analyzed and understood."[39] Energy humanists have argued that "while it would be reductive to see in the expanded use of energy an explanation for every aspect of modernity, it is equally problematic *not* to include energy in our narratives of historical change and development, including social and cultural shifts and transitions."[40] Here, reflecting on petroleum means partaking in a larger analysis of the social and cultural implications of energy transitions, meaning the values, practices, affects, hopes, beliefs, aesthetics, modes of vision, and representation that petroleum enables. In light of future scenarios "after oil," we need to recognize and reconsider the paramount role fossil energy has played in the "historical formation" of modernity.[41] Especially because there is a high chance that petroleum will not be gone as quickly or completely as usually insinuated with terms such as "post-oil" or "after oil." Michael T. Klare, a professor of peace and world security studies at Hampshire College, convincingly argues that the upcoming "Third Carbon Age" will mean the even more noxious exploitation of unconventional oil and gas reserves, such as tar sands, extra-heavy crudes, and arctic off-shore deposits.[42] However, in light of a possible decline of fossil energy demand following COVID-19, the petroleum market might in fact not have such a stable future ahead after all. However, despite the fundamental rifts across many different economies, hardly any bailout proposal has so far anchored the reduction of carbon emission and of fossil energy as paramount.

[38] See, for instance, Andrew Pendakis, "Being and Oil: Or, How to Run a Pipeline through Heidegger," in Wilson, Carlson, and Szeman, *Petrocultures*.

[39] Sheena Wilson, Imre Szeman, and Adam Carlson, "On Petrocultures: Or, Why We Need to Understand Oil to Understand Everything Else," in Wilson, Carlson, and Szeman, *Petrocultures*, 4.

[40] Ibid., 5 (italics in the original).

[41] Barrett and Worden, "Oil Culture," 271.

[42] Michael T. Klare, "The Third Carbon Age," *Huffington Post*, August 8, 2013, updated December 6, 2017, accessed January 27, 2021, https://www.huffingtonpost.com/michael-t-klare/renewable-energy_b_3725777.html.

Iridescence, as analytical concept, acknowledges humankind's complex and highly affective historical relationship with petroleum, in which petroleum is not just hydrocarbons but also plays out as energy, money, power, mobility, speed, destruction, and contamination. It accounts for oil's historical and material legacy of being not one but many different things at once, which has given it a sense of overwhelming and at times magical or haunting potency. Petroleum is *the* substance that has fueled the highest hopes and the greatest tragedies of modernity as the case study of Kuwait emphasizes.

Petro-modernity is situated in the Anthropocene, the ongoing era of human-induced environmental change, whose "scale of burning ambitions of fossil-making man … is hard to comprehend."[43] Petro-modernity is also difficult to investigate in relation to visual culture given "how deeply embedded in our very sensorium and modern ways of seeing the Anthropocene-aesthetic-capitalist complex of modern visuality has become" and how fundamentally it relies on the burning of fossil fuels as Mirzoeff has high-lighted.[44] Conceptually, the experience of living with oil has been described as "petrofictions" (Imre Szeman), "petromodernity" (Stephanie LeMenager), "oil modernity" (Nelida Fuccaro), "petroleumscape" (Carola Hein), and as "oil culture," which art historian Ross Barrett and literature scholar Daniel Worden define as "the broad field of cultural representation and symbolic forms that have taken shape around the fugacious material of oil."[45] Historian Bob Johnson speaks about "mineral rites" that highlight the "embodiment of fossil fuels, including our affective attachments to them."[46] Energy humanist Stephanie LeMenager describes living in petro-modernity as living in a modern world "based in the cheap energy systems made possible by oil."[47]

Building on LeMenager's definition, in this study the term petro-modernity is expanded (1) to also describe the historical period since the mid-nineteenth century, when modern oil production started and the use of petroleum products increased rapidly around the world, the "fossil economy"[48] and (2) to characterize a world in which petroleum and petroleum-derived products (and the set of practices associated

[43] For a thought-provoking discussion of the fossil-burning concept of the Anthropocene and alternative proposals for characterizing our time and our relationship to nature, see Donna Haraway, "Tentacular Thinking: Anthropocene, Capitalocene, Chthulucene," *e-flux journal*, no. 75 (September 2016), accessed January 27, 2021, https://www.e-flux.com/journal/75/67125/tentacular-thinking-anthropocene-capitalocene-chthulucene/.

[44] Mirzoeff, "Visualizing the Anthropocene," 213.

[45] Szeman, "Introduction to Focus," 3; Stephanie LeMenager, *Living Oil: Petroleum Culture in the American Century*, Oxford Studies in American Literary History (New York: Oxford University Press, 2014), 67; Nelida Fuccaro, "Visions of the City: Urban Studies on the Gulf," *Middle East Studies Association Bulletin* 35, no. 2 (2001): 179; Carola Hein, "Oil Spaces: The Global Petroleumscape in the Rotterdam/The Hague Area," *Journal of Urban History* 44, no. 5 (2018): 888; Barrett and Worden, "Oil Culture," 269.

[46] Bob Johnson, *Mineral Rites: An Archaeology of the Fossil Economy* (Baltimore: Johns Hopkins University Press, 2019), 2.

[47] LeMenager, *Living Oil*, 67.

[48] Johnson, *Mineral Rites*, 9.

with prospecting for, discovering, controlling, producing, and refining petroleum) have infiltrated ways of living, beliefs, and especially images and aesthetics through which we experience and negotiate the world. Especially because we make sense of the world through cultural representations, text and images provide pivotal access points for the detection and disclosure of petro-modernity.

Developed over the last two or three decades but predominantly within the last ten years, the research on oil within the humanities and social sciences is impressive and has been extremely inspiring. Even mainly socioeconomically oriented anthologies on petroleum include discussions of artworks, and scholars often team up with artists to produce visual essays and academic research. This underscores the importance (and ongoing challenge) of the visual in the field of petroleum studies.[49] However, systematically tracing the (in)visibilities, imagery, and imaginaries that the world of petroleum produce in relation to a particular visual medium has predominantly been done in relation to film.

Petroleum has in fact proven essential to (the history of) film: not only were early film rolls petroleum-derived products, but, as Mona Damluji has shown, oil companies were important producers of documentary films to promote their extractive operations and to control their public image.[50] Rising numbers of documentaries attempt to come to terms with the global fossil dependency and its environmental consequences, but, as Imre Szeman argues, they struggle to formulate a clear political agenda in the face of oil.[51] Films like Werner Herzog's *Lessons of Darkness* (1992) on the burning of oil fields in Kuwait after the Operation Desert Storm and George Stevens's *Giant* (1956), which portrays the experience of the oil boom in Texas, have become key filmic dioramas from which to analyze visual representations of the petroleum experience.[52]

Artists like Ursula Biemann have been pivotal contributors to a critical understanding of petroleum through artworks and text.[53] In *Black Sea Files* (2005), Biemann investigates

[49] For example, the anthology *Subterranean Estates* includes an article on the photographs of Ed Kashi. On other scholar-artist teams, see Biemann and Pendakis, "This is Not a Pipeline"; Michael Watts and Ed Kashi, "Oil City: Petro-Landscapes and Sustainable Futures," in *Ecological Urbanism*, ed. Mohsen Mostafavi and Gareth Doherty (Baden: Lars Müller, 2010); Imre Szeman and Maria Whiteman, "Oil Imaginaries: Critical Realism and the Oil Sands," *Imaginations: Journal of Cross-Cultural Image Studies* 3, no. 2 (2012).

[50] Damluji, "Petroleum's Promise."

[51] Imre Szeman, "Crude Aesthetics: The Politics of Oil Documentaries," *Journal of American Studies* 46, no. 2 (2012).

[52] Herzog filmed *Lessons of Darkness* during the oil field burnings in Kuwait immediately after the Iraqi invasion had ended. See Imre Szeman, "The Cultural Politics of Oil: On *Lessons of Darkness* and *Black Sea Files*," *Polygraph*, no. 22 (2010); Daniel Worden, "Fossil-Fuel Futurity: Oil in *Giant*," *Journal of American Studies* 46, no. 2 (2012).

[53] Examples include Per Barclay's photographic series *Oil Room* (1989), which shows oil-flooded interior spaces; Christo and Jeanne-Claude's *The London Mastaba* (2018), an installation of multi-colored oil barrels stacked on a floating platform in Serpentine Lake, London; and Edward Burtynsky's photography of petroleum landscapes, in Edward Burtynsky and Michael Mitchell, *Edward Burtynsky: Oil* (Göttingen: Steidl, 2009).

the networks, flows, infrastructures, and social communities that embody oil culture in everyday spaces of the Caspian oil geography. She argues that "the discovery of the vast potential of oil for the creation of new materials mustering an extraordinary range of qualities has fueled our imagination to create a synthetic world and overcome natural limits."[54] However, many exhibitions and artworks that deal with petroleum tackled the issues of pollution, sustainability, and violence, often under the label of Eco Art, although seldom asking questions how the aesthetics of petroleum and the ways in which it has historically shaped vision and imaginations, are part and parcel of an iridescent, ambivalent petro-modernity. A notable exception is the exhibition *Crude* (2019), which Murtaza Vali curated at the Jameel Arts Centre in Dubai, and which explores the ways in which contemporary artistic practices negotiate the experience of petro-modernity within the Arab world.[55] The fact that two large exhibitions on the historical artistic and cultural implications of petroleum are scheduled for 2021–22 indicates the rising interest in petroleum as a visual phenomenon and the exhibition as a medium to investigate and discuss it in a broader public sphere.[56]

Astonishingly, although art historians are intimately familiar with "oil" on canvas, they have not (yet) focused on the petro-experience of the world, as the scarcity of the research output shows.[57] Notable exceptions are the work of Amanda Boetzkes, who tackles plastics and waste in contemporary art, and of Heather M. Davis, who works on plastic as cultural practice and art material.[58] These works help reflect on petroleum-derived materials in artistic practice but are mostly limited to plastic. Focusing on a different material aspect, architect Mirko Zardini's poetic and thought-provoking essay "Homage to Asphalt," which unravels the bituminous "second crust of the Earth" as something that signifies urbanity and facilitates speedy movement, is also worth mentioning.[59] Recently established research projects such as Ecology and Aesthetics: Environmental Approaches in Art History at Kunsthistorisches Institut in Florenz – Max-Planck-Institut

[54] Biemann and Pendakis, "This is Not a Pipeline," 9.

[55] Murtaza Vali, *Crude* (Dubai: Art Jameel, 2019), exhibition catalog published in conjunction with the exhibition of the same name, shown from November 11, 2018, until March 30, 2019.

[56] The exhibition *Oil: Schönheit und Schrecken des Erdölzeitalters* (*Oil: Beauty and Horror in the Petrol Age*) is shown at Kunstmuseum Wolfsburg, Germany, starting in September 2021, and is curated by Alexander Klose and Benjamin Steininger together with Andreas Beitin. The exhibition *Experiences of Oil* will open at Stavanger Kunstmuseum, Norway, in November 2021 and is curated by Anne Szefer Karlsen and Helga Nyman.

[57] The oil paint used in oil paintings is actually not a petroleum derivative at all; instead, it consists of color pigments suspended in a drying oil, such as linseed oil. In contrast, acrylic paint, which was invented in the first half of the twentieth century, and which is today often used as a cheaper alternative to oil paint, is made from pigments suspended in an acrylic polymer emulsion, which is a petroleum-based synthesized product.

[58] Amanda Boetzkes, *Plastic Capitalism: Contemporary Art and the Drive to Waste* (Cambridge, MA: MIT Press, 2019); Heather M. Davis, "Life & Death in the Anthropocene: A Short History of Plastic." In *Art in the Anthropocene: Encounters Among Aesthetics, Politics, Environments and Epistemologies*, ed. Heather Davis and Etienne Turpin (London: Open Humanities Pres, 2015).

[59] Mirko Zardini, "Homage to Asphalt," *Log*, no. 15 (2009).

or Mediating the Ecological Imperative at the University of Bern are promising to open up the discipline's canon for environmental and ecological perspectives already established in various humanistic disciplines.[60]

Another important thematic cluster related to the multidisciplinary research on oil is centered around motorized speed and mobility. In the twentieth century, car culture and other forms of motorized mobility like air travel have emerged as crystallization points from which to tackle petroleum. As one research group puts it, "as oil and gas move through our lives, our movement is in turn enabled by them, in cars, planes, asphalt, the plants that make our bicycles, electric cars, and public transportation vehicles."[61] Existing studies with a focus on the Arabian Peninsula have, for instance, concentrated on car drifting and youth revolts in Saudi Arabia, on the promotion of driving as a part of US national identity, and on the "nationalization" of space in the UAE through infrastructures such as highways and suburban neighborhoods that demand automobility.[62]

Not only does petroleum enable all sorts of mobility, but it is also itself extremely mobile, frequently crossing language boundaries and national borders on its way from extraction site to refinery and local as well as global consumers. Oil's mobility is also methodologically challenging because it "complicates not only historical periodization but also the national boundaries that conventionally limit scholarly inquiry."[63] Therefore, the field of petro-culture or petro-modernity studies demands transnational and transdisciplinary research into the experiences with and of petroleum of various geographical areas.

Bridging fossil-fueled movement with petroleum-related infrastructures, Andrew Pendakis remarks that "our conception of oil is usually oriented by this wide-angle image of the silently running oil refinery or platform," through which, he warns, "oil is … dangerously literalized, wrongly conceived as simply coextensive with a highly simplified figure of its own productive apparatus."[64] Contrary to this, the fields of "infrastructure studies" or science and technology studies (STS) have undertaken challenging investigations into the material, cultural, social, economic, and political entanglements

[60] The research project Ecology and Aesthetics: Environmental Approaches in Art History is directed by Gerhard Wolf und Hannah Bader in collaboration with Sugata Ray, accessed January 27, 2021, https://www.khi.fi.it/en/forschung/abteilung-wolf/ecology-and-aesthetics-environmental-approaches-in-art-history.php. Mediating the Ecological Imperative is a multidisciplinary project including art history that is funded by the Swiss National Science Foundation for the period 2021–24, accessed January 27, 2021, https://ecological-imperative.ch/.

[61] Appel, Mason, and Watts, "Oil Talk," 27.

[62] Pascal Menoret, *Joyriding in Riyadh: Oil, Urbanism, and Road Revolt* (New York: Cambridge University Press, 2014); Sarah Frohardt-Lane, "Promoting a Culture of Driving: Rationing, Car Sharing, and Propaganda in World War II," *Journal of American Studies* 46, no. 2 (2012), special issue: Oil Cultures; Matthew MacLean, "Suburbanization, National Space and Place, and the Geography of Heritage in the UAE," *Journal of Arabian Studies* 7, no. 2 (2017).

[63] Barrett and Worden, "Oil Culture," 271.

[64] Biemann and Pendakis, "This Is Not a Pipeline," 8.

of infrastructures, focusing on roads, dams, and other structures.[65] The infrastructure of the oil industry itself—the oil towers, pipelines, oil tanks, oil tankers, refineries, petrol stations, and so on—is nevertheless crucial to simultaneously highlight petroleum and hide it in plain sight, disguising its mobility, transformation, and impact.[66] For example, the authors of the anthology *Subterranean Estates* have called for an acknowledgment of the site-specificity of the oil industry despite its apparent global normalization and standardization.[67] Architect and cultural theorist Rania Ghosn has unraveled the pipeline as a key spatial site in the maintenance of oil, and Carola Hein has attempted to establish a spatial typology that highlights the entanglements between oil well and oil company office with the concept of the "petroleumscape."[68]

Urban space has been petroleum's favorite stage and preferred playground. Many studies investigate the spatial, urban, and architectural implications of petroleum, and some of these focus on the Gulf. Social historian and Gulf specialist Nelida Fuccaro has been a particularly thought-provoking voice; her work comprises studies that examine the complex sociopolitical historical relationships between the "pearl towns" and "early oil cities" and explores the ways in which "cities and urban environments [have] constituted the primary setting where oil modernity unfolded."[69] Fuccaro's approach has helped shape the present study's conceptualization of the oil-fueled urban transformation of Kuwait City.

1.3 Modernization and Urban Transformation

The analysis of urban images in relation to Kuwait City in the mid-twentieth century implies focusing not only on modes of pictorial depiction but also on the *image*, the reputation, and the external and self-representation of oil states. This is because understanding the common ways of framing the Gulf region and other oil-producing

[65] Penelope Harvey and Hannah Knox, eds., *Roads: An Anthropology of Infrastructure and Expertise* (Ithaca: Cornell University Press, 2015); Maria Kaika, "Dams as Symbols of Modernization: The Urbanization of Nature between Geographical Imagination and Materiality," *Annals of the Association of American Geographers* 96, no. 2 (2006).

[66] On this point in relation to refineries, see Steininger, "Refinery and Catalysis," 111.

[67] Appel, Mason, and Watts, "Oil Talk," 18.

[68] Rania Ghosn, "Territories of Oil: The Trans-Arabian Pipeline," in *The Arab City: Architecture and Representation*, ed. Amale Andraos, Nora Akawi, and Caitlin Blanchfield (New York: Columbia Books on Architecture and the City, 2016); Hein, "Oil Spaces."

[69] Nelida Fuccaro, "Pearl Towns and Early Oil Cities: Migration and Integration in the Arab Coast of the Persian Gulf," in *The City in the Ottoman Empire: Migration and the Making of Urban Modernity*, ed. Ulrike Freitag et al., SOAS/Routledge Studies on the Middle East 14 (London: Routledge, 2011); Nelida Fuccaro, "Introduction: Histories of Oil and Modernity in the Middle East," *Comparative Studies of South Asia, Africa and the Middle East* 33, no. 1 (2013): 1; and also Fuccaro, "Visions of the City."

countries at the time—from the outside as well as from the inside—are crucial for the historical contextualization of the visual materials.

These extended 1950s, the period between Kuwait's first oil export in 1946 and its independence from Britain in 1961, coincided with the heyday of Anglo-American modernization and development theory, which influenced the way in which Kuwait's petro-modernity was (inter)nationally interpreted and (visually) represented. These theories were built on grand historical-comparative concepts and strategies of macro-social change that attempted to provide historical explanations of why some nations were more advanced than others and to deliver schemes of how to develop the world, especially targeting so-called developing countries like Kuwait.[70] It is no surprise that fossil energies played a role already in projecting progress in this context.

Kuwait was neither an empirical nor a political focus of Anglo-American modernization efforts, as seminal publications on modernization in the Middle East did not include Kuwait in any significant way.[71] Yet, as a British quasi-protectorate since 1899 and neighbor of Saudi Arabia, America's prime petroleum partner, Kuwait was situated within a regional sphere of declining British power and rising US influence. This also infused Kuwait and its external but also internal *image* with the prevailing modernization and development ideologies of the time.[72]

Broadly speaking, modernization theory describes society's accelerated, linear, and unilateral development path from a traditional, agrarian, and rural stage to a modern, industrial, urban, and democratic one through the injection of Western technological, economic, and political assistance; this process was famously called "take-off" by modernization theorist Walt Whitman Rostow.[73] Economic growth and industrialization were hailed as prime instruments to stimulate transformation processes toward a Western (West European and Anglo-American) modernity characterized by free-market capitalism, liberal democracy, institutional differentiation, urbanization, rationalization, welfare, mass consumption, and so on.[74] Sociologist Wolfgang Knöbl has asserted that the inherent ethnocentrism is highly problematic, insofar as "the sociopolitical structure

[70] However, Knöbl cautions that US sociologists, who laid the founding stones for theories of modernization, did not in fact analyze the historical development of American society in order to project a path model, but instead developed historical explanation models of how other (underdeveloped) countries should develop by empirically researching their "still traditional" status quo. Wolfgang Knöbl, *Spielräume der Modernisierung: Das Ende der Eindeutigkeit* (Weilerswist: Velbrück Wissenschaft, 2001), 34.

[71] Daniel Lerner, *The Passing of Traditional Society: Modernizing the Middle East* (New York: Free Press, 1958); Manfred Halpern, *The Politics of Social Change in the Middle East and North Africa* (Princeton: Princeton University Press, 1963).

[72] See Simon C. Smith, "Power Transferred? Britain, the United States, and the Gulf, 1956–1971," *Contemporary British History* 21, no. 1 (2007).

[73] Walt Whitman Rostow, *The Stages of Economic Growth: A Non-Communist Manifesto* (Cambridge, UK: Cambridge University Press, 1960), chapter 4.

[74] Doubts over a directly quantifiable interdependency between economic-industrial change and democratization were formulated early on; see Knöbl, *Spielräume der Modernisierung*, 190–96.

of the West represented a kind of end point" that non-Western states were pressured to follow.[75] Moreover, modernization implied catching-up with something already achieved by others instead of inventing new and original future scenarios tailored to site-specific conditions on the ground. Modernization often meant nothing else than working with or toward the current standards set by others by means of foreign aid.

A certain geo-political or economic relevance to Anglo-American interests was needed for a country to become a target of foreign modernization efforts. Kuwait entered the modernization picture only when oil was struck. Petroleum extraction and export started in 1946 and by 1951 a new 50/50 profit-sharing oil deal between the Kuwaiti government and the Kuwait Oil Company had been agreed upon. Suddenly, the country's oil revenues provided the capital needed to both stimulate and finance the city-state's modernization. Ironically, it was Kuwait's sudden affluence and not its previous (relative) poverty that triggered the strong increase of British, and generally foreign, interest in modernizing Kuwait.[76]

Britain intended to control Kuwait's oil-fueled development to shore up its own financial and political interests. A development board with two British advisors as controller of finances and controller of development was established in 1950 and was expected to effectively monitor and channel the spending of surplus oil revenues according to British interests.[77] Another typical strategy was the (temporary) posting of mostly British advisors and experts, among them architects and urban planners, to advise and simultaneously steer Kuwait's development. However, in the 1950s, Britain's power in the Middle East and the Persian Gulf was rapidly declining. Additionally, Britain suffered so greatly from the weak sterling area that it in effect froze Kuwaiti surplus oil revenues in London in order to secure stabilization. Therefore, a strong discrepancy between British development aid rhetoric and the partial blocking of capital needed to initiate large-scale projects existed at the time.[78] Terms like "modernization" and "development" often functioned as a political disguise for British interests in the Gulf; development consisted mainly of advising and ensuring commissions of British firms, thus securing additional shares of oil revenues, instead of providing British state-funded development investments or initiatives tailored predominantly to Kuwaiti needs.[79]

[75] Ibid., 11 (author's translation).

[76] Simon C. Smith, "'A Vulnerable Point in the Sterling Area': Kuwait in the 1950s," *Contemporary British History* 17, no. 4 (2003): 37, https://doi.org/10.1080/13619460308565456.

[77] See Al-Nakib, *Kuwait Transformed*, 105–7.

[78] Paul W. T. Kingston, *Britain and the Politics of Modernization in the Middle East*: 1945–1958, Cambridge Middle East Studies 4 (Cambridge, UK: Cambridge University Press, 1996), 42–45.

[79] Ali Karimi and Frederick Kim, "On Protectorates and Consultanates: The Birth and Demise of Modernization in the Gulf States," in *Unsettling Colonial Modernity in Islamicate Contexts*, ed. Siavash Saffari et al. (Newcastle-upon-Tyne: Cambridge Scholars, 2017), 96; J. E. Peterson, "Britain and the Gulf: At the Periphery of Empire," in Potter, *The Persian Gulf in History*, 284; Rosemarie Said Zahlan, *The Making of the Modern Gulf States: Kuwait, Bahrain, Qatar, the United Arab Emirates and Oman* (London: Unwin Hyman, 1989), 33.

Petroleum also played a crucial role in the theoretical conceptualization of modernization. Apart from the importance of oil revenues as capital to stimulate economic growth and industrialization, petroleum was acknowledged as being relevant to motorized mobility, electrification, and urbanization—basically to pivotal markers of being modern. For example, American sociologist Marion J. Levy characterized modern societies not only by industrialization and rationalization, but also by their high consumption of energy and the use of non-animated matter (like coal and petroleum) for power generation.[80] One of the most prominent scholars of modernization, the American economist and political theorist Walt Whitman Rostow, proposed that the automobile was the key to becoming modern or to reaching what he called the "age of high mass consumption."[81] As early as the 1950s, modernization had already become clearly unthinkable without fossil energy and thus petroleum, independently of the question of whether a country was an oil producer or not. In this logic, development was tied to the accessibility of fossil energy, petroleum-derived materials and consumer goods, and (petro)capital.

The modernization of the city-state Kuwait was measured especially by its level of oilstimulated urban growth, which increased considerably from the late 1940s onward. This urban transformation involved a complex shift in labor migration (attracted by the growing economy) and higher birth rates, which, along with other factors, accounted for the explosive growth of Kuwait City. The transformation also included a radical change of the city's layout, form, and silhouette. The economy transitioned from seafaring, shipbuilding, and trading to a welfare system that relied almost exclusively on oil revenues distributed by the rulership. The vernacular architectural style gave way to idioms typical of the International Style and manifested in industrial building materials. Professions, ways of living and socializing, education trajectories, and social cohesion all changed. These are just a few of the aspects associated with Kuwait's complex urban transformation.[82]

It was only in the 1980s that the relationship between oil (booms) and urbanization was systematically analyzed on a macro level for the first time. One important triggering event for this was the startling 1973 "oil crisis," which unfolded in the form of skyrocketing oil prices in the West and resulted in soaring revenues and building booms in the oil-producing OPEC countries. Subsequently, economists, political scientists, and geographers examined the spatial and socioeconomic characteristics of the sudden impact of oil on urban space, which was predominantly observed within the rapidly transforming

[80] Marion J. Levy, Jr., "Some Sources of the Vulnerability of the Structures of Relatively Non-Industrialized Societies to Those of Highly Industrialized Societies," in *The Progress of Underdeveloped Areas*, ed. Bert F. Hoselitz (Chicago: University of Chicago Press, 1952), 115. Levy's take on modernization is analyzed in Knöbl, *Spielräume der Modernisierung*, 160–73.

[81] See Nils Gilman, *Mandarins of the Future: Modernization Theory in Cold War America*, New Studies in American Intellectual and Cultural History (Baltimore: Johns Hopkins University Press, 2003), 190–202.

[82] Urban transformation entails always more than just urban growth. Still, at the time, (Kuwait's) urban transformation was often subjected to such limited definition. See Josef Gugler, ed., *The Urban Transformation of the Developing World* (Oxford: Oxford University Press, 1996).

OPEC member states, including Kuwait and other Gulf states.[83] Coined "petro-urbanism" or "oil urbanization," such transformation was generally characterized as an extremely rapid, large-scale, and in this form unprecedented acceleration of urbanization that resulted from the surge in oil revenues and the subsequent economic boom in the small oil-producing states of the Gulf of the 1970s.[84] Other important factors were the shift in demographics toward an extremely heterogeneous, non-citizen majority and the strengthening of existing urban centers. Geographers Michael E. Bonine and Rainer Cordes also emphasized the adaptation of urban space to motorization, the energy-intensive climate-controlling of architecture, and the influence of Western consultants on building and planning.[85] To this day, as Laure Assaf and Clémence Montagne have recently observed, "The urban phenomenon"—and one should add the petroleum-fueled urban phenomenon—"has been the main lens through which the idea of an exceptionality of the Arab Gulf states was elaborated in academic scholarship."[86]

Although scholars agree that the 1970s marked the core phase of "petro-urbanism," they differ on when exactly to place the starting point of the petroleum-induced change in urbanization patterns in the Gulf. That this starting point was considered a watershed moment is shown in the temporal categories of "pre-oil" and "post-oil" that became firmly established in the 1980s. In the assessment of Mohamed Riad, an Egyptian geographer, the understanding of time and history in this regard had already been affected by oil in 1981:

> One should be aware that the term "past," in the Gulf area does not necessarily refer to any appreciable time distance. It simply refers to pre-oil periods which ended around the fifties of this century. Since it is so near, it is vivid and nostalgic in the lore of the people, but to the new generation it is antiquated.[87]

[83] The Organization of the Petroleum Exporting Countries (OPEC) was established in 1960 in Baghdad by the founding members Iran, Iraq, Kuwait, Saudi Arabia, and Venezuela. OPEC's goal is to regulate oil market prices and represent the economic and political interests of these national oil producers. By 1973, Algeria, Ecuador, Indonesia, Libya, Nigeria, Qatar, and the United Arab Emirates had also joined.

[84] See, for example, Mohamed Riad, "Some Aspects of Petro-Urbanism in the Arab Gulf States," *Bulletin of the Faculty of Humanities and Social Sciences*, no. 4 (1981): 17; Michael E. Bonine and Rainer Cordes, "Oil Urbanization: Zum Entwicklungsprozess eines neuen Typs orientalischer Städte," *Geographische Rundschau* 35, no. 9 (1983): 465.

[85] See Riad, "Some Aspects of Petro-Urbanism in the Arab Gulf States"; Bonine and Cordes, "Oil Urbanization," here 465; Salih A. El-Arifi, "The Nature of Urbanization in the Gulf Countries," *GeoJournal* 13, no. 3 (1986); Sulayman Khalaf and Hassan Hammoud, "The Emergence of the Oil Welfare State: The Case of Kuwait," *Dialectical Anthropology* 12, no. 3 (1987); Richard I. Lawless and Ian J. Seccombe, "Impact of the Oil Industry on Urbanization in the Persian Gulf Region," in *Urban Development in the Muslim World*, ed. Hooshang Amirahmadi and Salah S. El-Shakhs (New Brunswick: Rutgers University Press, 1993).

[86] Assaf and Montagne, "Urban Images and Imaginaries," 6.

[87] Riad, "Some Aspects of Petro-Urbanism in the Arab Gulf States," 10.

Depending on each oil-producing country's specific experience with oil, authors tend to draw the line of the pre-oil period around the 1950s or the 1960s.[88] For the case of Kuwait, the end of the pre-oil period can be determined with the first export of oil in 1946. While pre- and post-oil seem to be useful categories, the latter causes confusion because it is sometimes used to refer to a time "after" the discovery of oil and sometimes to a time in the future when oil is no longer (as) necessary. To provide a clear differentiation when speaking about Kuwait's history, in the present study the terms "pre-oil" and "oil" are used to describe the periods before 1946 and after 1946 respectively, while the term "after oil" is used to refer to a future in which oil will not be the dominant energy and material base of our world. The dominant characteristics of oil urbanization might have manifested most intensely during the 1970s, but the case of Kuwait City clearly shows that from the late 1940s onward (and especially during the 1950s) all of the above-mentioned factors of petro-urbanism already impacted the city majorly.

Descriptions of "petro-urbanism" or "oil urbanization," have established a narrative of Kuwait's urban transformation as a radical break from the past. In line with the logic of modernization theory, the notion of urban transformation often implies firm binaries of the old and traditional versus the new and modern in urban form and social structure. This is also the case when developments in Kuwait are described along the lines of without oil vs. with oil. Instead of thinking of the pre-oil and the oil periods as totally separated eras, however, the concept of "transformation" put forward by German social and political scientist Rolf Reißig stimulates a more refined understanding.

Reißig defines transformation as a "change that always includes continuity as well."[89] He describes it further as "an intentional, intervening, organizing, and at the same time self-stimulated, organic-revolutionary process of development. Historical processes that take on the character of transformation are as a rule driven by both processes [change and continuity]."[90] Consequently, Kuwait City's urban transformation is not analyzed according to existing macro-level typologies or concepts of oil-induced modernization and urbanization. Instead, the architectural and spatial outcomes and visual expressions and representations of this complex, ambiguous, and impactful process are understood as containing both change and continuity. This approach also considers that oil cities are no longer analyzed merely as the spatial products of petro-urbanization but rather, on the

[88] In favor of the 1950s see ibid., 17; El-Arifi, "The Nature of Urbanization in the Gulf Countries," 224. In favor of the 1960s see Nelida Fuccaro, "Visions of the City: Urban Studies on the Gulf," *Middle East Studies Association Bulletin* 35, no. 2 (2001): 176–77. Khalaf situates the end of the pre-oil period for Kuwait, Bahrain, and Qatar in the 1950s and for the UAE and Oman in the 1960s; see Sulayman Khalaf, "The Evolution of the Gulf City: Type, Oil, and Globalization," in *Globalization and the Gulf*, ed. John W. Fox, Nada Mourtada-Sabbah, and Mohammed A. Mutawa (London: Routledge, 2006), 248.

[89] Rolf Reißig, "Transformation – ein spezifischer Typ sozialen Wandels: Ein analytischer und sozialtheoretischer Entwurf," in *Futuring: Perspektiven der Transformation im Kapitalismus über ihn hinaus*, ed. Michael Brie (Münster: Westfälisches Dampfboot, 2014), 54 (author's translation).

[90] Ibid.

micro-level, as multi-sensory environments or stages of the urban visual culture of petro-modernity as this book does. For instance, Michael Watts and Ed Kashi's definition of the "oil city" implies that "much of what is modern in the modern city is the by-product of oil. The city as a way of life is, in this specific sense, petro-urbanism *a la lettre*."[91] Moreover, Kuwaiti architectural historian Asseel Al-Ragam has emphasized that Kuwait City's development "was intimately connected with its determination to reuse existing sites for modern functions."[92] This can be seen in the fact that the modern oil city was conceived both visually and physically on top of the existing coastal settlement, a development that is emblematic of urban transformation as a process of change and continuity.

As Kuwait City was physically altered it was simultaneously created in visual representations which in turn shaped the further course of urban planning and rebuilding and constructed how the city was perceived while it was continuously changing. Still, many authors argue that image creation and "city branding" is something that only comes *after* the basic infrastructure of a city and a certain level of "modernization" has been established. For example, a 2017 article on Dubai discussing the "Birth and Demise of Modernization in the Gulf States" states:

> Whereas thirty years prior, the main concerns were the provision of water, electricity, and healthcare, the preoccupation now [around 1979] became how to purchase an identity and create a brand for the city that would make it known throughout the world. This is not to be understood as a breaking away from the trajectory of modernization, but in fact its apotheosis. Once the basic provisions of civilization had been fulfilled, the project of modernization became one of capitalist consumption driven by the pace that had been set years prior, but also one of self-reflection and the need to prove to the world that the developing countries had modernized.[93]

In contrast, the example of the urban transformation of Kuwait City during the extended 1950s shows that the forging of visual representations of modern architecture, urban space, and infrastructures served as effective proof of the city-state's modernization while it was still ongoing. Furthermore, it indicates that such imagery was therefore an intrinsic part of the fast-paced modernization in the Gulf region and continues to be as Laure Assaf and Clémence Montagne have demonstrated.[94] Moreover, many projected development projects were even foreshadowed by images and at times have remained as images only. These visual representations were influential in the way that they created the *image* of the city according to different agendas; a quasi-forerunner of the prevalence of city branding in relation to the Gulf cities today.[95]

[91] Watts and Kashi, "Oil City," 93 (italics in the original).

[92] Asseel Al-Ragam, "Towards a Critique of an Architectural *Nahdha*: A Kuwaiti Example," (PhD diss., School of Architecture, University of Pennsylvania, 2008), accessed September 29, 2019, https://repository.upenn.edu/dissertations/AAI3309387/, 34.

[93] Karimi and Kim, "On Protectorates and Consultanates," 97.

[94] Laure Assaf and Clémence Montagne, "Urban Images and Imaginaries: Gulf Cities through Their Representations," *Arabian Humanities*, no. 11 (2019).

[95] Ibid., 1.

In Kuwait, just like in other oil-producing countries, the interest in visual representation was also triggered by the competitive, comparative, and international nature of the oil industry. Projecting "correct" development was obviously a valuable currency of an oil state's self-representation to the outside that facilitated good relations with other states, prominence, and simply presence. (Portable) visual artifacts affected and facilitated the nation-building process and allowed for transnational and transcultural communication, in many ways flowing through the same networks that the oil companies and petro-modernity had opened up.[96] The Kuwait Oil Company actively partook in the project to visualize and thereby curate Kuwait City. Even more marginal agents, ordinary people, living in Kuwait engaged visually and aesthetically to various ends; visual artists established shared practices, networks, and spaces for the visual arts; homeowners engaged in architectural explorations by commissioning spectacular designs; Arab and Kuwaiti writers forged new, often illustrated magazines and the city became itself a popular display for posters, illuminated advertising, shop windows, and billboards—increasingly experienced while driving a car. Yet, the new petro-fueled imagery needs to be read against the pre-oil background of the coastal town, its pre-oil visual and material culture and urban history, too. Only in this way can justice be paid to understanding the complexities of Kuwait's urban transformation as a "change that always includes continuity as well."

[96] Similarly, Mona Damluji has based her analysis of oil company films on the understanding "that the context of nation building was being actively produced through the content of oil company films." Damluji, "Petroleum's Promise," 9.

2. A (PRE-)OIL HISTORY OF KUWAIT

Kuwait City is not built on sand, as is often claimed.[1] Rather, the coastal location has been inhabited since the eighteenth century. Therefore, the city's mid-twentieth century urban transformation represents a transition phase within a longer urban history. As a port town of the Arabian Peninsula, Kuwait, like other Gulf states, has historically been considered a border zone of the Arab World, or today the MENA region, and has consequently been understudied. The often scarce archival situation and the demise of much of the pre-oil architecture have enhanced this neglect.[2] Nevertheless, the history of Kuwait belongs within the transcultural and transregional history of the Persian Gulf,[3] which, as historian Rosemarie Said Zahlan emphasizes, "is one of the oldest continuously inhabited places in the world."[4] Kuwait owes its emergence as a successful seaport town to the Gulf as "a key international trade route connecting the Middle East to India, East Africa, Southeast Asia, and China."[5] Acknowledging Kuwait's dynamic pre-oil history therefore challenges persisting perceptions of the Gulf States as having neither a long history nor, in particular, a long urban tradition; it also allows for a re-situating of the often decontextualized petro-fueled urban transformation that has taken place since the late 1940s. In fact, a growing number of recent studies has investigated the modern histories of the Arabian Peninsula

[1] This superficial assertion is made regarding all Gulf cities, often when comparing cities like Kuwait City to other Arab cities like Damascus or Cairo, or to major European cities; it downgrades material, oral, and archaeological evidence. See for example Shumon Basar, ed., *Cities From Zero* (London: Architectural Association, 2007); Elisabeth Blum and Peter Neitzke, eds., *Dubai: Stadt aus dem Nichts,* Bauwelt Fundamente 143 (Basel: Birkhäuser, 2009). For a critique of the Gulf's ahistorical reading see Karen Exell and Trinidad Rico, "'There Is No Heritage in Qatar': Orientalism, Colonialism and Other Problematic Histories," *World Archaeology* 45, no. 4 (2013).

[2] Lawrence G. Potter, "Introduction," in Potter, *The Persian Gulf in History*, 1.

[3] Despite the preference of many Arab Gulf states to refer to the waters of the Gulf as the "Arabian Gulf," the region is here referred to as the "Persian Gulf" according to established convention in the historiography of the region in the English language. No political connotation is intended. For a detailed analysis of this politically charged "name game" see ibid., 15–16.

[4] Zahlan, *The Making of the Modern Gulf States*, 1. A similar description of the Persian Gulf is found in Arnold T. Wilson, *The Persian Gulf: An Historical Sketch from the Earliest Times to the Beginning of the 20th Century*, rev. ed. (Westport: Hyperion, [1928] 1981).

[5] Lawrence G. Potter, "Introduction," in Potter, *The Persian Gulf in History*, 1.

https://doi.org/10.1515/9783110714739-004

and the Gulf through the complex twentieth-century urban trajectories of Gulf cities.[6] Among these, this book is the first dedicated to the urban visual culture of the Gulf city, in this case Kuwait, as part of a rising petro-modernity in the mid-twentieth century.[7]

2.1 Kuwait's Pre-Oil History

Before Kuwait existed as a nation-state, it existed as a town of the same name. Historians generally agree that Kuwait was first settled by the al-ʿUtūb, a group of families said to be descendants of the ʿAniza tribe. Seeking relief from heavy drought and a difficult political climate, the al-ʿUtūb emigrated from the Nejd region in the early eighteenth century, first via al-Ḥasāʾ to al-Zubāra on the Qatar peninsula and subsequently to Kuwait, where they settled in an already existing small fort built by the Banū Khālid tribe.

As early as 1709, Syrian traveler Murtaḍā. ʿAlī b. ʿAlwān is reported to have stayed in a coastal settlement called al-Kuwayt on his way to Mecca for the *ḥajj*.[8] He outlined that the name of the town is derived from the diminutive form of *al-kūt* (fort), hence al-Kuwayt, meaning "small fort." He described a port town with strong trading ties to Basra, one day away by boat; most of the food was imported as the soil was not fertile. He also noted that the architecture was similar to that of al-Ḥasāʾ (today's Al Hofuf), but that Kuwait was smaller in size.[9] Murtaḍā's observations capture some of the essential elements of Kuwait's

[6] Among these publications are, for example: Al-Nakib, *Kuwait Transformed*; Alamira Reem Bani Hashim, *Planning Abu Dhabi: An Urban History* (Abingdon: Routledge, 2018); Yasser Elsheshtawy, ed., *The Evolving Arab City: Tradition, Modernity and Urban Development* (London: Routledge, 2008); Yasser Elsheshtawy, *Dubai: Behind an Urban Spectacle* (London: Routledge, 2010); Yasser Elsheshtawy, ed., *Planning Middle Eastern Cities: An Urban Kaleidoscope in a Globalizing World* (London: Routledge, 2010); Nelida Fuccaro, *Histories of City and State in the Persian Gulf: Manama since 1800* (Cambridge: Cambridge University Press, 2009); Claudia Ghrawi, "A Tamed Urban Revolution: Saudi Arabia's Oil Conurbation and the 1967 Riots," in *Violence and the City in the Modern Middle East*, ed. Nelida Fuccaro (Stanford: Stanford University Press, 2016); Stefan Maneval, *New Islamic Urbanism: The Architecture of Public and Private Space in Jeddah, Saudi* Arabia (London: UCL Press, 2019); Menoret, *Joyriding in Riyadh*.

[7] The only exception to this is Mona Damluji's PhD thesis on documentary films, which however only focuses on oil company commissioned film productions. See Damluji, "Petroleum's Promise." The urban visual culture of Iran, another petro-state, in general (i.e., without a particular focus on petroleum) has been explored in two notable publications: Pamela Karimi, *Domesticity and Consumer Culture in Iran: Interior Revolutions of the Modern Era* (London: Routledge, 2013); Staci G. Scheiwiller, ed., *Performing the Iranian State: Visual Culture and Representations of Iranian Identity* (London: Anthem, 2013).

[8] Ulrich W. Haarmann has been able to show that this source—and not, as assumed until then, the travel accounts of Carsten Niebuhr—contains the earliest mention of Kuwait. See Ulrich W. Haarmann, "Early Sources on Kuwait: Murtaḍā b. ʿAlī b. ʿAlwān and Carsten Niebuhr: An Arab and a German Report from the Eighteenth Century," *Hadīth al-Dār* 3 (1995); Ulrich W. Haarmann, "Two 18th-Century Sources on Kuwait: Murtaḍā b. ʿAlī b. ʿAlwān and Carsten Niebuhr," in Slot, *Kuwait*.

[9] Ulrich W. Haarmann, "Two 18th-Century Sources on Kuwait: Murtaḍā b. ʿAlī b. ʿAlwān and Carsten Niebuhr," in Slot, *Kuwait*, 37–39. Haarmann provides a translation of the original Arabic text.

pre-oil lifeworld: while the locality was not particularly blessed in terms of local produce, lacking good water supplies, wood, and farmable land, it was endowed with a favorable natural harbor in a suitable strategic location, which the formerly pastoral nomads put to good use by becoming seamen trading with Basra and many other places. Murtaḍā also mentioned Kuwait's alternative name al-Qurayn (sometimes written as Grain or Grän). Later, Lewis Pelly, the Political Resident of the Persian Gulf (1862–1872), suggested that the name al-Qurayn derived "from Gern, a horn, which the bay is said to resemble in shape."[10] In fact, the name is the diminutive form of *qarn*, Arabic for horn.

The name al-Qurayn was frequently used in European documents, for example those of the German cartographer Carsten Niebuhr, who provided another pivotal, although second-hand account of Kuwait dating from the second half of the eighteenth century.[11] Niebuhr, who located Kuwait on a map of the Persian Gulf, described the location by referencing both of its names: "Koweit s[ive] Grän" (Koweit/Kuwait equaling Grän/al-Qurayn).[12] Kuwait was thus first known as a settlement with a small fort at a horn-shaped bay.

To the east, the town of Kuwait was delineated by the Persian Gulf. From the northwest to the southwest, mostly flat desert surrounded the settlement; as one traveler noted in the 1830s, "nothing is to be seen but vast sandy plain, extending to a distance of more than sixty miles. Not a tree, not a shrub affords the eye a momentary relief."[13] While framed on one side by a waterfront and natural harbor, landward Kuwait used to be enclosed by a wall that, together with its subsequent extensions, decisively shaped the town's urban morphology. It is assumed that Kuwait's first wall was built during the reign of the first ruler, Shaykh Sabah I (d. 1762), around 1760 or earlier, which indicates that the Al Sabah (Āl Ṣabāḥ), which continue to rule Kuwait today, already held some authority over the affairs of the town at the time.[14] The wall was built to protect the settlement against sand storms and hostile intruders like the Wahhabi raiders, who attacked it in 1793 and 1797,

[10] Lewis Pelly, *Report on a Journey to Riyadh in Central Arabia (1865)*, repr. ed. (Cambridge: Oleander, [1866] 1978), 10.

[11] Niebuhr, a mathematician and civil servant, participated in the orient expedition of the Danish King Frederick V in 1761 and returned six years later. He then published his geographical manual as *Beschreibungen von Arabien* (1772) and his first-hand experiences in *Reisebeschreibungen nach Arabien* (1774, 1778, and 1837), in which he wrote about Kuwait, a city he had in fact never visited. Carsten Niebuhr, *Beschreibung von Arabien: Aus eigenen Beobachtungen und im Lande selbst gesammleten Nachrichten abgefasset* (Copenhagen: Nicolaus Möller, 1772), 341–42; For a discussion of Niebuhr and Kuwait see Ben J. Slot, *The Origins of Kuwait* (Leiden: Brill, 1991), 69–100, 103–8.

[12] As detailed in Niebuhr's map of the Sinus Persicus, 1764, Niebuhr, *Beschreibung von Arabien*, plate xix.

[13] Joachim Hayward Stocqueler, *Fifteen Months' Pilgrimage Through Untrodden Tracts of Khuzistan and Persia: In a Journey from India to England, through Parts of Turkish Arabia, Persia, Armenia, Russia, and Germany; Performed in the Years 1831 and 1832* (London: Saunders & Otley, 1832), 18.

[14] Kuwait's first ruler was Abū ʿAbdillāh Ṣabāḥ I bin Jābir Āl Ṣabāḥ (ca. 1700–1762), who reigned from 1752 to 1762. Facey and Grant suggest that the wall was constructed before 1760; see William Facey and Gillian Grant, *Kuwait by the First Photographers* (London: I. B. Tauris, 1999), 8. Abu-Hakima and Al-Nakib give the

but also to control the movement in and out of the town, thereby managing the collection of customs.[15] Carsten Niebuhr reports that, in the second half of the eighteenth century, Kuwait had eight hundred ships and, when all had returned from their maritime voyages and caravan journeys, around ten thousand inhabitants.[16]

During the rule of Sabah's son Abdallah I (r. 1763–1814), the Al Sabah began focusing exclusively on the government of the town and no longer participated in trade.[17] In exchange for their supervision, the other large merchant families provided sustenance for the Al Sabah, creating a system of mutual dependence with the majority of power in the hands of the merchants.[18] Until the mid-twentieth century, the higher strata of Kuwait's society consisted of the ruling family and the merchant families, of which a few very wealthy families owned most of the ships and the larger number were small shop owners. There were also the sailors that seasonally worked on the boats as well as Bedouin herdsmen and traders; these made up most of the pearl divers and also contributed to the defense of Kuwait during times of conflict by providing men for the armed forces.[19] The sailors, herdsmen, and divers lived in the town only seasonally or visited irregularly and belonged to the lower social strata. Overall, the majority of Kuwaitis were involved in a maritime economy consisting of fishing, pearl diving, shipping, shipbuilding, and trade.[20] All groups were tied together in a complex system of debt caused by the nature of the pearling economy, which some authors argue created a strong (and rather supportive) network, but others reject as exploitative.[21]

year 1760; see Ahmad Mustafa Abu-Hakima, *The Modern History of Kuwait: 1750–1965* (London: Luzac, 1983), 7; Al-Nakib, *Kuwait Transformed*, 22.

15 Abu-Hakima, *The Modern History of Kuwait*, 46–47, 59; Facey and Grant, *Kuwait by the First Photographers*, 8.

16 Niebuhr, *Beschreibung von Arabien*, 341–42.

17 Kuwait's second ruler was 'Abdullāh I bin Ṣabāḥ Āl Ṣabāḥ (1740–May 3, 1814).

18 Jill Crystal, *Oil and Politics in the Gulf: Rulers and Merchants in Kuwait and Qatar* (Cambridge, UK: Cambridge University Press, 1990), 36–45; Eran Segal, "Merchants' Networks in Kuwait: The Story of Yusuf al-Marzuk," *Middle Eastern Studies* 45, no. 5 (2009); Suhail Shuhaiber, "Social and Political Developments in Kuwait Prior to 1961," in Slot, *Kuwait*, 100.

19 Suhail Shuhaiber, "Social and Political Developments in Kuwait Prior to 1961," in Slot, *Kuwait*, 102–4; Farah Al-Nakib, "Revisiting *Ḥaḍar* and *Badū* in Kuwait: Citizenship, Housing, and the Construction of a Dichotomy," *International Journal of Middle East Studies* 46, no. 1 (2014): 8; Robert S. Fletcher, "'Between the Devil of the Desert and the Deep Blue Sea': Re-orienting Kuwait c. 1900–1940," *Journal of Historical Geography* 50 (2015): 54.

20 Frank Broeze, "Kuwait Before Oil: The Dynamics and Morphology of an Arab Port City," in *Gateways of Asia: Port Cities of Asia in the 13th–20th Centuries*, ed. Frank Broeze, Comparative Asian Studies Series 2 (London: Kegan Paul International, 1997), 152.

21 Among the authors who describe pre-oil Kuwait's social structure as mutually supportive are: Farah Al-Nakib, "Inside a Gulf Port: The Dynamics of Urban Life in Pre-Oil Kuwait," in *The Persian Gulf in Modern Times: People, Ports, and History*, ed. Lawrence G. Potter (New York: Palgrave Macmillan, 2014), 204–7; Suhail Shuhaiber, "Social and Political Developments in Kuwait Prior to 1961," in Slot, *Kuwait*, 103. Those

Stimulated by maritime activities and trade, the town grew larger, and a second wider wall was built in 1811; this new wall "reflected the extent of the town's achieved and anticipated spatial expansion."[22] English traveling journalist Joachim Hayward Stocqueler, who spent a few nights in Kuwait in April 1831 on his ship passage from Bombay to the Shatt al Arab, found the town—which now had over twenty thousand inhabitants—disappointing, being so "sterile, it literally yields *nothing*."[23] Lewis Pelly, however, stated upon his visit in 1865 that despite the lack of sweet water, "Kowait [*sic*] is one of the most thriving ports in the Persian Gulf. Its craft are large and numerous, trading with India and the Arabian coast."[24] He reported that Kuwaiti merchants imported a wide array of goods such as rice, corn, dates, timber, wool, horses, coffee, and tobacco.[25]

Attention for Kuwait increased during the second half of the nineteenth and the early twentieth century due to imperial interest in securing influence over (the port of) Kuwait. In 1871, Kuwait came under Ottoman rule as a *kaza* of Baghdad, a provincial sub-district, and thus formally integrated into the Ottoman Empire, eventually becoming part of a new administrative province, the *vilayet* Basra. Claiming power in 1886, Shaykh Mubarak, who is considered "the founder of modern Kuwait," strove to gain confirmation as the ruler (*kaymakam)* of this *kaza*.[26] However, as Ottoman recognition was a long time in coming, Mubarak turned to another foreign power eager to increase its presence in the Gulf, the British, for protection and alliance, asking for the establishment of a British protectorate in Kuwait in 1897.[27] In *The Ottoman Gulf*, Frederick F. Anscombe shows that the immediate period after Mubarak's claim of power was a clever time to play the Ottomans against the British and vice versa for Mubarak's own benefit. Despite Kuwait's nominal status as a part of the Ottoman empire and Mubarak's eventual recognition as *kaymakam*, he signed a secret "nonalienation bond" with Britain in 1899 that secured him protection and more independence from the Ottomans, especially as the British did not firmly exert their rule. However, the bond stipulated that Kuwait would only maintain relationships with other countries through Britain or with British approval, with Britain's interference supposedly

who describe the debt system as exploitative are Khalaf and Hammoud, "The Emergence of the Oil Welfare State," 345–48.

22 Al-Nakib, *Kuwait Transformed*, 22.

23 Stocqueler, *Fifteen Months' Pilgrimage Through Untrodden Tracts of Khuzistan and Persia*, 19 (italics in the original). On the number of inhabitants see Suhail Shuhaiber, "Social and Political Developments in Kuwait Prior to 1961," in Slot, *Kuwait*, 101.

24 Pelly, *Report on a Journey to Riyadh in Central Arabia (1865)*, 10.

25 Ibid.

26 Mubārak Ṣabāḥ II al-Jābir I Āl Ṣabāḥ (1839—November 28, 1915) ruled Kuwait from 1896 to his death in 1915. See Ben J. Slot, *Mubarak Al-Sabah: Founder of Modern Kuwait 1896–1915* (London: Arabian Publishing, 2005).

27 Frederick F. Anscombe, *The Ottoman Gulf: The Creation of Kuwait, Saudi Arabia, and Qatar* (New York: Columbia University Press, 1997), 101. Anscombe explains the treaty's special nature: "in practice the primary difference between a bond and a protectorate was that the former could be better kept secret." Anscombe, *The Ottoman Gulf*, 111–13.

constrained to foreign policy only. From the British point of view, this treaty prevented the Germans, an Ottoman ally, from having the Baghdad railway terminate in Kuwait, the best port of the Persian Gulf, and hence from gaining more strategic presence in the region. The Persian Gulf was precious to the British for its status as best gate to reach its "crown jewel" India. Interestingly, the exact scope of the treaty remained secret until 1912 and the status of Kuwait as "quasi-protectorate" stayed intact until independence despite many debates about its nature.[28]

Travel reports are one of the most valuable sources on the pre-oil history of Kuwait. They provide first-hand information in text and, often, images, about the urban conditions, lifestyles, and connectedness of Kuwait. For example, in December 1903, the German scholar and traveler Hermann Burchardt took a *būm* (wooden boat) from Basra to Kuwait and, upon his arrival, Shaykh Mubarak invited him to stay at his palace. The traveler acknowledged that his room was equipped with a mattress and bed linen as well as a towel and a piece of German soap.[29] He experienced Kuwait as a "very expansive city, certainly numbering 30,000 inhabitants, whose streets are kept clean. As I noticed, they are regularly swept and sprinkled in the early morning. The Shaykh inspects the city several times daily in a coach or on horseback."[30] Three years later Alfred Stürken, a German merchant from Hamburg, arrived on a steamboat of the British India Steam Navigation Company, which had begun calling at Kuwait every two weeks. He provided observations similar to Burchardt's on the city's cleanliness and emphasized the impressiveness of Kuwait's wharves, where many of the dhows sailing the Persian Gulf were built.[31]

Stopping in Kuwait in 1912, Danish writer and explorer Barclay Raunkiær similarly described a bustling port town, which by this time had grown to include a two-kilometer coastline and had a landward width of no more than one kilometer. He listed in great detail that while Kuwait exported pearls, wool, salted sheep meat, and goat skins, it imported basically everything else, including wood, butter, charcoal, fruit, sugar, tee, matches from Austria and Sweden, and coffee pots from Al Hofuf and Baghdad. Notably, the white cotton fabric used to tailor the men's *dishdāsha*, the most important piece of male clothing, came via Aden all the way from a company in Boston, while other colored cotton fabrics arrived from England.[32] Given Kuwait's magnitude of regional and international exchange, Raunkiær concluded that "Kuwait is the most important trading town on the east coast of Arabia," both for caravan trade with central Arabia and Iraq and seaborne

[28] Anscombe, *The Ottoman Gulf*, 113.

[29] Hermann Burchardt, "Ost-Arabien von Basra bis Maskat auf Grund eigener Reisen," *Zeitschrift der Gesellschaft für Erdkunde zu Berlin*, no. 21 (1906): 207; reprinted in Nippa and Herbstreuth, *Along the Gulf* (Berlin 2006), 203–27.

[30] Ibid.

[31] Alfred Stürken, "Reisebriefe aus dem Persischen Golf und Persien," *Mitteilungen der Geographischen Gesellschaft in Hamburg* 22 (1907): 92.

[32] Barclay Raunkiær, *Through Wahhabiland on Camelback (1913)* (New York: Frederick A. Praeger, 1969), 33–51 (on Kuwait), here 44.

trade with Iraq, Persia, India, East Africa, and East Arabia.[33] The Gulf was now also served by the Hamburg-America-Line and some other English ship lines, but only British-Indian shipping companies such as the British India Steam Navigation Company were allowed to call at Kuwait, which by then the company did weekly.[34] The town of Kuwait was clearly a dynamic, bustling, and well-connected coastal settlement even prior to the arrival of oil production. Transregional trade was already common, and the livelihood of Kuwait depended on these exchanges of produce, pointing to not only a certain boldness required to strive in such an environment but also to the ecological fragility of the setup.

Until the early twentieth century, the town of Kuwait experienced more or less continuous economic stability, steady urban growth, and peace. Due to a peak in pearling from increased, mostly Western, demand in luxury goods such as pearls and mother-of-pearl, the period between the 1890s and the year 1920 was the most prosperous.[35] Profiting from the geopolitical assets of location and its fine natural harbor, Kuwait also thrived due to its strategic political maneuvering between regional and imperial powers. This negotiating was aimed at securing Kuwait's independence and political neutrality as much as possible.[36]

In sharp contrast, the 1920s and 1930s heralded a phase of great economic hardship, galvanized by several events colliding at once. Abdul Aziz ibn Saud, then emir of Nejd, attacked Kuwait at Jahra, an oasis village to the northeast, in October 1920 and continued raids on Kuwaiti territory until 1930. Just a little earlier, the third, last, and longest town wall was constructed that delineated and shielded the town of Kuwait to a certain extent.[37] With the British-mediated Uqair Protocol in 1922, Kuwait lost two thirds of its territory to the Nejd (today part of Saudi Arabia). From 1923 to 1937, Ibn Saud imposed an embargo on Kuwait due to a customs dispute and consequently deprived Kuwait's harbor of its historic role of providing Eastern Arabia with everyday goods and transportation. Moreover, Japan successfully brought the first cultured pearls to market in the late 1920s against the background that the economic depression that had followed World War I culminated in the Great Depression. Consequently, the demand for Gulf pearls decreased and the value of natural pearls declined heavily, and so did pearl fishing in the Persian Gulf.[38] Pearls and with them the pearl merchants were left without a market; and without their circulation, the commodity pearl became useless and even ruinous.

When Alan Villiers, an acclaimed Australian photojournalist and experienced seaman, visited Kuwait in 1939, pearling was heavily on the decline, with some of the

33 Ibid., 46.

34 Ibid., 44.

35 Al-Nakib, *Kuwait Transformed*, 23, 27–28.

36 Abu-Hakima stresses this factor throughout his book. See Abu-Hakima, *The Modern History of Kuwait*.

37 Ibid., 133 and fn. 11. Al-Nakib emphasizes that it was not built to ward off Bedouin raiders, as is sometimes insinuated in popular Kuwaiti discourse, see Al-Nakib, "Revisiting Ḥaḍar and Badū in Kuwait," 8–10.

38 Bowen, "The Pearl Fisheries of the Persian Gulf," 164; Dickson, *The Arab of the Desert*, 484; Zahlan, *The Making of the Modern Gulf States*, 22.

pearling merchants' houses abandoned and derelict.[39] At that time, Kuwait consisted of around eight thousand houses and seventy thousand inhabitants; Villiers reported that only onehundred-and-fifty boats of all kinds and sizes had gone out that year, while forty years ago they would have numbered six hundred.[40] Historian Robert S. G. Fletcher asserts that "amidst the general crisis of the pearl trade between the wars, it was the desert and its opportunities that helped the state survive into the oil age."[41] As a result of these events, Kuwait's maritime economy shrunk and was subsequently reduced to deep-sea carrying trade and shipbuilding only. Against this background, the discovery of massive oil deposits in an area of the desert called Burgan on February 22, 1938, stirred high hopes for relief from economic hardship but also offered a chance to reconnect with Kuwait's rather cosmopolitan, mercantile, and dynamic recent past.

In light of early twentieth-century descriptions of Kuwait's prosperity, later assessments of the town as stagnant on the eve of oil production, only a few decades later, are surprising. They reveal an ideological bias toward an oil-based economy. An article in *National Geographic*, for example, explained: "Kuwait, the former *sleepy* village, *has awakened* with the coming of oil and is stretching its strong new limbs."[42] Such comments remain superficial given the extremely successful entrepreneurship of Kuwaitis over the centuries in an utterly hostile environment. Yet, they reflect the prevailing logic of modernization and development theories at the time, which used orientalist tropes to exacerbate the "positive" impact of the petro-industry to advance the "developing" world.

2.2 Oil Industrialization in Kuwait and the Persian Gulf

From the mid-twentieth century onward, the oil boom around the Persian Gulf created a new epicenter of international attention, with Kuwait at its center. Yet the country was not the first in the region to strike oil. On the Iranian side of the Persian Gulf, oil in

[39] Pearling was not only centered on the pearls themselves but also on the oyster shells. Therefore, as Kate Lance has argued, the decline of the pearling economy in the Persian Gulf was caused not only by the invention of the cultured pearl in Japan (as Villiers thought and what is still commonly argued), but from Japanese industrialized ships fishing *en masse* for pearl shells in Australian waters. Furthermore, (luxury) products like buttons made from mother-of-pearl were increasingly substituted by (petroleum-based) plastic imitating the iridescent sheen, such as pearloid. See Kate Lance, *Alan Villiers: Voyager of the Winds* (London: National Maritime Museum, 2009), 163.

[40] Alan Villiers, *Sons of Sindbad: An Account of Sailing with the Arabs in Their Dhows, in the Red Sea, round the Coasts of Arabia, and to Zanzibar and Tanganyika; Pearling in the Persian Gulf; and the Life of the Shipmasters and the Mariners of Kuwait*, rev. ed. (London: Arabian Publishing, [1940] 2006), 313, 324; on pearling in general see 324–47.

[41] Fletcher, "Between the Devil of the Desert and the Deep Blue Sea," 65; on the "profound crisis" of the 1920s and 1930s see 57–60.

[42] Paul E. Case, "Boom Time in Kuwait," *National Geographic Magazine* 102, no. 6 (December 1952), 802 (author's emphasis); photographs by George Rodger.

massive quantities was first discovered in Masjed Soleyman as early as 1908. This resulted in the establishment of the London-based Anglo-Persian Oil Company (APOC) in 1909, which was renamed the Anglo-Iranian Oil Company (AIOC) in 1935 and finally British Petroleum (BP) in 1954.[43] In 1913, the British-run Persian oil industry started from a newly built refinery at Abadan, which became the oil center of the Gulf for the first half of the twentieth century. On the Arabian side, the first successful oil well tapped the black gold at Baba Gurgur near Kirkuk in British-mandated Iraq in 1927 and at Jebel Dukhan, Bahrain, in 1931; oil exports commenced in 1938 and 1934 respectively.[44] Battling to be granted the oil concession in Kuwait, the AIOC and the American company Gulf Oil eventually jointly founded the Kuwait Oil Company (KOC) in December 1934. The oil concession delineated all of Kuwait's territory as land available for oil explorations for the next seventy-five years.[45] The oil companies negotiated a deal to pay the then-ruler, Shaykh Ahmad al-Jaber Al Sabah, "a royalty of three rupees per ton plus four annas in lieu of tax," which was at the time as little as 0.2 British pounds.[46]

Prior to the discovery of large oil deposits in Kuwait, it was known that bitumen seepages lay openly like little sticky, dark lakes amid a sea of sand at some locations in the desert.[47] Shipbuilders in Kuwait used the viscous material or, alternatively, fish oil from Hadhramaut to seal ship planks as was also done, for instance, in Iraq.[48] Petroleum and petroleum-derived products, however, were mostly known in the form of imported goods like lubricants and paraffin for oil lamps brought from India and, later, from the refinery in Abadan across the Gulf.[49] Empty oil tins were in turn used as transport containers and measuring units for drinking water imported from the Shatt al Arab; a common sight that Kuwaiti sculptor Sami Mohammed captured in a bronze sculpture of a woman carrying such a water-filled oil tin (fig. 2.1). Petroleum products such as Pennzoil (lubricants) and Oilzum (motor oil) were prominently advertised on signs mounted on, for example,

43 See Ronald W. Ferrier and James H. Bamberg, *The History of the British Petroleum Company*, vol. 1: *The Developing Years 1901–1932*; vol. 2: *The Anglo-Iranian Years, 1928–1954* (Cambridge, UK: Cambridge University Press, 2009); James H. Bamberg, *British Petroleum and Global Oil 1950–1975: The Challenge of Nationalism* (Cambridge, UK: Cambridge University Press, 2000).

44 In Iraq, the Turkish Petroleum Company, a multinational consortium of European and American firms, was in charge of the oil industry, its concessions and operations; in 1929 it was renamed the Iraq Petroleum Company. The same year, the Bahrain Petroleum Company was established in Canada by the Standard Oil Company of California.

45 Mary C. van Pelt, "The Sheikdom of Kuwait," *Middle East Journal* 4, no. 1 (January 1950): 23.

46 Elizabeth Monroe, "The Shaikhdom of Kuwait," *International Affairs* 30, no. 3 (July 1954): 274. Shaykh Ahmad (1885–1950) ruled from March 29, 1921 until his death on January 29, 1950.

47 For the first photographs of oil in Kuwait, see Laura Hindelang, "Photographing Crude in the Desert. Sight and Sense among Oilmen," in *The Life Worlds of Middle Eastern Oil*, ed. Nelida Fuccaro and Mandana E. Limbert, Edinburgh: University of Edinburgh Press, forthcoming.

48 Broeze, "Kuwait Before Oil," 153.

49 Ministry of Energy, Electricity and Water, *Water and Electricity in the State of Kuwait* (Kuwait: Center for Research and Studies on Kuwait, 2005), 41.

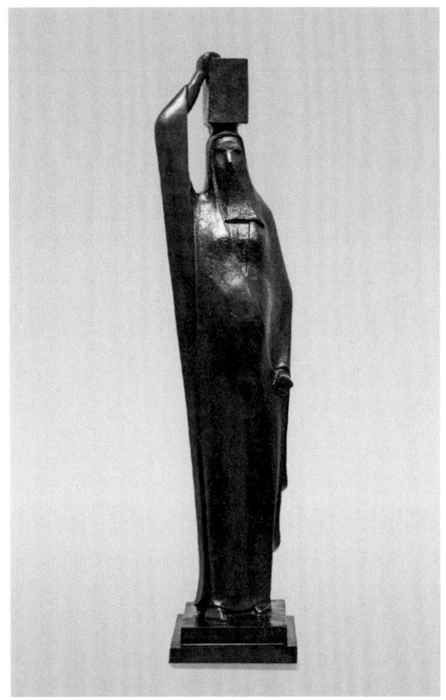

2.1 Sami Mohammed, *The Water Carrier*, undated. Bronze, 83.5 × 18 × 18 cm. Barjeel Art Foundation.

Shamiya (Naif) Gate and Jahra Gate and, as postcards from the 1940s and 1950s show (figs. 2.2, 2.3).

The discovery of the massive Burgan Oil Field, around forty-five kilometers south of Kuwait City, occurred in February 1938, two years after drilling had started. Only a month earlier, oil in commercial quantities had been found in Saudi Arabia, where the American company CaliforniaArabian Standard Oil immediately exported its first tanker load in 1939.[50] It became quickly evident that Kuwait's petroleum was especially attractive because the deposits were enormous and extremely productive—they lay close to the surface and were pressurized enough to be tapped without pumping, making the production of oil fairly cheap.[51] Nevertheless, due to restrictions on equipment and workforce during World War II, Kuwait's petroleum industrialization was suspended. Soon after the war had ended, Kuwait publicly celebrated its very first oil shipment to Britain in 1946. This event

[50] In Saudi Arabia, the American company California-Arabian Standard Oil gained the oil concession in 1933 and the Texas Oil Company took over 50 percent of its shares. From 1944 onward, the company was called Arabian-American Oil Company (ARAMCO) and, after nationalization between 1972 and 1980, eventually renamed Saudi Aramco in 1988.

[51] Stephen Longrigg, "The Economics and Politics of Oil in the Middle East," *Journal of International Affairs* 19, 1, special issue, The Arab World: Paths to Modernization (1965): 112–13.

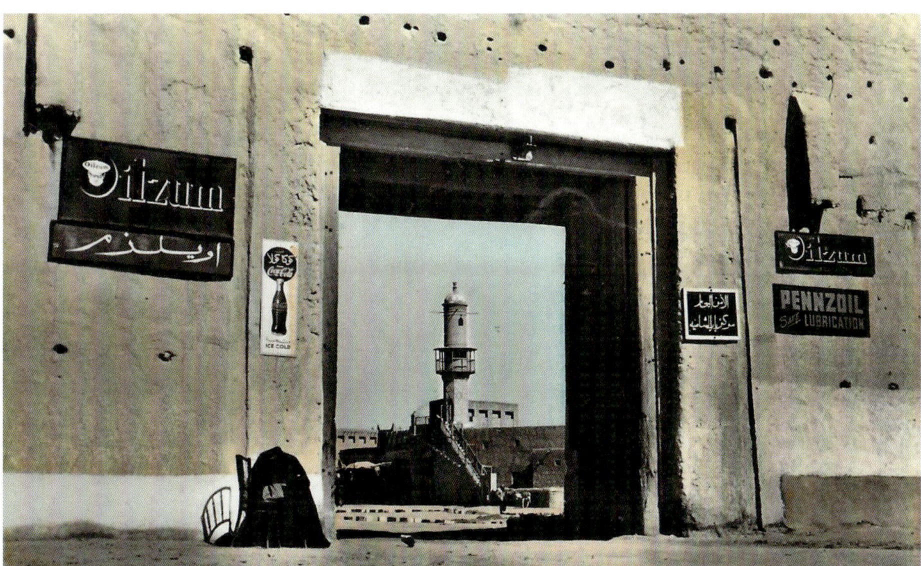

2.2 Shamiya (Naif) Gate with Pennzoil and Oilzum advertisements. Postcard mailed to the Netherlands in 1954 with a hand-colored photograph dating from the 1940s.

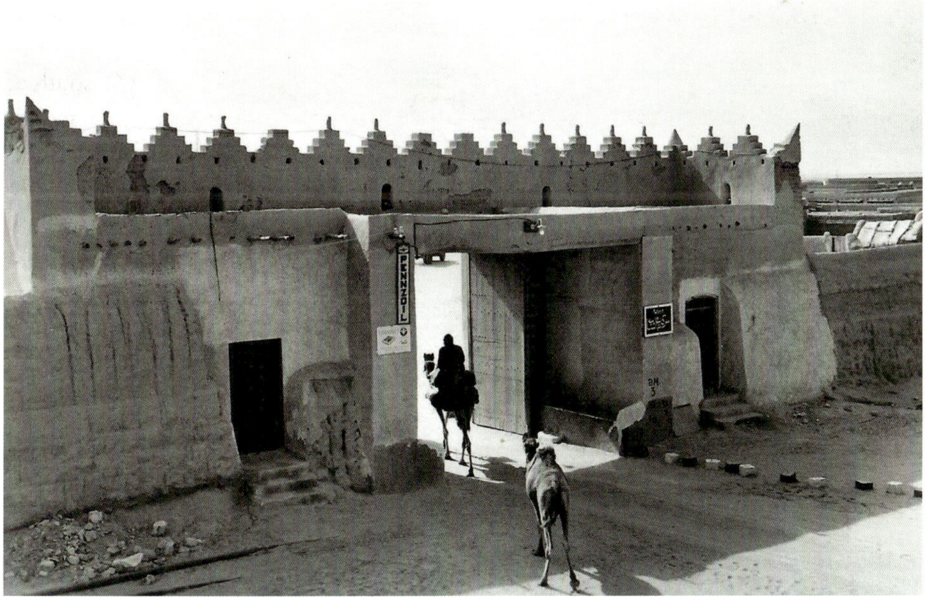

2.3 Jahra Gate with Pennzoil advertisement. Postcard from the 1950s with black-and-white photograph by Studio Badran, Kuwait City.

marked the arrival of Kuwait's petro-modernity, as the flows of petroleum were clearly not restricted to the oil-producing sector alone.

Global demand for oil skyrocketed in the late 1940s, as war-torn economies picked up again after World War II. Meanwhile, Qatar had also struck petroleum (1940) and started exporting by 1949.[52] At the time, the unequal oil concession deals stirred heavy discord, and not just in Kuwait. First the government of Venezuela (1948) and then Saudi Arabia (1950) reached a fifty-fifty oil profit-sharing agreement with their respective oil companies. Following closely, Kuwait, now ruled by Shaykh Abdullah al-Salem al-Mubarak Al Sabah, brokered a new fifty-fifty share deal with the Kuwait Oil Company by December 1951, securing an unprecedented income from oil revenues going straight to the account of the Shaykh and the Al Sabah as the sole contractor with the KOC.[53] Consequently, although Abadan (and therefore Iran) had dominated oil production in the Gulf prior to World War II, it had never gained such substantial revenues due to the nature of the oil concession deal with the APOC at the time—and thus never the same international visibility.

In this already heated atmosphere, Iran had earlier that year decided to nationalize its petroleum industry, effectively expelling the AIOC (formerly APOC), which led to an international boycott of Iranian oil. Therefore, Britain lost one of its main oil suppliers overnight, and other oil-producing British allies, protectorates, and colonies had to jump in and satisfy the petroleum demand. This historical context stimulated an explosive increase of Kuwaiti oil production and, subsequently, a dramatic surge in income from oil revenues for the ruler's household. Consequently, the power balance between the Al Sabah and the merchant families radically shifted in favor of the former.

Initially, Kuwait was by far not the biggest oil producer in the world, nor did it have the biggest proven oil reserves. By 1955, however, it was producing 15 percent of the world's petroleum output.[54] Given Kuwait's demographically and geographically small size in the early 1950s (around 100,000 people living in around 15,500 square kilometers, the size of the German federal state of Schleswig-Holstein), the amount of oil royalties per capita was enormous and unprecedented on a global scale, which stirred up much (orientalizing) excitement. As one British newspaper article from 1952 put it, "Kuwait will be, per head of

[52] An associate company of the multinational Iraq Petroleum Company (IPC) operated in Qatar and established the Petroleum Department of Qatar, which was in charge of concessions and operations. In the Trucial States (later the United Arab Emirates), the first onshore and offshore oil fields were opened up in 1958 and commenced exports in 1963 from Abu Dhabi. In charge of onshore operations was the IPC-subsidiary company, Petroleum Development (Trucial Coast), established in 1936. For the offshore explorations, another company was founded in the 1950s, the Abu Dhabi Marine Areas Ltd, which was jointly owned by British Petroleum and Compagnie Française des Pétroles (which later became Total).

[53] This salient story was immediately exploited in the international press; see, for example, "The Fabulously Rich Oilfield of Kuwait: Aspects New and Old of the Tiny State," *Illustrated London News*, December 22, 1951, 1030–31.

[54] R. L. Banks, "Notes on a Visit to Kuwait," *Town Planning Review* 26 (April 1955): 49.

its population, the richest state in the world. It is a transition more dramatic than any fable of the *Arabian Nights*."[55] From 1950 to 1961, oil production increased from 17 million to 87 million metric tons, while state revenues jumped from 16 million to 467 million dollars.[56] Within fewer than six years since the first oil export, the city-state of Kuwait had become the richest country in the world in per capita income. Suddenly Kuwait, like other Gulf states who followed in the 1960s and 1970s, was plunged into and intrinsically tied into the industrial capitalist world, as "wealth earned through oil revenues depends on world trade and fluctuating oil prices, as well as the capacity for energy consumption of the industrialized societies."[57]

2.3 Petro-States and the "Kuwaiti Model"

One of the immediate and tangible outcomes of oil production in Kuwait was a demographic surge. This surge was mostly caused by an influx of foreign skilled and unskilled labor to work in the oil industry, the quickly expanding government sector, and of course the construction industry. Visiting the country in 1953–54, young anthropologist Peter Lienhardt observed that:

> It was not, however, the Oil Company that was attracting most of the immigrants to Kuwait by this time, but rather the development of the city. Once an oil company had completed its installations, it was not a great employer of labour, unless there was a refinery, as in Bahrain. The city, on the other hand, had to produce all the services that had not been there before—metalled roads, pavements, sewers, piped water, electricity and telephone cables and new buildings—and to produce them all at once.[58]

And construction never seemed to cease. Workers, at the time mostly from other Arab and Gulf countries, were greatly attracted by "the highest money wage-scale in the Middle East" as well as free health care, education, and other services that the newly-established welfare state initially offered irrespective of citizenship.[59] By 1957, the first demographic census noted a doubling of the estimated total population of around 100,000 at the beginning of that decade, and 45 percent of the total population of 206,473 were non-Kuwaiti. Four years later Kuwait already counted 321,621 inhabitants, the majority of which lived in Kuwait City itself.[60]

[55] Lord Kinross, "The Richest State in the World," *The Listener*, December 11, 1952, 407 (italics in the original).

[56] Suhail Shuhaiber, "Social and Political Developments in Kuwait Prior to 1961," in Slot, *Kuwait*, 105.

[57] Khalaf and Hammoud, "The Emergence of the Oil Welfare State," 352.

[58] Peter Lienhardt, *Disorientations: A Society in Flux: Kuwait in the 1950s* (Reading: Ithaca Press, 1993), ed. Ahmed Al-Shahi, 35.

[59] Suhail Shuhaiber, "Social and Political Developments in Kuwait Prior to 1961," in Slot, *Kuwait*, 105.

[60] While demographics were only estimated before 1957, proper national censuses were carried out in 1957, 1961, 1965, 1970, and 1975. See the Annual Statistical Abstract by the Ministry of Planning, Kuwait 1977,

Because the growing number of people and oil revenues needed organization, in the logic of development and modernization, the government of Kuwait was institutionalized and expanded into a modern bureaucratic apparatus. A central goal of the government was to provide the (built) infrastructure for schooling, medical care, employment, and housing, all of which was offered for free to people living in Kuwait. Bedouin received incentives for sedentation. The influential merchants, who also had the best formal education, received important government posts. Former seamen and pearl divers found new employment in the lower ranks of the governmental institutions but also in the oil industry.

A fascinating testimony is Nasser Al-Othman's book *With Their Bare Hands: The Story of the Oil Industry in Qatar*, for which he collected interviews with Qatari men who had been the first to work in the oil industry. Several men recall shifting from pearling to working for the oil company in Qatar in the late 1930s and early 1940s—similar changes in professional biographies can be assumed in Kuwait, too.[61] Many of the men interviewed explained their motivation due to the fact that aside from pearling, there was no other form of employment until the oil sector opened up and offered lucrative jobs. For example, Muhammad Muftah recalled: "I was paid 25 rupees for three months at sea compared with 30 rupees a month while working for the company."[62] Not only in Qatar, but across the Gulf and in Kuwait, the workforce who once toiled the pearling ships often found new employment in the oil industry, underlining the fact that the oil companies also played a crucial role in the overall modernization and nation building process by providing jobs and income to the local population.[63]

After World War II, the Kuwaiti government began distributing the new wealth gained from oil revenues not only by establishing an impressive welfare state but also other channels. One important strategy was purchasing privately-owned land within the third town wall at increasingly inflated prices and then resettling the inhabitants within the newly emerging suburban neighborhoods outside the wall and the historical core on the basis of the first master plan, which had been introduced in 1952. To give an idea of the scope of this project, in 1961 the government still spent a third of its annual budget on land acquisitions, while 20 percent of the budget financed public works.[64] Moreover, the government allocated land, developed and distributed it either as building plot or as

reprinted in Abdullah Abu-Ayyash, "Urban Development and Planning Strategies in Kuwait," *International Journal of Urban and Regional Research* 4, no. 4 (1980): 553–54 and table 1.

[61] See David Finnie, "Recruitment and Training of Labor: The Middle East Oil Industry," *Middle East Journal* 12, no. 2 (1958).

[62] Nasser Al-Othman, *With Their Bare Hands: The Story of the Oil Industry in Qatar* (London/New York: Longman, 1984), 91.

[63] Bowen, "The Pearl Fisheries of the Persian Gulf," 179–80.

[64] Suhail Shuhaiber, "Social and Political Developments in Kuwait Prior to 1961," in Slot, *Kuwait*, 106–7. The author draws on the World Bank report *The Economic Development of Kuwait* (Baltimore: John Hopkins, 1965).

state-built housing to Kuwaitis. To this day, "housing has become the currency through which the state physically transfers its wealth to its citizens," argues architect and urban researcher Sharifa Alshalfan.[65]

In this "oil mode of production," as social scientists Sulayman Khalaf and Hassan Hammoud call it, "wealth is not generated by productive social forces from within society itself, but it is distributed to the population by a new and continually expanding state bureaucratic apparatus."[66] Here, the government as well as "economic life … became almost entirely dependent on oil revenues, … shaping in an accelerated form all aspects of social life in these 'old societies.'"[67] This constellation, usually described as an oil rentier state, implies that the government is not dependent on the citizens for taxes and is also not politically accountable to them, but receives its budget to a large extent from oil revenues, of which it is the principal recipient.[68] While only a few are involved in the generation of oil revenues, the majority are involved in its dissemination and spending.[69] In an oil rentier state, citizens usually fully depend on the government, and therefore almost exclusively on the economic monopoly of oil production.

Eventually, a new Nationality Law, written in 1959 and amended in 1960, sharply defined and limited the conditions for entitlement to Kuwaiti citizenship and the access to much of the state's welfare system; one crucial factor was whether someone had lived within Kuwait (as delineated by the third town wall) prior to 1920, as the wall eventually served as the benchmark of citizenship entitlement, and hence also became a symbolic marker of Kuwaiti national identity.[70] Another new law provided that all foreign companies operating in Kuwait had to be 51 percent Kuwaiti-owned and run jointly with a Kuwaiti partner. Peter Mansfield, a British political journalist visiting Kuwait in the late

65 Sharifa Alshalfan, "The Aftermath of a Masterplan for Kuwait: An Exploration of the Forces that Shape Kuwait City," in *"Wise Cities" in the Mediterranean? Challenges of Urban Sustainability*, ed. Eckart Woertz (Barcelona: CIDOB edicions, 2018), 217–20, here 219; for a detailed discussion of housing and the Kuwaiti oil welfare state see Sharifa Alshalfan, *The Right to Housing in Kuwait: An Urban Injustice in a Socially Just System,* Kuwait Programm on Development, Governance and Globalisation in the Gulf States 28 (London: London School of Economics, 2013).

66 Khalaf and Hammoud, "The Emergence of the Oil Welfare State," 350.

67 Ibid.

68 First introduced by Hossein Mahdavy, the rentier state concept was subsequently refined and adapted to describe oil-producing and exporting (Arab) countries including Kuwait. Although much debated, it continues to be one of the dominant explanatory models in economic and political studies. Hossein Mahdavy, "The Pattern and Problems of Economic Development in Rentier States," in *Studies in the Economic History of the Middle East: From the Rise of Islam to the Present Day*, ed. Michael A. Cook (London: Oxford University Press, 1970), 428–67; Jacqueline S. Ismael, *Kuwait: Dependency and Class in a Rentier State*, 2nd ed. (Gainesville: University Press of Florida, [1982] 1993); Hazem Beblawi, "The Rentier State in the Arab World," in Beblawi; Luciani, *The Rentier State*; Giacomo Luciani, "Allocation vs. Production States: A Theoretical Framework," in Beblawi; Luciani, *The Rentier State*.

69 See Hazem Beblawi, "The Rentier State in the Arab World," in Beblawi; Luciani, *The Rentier State*, 51.

70 See Fuccaro, "Pearl Towns and Early Oil Cities," 111.

1950s, observed that "although Kuwait was physically changing at an astonishing pace in the 1950s and an inexorable shift was taking place in its population structure, the country was far from losing its individual character. On the contrary, this character was becoming stronger and more self-confident."[71] Indeed, the 1950s provided for the nationalization or "Kuwaitization" of the economy and the country, which resulted in an overall enhancement of a Kuwaiti national identity. The evolving system of "reverse taxation"—whereby the government paid the citizens through direct payments, government jobs, public services, property, and other welfare benefits in combination with a protection scheme in order to prevent certain groups considered "alien" (such as expatriates, residents without Kuwaiti citizenship) from accessing many of the oil-funded benefits—became known as "Kuwaiti model"; with some modifications, it was adopted by the other Gulf states once they started oil production.[72]

Given the unprecedented speed and magnitude of change while moving from being a pre-oil community to being one of the world's most significant oil producers, the level of political and socioeconomic stability in Kuwait was remarkable but not unusual for petro-states during this earlier oil-producing period.[73] In *The Paradox of Plenty: Oil Booms and Petro-States* (1997), Terry Lynn Karl has assessed the impact of oil booms, especially those occurring throughout the 1970s (of which Kuwait's 1950s boom is a forerunner), on oil-exporting countries and found that many apparently diverse oil countries shared strong similarities. First, all of them came to depend heavily on the same commodity (oil) as their prime export product. Secondly, the development of the petroleum industry very often also coincided with state formation, making petroleum the common denominator: "The petro-state's technical and administrative resources, its *symbolic* content, its institutional separateness, and its own interests are most fundamentally shaped by its leading export activity [petroleum]," effectively interlinking the formation of a national identity also ideologically with oil.[74] Thirdly, the petro-states had difficulties exerting political authority in a rentier setting. Fourthly and finally, despite the wealth of oil and especially oil revenues during oil booms, they all struggled to cope with managing the money and, subsequently, to adapt their expenditures from periods of abundance to periods of stagnation caused by fluctuations in the global oil market. Karl subsequently refined the resource curse theory for the case of petro-states—which today is referred to as the "oil curse"—in order to explain the harsh downsides of this phenomenon.[75] In the mid-twentieth century, Kuwait,

[71] Peter Mansfield, *Kuwait: Vanguard of the Gulf* (London: Hutchinson, 1990), 47.

[72] Hazem Beblawi, "The Rentier State in the Arab World," in Beblawi; Luciani, *The Rentier State*, 54; E. R. Owen, "One Hundred Years of Middle Eastern Oil," *Middle East Brief*, no. 24 (2008): 3, accessed January 25, 2021, https://www.brandeis.edu/crown/publications/middle-east-briefs/pdfs/1-100/meb24.pdf.

[73] Terry Lynn Karl, *The Paradox of Plenty: Oil Booms and Petro-States*, Studies in International Political Economy 26 (Berkeley: University of California Press, 1997), 58.

[74] Ibid., 46 (author's emphasis).

[75] First introduced by Richard Auty in 1993, resource curse theory was subsequently applied to oil-producing countries in the work of Terry Lynn Karl in the 1990s. Richard M. Auty, *Sustaining Development in*

Venezuela, and many other petro-states for the time being enjoyed affluence, capital, and political stability—with petroleum affirmatively infusing also much of their *symbolic* and thus visual representation.

Just as the Gulf states share the oil industry as common history, they used to share pearling as their socioeconomic history of boom and bust, as "pearls tied the Gulf to the regional and global market."[76] Victoria Hightower argues that "the pearl was a valuable commodity throughout history because it was low bulk, high value, and relatively easy to acquire and transport."[77] Pearls have always been a commodity and an export product, similar to petroleum. Birgit Krawitz's statement that "those for whom pearling was a lucrative business were globally networked entrepreneurs who met their peers in commercial metropolises" could equally serve to describe the subsequently emerging oil industry networks, which were of course much more corporate.[78]

Accordingly, in 1950s Kuwait it became petroleum, and no longer the complex debt system typical of the maritime pre-oil economy, that now held society together.[79] Kuwait's riches no longer lay in the pearl banks out at sea but in fossil deposits underneath the desert sand, a shift from pearlescence to iridescence. It appears that the oil concessions and finally the successful launch of the oil industries across the Arab Gulf states came just in time to ease the life-threatening depression after the demise of the pearling industry. Kuwaiti historian Mohamad Abdul Hadi Jamal argues:

> Had it not been for the discovery of oil during that period and the turning of big numbers of Kuwaitis to work in the Oil Company as well as the flourishing of the commercial activity, it would have been difficult to imagine the living conditions of Kuwaitis as a result of halting of the pearl diving business and traveling to India. The discovery of oil has led, in a few years, to changing the life of Kuwaitis and

Mineral Economies: The Resource Curse Thesis (London: Routledge, 1993); Karl, *The Paradox of Plenty*. In current anthropological research, the oil curse is conceptualized as "the triple conjuncture in petro-states of stagnating social development and poverty; high conflict, often violent; and a tendency towards authoritarian regimes." The authors call it the "crazy curse" because of the paradox of oil money producing more of a "petro-curse" than a "petro-utopia." Stephen P. Reyna and Andrea Behrends, "The Crazy Curse and Crude Domination: Towards an Anthropology of Oil," in *Crude Domination: An Anthropology of Oil*, ed. Andrea Behrends, Stephen P. Reyna, and Günther Schlee (New York: Berghahn, 2011), 6.

[76] Victoria Hightower, "Pearls and the Southern Persian/Arabian Gulf: A Lesson in Sustainability," *Environmental History* 18, no. 1 (2013): 46.

[77] Ibid., 45.

[78] Birgit Krawietz, "The Sports Path Not Taken: Pearl Diving Heritage and Cosmopolitanism from Below," *Sport, Ethics and Philosophy* 14, no. 3 (2020): 11.

[79] In her comparative study of Venezuela, Iran, Nigeria, Algeria, Indonesia, and Norway, Terry Lynn Karl defines this radical substitution of former economic systems as a common denominator of petro-states. See Karl, *The Paradox of Plenty*. Jill Crystal also emphasizes that the political continuity and smoothness of transition "from pearling to petroleum" was achieved "because of oil, not despite it." See Crystal, *Oil and Politics in the Gulf*, 1

> their living style radically, after which the years of hardship had only become memories, and those who lived through them could hardly believe that such a nightmare had vanished.[80]

All social groups in Kuwait soon depended on the revenues from oil production, while the sea as livelihood (together with boatbuilding and pearling as professions) rapidly lost its importance. Conversely, the historical importance of imports was reinforced during the oil period to cover everything from basic supplies to the latest luxury goods. Through the diverse channels of pumping oil monies into society, the connecting maxim became partaking in the spending of this money. Kuwaiti society itself turned out to be implicit in fueling the demand (and justification) of oil production, as Kuwaitis immersed themselves in a lifestyle drenched in fossil energy, petroleum-derived products, and the iridescent attractions of petro-modernity.

All petro-states in the Gulf relied on foreign oil companies to initiate the capital-intensive and large-scale oil industry. These foreign firms became highly influential due to their monopolistic, internationally well-connected, and indispensable role in maintaining the petro-state.[81] They claimed an ambivalent but powerful position within each Gulf state in the second half of the twentieth century. "On the one hand, they upheld and perpetuated the political units which had evolved and developed under British aegis; on the other, they acted as agents of major change. The two effects were mutually reinforcing," suggests Rosemarie Said Zahlan.[82] In the mid-twentieth century, the major players in the Kuwaiti oil state were, besides the oil company, the ruling family as sole oil-revenue receiver and powerful distributor, and the still-influential merchant families. The latter would establish business empires with exclusive licenses for international brands, as, for example, Yousef Ahmed al-Ghanim, who was the Kuwaiti representative of BP products like Energol, which he advertised prominently in the Kuwaiti magazine *al-ʿArabī*.[83] Political power, however, had shifted in favor of the Al Sabah, who no longer depended (as much) on the merchants.

Most areas of social and economic life in Kuwait felt the impact of petroleum drastically and the two formerly most important environments of Kuwait, the sea and the desert, were radically subverted. As early as 1954, for instance, Peter Lienhardt noted that all of the old seafaring activities had substantially declined and that "only fishing continued to flourish in the old way," but that "even that had changed a little with the addition of diesel engines to convert the old sailing boats into launches."[84] Harold Dickson, when explaining the sinking demand for pearls, suggested: "A girl to-day asks for a car, where formerly she

[80] Mohamad Abdul Hadi Jamal, *The Old Crafts, Trades, and Commercial Activities in Kuwait* (Kuwait: Center for Research and Studies on Kuwait, 2009), 118.

[81] Karl, *The Paradox of Plenty*, 47, 49–52.

[82] Zahlan, *The Making of the Modern Gulf States*, 16.

[83] Back cover of the November 1964 issue of *al-ʿArabī* magazine, no. 72.

[84] Lienhardt, *Disorientations: A Society in Flux*, 94.

craved a pearl necklace."[85] This suggestion is astonishing as it suggests a similar economic value between a pearl necklace and a car. Nevertheless, the observation indicates the sharp rise in petroleum demand, and the lifestyles it stimulated went somewhat hand in hand with a decreasing interest in traditional commodities such as pearls.

Around the same time, American Foreign Service officer Richard Sanger described the change stimulated by the petroleum (industry) of the Saudi Arabian desert landscape close to the Kuwaiti border:

> For some distance inland the dunes and gravel plains, which a few years ago recorded only the footprints of infrequent caravans the unmistakable traces of Bedouin encampments, are crisscrossed with motor and railroad tracks, telephone wires, and pipe lines. Oil drums used as markers and road signs in English and Arabic give new character to the landscape in the daytime, while giant gas flares light up the landscape at night.[86]

Yet the field where petro-modernity struck most heavily and visibly, and where change was most felt and seen, was in the urban space of Kuwait. To assess the 1950s urban transformation and its resonance in urban visual culture, the following section provides an architectural and socio-spatial inventory of the town of Kuwait and the urban visual culture that existed until around the mid- to late 1940s.

2.4 Pre-Oil Architecture and Visual Culture: An Inventory

The bustling pre-oil town of Kuwait was nested between the Gulf and the 1920 town wall, between the sea and the desert.[87] Given the extensive maritime economy, the waterfront (*sāḥil*) formed one of the busiest parts of the town. Here, ingoing and outgoing ships of all shapes and sizes were lined up, either propped up on the beach or moored along the shore, where low man-made coral walls functioned as breakwaters and created tidal basins for the dhows. Shipwrights were at work in the wharves and goods were loaded, unloaded, and inspected around the Customs House built in 1904 and the nearby *al-furḍa* market. Close by and roughly in the middle of the shoreline, Seif Palace stood on the site of the former Banū Khālid fort. It was considered the town house of the ruler, who

[85] Dickson, *The Arab of the Desert*, 485.

[86] Richard H. Sanger, *The Arabian Peninsula* (Ithaca: Cornell University Press, 1954), Photographs by courtesy of ARAMCO, California Texas Oil and Gulf Oil, 113; for a similar but not as illuminating description of Kuwait's desert see 164.

[87] The following description is mainly based on the analysis of historical photographs from the KOC photographic archives as well as published photo collections, such as Basem E. Alloughani, *Kuwait in Black and White: A Rare Collection of Pictures of Kuwait Before Oil* (Kuwait: Xlibris, 2008) and ʿAlī G. al-Raʾīs, *Ṣuwar min aswāq al-Kuwayt al-qadīma: 1916–1966 milādī* [*Pictures of the Souks of Old Kuwait: The Years 1916–1966*] (al-Kuwayt: Markaz al-Buḥūth wa-l-Dirāsāt al-Kuwaytiyya, 2017). The description also relies on these analyses of pre-oil Kuwait: Al-Nakib, *Kuwait Transformed*; Al-Nakib, "Inside a Gulf Port"; Broeze, "Kuwait Before Oil."

otherwise lived in Dasman Palace at the northeastern edge of the town.[88] In 1912, Barclay Raunkiær described Seif Palace as a large complex of various architectural styles indicative of the building's gradual adaptation and expansion. He recalled that it included the ruler's personal chambers, the facilities of his servants, and a governmental building, on the second floor of which there were large reception spaces with arcaded glass windows and furnished with European-style chairs and sofas.[89] A small road called Seif Street (today the Arabian Gulf Road, a massive three-lane highway) led directly along the waterfront, and across the road was a line of storehouses, coffee shops, and imposing merchant houses, the largest houses in Kuwait besides the Al Sabah properties.[90]

Seif Palace also stimulated descriptions by Western travelers visiting Kuwait and these travel accounts shed light on the first spaces of accumulated image display and the kind of images that were present in Kuwait in the early twentieth century prior to the image-world of petro-modernity. Hermann Burchardt noted the reception rooms decorated *à la franca* with photographs of the English royal couple in December 1903, and in the 1930s Alain Villiers recounted: "Later in the day we had coffee with His Highness at his waterside palace, the one in the heart of the city where his grandfather, the Lion Mubarak, had decorated the bedrooms with ceilings filled with the lithographs of actresses and queens."[91] He also noted the presence of some photographs.[92] Based on his extensive photography and postcard collections, Kuwaiti historian Ali AlRais ('Alī Ghulūm al-Ra'īs) has shown that early postcards depicting Kuwait's harbor front and Bedouins at Safat Square were printed in Bombay as early as 1916.[93] However, no permanent photographer resided in Kuwait until the mid-1930s.

Besides Seif Palace on the shoreline, the large souk was another focal point of Kuwait's morphology that extended from the *sāḥil* to the town's center. Branching out landward from the port and waterfront alongside the souk were the honeycombed residential quarters.[94] To the east and west lay the mercantile quarter Jibla and the maritime and

[88] See Al-Nakib, *Kuwait Transformed*, 117–18.

[89] Raunkiær, *Through Wahhabiland on Camelback (1913)*, 33–34. Al-Nakib states that Seif Palace was built in the 1890s. Al-Nakib, *Kuwait Transformed*, 29. It is commonly said that the main diwan was built by Mubarak I. in 1905–06 and that the palace was substantially refurbished in 1917.

[90] Broeze, "Kuwait Before Oil," 174.

[91] Annegret Nippa and Peter Herbstreuth, *Along the Gulf: From Basra to Muscat: Photographs by Hermann Burchardt* (Berlin: Hans Schiler, 2006), 62–63; Villiers, *Sons of Sindbad*, 312. In 1913, Barclay Raunkiær also saw and described this room's decoration in detail: "The ceiling is divided into panels by wooden fillets. Each panel is occupied by a polychrome lithograph, representing a young and appetizing [*sic*], including European, female beauty." Raunkiær, *Through Wahhabiland on Camelback (1913)*, 34.

[92] Alan Villiers, *Sons of Sindbad: The Photographs* (London: National Maritime Museum, 2006), 312.

[93] Al-Ra'īs, *Ṣuwar min aswāq al-Kuwayt al-qadīma*, 22–23; see also 'Alī G. al-Ra'īs, *Kuwait in Postcards* (Kuwait: Center for Research and Studies on Kuwait, 2009).

[94] Farah Al-Nakib describes these residential quarters in great detail; see Al-Nakib, "Inside a Gulf Port," 218–21.

pearling quarter Sharq, while Mirqab, which was developed by Nejdi Arabs employed in construction, extended from the souk southwestward.

Until the 1940s, when corrugated metal roofing sheets (locally called *shinko*) were added to provide shade, the souk was either open or covered by awnings made of wood or woven palm mats. Side by side and accessible by wooden doors, merchants' offices and vendors' shops clustered in specialized markets according to the kind of goods sold; there were, for instance, markets which specialized in corn, water, rugs and cloaks, or bookbinding. The ruler also conducted his everyday business in a two-story kiosk (*kishk*) within the souk.[95] Historical photographs show that, from the late 1940s onward when oil revenues began sweeping the country, adverts for Western goods became more frequent and items such as refrigerators and gas-powered stoves were put on display.[96] Cars, from Volkswagen to Chevrolet, also increasingly frequented the few wider streets.

According to one account, the first car (together with an Indian driver) had arrived in Kuwait as a gift to Shaykh Mubarak in 1912.[97] Over the following two decades, a number of wealthy merchants also purchased cars with drivers, which resulted in a small fleet of taxis in the 1920s and a group of lorries servicing the roads to Saudi Arabia and Iraq during the 1930s. Around this time, car caravans were initiated to transport pilgrims in convoys across the desert from Kuwait to Mecca and Medina, a business which eventually became substituted by more comfortable air travel. On a larger scale, along with the expanding oil industry, privately owned cars rapidly increased in popularity and, of course, affordability in the late 1940s stimulating corresponding infrastructure of petrol stations, car workshops, and automobile salesrooms typical of twentieth-century petro-modernity.

Another element of urban importance was Safat Square (*Sāḥat al-Ṣafāt*), which was connected with the market and the residential areas via several access points. As historian Farah Al-Nakib observes, "the Safat was the counterpoint to the *sahel*: whereas the latter was where the town interacted with the sea, the former was where the urban met the desert."[98] From here toward the town wall there lay more or less open land for Bedouin tribesmen to camp in. Additional unbuilt spaces in the urban morphology included several cemeteries, which were located here and between residential areas.

Situated on an axis from Seif Palace to Naif Gate (part of the 1920 town wall), Safat Square lastingly shaped the urban morphology of Kuwait Town. The big open-air space was framed by small shops and served as the gathering point of three historic caravan routes. Caravans and Bedouins used the space to trade camels and other livestock and sell

95 Raunkiær, *Through Wahhabiland on Camelback (1913)*, 35 and 50.

96 Al-Ra'īs, *Ṣuwar min aswāq al-Kuwayt al-qadīma*, 172–73.

97 Jamal, *The Old Crafts, Trades, and Commercial Activities in Kuwait*, 471–76.

98 Al-Nakib, "Inside a Gulf Port," 214 (italics in the original).

goods such as brushwood, leather, and camel thorn.[99] Public celebrations also took place here, including Shaykh Abdullah's coronation on February 25, 1950.[100] From the 1930s onward, the Department of Finance, the police station, the British Bank of the Middle East, the Security Department, coffee shops and the *baladiyya*, the municipality founded in 1930, began framing the always-busy square.[101] Later, car showrooms and rental agencies also opened here. Safat Square became notorious for being congested by cars and local taxis, which used the area both for parking and as a thoroughfare. Gradually evolving as an urban nexus in the 1950s, Safat emerged as a motif of Kuwait's petro-modernity in visual representations as will be discussed later.

Until its demolition in 1957, the third town wall effectively marked the boundary of Kuwait Town, enclosing an area of 7.5 square kilometers. The wall not only delineated jurisdiction but effectively shaped the (visual) urban form of both the pre-oil *and* the oil city, as the next chapter will analyze in detail. The wall comprised four gates and the mud-based construction was apparently a community effort to which every Kuwaiti was conscripted and thus became an important historical reference within the urban space and also in popular memory.[102]

Imagining a view of Kuwait from afar with its mainly one-story houses clustering over relatively flat terrain, the town's silhouette seems to have been rather plain. This included the town's religious buildings; according to historian Frank Broeze, "[the mosques' minarets] were such low structures that they were hardly visible above the houses of the city. Not even Kuwait's great mosque, close to the *suq*, possessed a dome or prominent minaret; instead it had a kind of architraved gate-tower over its entrance."[103] If anything, as Al-Nakib describes, "the roof of the palace became the highest point in the town, giving the ruler and his guards a clear view of the sea, port, market, and residential areas."[104] However, on the ground, Al-Nakib argues that "it was the town harbor rather than a mosque, palace, or citadel that served as the locus of expansion, making it similar to port towns from the Mediterranean to the Red Sea and Indian Ocean."[105] In summary, the town of Kuwait comprised a tightly knitted, walled-off urban fabric whose focal spaces were the waterfront with the Sief Palace, the souk, the residential areas, and open spaces such as Safat Square and several cemeteries.

[99] Villiers, *Sons of Sindbad*, 359. On the caravan routes see Al-Ragam, "Towards a Critique of an Architectural Nahdha," 34, 39–42.

[100] Al-Ragam, "Towards a Critique of an Architectural Nahdha," 35.

[101] On the historical development of the *baladiyya* into an "agent of change in Kuwait" see ibid., 35–37, here 35.

[102] Abu-Hakima, *The Modern History of Kuwait*, 133.

[103] Broeze, "Kuwait Before Oil," 172 (italics in the original).

[104] Al-Nakib, *Kuwait Transformed*, 31. The name is derived from *al-saif*, the Arabic word for seafront.

[105] Al-Nakib, "Inside a Gulf Port," 210–11.

Vernacular Architecture

Shifting from a distant horizontal viewpoint to a close-up perspective, the pre-oil, mostly domestic architecture of Kuwait can be characterized as follows:[106] houses were clustered in quarters (*farīj; pl. firjān*) around a local mosque and a little square with a few shops. Given that the main means of transportation before the mid-1940s were going on foot or by donkey, streets consisted primarily of small lanes and blind alleys. The tight-knit arrangement was also influenced by the fact that building houses in dense clusters increased the available shade, which could be enjoyed on the outdoor benches, called *maṣṭaba*, protruding from many houses.

Groups of houses inhabited by an extended family were usually built around a central courtyard. Most windows would have opened into the yard, which sometimes included "Sidr" trees and a cistern to collect rainwater. Most of the buildings in Kuwait were constructed using some kind of sun-dried mud bricks. More important structures like mosques, some merchant houses, and the Seif Palace were built using hard coral stone, which was locally mined at the shore. The often windowless outside walls were occasionally left unplastered, but were usually coated with locally found mud or gypsum.

The roofs of ordinary houses were lined by carved wooden or mud-brick parapets to shield the open rooftop space visually and to allow for air circulation. Wooden horizontal waterspouts or roof gutters (*badgeer*) pierced the outer walls to circulate cooling air but also to direct water from the flat roofs into the cisterns or onto the streets. The roof itself was supported by mangrove poles (locally known as *jandals*) usually imported from Lamu Island off the Kenyan coast or from the Rufiji Delta in today's Tanzania. Used as beams, their lengths determined the width of Kuwaiti houses. On top of these poles, mats made of reed or Iraqi date palm leaves held a mixture of mud and straw that formed the ceiling and roof as one. Teak wood imported from India was used in the pillars supporting the courtyard houses' verandas and for the richly carved wooden doors Kuwait and other Gulf towns were known for. The common architectural style, made up of building techniques, specific materials, and ornamentation found in wooden carvings (doors, furniture) constituted what can be called one aspect of the pre-oil urban visual culture prevailing in Kuwait that effectively shaped Kuwait's overall appearance, its image.

Pearls also played a role in this regard. In a way, the remains of pearling formed the sediment on which the modern Gulf cities were built on. Richard L. Bowen, a chemical engineer by profession who worked for the Arabian American Oil Company in Saudi Arabia between 1945 to 1947, reported the following story:

[106] For detailed descriptions of the vernacular pre-oil architecture in Kuwait and in the Gulf, see Ronald Lewcock and Zahra Freeth, *Traditional Architecture in Kuwait and the Northern Gulf*, Art and Archaeology Research Papers (London: United Bank of Kuwait, 1978), 15–24; Stephen Gardiner, *Kuwait: The Making of a City* (Burnt Mill: Longman, 1983), 16–19; Huda Al-Bahar, "Traditional Kuwaiti Houses," *Mimar*, no. 13 (1984); Evangelia S. Ali, "Retracing Old Kuwait," in *Kuwait Arts and Architecture: A Collection of Essays*, ed. Arlene Fullerton and Géza Fehérvári (Kuwait: Oriental, 1995); Al-Nakib, *Kuwait Transformed*, 54–69.

> When the refinery at Ras Tanura [in Saudi Arabia, completed 1945] was being built, a low hill was leveled by bulldozers. Cutting through many ancient graves they turned up a stone diving weight among the numerous bones and pottery. Between Jubail and Ras Tanura, several more ancient shell heaps have been located high on the beach. Some of these are composed *entirely* of the large plate-sized species of pearl oysters.[107]

Given that all Gulf states participated in pearling, bulldozers that demolished the old town of Kuwait during the 1950s likely encountered such pearling remains, too.

Overall, this vernacular style and method of building was practiced until well into the 1940s. As Alan Villiers reported in 1939, despite heavy rainfalls that had destroyed over 2,000 houses,

> this disaster had not brought about any improvement in the style of building. Houses were still without foundations, still only walls of coral stones. Here and there I saw new houses laced with Japanese cement, and some of these looked a little better. The habit of using cement was on the increase he [Nejdi, a Kuwaiti captain] said; but he doubted its value, for the local builders put too much sand in the cement.[108]

From these observations it can be established that imported cement was occasionally used in construction by the late 1930s. It is noteworthy that not only modern reinforced concrete (or cement) architecture relied on building material imports, but also pre-oil architecture depended heavily on imported goods. In addition, it was common for Kuwaiti architecture to be regularly renovated and even rebuilt after heavy rain, thus designating a certain temporality as characteristic concept of coastal architecture in the Gulf.

Western businesses were largely absent from Kuwait before the establishment of the KOC in 1934. Until that time, only a few Westerners had stayed for longer periods in Kuwait; among these were the British Political Agents, the staff of the American Mission, and oilmen engaged in prospecting oil and brokering licenses, such as the geologists Arnold Heim and Frank Holmes.[109] However, until the first export of oil in 1946 and the subsequent incoming oil revenues, oil business was conducted outside Kuwait City in the oil company town of Ahmadi, around forty kilometers south of the capital, and "little of its impact was felt there."[110] In Kuwait Town, the first two houses with strong Western architectural influence in terms of style, building materials, and construction method, were the Political Agency and the American Mission hospital.[111] Some of the early civic buildings, including the *baladiyya* and the Departments of Finance and Public Security, projected the earliest shift in local architectural style, notably the embellishment of the façade and the roof parapet.[112] In the late 1940s, Kuwait Town's urban form still consisted

[107] Bowen, "The Pearl Fisheries of the Persian Gulf," 177 (italics in the original).

[108] Villiers, *Sons of Sindbad*, 314.

[109] Broeze, "Kuwait Before Oil," 161.

[110] Ibid.

[111] Ibid., 178. Arguably, these buildings did not have a strong influence on subsequent architectural styles.

[112] See Al-Ragam, "Towards a Critique of an Architectural Nahdha," 37–38.

of a honeycombed cluster of low buildings of a fairly homogenous vernacular style, typical of the Gulf coast, that encompassed the historically grown focal points of the waterfront, the souk, and, in Kuwait especially, Safat Square.

The Emergence of Visual Arts

Besides the scarce appearance of photography and portrait lithographs as displayed at Sief Palace, Kuwait's pre-oil visual culture was rooted in material forms and cultural practices such as pearling, wood carvings, metal work, textiles, and in architecture—contexts where the visual and the material went hand in hand.[113] However, "Western" art forms such as linear perspective drawing and easel painting as well as institutionalized art education were not unknown. Around 1936–37 when the oil explorations were in full swing, the formal school system in Kuwait was revised and art as an extracurricular subject was introduced at the prestigious Al Mubarakiyya School (*al-Madrasa al- Mubārakiyya*).[114] Still, Tareq Sayid Rajab (1935–2016), a passionate painter, photographer, and later founder of the Tareq Rajab Museum displaying Islamic art, argued that "painting and drawing had virtually no role and except for the few pictures we saw in imported magazines, we had no idea at all," when he was a student at Al Mubarakiya in the late 1940s, early 1950s. Probably during the 1940s, the Kuwaiti government initiated a scholarship program to study abroad that allowed its recipients to obtain a formal art education, mostly in Egypt and Great Britain. The biography of Mojeb al-Dousari (1922–1956), today considered a pioneering artist and who later became the art teacher to Rajab at Al Mubarakiya, reflects these early educational opportunities for Kuwaitis.[115] Although there was no full-fledged art scene in Kuwait during the first half of the twentieth century, the early rudimentary,

[113] For a broad overview of pre-oil material cultures of the Arabian Peninsula, see Ileana P. Baird and Hülya Yağcıoğlu, eds., *All Things Arabia: Arabian Identity and Material Culture*, Arts and Archaeology of the Islamic World 16 (Leiden/Boston: Brill, 2021).

[114] The interest of notable families in Kuwait to reform their children's education led to the opening of Al Mubarakiyya School on December 11, 1911. It became the first formal school in Kuwait with its own premises, a curriculum, and staff, many from Palestine and Egypt. Initially, only boys were allowed, but an additional girls' school was opened in 1937–38. Kuwait National Council for Culture, Arts and Letters, *Mubarakiya School: 100 Years' History of Education in Kuwait* (Kuwait: Kuwait National Council for Culture, Arts and Letters, 2011). On art education in Kuwait see Muayad H. Hussain, "Modern Art from Kuwait: Khalifa Qattan and Circulism" (PhD diss., University of Birmingham, 2012), accessed January 21, 2021, https://etheses.bham.ac.uk/id/eprint/3909/1/Hussain_12_PhD_v1.pdf, 30–33; "Kuwait," in *The Grove Encyclopedia of Islamic Art and Architecture*, ed. Jonathan Bloom and Sheila Blair, 3 vols. vol. 2 (New York: Oxford University Press, 2009), 405.

[115] Sultan S. Al Qassemi, "Correcting Misconceptions of the Gulf's Modern Art Movement," *Al-Monitor*, November 22, 2013, accessed January 22, 2021, https://www.al-monitor.com/pulse/originals/2013/11/gulf-visual-arts-modern-indigenous-tradition-misconception.html; Tareq Sayid Rajab, *Tareq Sayid Rajab and the Development of Fine Art in Kuwait* (Kuwait: Tareq Rajab Museum, 2001), iii–iv.

and later evolving art infrastructure can provide clues to understand assessments such as the following statement made by the Grove Encyclopedia of Islamic Art and Architecture that "the modern art movement in Kuwait is the oldest among those in the Arabian Peninsula."[116] Also Sultan Sooud Al Qassemi, art collector, educator, and founder of Barjeel Art Foundation, and the art historian Wijdan Ali have stressed Kuwait's historic role for the proliferation of modern art in the Gulf.[117]

A generation and more after al-Dousari, Khalifa Qattan (1934–2003), Sami Mohammed (*1943), Munira Al-Kazi (*1939), Abdullah Al Qassar (1941–2003), Ibrahim Ismail (*1945), Thuraya Al-Baqsami (*1952) and others were able to forge artistic careers as visual artists and sculptors and gained national and international attention to various degrees.[118] Besides strong figurative tendencies among Kuwaiti artists, Surrealism was favored by Al Qassar and others, and Qattan developed his own style and aesthetic theory called Circulism.[119]

No comprehensive research has been done on the early modern history of visual arts in Kuwait so far. However, it is known that from the mid-twentieth century onward, governmental efforts to establish art education and an art scene in Kuwait increased.[120] Besides the scholarships, of which also Rajab profited, the Department of Education focused on establishing professional artistic training opportunities and spaces for artists to work and exhibit, such as the Free Studio (*al-marsam al-ḥurr*) founded in 1960. In 1967, Sami Mohammed and others established the Kuwaiti Association of Plastic Arts. And that year or 1968, Khalifa Qattan initiated the Society of Formative Arts as an independent exhibition platform.[121]

In March 1969, Kuwait's, and in fact the Gulf's, first art gallery opened in the iconic Thunayan Al Ghanim Building on the roundabout leading to Fahad al-Salem Street with a show of works by Munira Al-Kazi (Kuwait) and Issam al-Said (Iraq). The Sultan Gallery—founded by the siblings Najat and Ghazi Sultan, she a teacher, he an architect—would continue to show "modern young Arab artists" and sometimes also Western artists, such as Andy Warhol in 1977, to create networks of artistic exchange across the Arab world and

[116] "Kuwait," in *The Grove Encyclopedia of Islamic Art and Architecture*, ed. Jonathan Bloom and Sheila Blair vol. 2 (Oxford/New York: Oxford University Press, 2009), accessed February 2, 2021, https://www.oxfordreference.com/view/10.1093/acref/9780195309911.001.0001/acref-9780195309911-e-525?rskey=bSbVLs&result=1.

[117] "Kuwait," 405; Al Qassemi, "Correcting Misconceptions of the Gulf's Modern Art Movement" Wijdan Ali, *Modern Islamic Art: Development and Continuity* (Gainesville: University Press of Florida, 1997), 121, 123.

[118] All of them exhibited in the Gulf and across the Arab World, at times even in Europe, the Soviet Union, or the US.

[119] On Qattan and Circulism see Hussain, "Modern Art from Kuwait"; Anneka Lenssen, Sarah Rogers, and Nada M. Shabout, eds., *Modern Art in the Arab World: Primary Documents* (New York: Museum of Modern Art, 2017), "294. Circulism and Kinetics in Kuwait."

[120] See Ali, *Modern Islamic Art*, 121–23.

[121] Hussain, "Modern Art from Kuwait," 44.

beyond.[122] Obviously, a thriving, even if small, local and regional art scene emerged in the second half of the twentieth century in Kuwait that was very well-connected. Its history still awaits comprehensive research efforts to bring it to light, especially as there have only recently been efforts to systematically collect modern artworks from the region.[123]

2.5 As Petro-Modernity Unfolds, Urban Visual Culture Is Fueled

In the mid-twentieth century, Kuwait City's fossil-fueled urban transformation and petro-modernity's image-world unfolded against this historical, architectural, and visual background, as the following three main chapters will show. The speed of urbanization and the magnitude of urban transformation from the late 1940s onward was completely unprecedented, all-encompassing, and radical, yet nevertheless part of a certain continuous urban and social renewal Kuwait was historically acquainted with. The proliferation of modern visual media in public and private spaces and the emergence of a vivid visual and architectural culture strongly enhanced an experience of change that coincided with the growth of an affluent consumerist society and the development of a governmental body that demanded national and international representation through a visual language of national symbols and other imagery. Furthermore, also the Kuwait Oil Company, which spearheaded the country's most important economy, felt the need to both legitimize its lucrative operations and fuel the consumption of petroleum through attractive (visual) narratives.

The rise of a broad urban visual culture that encompassed the visual arts and (vernacular) architecture amid the expanding petroleum business in the Gulf is neither a singular nor an accidental case to be made about Kuwait; rather, it has revealed itself to be emblematic of petro-modernity in the Gulf and elsewhere. Probably one of the best informed people on modern art in the Gulf, Al Qassemi has argued that, besides modern school systems, state art programs, and social open-mindedness, "another factor that contributed to the development of the region's visual arts industry was another industry altogether, the discovery of oil around the mid-20th century."[124] As example, Al Qassemi discusses the Bahrain Petroleum Company's commission of (local) artists, such as the

[122] Sultan Gallery closed in 1990 during the Iraqi invasion until Farida Sultan, the siblings' younger sister, reopened it in 2006. Kristine Khouri has done extensive research on the gallery based on its archives. The results of which were first shown in an exhibition at Sultan Gallery titled *The Founding Years (1969–1973): A Selection of Works from the Sultan Gallery Archives* in 2012. Kristine Khouri, "Mapping Arab Art through the Sultan Gallery," *ArteEast Quarterly*, Spring 2014, accessed January 22, 2021, http://arteeast.org/quarterly/mapping-arab-art-through-the-sultan-gallery/.

[123] Many works of Sami Mohammed are on display at the Kuwait Museum of Modern Art, which was opened in 2003. Most Kuwaiti artists mentioned here are today in the collection of the Barjeel Art Foundation in Sharjah, established in 2010; some are also in the collection of the Mathaf: Arab Museum of Modern Art in Doha, established also in 2010.

[124] Al Qassemi, "Correcting Misconceptions of the Gulf's Modern Art Movement."

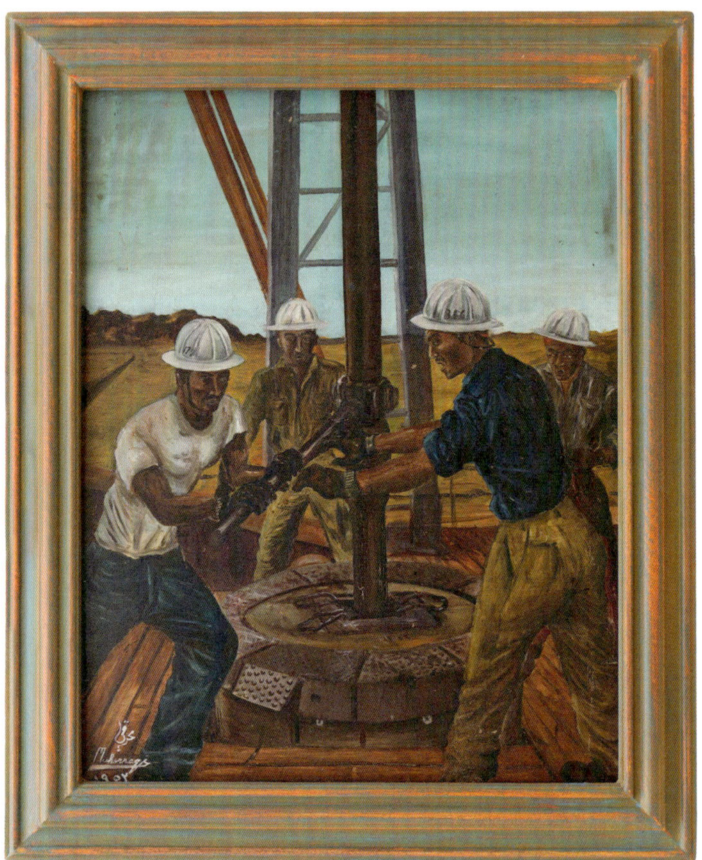

2.4 Adullah al-Muharraqi, *Oil Exploration*, 1953. Oil on hardboard, 75.5 × 60.5 cm. Mathaf: Arab Museum of Modern Art, Doha.

Bahraini Abdullah al-Muharraqi (*1939) for an oil painting in a figurative style that thematizes the oil industry, which is now in the collection of the Mathaf: Arab Museum of Modern Art in Doha (fig. 2.4). In al-Muharraqi's *Oil Exploration* (1953), we see four men working an oil drill at a well site in the desert. The artwork focuses on depicting the hard labor involved in the oil exploration and the harsh working conditions under the beaming sun and without any protection out in the desert.[125]

A similar story exists for Kuwait and the KOC: when parts of the collection of Neil Donaldson, a philatelic scholar and Gulf expert, were auctioned in spring 2018, the sale brought to light several hand-painted essays for an unpublished set of Kuwaiti stamps

[125] Ibid. Al Qassemi compares this painting to a similarly-themed oil painting by Saudi Arabian artist Abdul Halim Al Radwi (1939–2006) titled *Extraction of Oil* (1965).

dating from 1960.[126] According to the auction brief, Donaldson had made the design suggestions on behalf of the head of Kuwait's postal directorate, while Ramzi Kayello, who was a commercial artist who worked for the KOC, executed and painted the designs with motifs of a gazelle, the map of Kuwait, an oil tanker, and the ruler.[127] Kayello, a Palestinian of Lebanese-Canadian citizenship born in Haifa, was later also in charge of a stamp design commemorating the twentieth anniversary of the first shipment of oil in 1966 with the image of an oil tanker and the portrait of Shaykh Ahmad al-Jaber Al Sabah, which seems to have been a joint project by the Kuwaiti government and the oil company.[128]

Overall, visual representations became the currency of the country in relation to the world and other petro-states and they effectively worked to simultaneously expose and hide the politics of petroleum behind a façade of progress, modernity, and urban transformation for much of the second half of the century. Images of the city transitioning into a petropolis became the poster child of the country and were crucial to the *image* of Kuwait (City) that different actors sought to curate, negotiate, manipulate, and aestheticize in a myriad of ways. The following main chapters unlock the ways in which the visual representations emerging in the context of Kuwait City's urban transformation created an image-world that reified Kuwait's petro-modernity. The starting point, one could say, was the process of creating the first master plan.

[126] Auction house Christoph Gärtner, auction no. 39, February 2018, lot no. 6917, accessed January 22, 2021, https://www.auktionen-gaertner.de/?FTSearchHTML|Name=DetailsA&Cat=GP&UID=722045ABB-07445B1C125821D006C822F&Phase=AUCTION&Lang=DE&DetailDB=PHILNET/GAERTNER/GP-KATAUK39&CID=1&SessionID=PxcTH-h25QT0y0zteSvH.

[127] Considered the founding father of philatelic history of the Arabian Gulf states and especially of Kuwait, Neil Donaldson (1920–2012) had worked for the Kuwait Oil Company from 1948 to 1967, although it is unclear in which capacity. See the two special issues on Neil Donaldson, *al-Būsṭa (al-Posta)*, no. 23 (January 2012) and no. 24 (April 2012).

[128] Kuwait 1966, commem., MiNos. 323–24, referencing the catalog number of the stamp in *Michel Gulf States Catalogue 2013*. 2nd ed. (Unterschleißheim: Schwaneberger Verlag, 2012). Ramzi Kayello, artist's website, documents, accessed January 25, 2021, http://www.ramzikayelloartscapes.com/documents/Central-OfficeInterviewStamps.pdf. It remains unclear in which capacity Kayello worked for the KOC.

3. IMAG(IN)ING KUWAIT FROM ABOVE IN AERIAL PHOTOGRAPHY, URBAN PLANNING, AND CARTOGRAPHY

"[Kuwait City] is indeed a town planner's dream," wrote Peter W. Macfarlane, one of the British urban planners responsible for the first master plan of Kuwait.[1] "To drive along a splendid dual carriageway road, which only a year before was a line on paper, is an experience given to few in this country," he marveled, contrasting the far more restricted planning situation in "this country" (i.e., Britain) with the situation in Kuwait.[2] Published in 1954, two years into the implementation of the master plan, the comment demonstrates that the projected urban overhaul of the Gulf town focused on the creation of a motorized city in which the new architectural landscapes would be consumed as vistas in a drive-by (or even fly-over) mode in the logic of petro-modernity.

Town planning in the twentieth century relied on new technologies of seeing, evaluating, and representing space. While the ultimate goal was rebuilding Kuwait from scratch, the planning process also gave way to unprecedented and compelling visualizations of the town itself. First of all, a comprehensive aerial survey of Kuwaiti territory was undertaken, which resulted in a composite aerial photomosaic. Second, the country's first master plan, which envisioned a radically new Kuwait City based on the photomosaic as a prime source of information, was developed. In the context of Kuwait's urban visual culture, both the photomosaic and the master plan were new forms of visualization, as they pictured Kuwait in its vertical totality from above for the first time. The urban transformation of Kuwait City during the 1950s was therefore not only a translation from image to physical space as the master plan was implemented, but also the creation of the city in and as pictures that eventually became iconic yet highly ambiguous and ultimately iridescent symbols of Kuwait's petro-modernity.

Petroleum played a decisive role in respect to the technical, visual, and material conditions of seeing and picturing the coastal settlement of Kuwait from above in aerial photography and urban planning. The subsequent dissemination of the vertical

[1] Peter W. Macfarlane, "Planning an Arab Town: Kuwait on the Persian Gulf," *Journal of the Town Planning Institute* 40, no 5 (April 1954): 113. Town planning was used in British contexts at the time; urban planning is the term commonly used today. In the following the terms are used interchangeably.

[2] Ibid.

https://doi.org/10.1515/9783110714739-005

gaze in other visual media (such as modern cartography) and among other audiences established a normative form of representing Kuwait from above. While aerial-view imagery undoubtedly created a new visual identity for Kuwait, it also came to encompass an incommensurable tension between nostalgic affect for the pre-oil town as social habitat and the highly appreciated progressiveness of the oil city as material and visual symbol of its modernization. Unraveling the different readings of the aerial-view imagery in the 1950s and 1960s unlocks the visual strategies that characterize petro-modernity and account for its seductive iridescent effect.

3.1 Visualizing Kuwait in Aerial Photography

A short notification, published in the British aeronautic weekly *Flight* in early June 1951, announced the official commencement of a systematic survey of Kuwait City through aerial photography:[3]

> On May 24th a Hunting Aerosurveys expedition left Luton Airport in a Percival Survey Prince, bound for the Middle East territory of the Sheikh Abdulla as-Salim as-Subhah [*sic*], who has commissioned the company to prepare large-scale photomosaics of Kuwait and the surrounding 95 square miles.[4]

What the text did not communicate was that the photomosaics were to serve as the main source of information for the British town planners Anthony Minoprio, Hugh Spencely, and Peter W. Macfarlane, who were commissioned with creating the first master plan for Kuwait City. It also did not disclose the historical relationship between aerial photography and petroleum prospecting in the Gulf region.

Aerial surveying has been considered vital for exploring remote, difficult to access and/or vast areas and was especially recommended for "unmapped countries," a term usually applied to developing countries.[5] Rapidly devised in conjunction with heavier-than-air flight since the early 1900s and first applied in its modern form for the air reconnaissance of Palestine in 1918, aerial photography went through immense professionalization during World War I and World War II as it became a strategical tool of modern warfare

[3] *Flight* was first published in January 1909 as the official weekly journal of the Aero Club of Great Britain, which was founded in 1901 and renamed the Royal Aero Club (RAeC) in 1910. The RAeC established itself as the national coordinating body of ballooning and later aviation; until 1915 it also trained most military pilots. The journal was renamed *Flight International* in 1962. Today, it is considered the foremost aeronautical weekly in the world. See John Blake, "A Brief History of the Royal Aero Club," RAeC Homepage, section "History & Origins," accessed January 29, 2021, http://www.royalaeroclub.co.uk/history-and-origins.php.

[4] "Civil Aviation News," *Flight* 59, no. 2211 (June 1951), 685.

[5] One of the knowledge hubs to develop surveying technologies for developing countries was the International Training Centre for Aerial Survey (ITC) established in 1950 in Delft. See Willem Schermerhorn, "Planning in Modern Aerial Survey," *Photogrammetria* 17, no. 1 (1960); W. G. L. de Haas, "Aerial Survey for Developing Countries," *Build International*, no. 11 (November 1970).

and surveillance.[6] As a "powerful source of visual knowledge with connotations of control over the physical terrain," aerial surveying has played an important role in the development and control of colonial or quasicolonial territories since its inception.[7] For example, for the Levant and North Africa, topographic mapping, land registry, military control, archaeological surveys, and the exploitation of resources played a major and often negative role.[8] After World War I, oil companies and other actors—for example archaeologists, geologists, and eventually town planners—recognized the potential of air surveys to help them in their endeavors. They appreciated this technique for its quick, efficient, and detailed visual documentation of the Earth's surface, which provided an unprecedentedly rich set of information that was invaluable to anyone trained to interpret the aerials.[9]

According to William Facey and Gilian Grant, authors of *Kuwait by the First Photographers*, an oblique photograph taken in 1927 (probably as part of a series) is considered to be the earliest aerial record of Kuwait (fig. 3.1).[10] This photo was shot in the context of a British survey of the Persian Gulf that sought to find suitable landing spots for the air route to India.[11] The 1927 photo was taken from the seaside and depicts the harbor front, one of the big cemeteries, Safat Square, and substantial parts of the *intra muros* settlement. More obliques followed when a squadron of the British Forces in Iraq took photographs of Kuwaiti territory in December 1934 that included "the Town and the existing landing ground, also the site of the flying boat moorings and the site proposed for the new landing ground."[12]

[6] Frank Scarlett, "The Application of Air Photography to Architecture and Town Planning," *Journal of the Royal Institute of British Architects* 53, no. 8 (1946): 319. In recent years, Eyal Weizman and the team at Forensic Architecture have revisited the early aerial reconnaissance of Palestinian territory in light of contemporary political conflicts, which indicates the ongoing influence of such (historical) imagery not only in Kuwait but in other parts of the world, too. See Eyal Weizman and Fazal Sheikh, *The Conflict Shoreline: Colonization as Climate Change in the Negev Desert* (Göttingen: Steidl, 2015).

[7] Tanis Hinchcliffe, "'The Synoptic View': Aerial Photographs and Twentieth-Century Planning," in *Camera Constructs: Photography, Architecture and the Modern City*, ed. Andrew Higgott and Timothy Wray (Farnham: Ashgate, 2012), 135; Beaumont Newhall, *Airborne Camera: The World from the Air and Outer Space* (New York: Hastings House, 1969), 51.

[8] Scarlett, "The Application of Air Photography to Architecture and Town Planning," 323. See also Karen L. Piper's chapter on "Air Control, Zerzura and the Mapping of the Libyan Desert," in Karen L. Piper, *Cartographic Fictions: Maps, Race, and Identity* (New Brunswick: Rutgers University Press, 2002), 95–127.

[9] For an excellent overview of the proliferation of aerial photography in the US, see Roger E. Bilstein, *Flight in America: From the Wrights to the Astronauts*, rev. ed. (Baltimore: Johns Hopkins University Press, [1984] 1994).

[10] See Facey and Grant, *Kuwait by the First Photographers*, 24.

[11] Ibid., 23.

[12] Air Headquarters, British Forces in Iraq, to Political Resident, Bushire, July 24, 1934, and Political Agency, Kuwait, to Air Headquarters, British Forces in Iraq, January 21, 1935, both in "Air Photographs of Kuwait and Aerial Reconnaissance," file 6/11, 1934–1948, IOR/R/15/5/287, India Office Records and Private Papers,

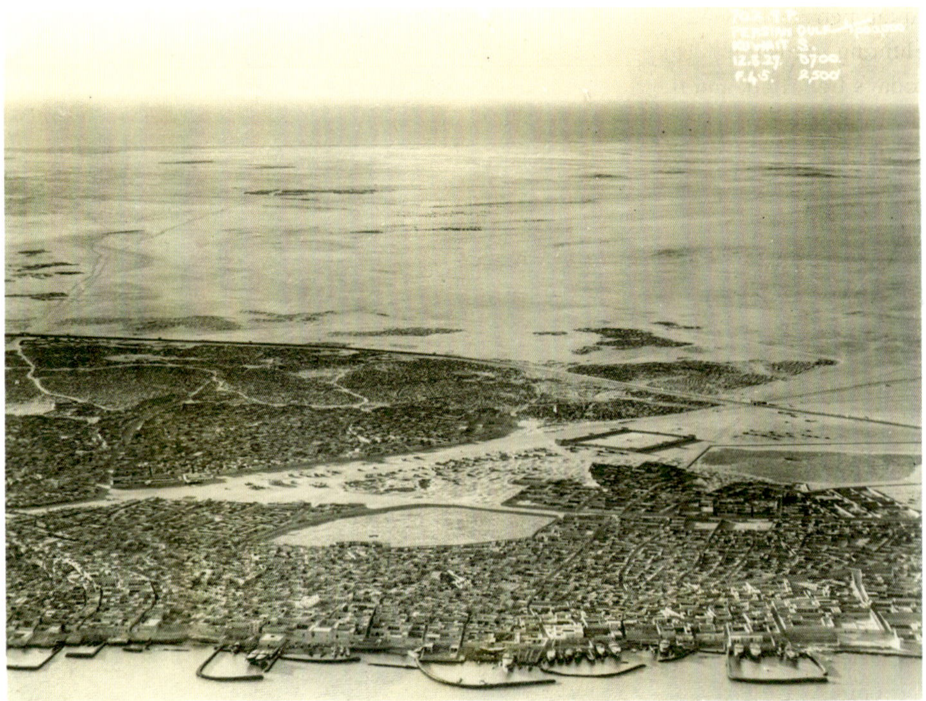

3.1 *Aerial view of Kuwait Town*. Photograph taken on August 12, 1927.

In contrast to these early sporadic oblique photos of the town of Kuwait, the exhaustive 1951 aerial survey was a novel approach. In its zeal to systematically and comprehensively explore Kuwait it was far more similar to the surveying approaches that oil companies applied to petroleum prospecting in the region. In fact, most of the aerial imagery of the Gulf taken before aerial photography, which became an essential tool in the modern town planning of Gulf cities from the midtwentieth century onward, had resulted from petroleum surveying.[13] Similarly, in the US after World War I, the oil industry was the commercial sector that dominated the use of aerial photography for geological prospecting.[14] In Canada and Alaska, oil exploration was also greatly dependent on aerial surveying.[15] In the 1930s, oil companies like the Shell group invested substantially in improving methods of aerial geology through photographic visualization technologies

British Library. Apparently, Shaykh Ahmad, then ruler of Kuwait, was pleased to receive a copy, but the photographs are not included in the British archival documents.

13 See Scarlett, "The Application of Air Photography to Architecture and Town Planning," 320.

14 Bilstein, *Flight in America*, 68.

15 Matt Dyce, "Canada between the Photograph and the Map: Aerial Photography, Geographical Vision and the State," *Journal of Historical Geography* 39 (2013): 69; on the contemporary entanglement of oil and aerial

to tap petroleum deposits in unexplored territories such as New Guinea.[16] In the Gulf, Hunting Aerosurveys emerged as the leading firm to fly aerial surveys over vast areas of today's Iran, Iraq, and the Arabian Peninsula for oil prospecting during the first half of the twentieth century. The view of Kuwait-from-above that Hunting Aerosurveys and its predecessor companies enabled thus intersected with petroleum (prospecting) in multiple ways.

Hunting Aerosurveys and the Petroleum Industry

The London-based company had multiple relationships with petroleum. It belonged to the Hunting Group, a leader in the field of commercial aerial photography, surveying, and film, but it was also a shareholder in the oil industry.[17] Prior to establishing Hunting Aerosurveys in 1942, the Hunting Group merged with the Aircraft Operating Company (AOC), which included the British company Aerofilms as a subsidiary. Registered in May 1919 by former Royal Air Force pilots Francis L. Wills and Claude Grahame-White, Aerofilms was one of the pioneers of commercial aerial photography, comparable only with Fairchild Aerial Surveys, founded by Sherman Fairchild in the US in 1920.[18] By 1929, the AOC had already undertaken various aerial surveys in Iraq, Brazil, and Southern Rhodesia on behalf of governments and private companies, and advertised its services for "empire development."[19] During the 1930s, the Anglo-Persian Oil Company (APOC) commissioned the company to fly aerial surveys over Persia.[20] In the course of World War II, the Air Ministry requisitioned the AOC to execute military air reconnaissance, interpretation of aerial photography, and mapping. By the end of the war, when the AOC (including Aerofilms) had become part of Hunting Aerosurveys, the company started offering commercial aerial photography for civilian services such as town planning and geological surveys. The sudden shift of customer orientation according to war or peace

surveying see Ila Tyagi, "Spatial Survey: Mapping Alaskan Oilfield Infrastructures Using Drones," *Synoptique* 8, no. 1 (2018).

[16] The "Bataafsche Petroleum Maatschappij," part of the Shell Group, undertook aerial prospecting for oil in New Guinea from 1935 to 1937; see Justus Krebs, "The Application of Aerial Geology and Aero-Photogrammetry in Petroleum Exploration," *Photogrammetria* 4, no. 2 (1941). On Justus Krebs, a Swiss geologist who was one of the pioneers of developing aerial geology and photogrammetry for oil exploration, see E. Ritter, "Nachruf: Krebs, Justus," *Verhandlungen der Schweizerischen Naturforschenden* 193 (1959).

[17] For a list of companies within the Hunting organization, see Aerofilms and Aero Pictorial, *Classified Index to the Library of Aerial Photographs*, rev. ed. (London: A Hunting Group Company Publication, [1954] 1962).

[18] Denis Cosgrove and William L. Fox, *Photography and Flight* (London: Reaktion, 2010), 46.

[19] Aircraft Operating Company, "Aerial Survey and Empire Development," ca. 1929, 68783, BP Archive, University of Warwick.

[20] In March 1940, the AOC supplied the War Office with aerial mosaics and individual vertical prints that the oil company had commissioned. See Military Protection of AIOC Interests in Iran, 1935–1940, 58997, BP Archive, University of Warwick.

time was typical for this area of business. Meanwhile, Aerofilms continued under its original name and specialized in oblique photography.

Continuing the AOC's prewar engagement, Hunting Aerosurveys quickly received commissions from oil industries operating in the Middle East and Latin America.[21] For example, the company conducted "aerial exploration of large areas of the uncharted mountains and deserts in Iran" for the Anglo-Iranian Oil Company between 1946 and 1949 and announcements such as "10,000 sq Miles Air Survey" in search of potential oil fields appeared frequently in *Flight* throughout this period.[22] The Kuwait Oil Company archives also hold various obliques approximately dated to the second half of the 1940s, which were probably taken by the company in the context of the start of oil exports in 1946.[23] British archival sources indicate that Hunting Aerosurveys conducted aerial surveys on the Iraqi/Kuwaiti frontier in preparation for potential new pipeline tracks and locations of pumping stations for the Kuwait Oil Company (KOC) around August 1948.[24] Eventually, the KOC acquired the necessary surveying equipment itself. In the late 1950s it owned a Viscount airliner and two Twin Pioneers, the latter a model often used for aerial prospecting. The company flew surveys on behalf of the Kuwaiti Public Works Department to document the urban development of Kuwait;[25] however, none of these surveys were as comprehensive as the one undertaken by Hunting Aerosurveys in May 1951. The history of Hunting Aerosurveys' engagement in the Arabian Peninsula provides a case in point that aerial photography arrived in this region along with the pursuit of petroleum by international oil companies.

Petroleum also played a decisive role in the development of aerial surveying on a material level. For example, the type of airplane used over Kuwait in May 1951 was a Percival Survey Prince (fig. 3.2). This all-metal twin-engine high-wing monoplane had been modified for aerial surveying with a lengthened transparent nose and by inserting two camera hatches covered by removable transparent panels in the fuselage.[26] With this setup, the photographer shot photos of potential oil-bearing grounds by remote control

[21] "Hunting Aerosurveys," *Flight* 51, no. 1994 (March 1947): 216.

[22] "Civil Aviation News: 10,000 Sq Miles Air Survey," *Flight* 52, no. 2035 (December 1947): 727; "Here and There: Oil Survey in Iran," *Flight* 54, no. 2084 (December 1948): 652–53; "Civil Aviation News: Surveying for Oil," *Flight* 56, no. 2129 (October 1949): 499.

[23] KOC Archive, Ahmadi, photographic holdings; see also Facey and Grant, *Kuwait by the First Photographers*, 29.

[24] List of air photographs recently taken at Kuwait, August 24, 1948, in John M. Pattinson, Kuwait: General (Photographs), 1946–1949, 59735, BP Archive, University of Warwick; Pattinson, AIOC London, to Southwell, KOC Ahmadi, January 4, 1949, in John M. Pattinson, Kuwait: General, 1946–1949, 59735, BP Archive, University of Warwick.

[25] Town Office monthly report, August 1958, Town Office, 1957–1958, 106975, BP Archive, University of Warwick. On KOC aircrafts see Rodney Giesler, "Memories of Kuwait 1958–1961," file 1/1, GB165-0508, Rodney Giesler Collection, Middle East Centre Archive, St Antony's College, Oxford.

[26] "Specialist Princes: New Variants of Percival Feederliner for Survey and Military Training," *Flight* 56, no. 2128 (October 1949): 476–77; "The Survey Prince," *Flight* 57, no. 2146 (February 1950): 196–97.

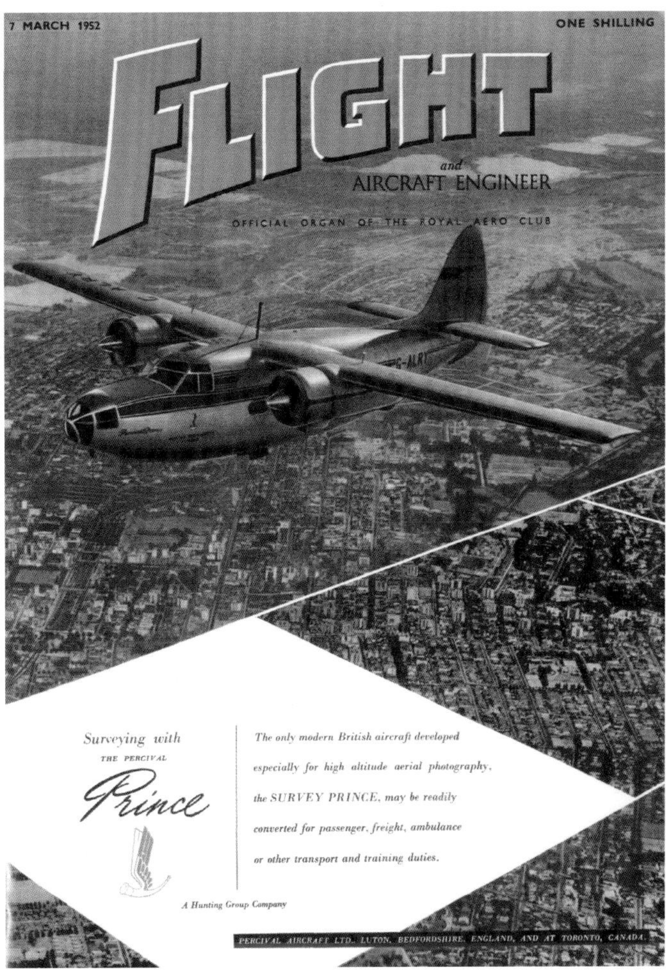

3.2 A Percival Survey Prince on the cover of *Flight* magazine, March 7, 1952.

while looking through transparent thermoplastic window screens made of Perspex, a petroleum-based polyacrylate derived from natural gas.[27] The airplanes ran, of course, on kerosene. Last but not least, chemicals used to produce film rolls and to develop the photographs usually contained petroleum derivatives. The fact that aerial photography depended materially and technologically on petroleum-derived products underscores this visualizing technology's intrinsic entanglement with the fossil material.

[27] Perspex was used in the aviation industry because of its clarity, stability, and thermo-resistance.

Kuwait from Above in 1951

For the 1951 Kuwait survey, Hunting Aerosurveys covered an area roughly equal to the total area of Kuwait City today (ca. 200 square kilometers) and produced both oblique and vertical aerial photographs. Obliques are aerials taken by a camera aimed at the ground at an angle of various degrees, like the 1927 aerial shot of Kuwait. They sometimes include the horizon (high oblique), which offers a more three-dimensional view. For verticals, the camera is directed perpendicularly toward the ground, creating photos with hardly any depth. In contrast to earlier *oblique* aerials that had shown only certain parts of Kuwait town, the novelty of the 1951 photomosaic was that it presented a composite *vertical* view of the town of Kuwait and its surroundings as a whole (fig. 3.3).

Generally speaking, a photomosaic is "any combination in more or less permanent mounted form of two or more vertical photographs."[28] Rectified, scaled, and assembled, the vertical photographs "quilt together a view of landscape."[29] The process of aerial surveying to generate verticals can be imagined as a macroscopic scanning process by an airplane. While the specially-equipped plane flies over the designated territory in adjacent parallel routes (or stripes), several cameras directed perpendicularly to the ground take photographs released by an automatic shutter on a continuous role of film. Ideally, each photograph overlaps with the adjacent ones by at least 30 percent. Thereby, each point on the ground is covered from at least two different angles, which enables a stereoscopic three-dimensional view. Two different media can subsequently be developed from verticals: photomosaics and maps.

Maps are produced by enriching the composite photo with additional topographic information from ground control, which in the case of Kuwait was provided by the Public Works Department. From this information it is possible to develop proper topographic maps in the form of line drawings. In contrast, the photomosaic (a composite picture) is rich in nuanced photographic information, but its content is not matched with additional sources, and therefore more ambiguous in its interpretation. Nevertheless, the 1951 photomosaic showed the built-up totality of the town in total perpendicularity reminiscent of modern topographic map standards that translated a lived environment into a fossil-fueled image.

The large-scale composite photograph of the town of Kuwait that was assembled from verticals taken in May 1951 visually encompasses part of Kuwait Bay, the town of Kuwait, and a substantial part of the area outside the town wall, where some urban sprawl was already visible in 1951 (see fig. 3.3). The photomosaic therefore does not include the complete surveyed area, but instead focuses on the town in line with its function to support town planning. The total landmass makes up around three quarters of the

[28] Melville C. Branch, Jr., *Aerial Photography in Urban Planning and Research,* Harvard City Planning Studies 14 (Cambridge, MA: Harvard University Press, 1948), 75. Photographs that are pasted together by eye measure form a so-called uncontrolled mosaic.

[29] Dyce, "Canada between the Photograph and the Map," 76.

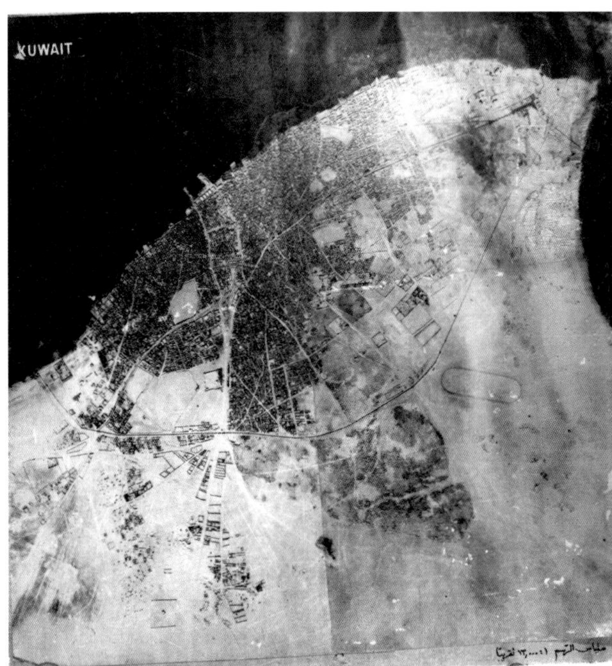

3.3 The 1951 photomosaic of aerial photographs of Kuwait, taken in May that year by Hunting Aerosurveys.

image, its various shades of gray contrasting with the surface of the sea, which appears in darker grays and even black. This stark black-and-white contrast makes the shape of the coastal land formation emerge prominently against the dark "background" of the sea and introduces the characteristically pointed shape of Kuwait City: the country's topography at this coastal section is shaped like a wave pointing right while the walled off town expands along the upper left of the wave crest and toward the inside of the wave, forming an almond-like shape.

"Kuwait" is written in typewritten capital letters in the upper left corner of the composite image and "scale of picture approximately 13,000" is handwritten in Arabic in the bottom right corner. By means of the integrated writing, the aerial image is aligned along the north-south axis and thus already organized according to modern topographic map standards. Depending on the accuracy of the photographs' alignment, the outcome is a picture disguising its composite nature to the viewer. Taken from a great height, the aerial perpendicular view flattens, abstracts, and formalizes real, physical, and urban space. For the untrained eye, it reduces the (urban) landscape to shapes and colors, to a single black-and-white image. The perpendicular verticality produces the flatness of space typical of modern cartography, which translates and subjugates a lived environment (in)to a measurable, easily controllable, and homogenous visual representation of space.

Aerial photography is a petro-fueled technology that objectifies space by turning it into pictures. This specific photomosaic amalgamates many hours of flying strips over the

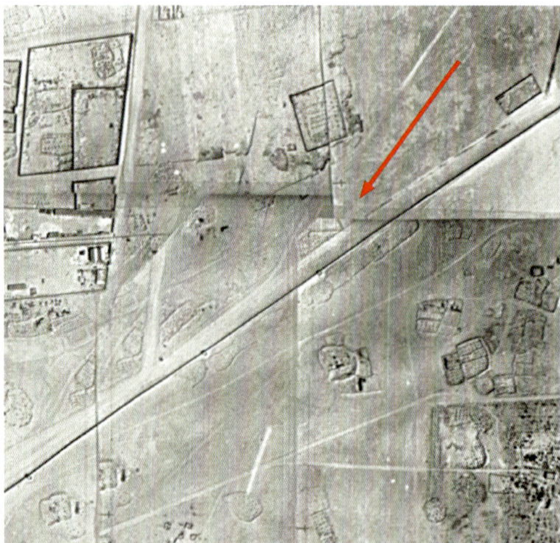

3.4 Detail of the 1951 photomosaic of aerial photographs of Kuwait with arrow indicating the edge of overlapping photographs.

territory and thus many different technically enhanced viewpoints into one photograph. The physical photo-collage still allows each photograph to be dissected from the others, thus disclosing its composite nature and the artificiality of its viewpoint (fig. 3.4). Later copies, images of the photo-collage, however, no longer provide for this physical and visual differentiation of the photographic mosaic stones. By way of bringing these multiple standpoints and timelines into one homogenous picture, the viewer is presented with an overwhelming yet condensed view that is humanly impossible to achieve. Nevertheless, the photographic image acts as apparent proof that it is in fact possible. Aerial photographs are fascinating as they convey the sense of looking at a miniature version of the world, which can convey to the viewer a feeling of total control. The fossil-fueled photomosaic synthetizes the world as a picture; an iridescent picture that depends on an artificial but extremely powerful and seductive position of unlimited vision. Here, the iridescent effect encapsulates the ambition to hide its multiple eyes, its composite nature, its fossil-fueled technical apparatus, and its specific temporality from view.

Aerial photography also becomes a powerful strategy to disembody lived space. On the one hand, it decouples images from their optical apparatus, economic-political interests, and the human bodies flying over Kuwait producing these images. On the other hand, it empties the urban space of the people, cultural narratives, and social experiences situated within it. Through aerial photography and the view from above, the urban space undergoes a petro-fueled optical and aesthetic translation. Simultaneously to the process of disembodiment, a space that is unfamiliar to the technicians and experts in charge of the seeing process is turned into a familiar visual representation for this professional viewership. As a result, aerial photos entail both the defamiliarization of space for people used to experiencing this particular space as lived environment and the familiarization of this space for people used to working with urban space in an abstract, external mode.

Once translated, disembodied, and objectified as urban-space-as-image, the image can now be modified as needed. This in turn gives way to an unrestricted vision that allows one to alter the depicted space as one pleases, as, for example, for town planning purposes. In her essay "Situated Knowledges: The Science Question in Feminism and the Privilege of Partial Perspective," Donna Haraway argues that if enhanced vision (as sight) is not openly situated as still somewhat individually embodied, technically mediated, and politically situated knowledge, it plays what she calls "the god trick." What she criticizes is that "the eyes have been used to signify a perverse capacity—honed to perfection in the history of science tied to militarism, capitalism, colonialism, and male supremacy—to distance the knowing subject from everybody and everything in the interests of unfettered power."[30] Similar to Foucault's analysis of the panopticon as a mechanism of surveillance, Haraway argues that this total view from above "[claims] the power to see and not be seen, to represent while escaping representation."[31] To understand how the god trick worked in the case of Kuwait it is necessary to trace the dissemination of the photomosaic and its pervasive aerial view in visual culture and to disclose the ways in which both the pre-oil town of Kuwait and the urban transformation were negotiated visually.

3.2 Envisioning Kuwait in Urban Planning

In 1951, three London-based town planners—Anthony Minoprio, Hugh Spencely, and Peter W. Macfarlane—received the assignment to conceptualize a development plan to modernize Kuwait. As their understanding of the existing town was based almost exclusively on the aerial imagery of May 1951, and thus on this particular view from above, their 1952 Master Plan projected what they called "New Kuwait City" on top of this flattened, abstracted, objectified, and "rationalized" vertical representation of Kuwait's existing urban space.

This planning commission formed one of the goals of Abdullah al-Salem Al Sabah's modernization reform for Kuwait in the early 1950s, which was nothing less than creating "the finest city in the Middle East and the happiest State."[32] He thereby placed the urban transformation of the coastal town of Kuwait at the center of his internal politics. His enthusiasm for the comprehensive urban development of Kuwait was initially not spurred by establishing an independent nation-state as part of decolonization or postwar reconstruction, as had been the case for many other countries rebuilding their capitals in the 1950s. Rather, the growth of Kuwait's oil industry—and the subsequent revenues reaching its ruler—provided both the economic means as well as the political independence

[30] Donna Haraway, "Situated Knowledges: The Science Question in Feminism and the Privilege of Partial Perspective," *Feminist Studies* 14, no. 3 (1988): 581.

[31] Ibid.

[32] "Preliminary Report on Development of Kuwait State," February 13, 1952, Kuwait State Development Board, file 101, 1952, FO 1016/217, The National Archives of the UK.

from the Kuwaiti merchant families required to steer urban reform at such a scale. Moreover, in line with British political aspirations in Kuwait, "it was also important that the city visually reflect the country's newfound prosperity and modernity—something the existing pre-oil landscape failed to do."[33] The reason for this was that the pre-oil landscape did not contain any established markers of this modernization trajectory as mentioned before, for example fossil-fuel based motorization and air-conditioned architecture, but it was also a shift that was expressed in new building typologies, industrially produced building materials and different architectural styles.

As scholars have rightly pointed out, combined with the rhetoric of modernization and the promotion of foreign expertise, architecture's and urban planning's primary use often came "to represent progress" within the Persian Gulf and in many other localities of the MENA region.[34] The plausibility of the success story depended not only on physical proof established by the material alteration of the built environment but also on visual proof. Esra Akcan highlights that it was especially "the canonic buildings and master plans of the 1950s and early 1960s [that] were perfect participants in modernization theory," since they served as not only material but also visual currency because they circulated as portable, reproducible images.[35] Shaping the built environment under Shaykh Abdullah's name provided—among other things—the opportunity to cement his personal power and the position of the House of Sabah within internal and external networks.[36]

The Politics of Commissioning the First Master Plan of Kuwait

Initially, Shaykh Abdullah had intended to engage a Palestinian town engineer for Kuwait's transformation; however, Herbert G. Jakins, the British Political Agent to Kuwait between 1948 and 1951, persuaded the ruler to consider a British expert.[37] Eventually, early in 1951, Shaykh Abdullah asked H. T. Kemp, his representative to the Kuwait Oil Company (KOC) in London, to find a suitable British town planner for Kuwait City.[38]

[33] Al-Nakib, *Kuwait Transformed*, 98–99.

[34] Karimi and Kim, "On Protectorates and Consultanates," 90; see also Panayiota I. Pyla, ed., *Landscapes of Development: The Impact of Modernization Discourses on the Physical Environment of the Eastern* Mediterranean (Cambridge, MA: The Aga Khan Program at the Harvard University Graduate School of Design, 2013).

[35] Esra Akcan, "Global Conflict and Global Glitter: Architecture of West Asia (1960–2010)," in *A Critical History of Contemporary Architecture: 1960–2010*, ed. Elie Haddad and David Rifkind (Farnham: Ashgate, 2014), 313.

[36] On the delicate balancing of power between the ruler and the merchants in the early 1950s, see Al-Nakib, *Kuwait Transformed*, 91–94.

[37] Jakins to Sir Rupert Hay, Political Resident in the Persian Gulf, January 2, 1951, FO 371/91270, reprinted in Richard Trench, ed., *Arab Gulf Cities: Kuwait City*, 4 vols. (Cambridge, UK: Archive Editions, 1994), 545.

[38] Ibid., 546. "Mr. Kemp was appointed under the Oil Concession as the Ruler's London representative with the Kuwait Oil Company. He has at present no official position vis-à-vis the Foreign Office and it was intended that he should deal exclusively with oil affairs…. In fact, however, he has come to be used more and

Appointing a British planner had ramifications that reached well beyond the walls of Kuwait City. Even though the British-Kuwaiti Protection Agreement of 1899 ensured that Britain's political relationship with Kuwait was constrained to foreign policy only, the commissioning of the first master plan for Kuwait City was deeply entangled in British imperial politics in the Persian Gulf and, on a larger scale, in modernization and development ideologies prevailing at the time. Advisors and experts in particular were the point of entry for British interests in Kuwait; the information and influence they gained allowed the British government to (directly or indirectly) guide important decision-making processes. Rather than providing capital, which Kuwait did not need anyway, posting "circulating experts" who made specialist knowledge portable and mobile had become "a common strategy of Cold War technopolitics."[39] On the Kuwaiti side, it was perhaps Britain's good reputation in town planning that made it plausible for Shaykh Abdullah to accept British town planners as urban experts. From a British perspective, securing this post for a British company as well as being involved in one of the biggest development projects in Kuwait—its urban transformation—was strongly politically and economically motivated.[40] It also had symbolic significance: by providing British expertise to Kuwait for a process of social and physical betterment (as urban planning was widely regarded), the British government could foster a positive image of their involvement in the Gulf. Similarly, Kuwait's ruler was able to do the same toward both his community and an international audience, fueling the petroleum promise, rather than being seen as using the oil revenues only for his private enjoyment.[41]

The correspondence between Sir Rupert Hay, Political Resident in the Persian Gulf from 1946 to 1953, Herbert G. Jakins, and the Foreign Office in London reveals that Kemp, encouraged by the Foreign Office, contacted the Colonial Office and the Ministry of Local Government and Planning in London, which suggested the British town planners Anthony Minoprio, Hugh Spencely, and Peter W. Macfarlane for the job.[42] Alternative town planners and consultant firms had been considered, but Kemp did not

more as the Agent for the Ruler of Kuwait in this country in a variety of matters, quite unconnected with oil, such as commercial transactions and the appointment of experts." C. M. Rose, Kuwait Government Agent in London: Mr. Kemp minutes, January 8, 1952, Recruitment of Experts for Kuwait Development, file 1052, 1951, FO 371/91271, The National Archives of the UK.

[39] Donna Mehos and Suzanne Moon, "The Uses of Portability: Circulating Experts in the Technopolitics of Cold War and Decolonization," in *Entangled Geographies: Empire and Technopolitics in the Global Cold War*, ed. Gabrielle Hecht (Cambridge, MA: MIT Press, 2011), 43–44.

[40] Gardiner, *Kuwait*, 33.

[41] See Stephan V. Ward, "Transnational Planners in a Postcolonial World," in *Crossing Borders: International Exchange and Planning Practices*, ed. Patsy Healey and Robert Upton (London: Routledge, 2010), 50.

[42] The Ministry of Local Government and Housing had just been formed in January 1951 as the central institution for organizing town planning in Britain. Its creation merged functions like housing and local government that had formerly been part of the Ministry of Health and the Ministry of Town & Country Planning.

approve of them.[43] Interestingly, all of the candidates under discussion had been taught at the Liverpool School of Architecture, one of the most influential and internationally-renowned university-based programs for architecture in Britain then headed by Charles Herbert Reilly.[44] This possibly indicates that suggestions were made from within this network, although British archival sources do not reveal who within the ministry in fact recommended Minoprio, Spencely, and Macfarlane (MSM) for the Kuwaiti job.

From the British perspective, besides fitting the "portable experts" brief, the evaluation of MSM's skills (as one of the possible selection criteria) is crucial for understanding the commission. In March 1951, Leslie A. C. Frey of the Foreign Office in London wrote to Hay:

> Kemp has been in touch, by our arrangement, with the Ministry of Local Government and Planning and after discussing requirements with them was advised to approach a firm of Town Planners named Minoprio, Spencely and Macfarlane. He has since seen all three partners in this firm and seemed to have been impressed with their enthusiasm and by reports he has received from the Development Officers of various towns which they have planned in this country, although we understand that they have had no previous experience of planning overseas. At all events, the three partners in the firm are anxious to visit Kuwait together, so that they will all be aware of the sort of problems they will have to tackle. We understand that Kemp has recommended to the Ruler that he should invite them to Kuwait for a fortnight towards the end of April, when all three can make themselves available at the same time. If the Ruler considers them suitable they would go ahead with the making of plans and then, individually or together, pay such other visits to Kuwait as may later be necessary.[45]

Apparently, Kemp selected these three town planners based on their enthusiasm as well as their experience and expertise with town planning in Britain. Their lack of experience in planning overseas was acknowledged but not given much weight in the decision. Rather, Frey stressed their willingness to visit Kuwait as a positive sign of their keen interest to tackle Kuwait's urban "problems," a phrasing clearly taken from development discourse.[46] Their selection, despite the fact that they had neither any prior knowledge of or expertise in Kuwait or the Persian Gulf or other British (quasi-)colonial spaces nor any

[43] For example, Group I Limited consisted of consultants and construction engineers but lacked a town planner; furthermore, they would have wanted to collaborate with William Holford, professor of town planning at University College, London, who was apparently too busy at the time. Maxwell Fry and Jane Drew, a British architect-planner partnership of international acclaim, were also discussed. However, "nothing seems to be known here of Mr. Maxwell Fry," as Jakins remarked, and their engagement was not pursued further for reasons unknown. Jakins to Hay, March 10, 1951, EA 1052/19, reprinted in Trench, *Arab Gulf Cities*, 550.

[44] Maxwell Fry (B.Arch. 1923), Anthony Minoprio (B.Arch. 1925, M.A. 1928), Hugh Spencely (B.Arch. 1926, Certificate of Civic Design 1928) and William Holford (B.Arch. 1930). See Joseph Sharples, ed., *Charles Reilly & the Liverpool School of Architecture 1904–1933* (Liverpool: Liverpool University Press, 1996).

[45] Frey to Hay, May 21, 1951, EA 1052/19, reprinted in Trench, *Arab Gulf Cities*, 551.

[46] On the terminology of the "problem" in development discourse see Arturo Escobar, *Encountering Development: The Making and Unmaking of the Third World* (Princeton: Princeton University Press, 1995), 6. Joseph Sharples also portrays Reilly (Minoprio's and Spencely's teacher in Liverpool) as someone who enthusiastically encouraged his students to undertake projects they had not trained for. See Joseph Sharples, "Reilly and

knowledge of Arabic, is reflective of the postwar shift which favored "portable experts" and "gave portable knowledge a higher priority than place-based knowledge (which might include local or indigenous knowledge) for many institutions."[47] Consequently, MSM's understanding of Kuwait City, as formulated in their subsequent town planning report of November 1951 and the master plan of May 1952, obviously derived predominantly from their town planning education and experience in Britain which was supplemented with their visits to Kuwait (April and July 1951) and the first-hand information they received there, as well as from the aerial survey of May 1951.

The town planners also recognized that two visits and the aerial survey as the core of the (visual) information and site-specific experience on Kuwait available was scarce. Anthony Minoprio himself explained in an interview conducted by fellow British architect Stephen Gardiner in the 1980s: "It was a difficult commission. We didn't know anything much about the Muslim world and the Kuwaitis wanted a city—they wanted a *new* city, hospitals, schools, housing and good communications… . All we could give them, was what we knew."[48] Acknowledging that their expertise lay elsewhere, the town planners resorted to aerial photography and visualization strategies typical of mid-twentieth century urban planning in order to provide a modern city by turning the unfamiliar space of Kuwait into a familiar picture—an aerial map-like view from above and a master plan. The special popularity of aerial photography among urban planners resulted from its perceived ability to provide an almost omniscient overview that allowed space to been seen primarily as a planning resource.

Aerial Photography as an (Omniscient) Urban Planning Tool

British architects and town planners had discussed aerial photography's potential both enthusiastically and skeptically since its introduction to the field in the interwar period. In general, aerials provided a quick, efficient, and seemingly objective means of photographically documenting topographies, both natural landscapes and built-up areas. Thus, depending on the kind of aerials taken, aerial surveys could support the planning and building process before, during, and even after its completion. At that time, oblique photographs were already attributed with a greater "pictorial" potential as they provided the volume of buildings in perspective, while verticals were considered "cartographic."[49] Town planners in Britain had begun analyzing aerial and especially vertical photographs

His Students, on Merseyside and Beyond," in *Charles Reilly & the Liverpool School of Architecture 1904–1933*, ed. Joseph Sharples (Liverpool: Liverpool University Press, 1996), 39.

47 Mehos and Moon, "The Uses of Portability," 68.

48 Gardiner, *Kuwait*, 33–35 (italics in the original).

49 Jack Whittle, "The Use of Air Photographs: Examination and Interpretation," in *Town and Country Planning Textbook: An Indispensable Book for Town Planners, Architects and Students*, ed. Association for Planning and Regional Reconstruction (London: Architectural Press, 1950), 561; Scarlett, "The Application of Air

as early as World War I, while oblique aerial shots of urban vistas began to illustrate professional magazines during the interwar period.[50] For example, aerial photographs, mostly obliques, appeared prominently in urban development campaigns by town administrations projecting attractive cities of the future as "place promotion."[51] Clearly, aerial photographs served to create a new and modern visual representation of cities.

As publications from the period show, architects and planners appreciated aerial photography's ability to contain a vast amount of very detailed information in one (composite) image, a complexity that complemented the growing comprehensive approach toward town planning.[52] Nevertheless, professionals also began cautioning that the interpretation of the information presented through aerials (especially verticals) demanded professional training and that planners should not lose sight of how projects would affect realities on the ground.[53] As surveying gained importance in the development of complex large-scale and increasingly systematic approaches to urban planning, aerial photographic surveys became established as the central tool.[54] By the early 1950s, aerial photography had become firmly integrated into British town planning curricula.[55]

Aerial photography's success among urban planners, however, was not exclusively rational. Advertisements by the company Hunting Aerosurveys toward the end of World War II demonstrate the enormous and almost supernatural potential that was attributed to aerial surveys. As the market was preparing to shift from a military to a civilian economy, the advertisements adopted the promotional strategy of ascribing a godlike ability of vision to aerial photography in order to sell the company's services to new customers.

Photography to Architecture and Town Planning," 319; see also Dyce, "Canada between the Photograph and the Map," 78.

50 Hinchcliffe, "'The Synoptic View,'" 138.

51 Peter J. Larkham and Keith D. Lilley, "Plans, Planners and City Images: Place Promotion and Civic Boosterism in British Reconstruction Planning," *Urban History* 30, no. 2 (2003); Peter Larkham and Keith Lilley, "Exhibiting the City: Planning Ideas and Public Involvement in Wartime and Early Post-War Britain," *Town Planning Review* 83, no. 6 (2012); see also Peter J. Larkham, "Selling the Future City: Images in UK Post-War Reconstruction Plans," in Whyte, *Man-Made Future*.

52 Whittle, "The Use of Air Photographs," 561.

53 Following architect Frank Scarlett's presentation on the application of air photography to architecture and town planning at the RIBA Architectural Science Board in 1946, Max Lock raised the question of keeping street-view reality in mind when using aerial planning technologies. See Scarlett, "The Application of Air Photography to Architecture and Town Planning," 322. Hinchliffe has discussed Scarlett's presentation in great detail; see Hinchcliffe, "The Synoptic View."

54 On the importance of surveying in interwar and wartime urban planning in Britain, see Michiel Dehaene, "Surveying and Comprehensive Planning: The 'Co-Ordination of Knowledge' in the Wartime Plans of Patrick Abercrombie and Max Lock," in Whyte, *Man-Made Future*.

55 See the chapter "The Use of Air Photographs" in the *Town and Country Planning Textbook: An Indispensable Book for Town Planners, Architects and Students* (1950), which served as the official study material for the examination of the Town Planning Institute; on this, see also Whittle, "The Use of Air Photographs." Aerial photography was also taught in US curricula, where it was described as an aid for town planning, as this book taught at Harvard University demonstrates: Branch, Jr., *Aerial Photography in Urban Planning and Research*.

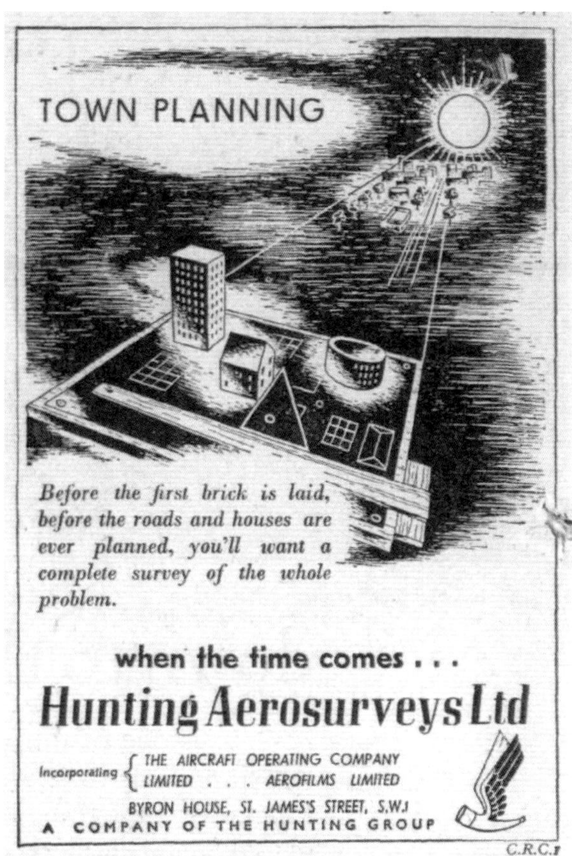

3.5 "Town Planning" advertisement published by Hunting Aerosurveys in June 1944 in *Flight* magazine.

Advertisements placed in *Flight* by Hunting Aerosurveys and Aerofilms indicate that their main target was the market of urban planning.

Hunting Aerosurveys' first such advertisement appeared in *Flight* in June 1944 and illuminates the way in which they affectively promoted their services (fig. 3.5). The graphic illustration shows the sun shining brightly in the background, its rays of light reaching a settlement in the far distance and extending toward a drawing board with models of various building types in the foreground of the image. A short text promotes the commissioning of an (aerial) survey prior to starting any building process; the phrase "when the time comes" alludes to the eventual end of the war. Through the combination of text and illustration, the advert symbolizes aerial surveying as sunlight, simultaneously drawing on photography as a light-sensitive technique and playing with the sun's symbolic implications of vision and godlike power, which connects with the idea of the view-from-above as an omniscient perspective. In its composition and its thematic focus on the process of seeing, this illustration resonates with the woodcut *Making a Perspective*

Drawing of a Reclining Woman by Albrecht Dürer from the mid-sixteenth century.[56] This print depicts a man drawing an almost-naked woman through a grid window that enables him to see the scene in perspective. Dürer brilliantly encapsulates the seduction that the power to see triggers in humans (symbolized by male-female attraction), especially technically enhanced modes of seeing—just like aerial photography.

After the end of the war, a new series of company adverts declared that "The time has come for Hunting Aerosurveys" (figs. 3.6, 3.7). With the slogan "Let's have a look at the problem," the company addressed their potential civil customers in a jovial tone.[57] In both adverts shown here, a winged eye—possibly understood as a symbol of godlike vision—hovers over the clipping of an aerial view.[58] Wherever the eye's cone of light touches the aerial photo, graphic illustrations of well-planned, future townscapes are revealed. The aerial views show either open land (new suburban development) or destroyed cities (rebuilding), the two aspects that dominated postwar town planning in Britain. The landscapes are thereby portrayed as being in dire need of planning. Aerial surveying is hyperbolized as the magic technique of visualizing and, by extension, solving urban problems best.

Aerial photography's magic drew on its (exaggeratedly) ascribed ability to uncover the hidden potentials of landscapes and spaces; in the adverts these were promising new planning and building possibilities in times of a severe postwar housing shortage. This echoed the way in which aerial photography was promoted by oil companies, who encapsulated the god trick with conviction: "A good aerial photograph is a real treasure-chest of information and may, within certain limits, be regarded as an absolutely complete record of anything and everything present and visible on the surface of the earth."[59] The fascination with the aerial view was twofold: the seductiveness of the omniscient vision inherent in especially vertical aerials experienced by the viewer and the captivation with the potential or even the promise of altering this landscape. For oil companies it is the tapping of petroleum reservoirs, for archaeologists it is the discovery of ruins and material remains, and for urban planners it is the transformation of space. The aerial vision (in its double meaning of sight and imagination) allows one to look past what is there in favor of imagining what else could be there; in this sense it is not an innocent documentary viewing.

[56] Dürer's famous woodcut "Der Zeichner des liegenden Weibes" ("Making a Perspective Drawing of a Reclining Woman") was included in his treaty *Underweysung der Messung mit dem Zirckel und Richtscheyt* (*The Painter's Manual*), first published in 1525, and was also reprinted independently.

[57] Hunting Aerosurveys' advertisements appeared in *Flight*, October 18, 1945, 26 (rebuilding) and *Flight*, December 6, 1945, 30 (town planning).

[58] The winged human eye also features Leon Battista Alberti's emblem. Scholars have offered various interpretations of this, for example that it symbolizes a father-like or god-like vision. See Laurie Schneider, "Leon Battista Alberti: Some Biographical Implications of the Winged Eye," *The Art Bulletin* 72, no. 2 (1990).

[59] Krebs, "The Application of Aerial Geology and Aero-Photogrammetry in Petroleum Exploration," 55.

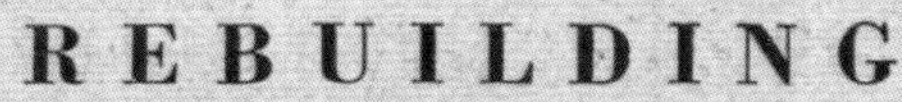

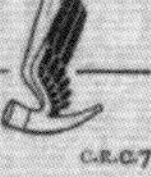

3.6 "Rebuilding" advertisement published by Hunting Aerosurveys in October 1945 in *Flight* magazine.

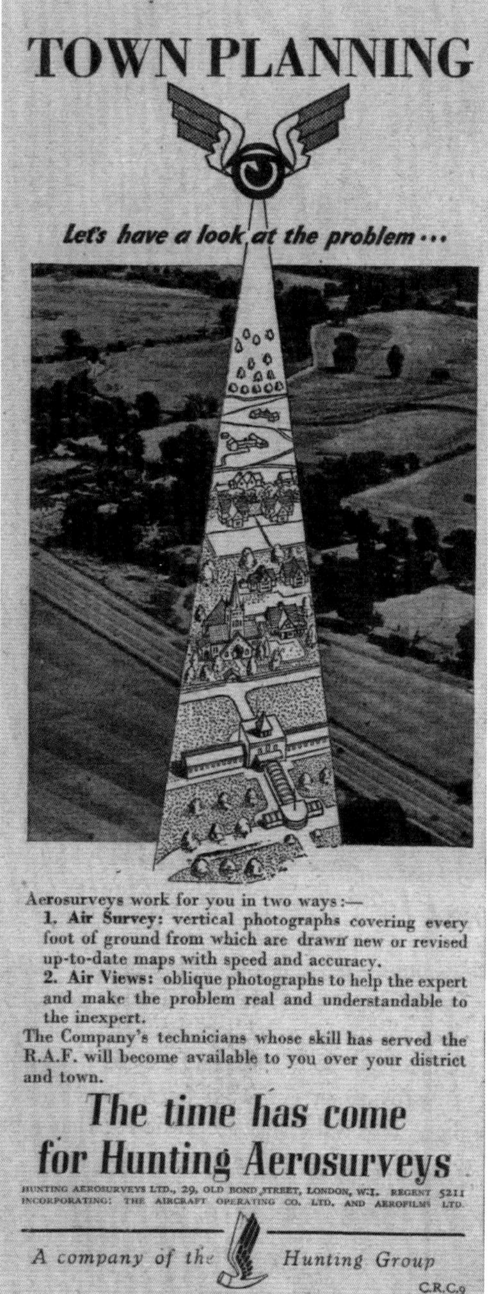

3.7 "Town Planning" advertisement published by Hunting Aerosurveys in December 1945 in *Flight* magazine.

MSM's aerial-affirmative approach resonated with commercial advertisements such as those by Hunting Aerosurveys. It also aligned with Anglo-American professional publications that readily embraced the potential of aerial photography to benefit town planning and justified it for remote (meaning little-known by the West) countries in particular. For example, American educator and urban planner Melville C. Branch claimed in 1948:

> In the type of urban research which seeks to explore the structural form and various characteristics of diverse towns and cities, air photos can provide that composite view which it is not practicable to obtain by direct visit or by an accumulation of material. When but little data are available concerning places in more out-of-the-way parts of the world, aerial photographs may serve as well for specific information or as the sole or most practical basis for the construction of a descriptive map or plan of the locality.[60]

For the three town planners, Kuwait was exactly such an "out-of-the-way" place that consequently required aerial surveying. As Peter W. Macfarlane's stated in one article: "Preparing a plan for such an area presented special problems. The town had never been mapped and the first step was an aerial survey ... from which a plan to a scale of 1:200 was prepared, together with mosaics and oblique photographs of points of importance."[61] The aerial survey not only provided factual information and a "mapping" of the territory—the photomosaic also became engraved into the master plan as a pictorial template and as specific visual-based knowledge.

The 1952 Master Plan's Aerial Vision of Kuwait

The 1952 Master Plan by Minoprio, Spencely, and Macfarlane (fig. 3.8) predominantly focuses on the same section of the Kuwaiti territory as the photomosaic (see fig. 3.3):[62] the town of Kuwait on the southern shore of Kuwait Bay and the bordering desert extending southwestward. It does, however, incorporate a substantially larger area than the photomosaic, thereby including more land to the south and the second eastern spit of Salmiya. The drawing is inscribed "A Development Plan for His Highness Shaikh Abdulla As Salim As Subah C.I.E." and "Kuwait." It thus establishes a visual and semantic *quid pro quo*: the development of Kuwait (the town) denotes the development of Kuwait (the country). Historically, the differentiation of the name "Kuwait" as two different topographical entities—the walled-off premises of Kuwait Town or *madīnat al-Kuwayt* and the territorial unit of Kuwait as a whole, which later became the nation-state

[60] Branch, Jr., *Aerial Photography in Urban Planning and Research*, 9.

[61] Macfarlane, "Planning an Arab Town," 112.

[62] The term "master plan" describes a single plan or a set of plans visualizing a comprehensive urban development concept. It can be understood as the macro-plan of an urban planning project aimed at combining all the major planned strategies, for example housing, traffic, and street layout.

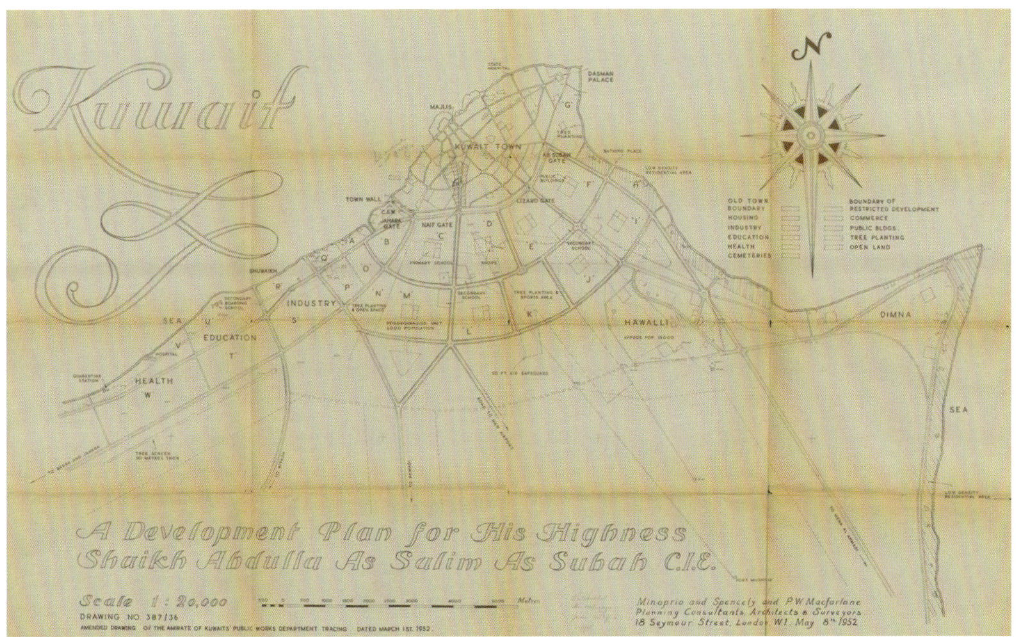

3.8 Development plan by Antonio Minoprio, Hugh Spencely, and Peter W. Macfarlane prepared in 1951/1952 as an urban planning blueprint of a new, modern Kuwait City.

Kuwait—followed the Uqair Convention in 1922 that negotiated the division of land between Saudi Arabia and Kuwait. The idea of Kuwait as a city-state and of modern Kuwait City as its flagship and signboard, that is, as the material, spatial, and visual representation of the country, is key to the master plan.

Based on a scale of 1:20,000 (a little larger than the photomosaic), the plan presents the overall structure and major aspects of the suggested development.[63] Given the color key in the upper right corner, the plan was originally most likely in color or used hatched patterns. Unfortunately, this rare archival copy preserved in The Postal Museum in London remains mostly blank. Also, the black-and-white illustrations of the master plan usually reproduced in primary and secondary literature show limited legibility; nevertheless, the key information is clearly visible.[64] Two basic techniques reorganize

[63] The following description is mainly based on the development plan, the document "Plan for the Town of Kuwait" (1951), and a 1954 article written by Macfarlane. See Minoprio, Spencely, and P. W. Macfarlane, "Plan for the Town of Kuwait: Report to His Highness Shaikh Abdullah Assalim Assubah, C.I.E., the Amir of Kuwait," November 1951, Center for Research and Studies on Kuwait; Macfarlane, "Planning an Arab Town," 112–13.

[64] To my knowledge the only color version of the master plan in print currently available was published as part of a small publication by the Kuwait Municipality in 1980. It provides information on the area outside

the space: first, the area is zoned functionally, with land identified for housing, industry, education, health, cemeteries, commerce, public buildings, tree planting, and open land; second, the road network—described as "boundaries"—is the crucial spatial organizer connecting or separating the functional zones and defining future (motorized) mobility. Using zones and road networks, the plan does not differentiate between already built-up land and "empty" desert. Instead, the projected urban expansion creates a homogenous space that spills across the historical urban demarcation of the town wall with ease.

Nevertheless, the zones and the new street network still differentiate qualitatively between the areas inside and outside the 1920 town wall. The projected thoroughfares within the perimeter of the "old town" are smaller and more irregular, while the area outside is organized by an expanding grid of wide radial and semicircular roads that compartmentalize zones of similar shape and size into "neighborhood units." While commercial and administrative zones are concentrated in the old town, the new residential areas are almost exclusively located beyond the town wall, systematically structured by the grid road system like quilted patches of habitat. Each block, called a "neighborhood unit," contains a multifunctional central area surrounded by private housing.[65] More blocks stretch along the coast to the spit of Salmiya (here still called Dimna) to the east. In addition, the zones for industry, education, and health are positioned along the shore to the west of Jahra Gate. Only a few buildings and localities are indicated by name, presumably underlining their importance, among them the state hospital, Seif Palace (here called Majlis), Dasman Palace, and Shuwaikh Secondary School. Once again, the information provided does not reflect the fact that some institutions already exist while some are merely projected.

Overall, the master plan proposed nothing less than turning Kuwait City inside out, as it were, by driving the entire population from inside the wall to outside of it. The honeycombed, walled-off town was substituted by clusters of suburban neighborhoods separated by distances that required motorization. In many ways, the vision of the future city of Kuwait paid tribute to a way of living saturated with petroleum and therefore resonates with Stefanie LeMenager's analysis of Los Angeles' urban transformation in the 1930s and 1940s as a manifestation of petroleum culture.[66] At the core of these processes was the creation of urban space that facilitates motorization, suburbanization,

the old town but—given the print's small size—only does so rudimentarily. See Rashid Al-Rashid, *Planning and Urban Development in Kuwait* (Kuwait: Kuwait Municipality, 1980), 27.

[65] The concept of the neighborhood unit was first developed by Clarence Perry in the *Regional Survey of New York and its Environs* in the 1920s, see Clarence Arthur Perry, *The Neighborhood Unit: Neighborhood and Community Planning; Regional Plan of New York and its Environs* (New York: Regional Plan Association, 1929). The concept became increasingly relevant for British urban planning in the 1940s, and is seen for example in Patrick Abercrombie's *The County of London Plan* (1943); see Michiel Dehaene, "Surveying and Comprehensive Planning: The 'Co-Ordination of Knowledge' in the Wartime Plans of Patrick Abercrombie and Max Lock," in Whyte, *Man-Made Future*, 45.

[66] LeMenager, *Living Oil*, chapter 2, The Aesthetics of Petroleum.

and, subsequently, the distanced consumption of landscape as vistas in a drive-by or even fly-over mode, as characteristic of petro-modernity.

Asphalted roads came to figure as prominent signifiers of such a transformation. For instance, *al-ʿArabī*, an illustrated Arab-language social and cultural magazine that was published in Kuwait and that was widely distribution across the MENA region, brought frequent updates on the road system in Kuwait when reporting on the country. In October 1959, the magazine highlighted the ongoing efforts to create 112 kilometers of smooth paved surface that would allow motorized travel at a speed of 120 kilometers an hour along "the first paved road linking Kuwait with the outside," which is today Highway 80 leading from Kuwait City to the northern border, and eventually Basra.[67] Such reports indicate the symbolic importance attributed to the development of (urban) space through roads that was of public interest. The urban planning policies introduced in Kuwait in the early 1950s resonated in the subsequent master planning of other Gulf cities and no matter how iridescently appealing they seemed then, Assaf and Montagne note in view of today's Gulf cities: "These policies have resulted in comparable landscapes: the urban morphology of Gulf cities today can be characterized by a scattered and discontinuous development where cars are the dominant mode of mobility."[68]

Despite these substantial construction works and changes, "old" Kuwait town remained indirectly visible exactly because of the new road system: the first semicircular ring road substituted the third town wall after it was demolished in 1957, thereby imprinting the outline of the (pre-oil) urban core on the master plan. As the consecutive ring roads were modeled on the first ring road (the former town wall), this pre-oil shape came to resemble a kind of halo in the subsequent urban expansion, a halo that the photomosaic had first brought to light. Yet, in the depiction of this urban vision (the 1952 Master Plan), the almond-shaped pre-oil urban form of the former town of Kuwait had become a mere placeholder for the depopulated new administrative and commercial city center. Conceiving of the pre-oil town as a mere shape or container was the result of seeing Kuwait through the photomosaic from above. However, this was not the only way in which the photomosaic resonated within the master plan. The photography also seemed to shine through the master plan as if it were made of tracing paper.

The 1952 Master Plan acknowledges the town of Kuwait as the epicenter of (national) urban growth and its almond-shaped urban form as its formal nucleus. From this core, various lines and delineated patches symbolizing "development" spread along the entirety of the coastline framed in the plan. This linear (originally colored or

[67] "Al-Kuwayt yataṭalaʿu ilā l-mustaqbal fī sabīl ghadd ʾafḍal [Kuwait Is Looking Forward to the Future on the Road to a Better Tomorrow]," *al-ʿArabī*, no. 11 (October 1959): 114. The same year, the magazine announced, "A million meters of roads are being paved yearly." "al-ʿImāra bi-l-Kuwayt [Architecture in Kuwait]," *al-ʿArabī*, no. 13 (December 1959): 62, 70.

[68] Laure Assaf and Clémence Montagne, "Urban Images and Imaginaries: Gulf Cities through Their Representations," *Arabian Humanities*, no. 11 (2019): 6, https://doi.org/10.4000/cy.4137.

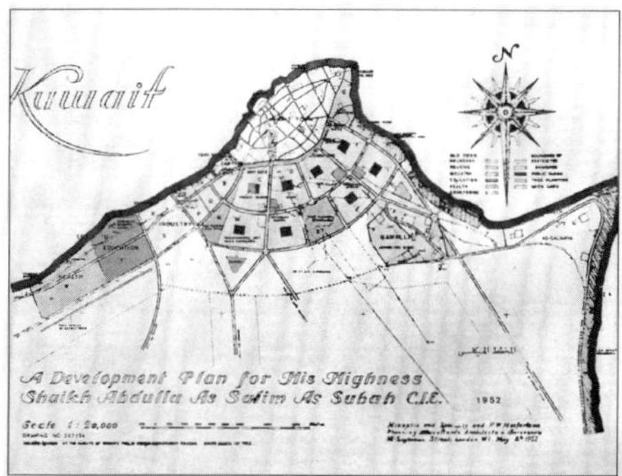

3.9 The development plan as reprinted in Gardiner's *Kuwait: The Making of a City.*

hatched) texture extends from the core and fans out into single lines (roads). A slightly more amended version of the 1952 Master Plan was subsequently reprinted in Stephen Gardiner's influential publication *Kuwait: The Making of a City* (1983) and it is here that the relationship between aerial and plan become most visible (fig. 3.9). The starkest contrast in this drawing is provided by the thick dark line that outlines the coastal formation along the two spits but lies beyond the land formation. The stark black-and-white contrast between the sea and the land mirrors the way in which sea and land are visualized in the photomosaic. Like in the composite photo, Kuwait's land mass rises against the darker undefined frame of the sea. As a result, the spitted shape with an almond-shaped nucleus protrudes from the image. This distinctive shape emerges as an independent form that comes to signify Kuwait (City) not only in the master plan drawing but also in the composite photo. Here, it is evident how much the aerial view has penetrated the planner's visual conception of Kuwait, how much the fossil-fueled, technologically enabled vision of aerial photography has infused the conventions of depicting new Kuwait City. Moreover, in comparison with the photomosaic, the white background of the drawing carrying the wind rose and the calligraphic writing "Kuwait" can be identified as another layer of the image, a layer that is superimposed onto the black area (the sea in the aerial photo), which has been reduced to a thick black line. In this future urbanized image of Kuwait, the sea has become a mere trace on paper, and a backdrop to the sensation of driving-by.

Harking back to the photogrammetric use of aerials, the relationship between the photomosaic and the plan could possibly be similar to that of the aerial survey and the resulting topographic map. Yet, without a grid, topographic details, and the exact geographic localization of such new urban features as neighborhood units, the first master plan cannot function as a topographic map, as a rational device of localization. Instead, it is the drawing of an urban vision that imitates some of the features of a map (northing, wind rose, verticality, color key). It also reflects the selective nature of maps, freely presenting some urban and geographical details while dismissing others, such as the differentiation between the existing built environment and unbuilt land. In this sense the first master plan depicts (new) Kuwait City not cartographically but as a pictorial representation of an urban utopia.

Aerial photography allows (urban) landscapes to be translated into images through the use of familiar photographic language. Characteristic of the use of aerial photography in urban planning is that it represents space as accessible, thereby allowing a future or utopian urban form to be imagined, conceived, and visually inscribed into these images of landscapes. This urban planning approach relies on the aerial view, especially the vertical view, to suggest that through aerial photography omniscient vision is possible and that the power to see creates the power to alter landscapes. Inscribed in both the master plan and the aerial photograph is the fundamental belief in landscape as a resource, a belief that is typical of development discourse and even embodied in the term "development plan" itself. The omniscient vertical view has made aerial photography "an increasingly privileged instrument of the double desire of planners—utopian and projective."[69] These are the seductive attributes that Hunting Aerosurveys readily recognized and promoted in their advertisements, and that clearly also shaped the urban planning approach to Kuwait City. Subjected to this view from above, new Kuwait City in the vision of the 1952 Master Plan became a free-floating form envisioned on the drawing board in remote London: it could have been anywhere and nowhere.

Taking the interpretation one step further, both images can be understood as establishing a continental or onshore image of Kuwait. The black-and-white contrast and the subsequent demarcation of spaces ultimately favors the land, severing it from the sea, which had been reduced to a mere thick black line. Hence, the respective technologies like aerial surveying, mapping, and planning also function as frontier technologies.[70] This is interesting insofar as the pre-oil history of Kuwait depended on the town's coastal location and maritime economy. These new visual representations forge a break from aligning Kuwait's urban identity with a connecting and nurturing sea; instead, they establish a Kuwaiti identity that is exclusively landbound. In many ways this reorientation is indicative of a socioeconomic and political shift from a society steered by a seafaring merchant class to a ruling family that is the main receiver of oil revenues; the onshore fixation of the oil-extracting economy in Kuwait may also play a part in this change of perception.

In the case of Kuwait, petro-modernity implied turning space into images—yet the resulting disembodied images also influenced the formation of Kuwait's urban space in

[69] Anthony Vidler, "Photourbanism: Planning the City from Above and from Below," in Bridge; Watson, *The New Blackwell Companion to the City*, 656.

[70] On frontier technologies in this context, see for instance Marionne Cronin, "Northern Visions: Aerial Surveying and the Canadian Mining Industry, 1919–1928," *Technology and Culture* 48, no. 2 (2007). Nelida Fuccaro also emphasized the concept of frontier urbanism for understanding the urban history of the Gulf region. See Nelida Fuccaro, "Middle Eastern Oil Towns as Petro-Histories," paper presented at the conference "The Global Petroleumscape," Technical University Delft, May 18, 2017.

return. In *Kuwait Transformed*, Farah Al-Nakib has analyzed how the implementation of the first master plan resulted in a new urban environment on the ground characterized by functional zones, neighborhood units, and road networks. Al-Nakib argues that the 1950s urban overhaul neglected and subsequently impaired the social coherence and interaction of people living in Kuwait, eventually leading to a "de-urbanization of society" today.[71] Viewing Kuwait from above, as projected in the photomosaic and the development plan, had already emptied the urban space of bodies, established movements, and familiar social interaction. The more such images infused Kuwait's urban visual culture, the more this perception became normalized and aligned with the changing urban reality on the ground.

The 1951 photomosaic and the 1952 Master Plan set precedents for perceiving and picturing Kuwait City from above (in the field of urban planning). Looking at the image-world emerging in the 1950s in Kuwait, the aerial view began to manifest as a dominant depiction of Kuwait City across a range of different media and outlets that worked to position Kuwait City firmly in the context of petro-modernity to lasting—yet ambiguous—effect.

3.3 Representational Ambiguities

In the 1950s, Kuwait was on everyone's lips. Articles in *The Times*, *Fortune*, *National Geographic*, and many others reported on Kuwait's development, its emerging cityscape, its civic transformation, its newfound wealth, and of course its oil industry. Dynamic postwar economies around the globe engaged in petro-modernity and shared a feverish interest in places where oil was produced. All reports about Kuwait talked about oil in one way or another and many were illustrated with aerial views of the transforming landscape to showcase Kuwait's story of oil to both local and foreign audiences. Yet it was not just in published images that the view of Kuwait from above proliferated: due to the rise of commercial air travel, this view speedily turned into a personal experience for many.

Kuwait encountered a strong increase in air travel in the postwar period, of which many passengers were involved in the oil business and more generally in the urban transformation of Kuwait. The city-state of Kuwait, surrounded as it was by either desert or the Gulf, became a frequented airport quickly. From 1948 onward, the British Overseas Airways Corporation (BOAC), among several other airlines, started flying to Kuwait every two weeks.[72] By 1954, BOAC served Kuwait twice a week.[73] Three years later, Kuwait was

[71] Al-Nakib, *Kuwait Transformed*. Al-Nakib's work is informed by the critique of "high modernism" as formulated by James C. Scott, *Seeing Like a State: How Certain Schemes to Improve the Human Condition Have* Failed (New Haven: Yale University Press, 1998).

[72] "Desert Pioneers: Aviation in Kuwait, the Impetus from Oil," *Kuwaiti Digest*, April 1973, 10.

[73] Macfarlane, "Planning an Arab Town," 110.

fully integrated in the commercial aviation network in the Middle East.[74] An enlarged transitional airport was built in 1961 and the commission for a new international airport was granted a year later.[75]

Despite the lack of precise figures, it can be safely assumed that, by the late 1950s, many people living and working in Kuwait were no longer traveling by boat or overland but by airplane. The harsh climate conditions during summer along with a new petro-dollar infused wealth readily promoted air travel not only as the fastest and most comfortable means of traveling but also as a lifestyle. Journalist Peter Mansfield, who visited Kuwait in 1958 and 1961, recalls that "with the first rush of affluence in the 1950s every Kuwaiti who could afford it left the country during the savage summer heat. It seemed to me at the time that Kuwait would in the future be actively deserted during July and August."[76] In fact, this is the case today. In addition, the significant population of workers and professionals from Europe and the US, but also increasingly from other Arab countries, India, and Pakistan living in Kuwait commuted by airplane.[77] As flying gradually turned into a mass phenomenon not only in Kuwait but in many countries, air travel was not just about mobility and affluence. It also introduced and eventually familiarized the positionality to view places from high above.

Together with new technologies of vision, fossil-fueled motorization and its unprecedented speed turned built environments into vistas of landscapes in a drive-by or fly-over mode. The resulting distant observer position is evident in Peter Lienhardt's observation when first arriving in Kuwait in 1953: "Reaching a strange place by air is like seeing it on television: the people who live there are just part of the scenery. Perhaps that is what 'international' has come to mean now."[78] Increasingly, petro-modernity meant experiencing space as image by petroleum-enabled means.

New Shapes in Kuwait's Cartography

The spatial visualizations of Kuwait that proliferated in articles discussing Kuwait in the mid-twentieth century reified the aerial view not only as reprinted photographs but also in the form of maps. These maps ranged from simplified figures to colorful and elaborate drawings. Many presented little more than the country's name, the national borders, and the location of the capital, and primarily indicated Kuwait's geographical position

[74] Keith Williams, "Commercial Aviation in Arab States: The Pattern of Control," *Middle East Journal* 11, no. 2 (1957): 134–35, table 2.

[75] Saba George Shiber, *The Kuwait Urbanization: Being an Urbanistic Case-Study of a Developing Country: Documentation, Analysis, Critique* (Kuwait: Kuwait Government Printing Press, 1964), 104; Fabbri, Saragoça, and Camacho, *Modern Architecture Kuwait*, 154–55.

[76] Mansfield, *Kuwait*, 125.

[77] Williams, "Commercial Aviation in Arab States," 134–36.

[78] Lienhardt, *Disorientations: A Society in Flux*, 23.

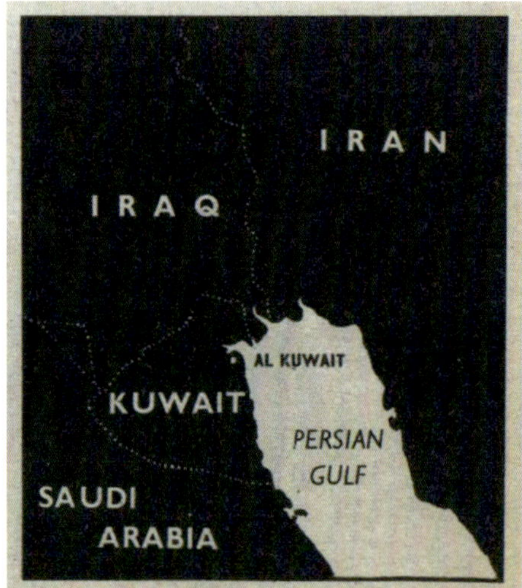

3.10 Simplified map of Kuwait published in July 1946 in *Picture Post*.

in relation to other countries. Most importantly, however, the cartography of this period had more than the aerial view in common with the aerial photography of May 1951 and the 1952 Master Plan. The new maps proliferated the iconic image of Kuwait City in the form of new emblematic shapes: the almond-like form (modeled on the 1920 town wall) of Kuwait town situated within the wave-shaped spit that is so characteristic of Kuwait's coastline. The emergence of these shapes was tied to the new visualization practices that aerial surveying and urban planning had given way to.

This popularization of depicting Kuwait City through shapes and the aerial view becomes most evident when comparing several such map-like drawings. A map illustration in a 1946 issue of the British magazine *Picture Post* presents "Al Kuwait" somewhere lost in the blackness of the landmass (fig. 3.10). With the dotted lines indicating the national borders like a string of lights, the illustration seems to resemble a night view of Kuwait, whereby Kuwait City accounts for merely one larger dot. These maps also served to affirm Kuwait's status as a bordered territory, one of the key characteristics of a nation-state (which Kuwait was in the process of becoming).

From mid-1951 onward, Kuwait City has frequently been represented as an almond-shaped area that is nested in the refined pointed spit of Kuwait Bay, as a figure in the *Illustrated London News* demonstrates (fig. 3.11).[79] The Kuwaiti government gazette also integrated this aerial representation of the almond-shaped town into its original 1953 cover (which has not changed since), thus suggesting the normalization of the aerial

[79] "The Mysterious Land of Kuwait," *Picture Post*, July 13, 1946, 14; photographs by N. Tim Gidal; "The World's Largest Single Oilfield: Kuwait and Its Fabulously Rich Ruler," *Illustrated London News*, June 30, 1951, 1061.

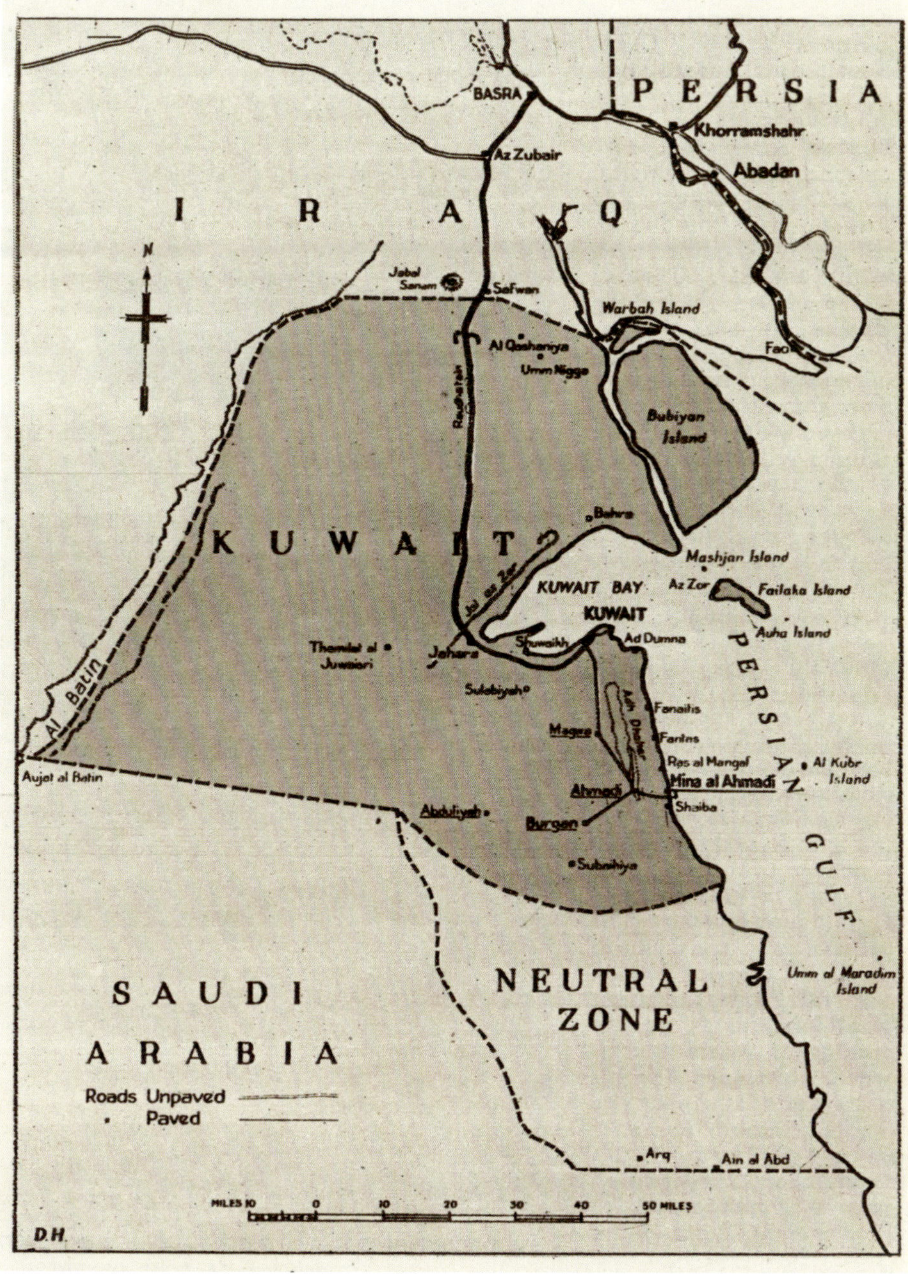

3.11 Map of Kuwait with road network published in June 1951 in the *Illustrated London News*.

viewing position and the integration of the view from above into Kuwait's national state-driven imaginary (see fig. 5.2).[80] Conceiving of Kuwait through/as a map-like icon resonates with Benedict Anderson's description of a "map-as-logo," which he considers a powerful visual vehicle of nation building.[81] Anderson suggests that, by being reproducible and transferable across media and spaces, such images gain influence by being "instantly recognizable and everywhere visible."[82] Processed through aerial photography and urban planning, the starkly simplified urban form of *pre-oil* Kuwait became the symbol of the *modern* oil city. Consequently, although the 1952 Master Plan set out to completely overhaul the existing town based on the aerial survey, the visual representation of this aerial vision fostered not only the preservation but also the popularization of the pre-oil urban form as iconic of New Kuwait City and the country as such. The inherent tension charged the visual representation of Kuwait City with that strongly affective ambiguity that characterizes petro-modernity's iridescence.

While traces of pre-oil Kuwait in the form of iconic shapes rapidly proliferated in all kinds of visual media, throughout the 1950s and 1960s much of what Kuwait's urban fabric had hitherto consisted of was erased according to the dictates of the first master plan. The 1951 aerial survey had produced the access points through which to conceive of landscapes as fit for drastic turnovers. Yet in the case of Kuwait, these aerials were simultaneously used to disguise, circumnavigate, and ignore the dramatic urban changes on the ground.

Kuwait Frozen in the 1951 Oblique Photography

MSM were among the first to publish the brand-new obliques taken of Kuwait during the aerial survey of May 1951. In contrast to the perpendicular comprehensiveness of the verticals (from which the photomosaic had been produced), these obliques captured the city in parts and from an inclined perspective. MSM's first article, titled "Planning Problems in Kuwait," appeared in *The Architect and Building News* in July 1951, shortly after MSM's second visit to Kuwait and only two months after the survey; the article was reprinted in *Town and Country Planning* in September.[83] Central to the article and its reprint—a status-quo report on Kuwait's oil-induced development and future urban

[80] For a detailed analysis of the government gazette see Chapter Five.

[81] Benedict Anderson, *Imagined Communities: Reflections on the Origin and Spread of Nationalism*, rev. ed. (London: Verso, [1983] 2006), 175.

[82] Ibid., 163–64, 170–78, here 175.

[83] While initially all three were named as authors, the September reprint indicates Macfarlane only. Hence, he was presumably the main author in the first place, possible being the writer in the team. Anthony Minoprio, Hugh Spencely, and Peter W. Macfarlane, "Planning Problems of Kuwait," *The Architect and Building News* 200, no. 4310 (July 1951); Peter W. Macfarlane, "Planning Problems of Kuwait," *Town and Country Planning* 19, no. 89 (September 1951).

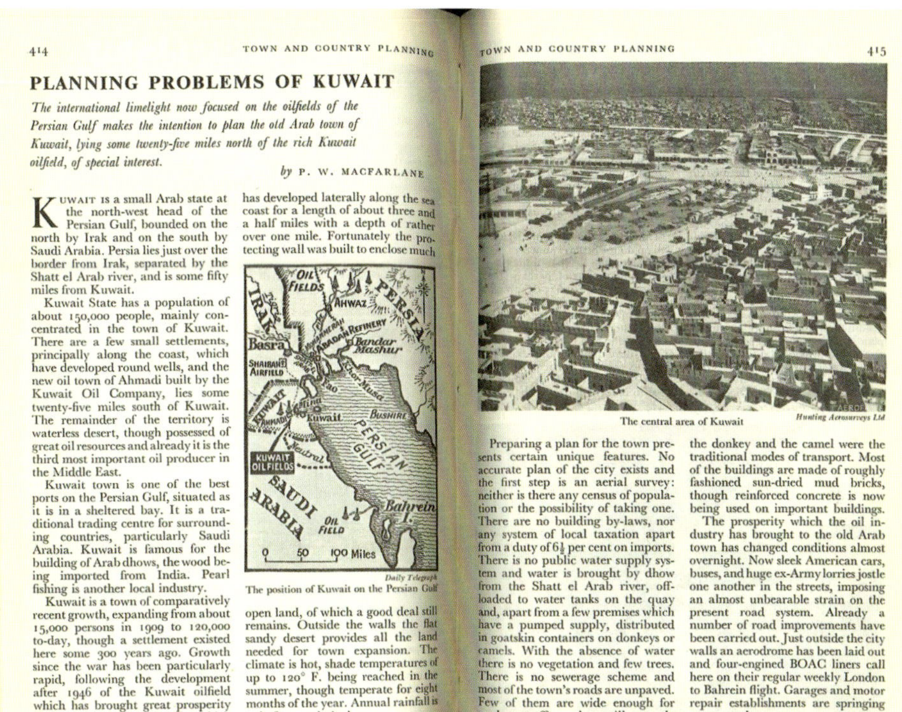

414 TOWN AND COUNTRY PLANNING

PLANNING PROBLEMS OF KUWAIT

The international limelight now focused on the oilfields of the Persian Gulf makes the intention to plan the old Arab town of Kuwait, lying some twenty-five miles north of the rich Kuwait oilfield, of special interest.

by P. W. MACFARLANE

KUWAIT IS a small Arab state at the north-west head of the Persian Gulf, bounded on the north by Irak and on the south by Saudi Arabia. Persia lies just over the border from Irak, separated by the Shatt el Arab river, and is some fifty miles from Kuwait.

Kuwait State has a population of about 150,000 people, mainly concentrated in the town of Kuwait. There are a few small settlements, principally along the coast, which have developed round wells, and the new oil town of Ahmadi built by the Kuwait Oil Company, lies some twenty-five miles south of Kuwait. The remainder of the territory is waterless desert, though possessed of great oil resources and already it is the third most important oil producer in the Middle East.

Kuwait town is one of the best ports on the Persian Gulf, situated as it is in a sheltered bay. It is a traditional trading centre for surrounding countries, particularly Saudi Arabia. Kuwait is famous for the building of Arab dhows, the wood being imported from India. Pearl fishing is another local industry.

Kuwait is a town of comparatively recent growth, expanding from about 15,000 persons in 1909 to 120,000 to-day, though a settlement existed here some 300 years ago. Growth since the war has been particularly rapid, following the development after 1946 of the Kuwait oilfield which has brought great prosperity to the area. It is a walled city which has developed laterally along the sea coast for a length of about three and a half miles with a depth of rather over one mile. Fortunately the protecting wall was built to enclose much open land, of which a good deal still remains. Outside the walls the flat sandy desert provides all the land needed for town expansion. The climate is hot, shade temperatures of up to 120° F. being reached in the summer, though temperate for eight months of the year. Annual rainfall is only four to six inches.

Daily Telegraph
The position of Kuwait on the Persian Gulf

TOWN AND COUNTRY PLANNING 415

The central area of Kuwait — Hunting Aerosurveys Ltd

Preparing a plan for the town presents certain unique features. No accurate plan of the city exists and the first step is an aerial survey: neither is there any census of population or the possibility of taking one. There are no building by-laws, nor any system of local taxation apart from a duty of 6½ per cent on imports. There is no public water supply system and water is brought by dhow from the Shatt el Arab river, off-loaded to water tanks on the quay and, apart from a few premises which have a pumped supply, distributed in goatskin containers on donkeys or camels. With the absence of water there is no vegetation and few trees. There is no sewerage scheme and most of the town's roads are unpaved. Few of them are wide enough for modern traffic and up till recently the donkey and the camel were the traditional modes of transport. Most of the buildings are made of roughly fashioned sun-dried mud bricks, though reinforced concrete is now being used on important buildings.

The prosperity which the oil industry has brought to the old Arab town has changed conditions almost overnight. Now sleek American cars, buses, and huge ex-Army lorries jostle one another in the streets, imposing an almost unbearable strain on the present road system. Already a number of road improvements have been carried out. Just outside the city walls an aerodrome has been laid out and four-engined BOAC liners call here on their regular weekly London to Bahrein flight. Garages and motor repair establishments are springing up everywhere.

3.12 *The Central Area of Kuwait [Safat Square]*. Oblique photograph taken in May 1951 by Hunting Aerosurveys/Aerofilms and reproduced in Peter W. Macfarlane's article "Planning Problems of Kuwait" in *Town and Country Planning*, September 1951.

rebuilding—is an almost identical oblique photograph of Safat Square, the town's center, viewed in the direction of the Persian Gulf (fig. 3.12).[84] Notably, this oblique—not the photomosaic or another vertical photograph—had been selected to provide a first impression of Kuwait to a wider audience, possibly because of the greater accessibility and pictorial quality attributed to oblique photography compared to verticals.

As one of the large open spaces within the surrounding neighborhoods of honeycombed groups of flat-roofed courtyard houses, Safat Square generally offered a clear point of orientation in Kuwait. At the time the photograph was taken, the open space was crowded with a makeshift market structure and pedestrians and some cars frequented the surrounding unpaved streets. When viewed in light of the "planning problems"

[84] Aerofilm is credited in the July issue, but Hunting Aerosurveys is credited in the September issue. In 1951, Aerofilm already belonged to Hunting Aerosurveys but continued under its original name and specialized in oblique photography. This shows that the aerial survey of Kuwait undertaken in May was not only used to take vertical photographs for a photomosaic but also for oblique photos.

Planning an Arab Town

Kuwait on the Persian Gulf

by P. W. Macfarlane, F.R.I.C.S. (M.)

It is a far cry from planning New Towns in Britain to preparing a plan for redeveloping and expanding the Arab town of Kuwait on the Persian Gulf. With the recent rapid development of the Burgan oilfield in the southern part of the State, Kuwait has, almost overnight, become the richest country in the world for its size, enjoying an annual income of many millions of pounds from oil royalties.

Its development is one of the romances of oilfield history. It was only in 1946 that the first barrel of oil was exported from Kuwait—now cumulative production has passed the 1,000 million barrel mark and today Kuwait takes its place with the great oil giants of the world. It is the largest individual producer in the Middle East and its proved reserves exceed one sixth of the world's known resources. The Kuwait Oil Company, which operates the concession, is a joint British-American enterprise in which the Anglo-Iranian Oil Company and the Gulf Oil Corporation are equal partners. The importance of this oilfield to Britain's economy can be appreciated from the fact that approximately 60% of our imports of crude oil in 1953 came from Kuwait.

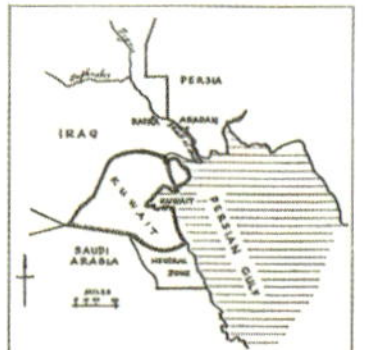

Kuwait State is a small independent Shaikhdom, about the size of Yorkshire, in close treaty relationship with Britain, situated at the north-west head of the Persian Gulf, bounded by Irak on the north and west, by Saudi Arabia on the south and by the Persian Gulf on the east.

The State has a population of some 180,000 persons, most of whom live in the town of Kuwait, a thriving port and walled city. Facing north into Kuwait Bay, it is one of the best natural sheltered harbours in the Persian Gulf and a traditional trading centre for surrounding countries, particularly Saudi Arabia. Besides their maritime commerce, the Kuwaitis are famous for boat building and before the war for pearl fishing. About 25 miles to the south is the oil town of Ahmadi, built by the Kuwait Oil Company to house several thousand employees and equipped with the most up-to-date services. Five miles to the east is the new port of Mena Ahmadi, where the world's largest oil tanker loading jetty handles the oil exports. Apart from a few small settlements served by shallow wells, mainly along the coast, the remainder of the State is an almost waterless desert with a rainfall of four to six inches a year. The climate is extremely hot in summer (the shade temperature rises to 125° Fahr.) but it is relatively temperate for the other eight months of the year.

The Ruler, His Highness the Shaikh, Sir Abdulla As Salim As Subah, K.C.M.G., C.I.E., is a man of high moral character who is following the wise and statesman-like policy of devoting his great wealth to improving living conditions for his people, and he aims at making Kuwait the best planned and most socially progressive city in the Middle East.

Up to quite recently conditions, according to Western standards, have been primitive. Much of the drinking water for the town was imported by dhow from the Shatt el Arab river, some 60 miles to the north, and distributed in tins or goat-skin containers on camels and donkeys. With the absence of water there is little vegetation and there has, hitherto, been no need for a sewerage system. Many of the town's roads are unpaved, and few are wide enough for modern traffic. Most of the older buildings are single storey, made of roughly fashioned sun-dried mud bricks or lumps of coral. Like most Arab cities, the town is densely built up and honeycombed with alleys and passageways which give shade against the hot sun and protection against sandstorms. Houses are flat-roofed and usually enclosed within courtyards by high walls. The Eastern custom of purdah is still strictly maintained.

Reconstruction and expansion

Prosperity is bringing great changes. Fleets of showy American cars, buses and huge ex-army lorries, throng the streets, imposing an almost unbearable strain on narrow roads more suited to the camel and donkey. B.O.A.C. Argonauts call twice weekly on their flight between London and Bahrein, landing at the airport just outside the town wall, whilst numerous local services are flying in freight and passengers from all over the Middle East. The number of shops, warehouses and cafés in the town is rapidly increasing and many houses are being converted to garages and motor repair shops. Opportunities for employment are attract-

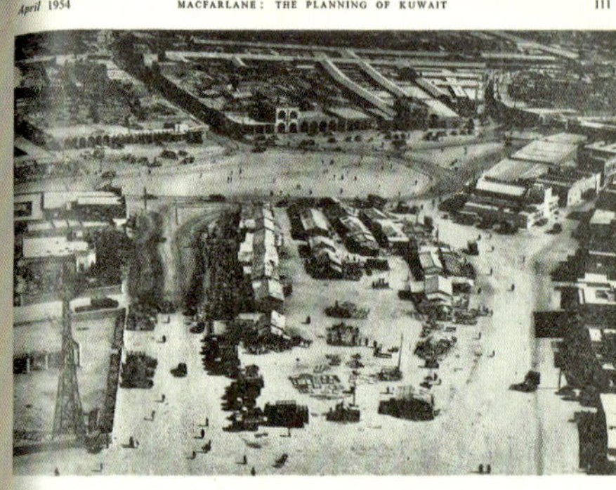

'The heart of the city,' a more extensive view of the picture shown on page 113.

ing the nomad Beduins, who are settling outside the city wall, building primitive houses of palm matting, kerosene tins and odd pieces of corrugated iron and wood.

Side by side with these changes the State is embarking on public works costing many millions. Already the first unit of a huge seawater distillation plant is in operation, supplying the town with drinking water. This, and an adjoining power station under construction, are fired by natural gases from the oilfield. Outside the walled town a modern harbour is being built, capable of handling ocean-going ships.

Kuwaitis already enjoy a free public health service which includes a well-equipped general hospital; another with 750 beds is proposed; a 250-bed T.B. hospital is nearly finished; mobile dispensaries will serve the villages; a fine block of old people's homes was recently completed. Many headquarter buildings for government departments are contemplated; and work will soon start on a large municipal abattoir, on a soil and building research station and on a plant for the manufacture of sand-lime bricks—at the moment virtually all modern building materials are imported. A state factory to make unit parts for small houses is already in production. Among other buildings proposed are a meat market, post office, Majlis, a hotel and a State guest house. At a not very distant date a new airfield will be required, as the present one will be absorbed into the expansion of the town. The town is to have a water distribution system—duplicate mains are required for drinking water and saline water for flushing. This will be followed by a sewerage scheme, and tenders have been invited for a comprehensive scheme of street lighting, whilst gas mains will distribute waste gas from the oilfield, which is suitable for domestic use. To accommodate the numerous Arab and British employees engaged on these building and engineering projects, two self-contained camps have been laid out west of the town.

Schools programme

Perhaps most important of all is the ambitious programme for universal education, for a population at present largely illiterate. Some thirty elementary schools are planned, of which three for 750 boys each will be completed early this year. Their facilities include gymnasium, library, scouts' rooms, assembly hall, laboratories, swimming pool, clinic, hostel for teachers, headmaster's flat, and soccer and basket-ball pitches. The cost of each school may well be between £300,000 and £400,000. Nursery schools, with similar generous

3.13 *The Heart of the City [Safat Square]*. Oblique photograph taken in May 1951 by Hunting Aerosurveys/Aerofilms and reproduced in Peter W. Macfarlane's article "Planning an Arab Town," in *Journal of the Town Planning Institute*, April 1954.

referenced in the article's title, the aerial supported the impression of a crowded, disorganized historical urban core that needed reorganization. Evidently this particular oblique was chosen to legitimize the urban planners' agenda overseas, as it justified the process of "rebuilding" according to Western town planning standards.

Three years later, in 1954, Peter W. Macfarlane, one of the town planners, published an article titled "Planning an Arab Town: Kuwait on the Persian Gulf" in the *Journal of the Town Planning Institute*.[85] Again, an oblique of Safat Square was featured, this time a close-up (fig. 3.13).[86] Close comparison reveals that the photo is a variation of the oblique published in the 1951 articles, which proves that MSM continued working with the set of obliques (and verticals) from 1951. Similarly, the magazine *Architectural Design* featured Kuwait's master plan as part of a special issue on "Architecture in the Middle East" edited

[85] Macfarlane, "Planning an Arab Town," 110–13.

[86] The photo's caption identifies Safat Square as the "heart of the city" and thus references the eponymous 8th CIAM congress (1951), but without reflecting its debates. See Sigfried Giedion, "CIAM 8: The Heart of the City: A Summing Up," *Ekistics* 52, no. 314/315 (1985). For an historical assessment of the metaphor "heart of the city," see for example Konstanze Sylva Domhardt, *The Heart of the City: Die Stadt in den transatlantischen Debatten der CIAM 1933–1951*, Architektonisches Wissen (Zurich: GTA Verlag, 2012), 330–48.

by Raglan Squire in March 1957.[87] Alongside the master plan and a neighborhood unit scheme a 1951 oblique photograph of the vernacular housing clusters close to the shore was published. Subsequently, not only MSM's understanding of Kuwait but also a larger professional audience's understanding of Kuwait remained, at least visually, limited to this one visual record of May 1951. This was problematic, because what in 1951 was an up-to-date visual document of Kuwait had by 1954 already become a historical record of Kuwait; by this time Kuwait was already undergoing major reconstruction and no longer resembled the images taken in 1951. Macfarlane himself underscored the change in the article.[88] Within the frame of just three years the aerials had aged dramatically: they now presented an image of Kuwait town that existed only as pictures and memory.

While the oblique in the 1954 article gave readers an impression of Kuwait's initial situation that was limited to the moment of the planners' first visit, the written text itself delivered a well-informed update about ongoing and planned rebuilding. That it included a detailed description of the 1952 Master Plan appears to suggest that MSM's town planning should continue to be read as a remedy to the urban situation as captured in the oblique (as already insinuated in the 1951 article). In combination with the oblique, the textual rendition of the master plan served to position the concept as the ultimate solution for change and development.

While the aerials encapsulated and simultaneously muted the preexisting (built) environment, the master plan unfolded a much stronger symbolic power: it gave at least the impression of being able to change this particular urban space irrespective of actual conditions on the ground. In this logic, the photograph no longer projects a status quo as a prerequisite to action but becomes subjected to photography's trap of conserving time and space in an eternal deadlock. The realistic aesthetic of the oblique photograph disguises the fact that it is basically no longer a sign of modernity, no longer a depiction of the present and projection of the future; rather, it now represents a past that has been arrived at overnight. Elsewhere, urban geographer Matthew Gandy has argued that "urban form can be interpreted as an accumulation of the past viewed through the concerns of the present."[89] However, in the case of Kuwait City and other petro-modernized cities that were so quick to "overhaul" their recent pasts, their physical urban form was almost too strained to provide for the past. Instead, in these spaces, visual representations such as aerial photographs, maps, and even master plans became images from which to interpret the past—and also to affectively access the past as Chapter Seven discusses. They thereby took the place of memory even for 1960s contemporaries as we will shortly see, which in other cases was tied to such architectural traces as physical ruins.

[87] Charles A. Minoprio, Hugh G. C. Spencely, and Peter W. Macfarlane, "Plan for Kuwait," *Architectural Design* 27, no. 3, special issue, Architecture in the Middle East, ed. Raglan Squire (March 1957): 75.

[88] Macfarlane, "Planning an Arab Town," 113. By "this country" the author was referring to Britain.

[89] Matthew Gandy, "Landscape and Infrastructure in the Late-Modern Metropolis," in Bridge; Watson, *The New Blackwell Companion to the City*, 58.

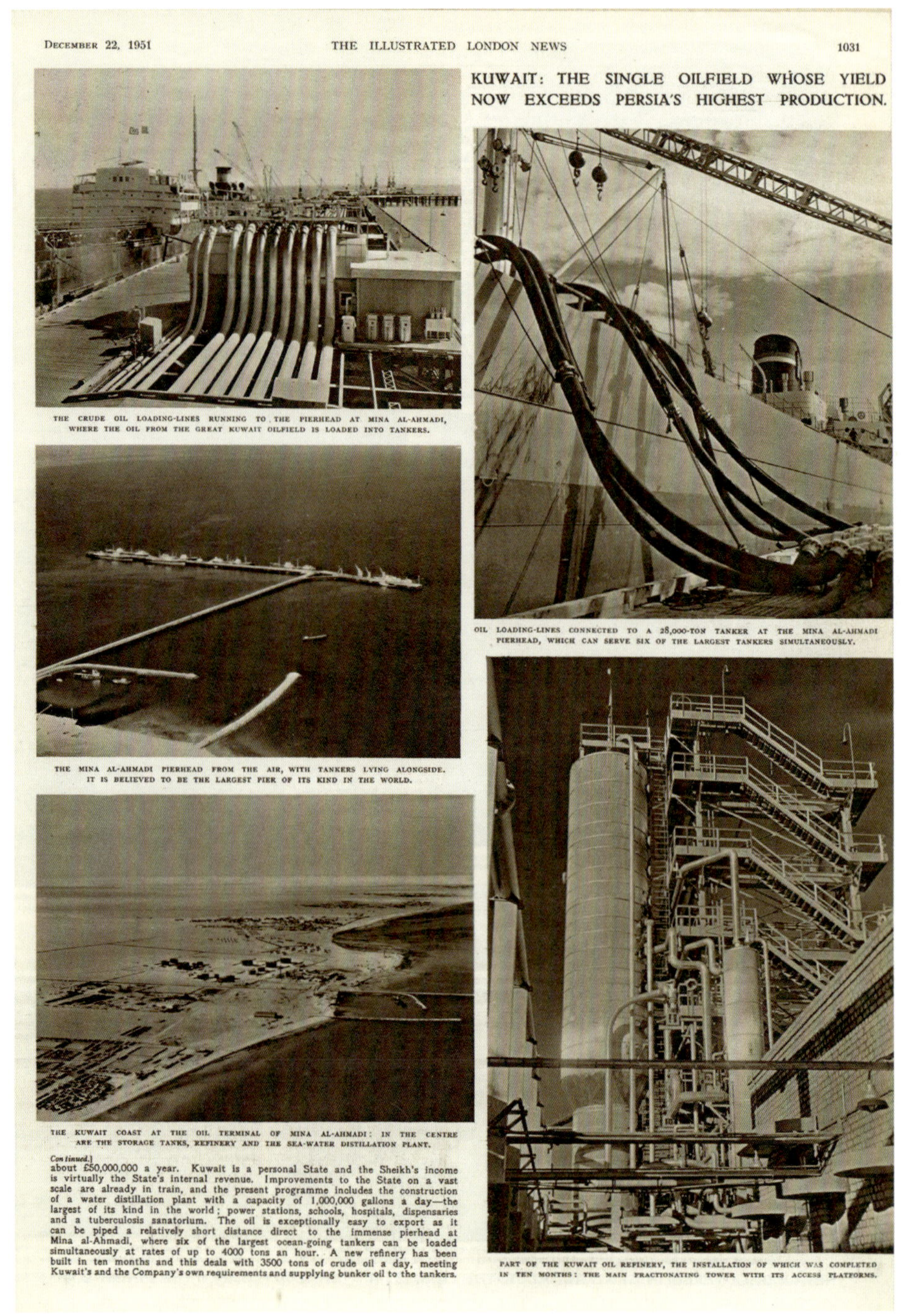

DECEMBER 22, 1951 THE ILLUSTRATED LONDON NEWS 1031

KUWAIT: THE SINGLE OILFIELD WHOSE YIELD NOW EXCEEDS PERSIA'S HIGHEST PRODUCTION.

THE CRUDE OIL LOADING-LINES RUNNING TO THE PIERHEAD AT MINA AL-AHMADI, WHERE THE OIL FROM THE GREAT KUWAIT OILFIELD IS LOADED INTO TANKERS.

OIL LOADING-LINES CONNECTED TO A 28,000-TON TANKER AT THE MINA AL-AHMADI PIERHEAD, WHICH CAN SERVE SIX OF THE LARGEST TANKERS SIMULTANEOUSLY.

THE MINA AL-AHMADI PIERHEAD FROM THE AIR, WITH TANKERS LYING ALONGSIDE. IT IS BELIEVED TO BE THE LARGEST PIER OF ITS KIND IN THE WORLD.

THE KUWAIT COAST AT THE OIL TERMINAL OF MINA AL-AHMADI: IN THE CENTRE ARE THE STORAGE TANKS, REFINERY AND THE SEA-WATER DISTILLATION PLANT.

Continued.]
about £50,000,000 a year. Kuwait is a personal State and the Sheikh's income is virtually the State's internal revenue. Improvements to the State on a vast scale are already in train, and the present programme includes the construction of a water distillation plant with a capacity of 1,000,000 gallons a day—the largest of its kind in the world; power stations, schools, hospitals, dispensaries and a tuberculosis sanatorium. The oil is exceptionally easy to export as it can be piped a relatively short distance direct to the immense pierhead at Mina al-Ahmadi, where six of the largest ocean-going tankers can be loaded simultaneously at rates of up to 4000 tons an hour. A new refinery has been built in ten months and this deals with 3500 tons of crude oil a day, meeting Kuwait's and the Company's own requirements and supplying bunker oil to the tankers.

PART OF THE KUWAIT OIL REFINERY, THE INSTALLATION OF WHICH WAS COMPLETED IN TEN MONTHS: THE MAIN FRACTIONATING TOWER WITH ITS ACCESS PLATFORMS.

3.14 A picture essay of Kuwait with oblique photos of Kuwait City (from the 1951 aerial survey), of the oil installations, and shipbuilding as published in the *Illustrated London News*, December 1951.

THE FABULOUSLY RICH OILFIELD OF KUWAIT: ASPECTS NEW AND OLD OF THE TINY STATE.

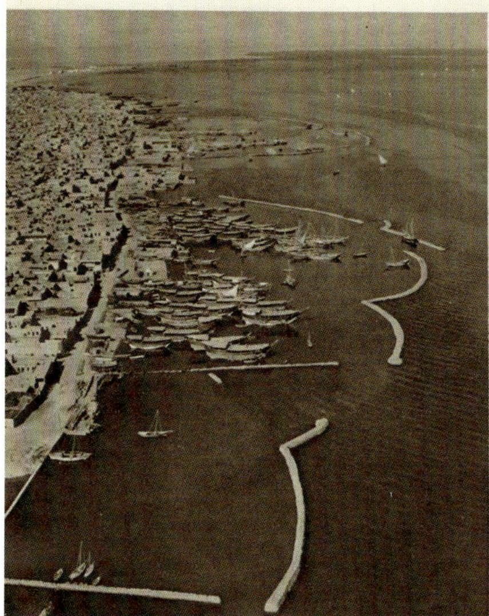

AN AERIAL VIEW OF THE HARBOUR OF KUWAIT, THE CAPITAL OF THE TINY PERSIAN GULF STATE, WHICH CONTAINS THE WORLD'S RICHEST SINGLE OILFIELD.

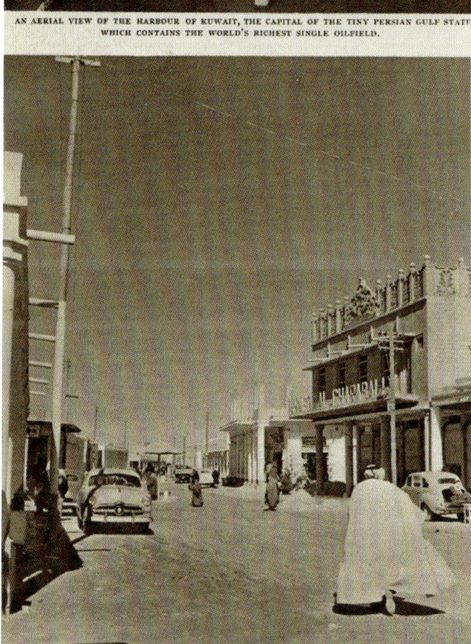

WITH ITS GREAT OIL BOOM, THE PROSPERITY OF KUWAIT HAS INCREASED FANTASTICALLY, AND NEW STREETS WITH MODERN SHOPS ARE BEING CARVED THROUGH THE OLD TOWN.

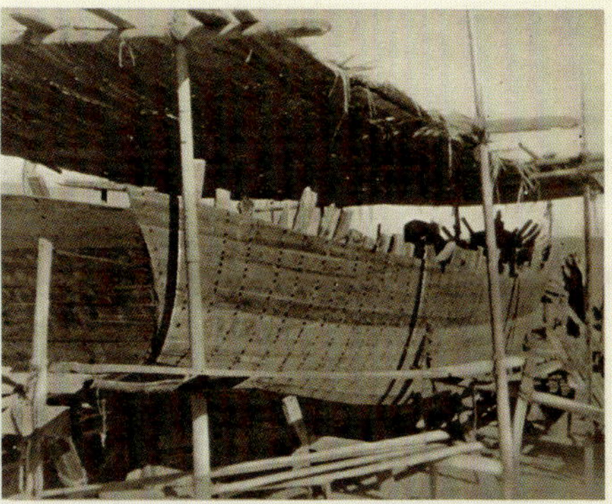

THE KUWAITIS HAVE BEEN FAMOUS FOR MANY YEARS AS SAILORS AND BOAT-BUILDERS; HERE A NATIVE SHIP IS BEING BUILT UNDER A PALM-LEAF AWNING.

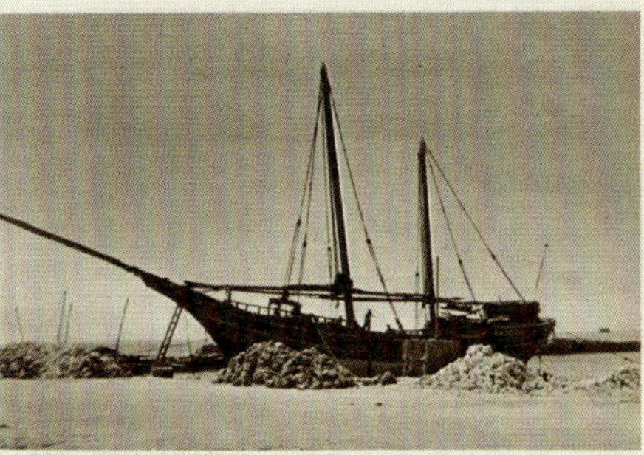

A TYPICAL KUWAIT TRADING-VESSEL. THESE SAILING-SHIPS SAIL AS FAR AFIELD AS INDIA AND ZANZIBAR, AND MANY OF THEM CAN BE SEEN IN THE UPPER-LEFT PHOTOGRAPH.

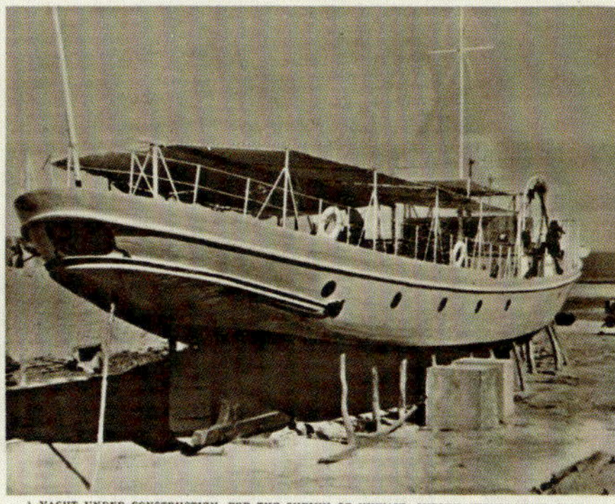

A YACHT UNDER CONSTRUCTION FOR THE SHEIKH OF KUWAIT, SHEIKH ABDULLAH AL SALIM AL SABAH, WITH WHOM THE NEW OIL ROYALTY AGREEMENT HAS JUST BEEN CONCLUDED.

ON December 3 it was announced that a new agreement had been reached between the Kuwait Oil Company and the Sheikh of Kuwait. The Kuwait Oil Company is jointly owned by the Anglo-Iranian Oil Company and the American Gulf Exploration Company, and under the new agreement the Sheikh becomes personally entitled to a 50 per cent. share of the Company's profits. The Kuwait oilfield at Burgan is the world's richest single oil structure, and the present production of oil there is at the rate of 3,000,000 tons a month—greater than the highest Persian rate. In 1946 the output was 797,350 tons; in the first six months of 1951 it was 13,657,689 tons. This fabulous expansion and the new agreement will, it has been estimated, raise the Sheikh's income to

[Continued opposite.

Through the frequent, although not exclusive use of the 1951 obliques that depicted the densely knit (pre-oil) urban fabric in the general press throughout the 1950s, Kuwait's aerial appearance was frozen in this visual status quo; despite the fact that, as one urban planner noted in 1964, "the building boom in Kuwait went berserk during especially the period 1954 to 1962."[90] This impression was amplified by the proliferation of another group of motifs in photographs of Kuwait that showed large and newly-completed building projects—and especially massive and sophisticated-looking oil infrastructure, often as singular structures. These were, for example, pictures of the oil jetty at Mina al-Ahmadi or a group of oil tanks in the desert, as shown on page 2 of a two-page article on Kuwait in the *Illustrated London News* of December 1951 (fig. 3.14).[91] Suddenly, the view from above of the pre-oil town of Kuwait was juxtaposed with these brand-new structures across the pages, even in these articles. This field of tension between old and new also resonated in the different types of ships currently under construction in Kuwait's wharves (see fig. 3.14).

While the sites of petroleum infrastructure and other building projects like schools emerged as organized, controlled, and recently built spaces of utmost productivity, the town of Kuwait became emblematic of an almost nostalgic or at least romantic notion of a dense, white-washed, and flat-roofed Middle Eastern coastal settlement. In such media outlets, the 1951 aerials played a crucial role in constructing the pre-oil town as inadequate, backward, inferior, and outdated, thereby not only fueling but justifying Kuwait's drastic rebuilding throughout the decade in the eyes of their readers. Although Kuwait's urban transformation was also visualized through individual photographs of newly built schools, government buildings, villas, and so on shot from street level, throughout the long 1950s the town—as a comprehensive unit—was frozen in time by means of these oblique photographs. This rapidly changed when a new comprehensive aerial survey was undertaken in October 1960 and the 1951 aerials were suddenly critically compared and reviewed.

Assessing the Urban Transformation in the 1960s

By the early 1960s the town of Kuwait had transformed into Kuwait City. Its population had tripled and the area of the city had expanded significantly beyond the town wall and become flooded with cars.[92] Suburbanization, motorization, abundant energy, and water supply, all made possible by oil revenues and fossil energy, had transformed the city lastingly and visibly. The most well-known view of Kuwait had become the aerial view from an airplane as captured by journalist Peter Mansfield in 1961:

[90] Shiber, *The Kuwait Urbanization*, 2.

[91] "The Fabulously Rich Oilfield of Kuwait."

[92] *Al-ʿArabī* called attention to the "twofold expansion of the city in four years," "*al-ʿImāra bi-l-Kuwayt* [*Architecture in Kuwait*]," *62.*

> Kuwait City already appeared at night from the air as a huge metropolis, with the lights of the new suburbs stretching for miles into the surrounding desert. Some of the new villas were uncompromisingly garish but their gardens greatly improved the city's appearance. Palms, tamarisks and acacia … were being planted along the city streets and kept alive at considerable cost.[93]

The 1951 aerial photographs were now undisputedly outdated but far from irrelevant. When the next comprehensive aerial survey was undertaken in October 1960, the 1951 aerials now provided a basis of visual comparison; they became both historical evidence of the existence of the pre-oil town and of the massive overhaul that had taken place.[94] While the small mud-plastered alleyways and courtyard houses vanished, multistory concrete buildings had begun appearing inside and futuristic detached villas outside the former town wall.

The new 1960 aerials confronted professionals with the fact that Kuwait's de facto urban expansion was already far greater than the template, the 1952 Master Plan, had envisioned just under a decade earlier and thus also revealed the practical limitations of such visualizations. Urban planner Saba Georg Shiber vividly recalled that the (comparative) view from above "came as a surprise to all responsible planning authorities and officials, engineers, and architects" in Kuwait in 1960.[95] Indeed, Kuwait's urban transformation was well under way, but instead of transitioning smoothly from a pre-oil coastal town into the neatly delineated shapes, roads, and forms of the master plan, it had gained a different dynamic altogether. In this context, aerials suddenly served to assess Kuwait's development in reverse, which meant that images were used to examine a spatial transformation, which had been based on images in the first place, through which new images were created in return. Evidently Kuwait was fully immersed in the symbolic process of petro-fueled visual representation characteristic of petro-modernity, a mirroring process insinuated by the (self-)reflecting iridescent sheen in the sculpture *Alien Technology*. How the aerials were discussed as highly ambiguous symbols of Kuwait's petro-modernity is best explored through the lens of Saba Georg Shiber's study of Kuwait's urban transformation: *The Kuwait Urbanization: Being an Urbanistic Case-Study of a Developing Country; Documentation, Analysis, Critique.*

Shiber (1923–1968), a Jerusalemite architect, planner, consultant, and writer who held several degrees from Arab and American universities in the field of architecture and planning, published *The Kuwait Urbanization* in both Arabic and English in June 1964.

[93] Mansfield, *Kuwait*, 43.

[94] Subsequently, updated obliques of Kuwait were also reprinted in the popular press, lifting Kuwait's visual standstill in aerial photography. "One of the Richest Cities in the World, Threatened by Iraqi Claims of Sovereignty: An Aerial View of Kuwait Town which Flourishes on Oil Revenues," *Illustrated London News*, July 8, 1961, 54–55; "Threatened by Iraq but Supported by the Other Arab Countries: Oil-Rich Kuwait and Its Ruler," *Illustrated London News*, July 8, 1961, 1.

[95] Saba G. Shiber, "Kuwait: A Case Study," in *From Madina to Metropolis: Heritage and Change in the Near Eastern City*, ed. L. C. Brown, Princeton Studies on the Near East (Princeton: Darwin, 1973), 183 (italics in the original).

At the time he had been working as an architectural and city planning adviser to several Kuwaiti government institutions such as the Public Works Department, the Development Board, and the Municipality over the past four years.[96] The publication can be considered the earliest comprehensive, first-hand assessment of the country's urban transformation over the by then past fourteen years and an important primary source of an Arabic debate on modern urban planning. Spread across 644 richly illustrated pages, *The Kuwait Urbanization* is a scholarly endeavor, history book, photo album, and artistic picture book for which Shiber drew on his professional education and long-standing experience and in which he attempts to settle the score with Kuwait's first master planning.

The mere fact of Shiber's employment marked a shift in urban planning politics in Kuwait and in fact in the Arab world at large, as his persona incorporated what Haraway describes as situated knowledge. Instead of British or American "circulating experts," circulating Arab professionals who worked and lived in Kuwait and eventually Kuwaitis became important players in the field. The nascent vernacular field of Arab urban experts manifested in conferences such as The New Metropolis in the Arab World that took place in Cairo in December 1960.[97] Shiber, who was a participant, developed a critical position toward Kuwait's development formula in the early 1960s. He was well aware of the necessity to modernize cities and also borrowed from Western theoretical models and techniques of visualization, yet, in contrast to MSM, he emphasized that the town of Kuwait as it had existed at the beginning of the 1950s would have provided an urban form with its own characteristics, good or bad, from which to start. As Aseel Al-Ragam has shown, "his intention was to position the Arab city as a model equal in value to its western counterpart" in order "to make way for a more sensitive design approach based on context" and appreciative of an earlier urban history.[98]

Long before "petro-urbanism" or "oil urbanization" was systematically analyzed and categorized, Shiber already described it as such by identifying oil and the car as the driving forces of Kuwait's rapid urban change and especially growth. Characterized by unprecedented speed, it was, in Shiber's words, "this unique and voracious urbanization

[96] The Jerusalemite had studied civil engineering at the American University in Beirut (B.A., 1944) and architecture at Cairo University (B.Arch., 1946), before moving to the US where he obtained an M.A. in architecture from MIT in 1947 and an M.A. in city planning from the same university in 1948. Six years later he completed a PhD in City and Regional Planning from Cornell University, apparently as the second Arab candidate in the whole of the US. He then worked in the US, in Lebanon, Syria, Jordan, and Saudi Arabia (for ARAMCO) before arriving in Kuwait. See Shiber, *The Kuwait Urbanization*, 643; Joe Nasr, "Saba Shiber, 'Mr. Arab Planner': Parcours professionnel d'un urbaniste au Moyen-Orient," *Géocarrefour* 80, no. 3 (2005), https://doi.org/10.4000/geocarrefour.1175.

[97] Morroe Berger, ed., *The New Metropolis in the Arab World* (New Delhi: Allied Publishers, 1963); papers prepared for an international seminar on City Planning and Urban Social Problems, Cairo, December 17–22, 1960; see also Asseel Al-Ragam, "Representation and Ideology in Postcolonial Urban Development: The Arabian Gulf," *The Journal of Architecture* 16, no. 4 (2011): 461, https://doi.org/10.1080/13602365.2011.598702.

[98] Al-Ragam, "Representation and Ideology in Postcolonial Urban Development," 460, 463.

that has witnessed one distinct urban form—that dictated by the scale of the car—'graft' itself on the distinct urban matrix and tissue of a tranquil, organic, typical desert Arab city."[99] And again and again Shiber also relied on aerial photography (and cartographic material) to make this point across the several hundred pages of the book.

The comparative aerial perspective stimulated Shiber to critique the 1952 Master Plan and the resulting rebuilding sharply. To him, MSM's plans were "rigid, geometric, two-dimensional plans: very simply and truly, drawings—drawings in an era when drawing, or geometry, had become an anathema."[100] Yet, on the one hand, Shiber argued almost sympathetically with MSM:

> Kuwait is unlike most other old Arab cities such as Cairo, Damascus, Baghdad, Jerusalem, Tunis and others in the sense that the old city contained few large religious, historic or architectural structures to act as starting-points or foci to planning. Often, the absence of such landmarks, or constraints, and a total "free rain" in a planning situation can cause challenges to the planner that are unusual, numerous and difficult. How does one create a significant new urban idiom?[101]

Here he conceded that the absence of significant historical landmarks, which would have emerged or protruded in the aerials, posed certain challenges for the new planning process due to the lack of urban orientation. On the other hand, he reproached MSM's planning solutions for obeying the car ad extremum and thereby sacrificing Kuwait's historical morphology and urban fabric:

> The old urban pattern, rendered in contemporary idiom, could have easily served as the inspiration for evolving the structure, grain, pattern, matrix, mosaic and texture of the new city. Instead, the almost childish happiness and preoccupation with superhighways, roundabouts and the haphazard, inorganic procedure in the choice of sites for major urban functions misted up basic considerations.[102]

In addition, Shiber criticized that the plan had neglected the climatic demands on architecture and urban planning, and the sociocultural needs of the Kuwaiti people.[103]

Most importantly, for Shiber, the 1960s aerial view of Kuwait City demonstrated that "uncircumscribed spread" had become the oil city's (or petro-urbanism's) dominant characteristic; this had resulted from the indefinite urban expansion beyond the former town wall that the master plan had stimulated.[104] In combination with the destruction of

99 Shiber, *The Kuwait Urbanization*, 5.

100 Ibid., 116. More precisely, he explained, "the basic planning of Kuwait, if a few rudimentary geometric lines and labels may be referred to as 'planning,' is not only alien to the habitat of Kuwait and therefore incorrect in the deep meaning of planning principles, but it must have emanated from minds—judging from the inorganicism [*sic*] of the 'planning'—that were purely the minds of civil engineers and surveyors. Those few lines that represent the 'Plans' of Kuwait could not have been any more rigid and inorganic vis-à-vis Kuwait and the Kuwaiti determinants of city formation." Shiber, *The Kuwait Urbanization*, 120.

101 Shiber, *The Kuwait Urbanization*, 5.

102 Ibid., 118.

103 Ibid., 115–21.

104 Ibid., 118.

the historic urban core, Shiber arrived at the conclusion that new Kuwait City had failed to acquire a unique identity—which the pre-oil town had had—and that it was still in the process of creating a new urban form for itself. Evidently, a major shift had occurred in that, from a professional perspective at least, pre-oil Kuwait was being appreciated.

This shift came to characterize subsequent disputes over the urban development of Kuwait, like the one that unfolded in *The Architects' Journal* between Kuwaiti planner Karim Jamal, Ghazi Sultan—the co-owner of Sultan Gallery, architect, and at the time the Director of the Master Planning Department—and the British town planning company Colin Buchanan and Partners, who had developed the second master plan of Kuwait in the 1960s.[105] First Karim Jamal, and later Ghazi Sultan, criticized the initial destruction of Kuwait's pre-oil urban morphology and architecture in the 1950s and accused Colin Buchanan and Partners of continuing the destruction. Similar to Shiber, the Kuwaiti planners used 1951 aerial photographs to contrast and contemplate the violent change induced by the aerial master planning. This debate reveals that the visual representations of pre-oil Kuwait triggered an affectionate mourning for its loss, despite the fact that it was the 1951 aerial photography itself that had been the catalyzer of pre-oil Kuwait's destruction. Although the 1952 Master Plan brought forth a new modern metropolis and thus a new urban face of petro-rich Kuwait, it did not necessarily create a more functional, more socially stimulating environment nor a climatically better adapted habitat.

3.4 An Aerial View of the Petroleum Playground

For Kuwait, the circular relationship between spatial visualizations and urban transformations was again sharply experienced during the Iraqi invasion 1990–91.[106] In *Close Up at a Distance: Mapping, Technology & Politics*, Laura Kurgan has described how, by August 1990, the GIS-based satellite image mapping of Kuwait had just produced one of the most detailed visual data sets ever available when the Iraqi army invaded Kuwait to occupy the oil fields. Once that happened, the brand-new aerial images became outdated overnight and suddenly represented "preservation images" from which to rebuild the

[105] Karim Jamal, "Kuwait: A Salutary Tale," *The Architects' Journal* 158, no. 50 (December 1973); Colin D. Buchanan, & Partners, "Kuwait," *The Architects' Journal* 159, no. 21 (May 1974); Colin D. Buchanan, & Partners, "Lifestyle Contrasts and Need for Planning Reform," *The Architects' Journal* 160, no. 40 (October 1974); Ghazi Sultan, "Kuwait," *The Architects' Journal* 160, no. 40 (October 1974); Karim Jamal, "Destruction of the Middle East?," *The Architects' Journal* 164, no. 30 (July 1976). Karim Jamal used a 1951 oblique photograph of the port area and a 1970s one with a similar view in juxtaposition to substantiate his reproach of the "ruthless destruction of the closely packed pattern" of pre-oil Kuwait and of the incoherent "rebuilding" strategy proposed by the 1952 master plan, "as if the country was in ruin or in a desperate situation." See Jamal, "Kuwait," 1453.

[106] Laura Kurgan, *Close Up at a Distance: Mapping, Technology, and Politics* (New York: Zone Books, 2013), 84–95.

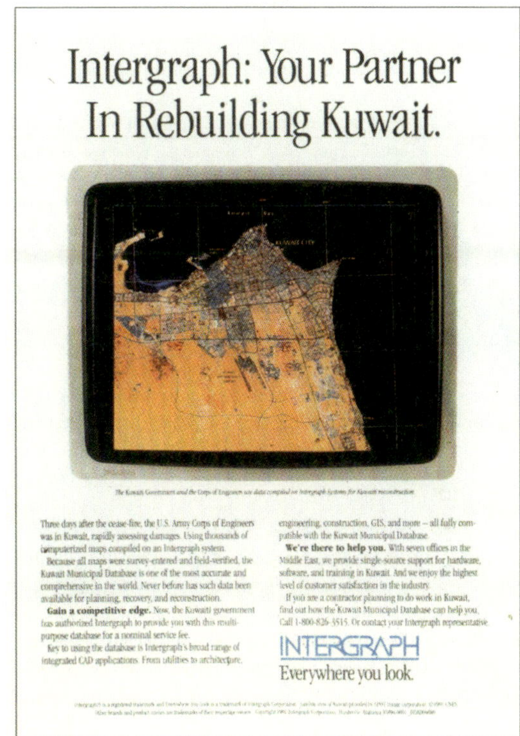

3.15 A GIS-based satellite image of Kuwait City. Advertisement for the software company Intergraph, 1991.

city once the Iraqi army and the US-led coalition forces had left.[107] Even before the war had ended, the software company Intergraph used the aerial view of Kuwait in the advertisement "Rebuilding Kuwait" (fig. 3.15). This advertisement is oddly reminiscent of Hunting Aerosurveys' adverts at the end of World War II, both in its aesthetic and in its demonstrative belief in the power of aerial omniscience. The proliferation of the view from above is a gesture of power that continues to be fueled in many ways by (the violent quest for) petroleum.

Today, reproductions of the 1951 photomosaic of Kuwait are often found on display in shops, offices, and various institutions in Kuwait, including the reading room of the Center for Research and Studies on Kuwait. The composite photo is not only considered as a historical document, but is also contemplated with affect. The enduring repercussions of the 1950s view from above can be substantiated not only here, but also in contemporary media forms. Images of Kuwait City from above, as seen for example on Google Maps and Google Earth, easily disclose the physical imprint of the 1952 Master Plan's road network (fig. 3.16). Even though MSM's plan required the demolition and hollowing out of the

[107] Ibid., 85.

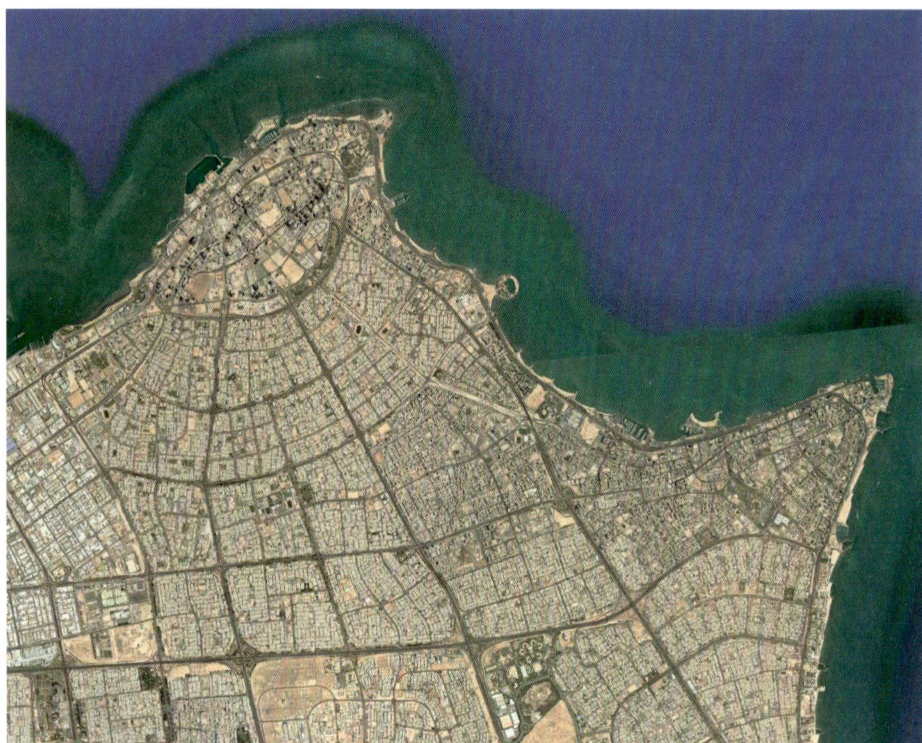

3.16 Composite satellite photograph of Kuwait City. Google Earth Pro 7.3.4.8248. Image taken on July 28, 2021.

pre-oil built-up area, such contemporary imagery is evidence of the fact that the almond shape of Kuwait's pre-oil historic core has remained engrained in the urban texture until the present day (despite several subsequent building booms and the Gulf War).

This assessment, however, is only possible through fossil-fueled technologically enhanced vision and the perpetuated visual representation of such gazing: the 1951 photomosaic, the 1952 Master plan, new cartography, map icons, drone footage, Google Earth, and so forth. Only when viewed from above is the almond-shaped form nested in the wave-like coastal formation recognizable. The fact that this view is acknowledged as iconic of Kuwait City, and by extension of the country, is caused by the continuous proliferation of the aerial view of Kuwait in a myriad of images that, despite all their differences, share a common denominator. Processed through aerial photography, urban planning, and cartography, the starkly simplified urban form of *pre-oil* Kuwait has become the symbol of the *modern* oil city, an iridescent symbol that has intrinsically interlinked the past and the present as well as the continuity and the change that has characterized Kuwait's urban transformation. In Kuwait it is not so much the physical urban form itself but rather its (historical) visual representation that allows for an assessment of the past.

Given the substantial loss of the built environment of pre-oil times, when viewed from above the almond-shaped form can offer traces of historical continuity, of memory, of belonging for 1960s audiences just as for today's.

The plethora of visual evidence has demonstrated the endless loop of visual mappings of Kuwait's space from above and subsequent attempts at assessing, altering, and picturing it anew. What the 1951 aerial imagery of Kuwait was able to depict and how it contributed to constructing meaning for Kuwait City changed rapidly throughout the 1950s. At first, the aerials were symbolic of a modern technology of perception and visualization. They allowed for the visual homogenization and subsequent future vision of transforming space in a kind of magic omniscience that led to the specific form of the 1952 Master Plan. Throughout the long 1950s, while the drawing of future Kuwait City was implemented on the ground, the circulating 1951 aerials (obliques and verticals) remained static images of a Kuwait frozen in May 1951. Only with an aerial update in 1960 were these aerials recognized as outdated and no longer representative of the status quo. They were subsequently used as historical records that encapsulated the pre-oil city, which by that time was already gone on the street level.

Images, especially photographic ones, have the ability to simultaneously realistically represent an object (to capture it in time and space) and to bury it (to freeze it in time and space). Petro-modernity has a similar double character. On the one hand, projections of almost unlimited progress and change at unprecedented speed have come to characterize petro-modernity. On the other, the toxic destruction contained in this progress is tangled up in a myriad of promotional strategies that enables petroleum's toxicity to remain hidden from view. Here, I see the ambiguous iridescence at play.

Is it only the familiarity with the aerial views of (pre-)oil Kuwait that allows us to see the old in the new, like a fleeting imprint of light on the retina? The gaze from above keeps seducing the viewer with its play of distance, of past and present, with its iridescent effect. While such a totalizing, disembodied view is humanly impossible and creates a remote visual dissociation from the urban landscape, it nevertheless also projects a sense of familiarity and of proximity through its aesthetic rendering across many visual representations, as each little detail becomes viewable and feels weirdly tangible. Like a miniature landscape, the town of Kuwait lies at one's feet and becomes available for being played with and altered as one pleases, without feeling affected by these changes oneself. It is a gaze that is confident in having the world subjugated to the pleasure of humans and to the comfort of splashing petroleum—a playground fueled by petro-desires. In contrast, reapproaching the historical photographs from time to time as traces of memory can become a method of nostalgic anachronism against the infectious spill of petro-modernity's proliferation of spatial images, which may one day have washed away the last trace of the pre-oil period, and maybe, once the final drop of petroleum has been extracted, even of the oil period.

4. THE KUWAIT OIL COMPANY, (COLOR) PHOTOGRAPHY, AND IRIDESCENT IMPRESSIONS

In the mid-twentieth century, Kuwaiti oil flowed in abundance, and the town of Kuwait experienced an unprecedented urban transformation that led to the creation of modern Kuwait City. Moreover, the transformation of urban space gained great visual momentum, and not just in the form of fossil-fuel fueled views from above. The Kuwait Oil Company (KOC) also favored urban images of Kuwait and presented the capital city as a symbol of the prosperity and progress that oil, and hence the oil company, was supposedly bringing to the country. To this end the KOC stimulated the text- and image-based metaphor of "making the desert bloom," which color photography was best able to communicate.

Initially, Kuwait City held no relevance for the oil company, for the firm's headquarters and operations were located in Ahmadi (the oil company town), the oil harbor (*Mīnā' al-Aḥmādī*), and the oil fields more than forty kilometers south of the capital. KOC's photographic scope, however, exceeded the choreography of oil fields, oil rigs, pipelines, storage tanks, refineries, oil harbors, oil workers, and Ahmadi. Other urban spaces and people of the country that the KOC was operating in were gradually incorporated into the KOC's visual cosmos, even if they were not directly related to the company's primary activities. In fact, a substantial share of the professional color photography commissioned by the oil company in the 1950s depicted Kuwait City exclusively.

One might imagine that the company was kept busy enough controlling the fast-flowing multimillion-dollar streams of petroleum but, in view of growing anti-imperialist and Arab-nationalist sentiments at the time, the curation of its public image became a pivotal concern. By visually claiming Kuwait's capital as part of its sphere of influence, the Anglo-American company attempted to stimulate acceptance of its own operations in the country by presenting the progress this coastal city-state was experiencing in positive terms, as this chapter will show.

To this end, the firm engaged professional photographers to shoot Kuwait City in expensive large-format color images. While these were not the first color images ever taken of Kuwait, the quality, format, size, and especially quantity of the new photographs was unprecedented: it was the first time that Kuwait City had appeared in such beaming colors in not one or a hand-full of shots, but in several albums of large-scale photographs. These images not only established Kuwait City as a beautified motif from which anything that could have challenged its positive progressive appearance was hidden from view.

https://doi.org/10.1515/9783110714739-006

They also relied heavily on the use of color. Color photography was crucial in conveying how the coastal village was apparently "awakening" to life once it started partaking in the consumerist lifestyle petro-modernity projected and the oil company encouraged. The photos, which wove a colorful picture of a modernizing Arab City, had one basic message: petroleum has switched on the lights. Fossil-fueled visualization technologies had made Kuwait viewable from above and, for passengers flying in at night, the expanding electrification had created breathtaking pictures of Kuwait City against the backdrop of the dark desert, a sight that many described with fascination. The KOC's framing of Kuwait City not only with light but with photographic colors represents another pivotal case in point of the visually seductive aesthetic effect of petro-modernity's iridescence.

The KOC created illustrated publications such as *The Story of Kuwait* and commissioned professional photographers to positively convey its operations in the country and the effect petroleum was having on Kuwait. Ever since the first issue, *The Story of Kuwait* metaphorized the promise of petroleum as "making the desert (meaning Kuwait) bloom." In subsequent issues, (black-and-white) photography was crucial in presenting Kuwait City's brand-new architecture as a concrete garden rising from the desert. When critique of the oil company climaxed around 1956–57, the company stepped up its game and commissioned a series of professional color photographs through which the idea of "making the desert bloom" could be depicted as "switching on the colorful lights." Now, Kuwait City emerged as an iridescent flower against the endless sand-colored background of the desert and the pre-oil town. The company no longer needed to say "This is what petroleum can do; we made this happen" because the color images spoke for themselves. As the corporate color photos of Kuwait subsequently proliferated in public displays and exhibitions outside the country, they were received as authentic representations of the city-state. Yet a closer inspection and a comparison with other photographic documentations, such as by Kuwaiti photographer Tareq Sayid Rajab, reveals that the corporate shots were highly selective in regard to which parts of Kuwait City's transformation were show and which parts were hidden from view.

4.1 Oil Company Photography

Oil companies operating across the world have gained tremendous influence by producing data and information on their concessional territories that go far beyond the actual scene of oil production. They have also made use of a wide range of often novel media not only for surveying and prospecting but also for product and corporate image promotion as well as to shape public opinion. For example, oil companies including the KOC have invested substantially in documentary film production in Iran, Iraq, and Kuwait in order to create a broad public acceptance of their operations as Mona Damluji has shown.[1]

[1] See Damluji, "Petroleum's Promise."

The case of the KOC indicates that photography, especially color photography, was another pivotal medium which, from the mid-1950s onward, the company started to use deliberately to improve its public relations. By the 1960s, many oil companies operating in the Gulf region and the Arabian Peninsula had already become substantial producers of photography and today, "they own the oldest collections in most of the oil producing countries visited. Their collections cover most aspects of local social life, and also include landscapes and city construction documentation."[2] They set up photographic archives, established in-house photographic units with staff photographers, or commissioned well-known professional photographers to take photographs on their behalf. They then utilized these pictures in their company publications and displays. They also offered their photographic collections to such other interested parties as governments, journalists, and writers, thereby infiltrating visual culture to an extent that has not yet been thoroughly examined.

The representational challenge that the oil companies encountered was that their product was crude oil. Sticky, smelly, usually dark black, and inflammable, the substance itself was not an easy or attractive product to display. Oil companies therefore preferred to show "everything *except* the product," as one industrial photographer pointedly summarized.[3] In a lecture on "Photography in Industry and Commerce" held in 1961, British photographer and later member of the photography faculty at the Royal College of Art, Michael J. Langford explained what oil companies, who were notorious for their extensive briefs, were looking for:

> With organizations such as the major oil companies a considerable volume of photography overseas is needed for large-scale internal public relations distribution. On these tours their staff photographers are expected to not only record the company's direct activities but also the way of life of the local peoples and the ways in which oil revenue is improving social conditions.[4]

Langford demonstrated that the industrial photographers grasped the complex issue of petroleum's (in)visibility. Besides showcasing the industrial operations, oil companies circumvented the representational ambiguity of oil by diverting the gaze toward "the way of life of the local peoples" and the ways in which oil revenues were "improving social conditions." To do so, the oil industry relied on a visually all-encompassing strategy that involved presenting its direct activities in the oil fields as clean and safe, and moreover it implied representing their activities indirectly by means of scenes far away from the

[2] Jean-Gabriel Leturcq, "Camera Arabia: An Introduction to the History of Photography in the Arab Peninsula," accessed December 4, 2017, https://leturcq.wordpress.com/2015/10/03/camera-arabia-1/#comments.

[3] Michael J. Langford, "Photography in Industry and Commerce," *Journal of the Royal Society of Arts* 109, no. 5061 (1961): 666 (italics in the original).

[4] Ibid., 675–76. In his obituary in *The Guardian*, Langford he was described as an "influential tutor whose best-selling books became standard texts for generations of photographers." Jenny May, "Obituary: Michael Langford," *The Guardian*, May 25, 2000, accessed January 30, 2021, https://www.theguardian.com/news/2000/may/25/guardianobituaries1.

oil fields. These motifs had to convey the impression of social improvement that could be linked to oil revenues, the oil company itself, and the growing reliance on petroleum-derived products without ever showing crude oil. Oil companies used photography both to divert the gaze away from petroleum extraction sites and to legitimize their presence by presenting the (positive) socioeconomic outcomes of petro-capitalism for the host country and society at large. In other words, the more Kuwait City made a good impression in such photographs, the better the image different audiences, such as Kuwait's ruler and inhabitants as well as people elsewhere, would have of the company; even if the two things, Kuwait City and the company, were not connected in the sense that the framing of the images insinuated.

The KOC was not the only oil company to rely on professional photographers for their public image. One of the most extraordinary cases—not just in the visual history of oil companies but in the history of corporate industrial photography—is the large photographic public relations campaign initiated by Standard Oil of New Jersey during World War II, around a decade earlier than the KOC's. The example of this photographic campaign underscores the fact that oil companies already considered almost anything to be suitable to represent them photographically, and that they tried to influence public opinion by instrumentalizing a visual medium on a mind-bending scale.

The Photographic Campaign of Standard Oil of New Jersey

In a 1942 poll, Standard Oil of New Jersey (SONJ), then a major US oil company, was cited as the most disliked firm after a secret 1929 cartel agreement with the German company I.G. Farben became public.[5] The enterprise decided to hire a public relations consultant with whom they developed "The Standard Oil (New Jersey) Photography Project," which was headed by Roy Stryker. Stryker, an economist and photographer, firmly believed in the power of the photographic medium to alter people's perception—even of SONJ.[6] The

[5] In fact, Standard Oil, SONJ's predecessor, had been the target of anti-monopolistic criticism since the late nineteenth century. This culminated in the court case *Standard Oil Co. of New Jersey vs. United States* (1911), in which the company was found guilty of monopolizing the petroleum industry through anti-competitive actions. The company was subsequently split into thirty-four competing firms, one of which became SONJ. Given the continuity in the name, SONJ did not possess a blank record in public opinion.

[6] Previously, in the 1930s, Roy Stryker had worked with a team of skilled photographers for the Resettlement Administration and later the Farm Security Administration on a project to document government efforts of fighting rural poverty. The public success of the project encouraged the management of SONJ to undertake a similar public relations campaign directed by Stryker. Cornell Capa, "Foreword, " in Steven W. Plattner, ed., *The Standard Oil (New Jersey) Photography Project* (Austin: University of Texas Press, 1983), published in conjunction with the exhibition *Roy Stryker: U.S.A, 1943–1950* presented at the International Center of Photography, New York, 7.

campaign specifically targeted white-collar, art-appreciating "thought leaders," a group of people that had been identified as most influential in opposing the oil company.[7]

Between 1943 and 1950, a group of permanently-employed SONJ photographers were sent out to take photographs. An objective, socially aware, and documentary style became the common denominator of practice, as Stryker was convinced that documentary photography with a visually conveyed narrative and a focus on the human element would appeal to the target audience.[8] Otherwise the photographers enjoyed great freedom in the selection of their motifs and the motifs' level of immediate connection with the oil industry. Project photographer Esther Bubley, for instance, explained, "Any way you could connect something to oil—that for Roy was a good enough excuse to photograph it. You could photograph anything having to do with oil."[9] Her colleague Russell Lee remembered the brief as anything to do with grease.[10] Basically, the goal was to shoot motifs and scenes that documented the "thriving producers and consumers of oil," meaning the modes of production and ways of living that oil enabled and petro-capitalism encouraged.[11] This very wide brief, the creative freedom, the high level of productivity over a seven-year term, the large geographic coverage, and the multitude of excellent photographic voices who took part were aspects that made SONJ's photo campaign so extraordinary.

The photographers generally captured the impact of petroleum at large, picturing bus stops (as an example of motorization thriving on fossil fuels), large transportations networks, oil tanker manufacturers, petrol stations, oilmen at work, in bars and restaurants, oil towns, agricultural landscapes using synthetic fertilizer, and common ways of living in the mid-twentieth century that were at first glance not obvious spheres of petro-influence and yet somewhat driven by fossil fuels and petroleum-derived products.

Apart from the few series shot abroad (for example in Saudi Arabia and Venezuela), most photos were taken in one of the many oil-producing and oil-refining US states, often in rural areas and small or medium-sized towns within the US. The survey therefore documented the oil industry's substantial share in the national economy and substantiated

[7] Public discontent was especially large because the agreement had hindered American industry from inventing synthetic rubber, thereby giving Nazi Germany a strategic lead in the war. A subsequent public opinion survey revealed that well-educated, intellectual "thought leaders" in particular were opposing Standard Oil. See ibid., 12–13.

[8] Ibid., 17. Hurley notes that "oil was always in the story, but under Stryker's direction, the emphasis was often on the people who drilled for it or transported it or sold it or used it." F. Jack Hurley, *Industry and the Photographic Image: 153 Great Prints from 1850 to the Present* (Rochester: George Eastman House, 1980), published in conjunction with an exhibition at George Eastman House, Rochester, in 1976, 101–2.

[9] Plattner, *The Standard Oil (New Jersey) Photography Project*, 20.

[10] Ibid.

[11] Ibid., 22. Among the staff photographers were Esther Bubley, John Collier Jr., Harold Corsini, Arnold Eagle, Russell Lee, Sol Libsohn, Gordon Parks, Edwin and Louise Rosskam, Charles E. Rotkin (as the aerial photographer), John Vachon, and Todd Webb.

the way in which oil consumption was even already nested in remote, rural areas, instead of tracing petroleum's rather obvious influence on urban life.

Showing the total infiltration of petroleum into modern life by photographically documenting everyday life as such was nothing less than visionary. Photographs that conveyed a vague connection to oil and carried the SONJ credit line held the most potential to catch the attention of viewers intent on finding the connection to petroleum that the pictures supposedly portrayed. As a result, the petro-intimacy insinuated in the images became normalized as a part of everyday life. But, as visual sociologist Douglas Harper points out, it was also "ironic" that, "because oil was in one way or another everywhere, the photographers were able to photograph virtually anything of a social nature."[12] In retrospect, the Standard Oil of New Jersey Photography Project was the first deliberate large-scale photographic investigation of petro-modernity at play. Its scope of almost sixty-seven thousand large-format black-and-white photographs and around one thousand color slides of (mostly) American life is photographic evidence of the way that "'oil seeped into every joint' of an increasingly technological nation."[13]

The sobering realization that oil was everywhere also underscored something else: the petro-*corporate* infiltration of everyday life in the mid-twentieth century. The Photographic Project reflected "the first major, long-range attempt by an industry to justify its role in society through visuals as well as written means."[14] As such, SONJ not only presented its operations across the US but proudly pictured US lifestyles as being entirely dependent on the oil industry. Although the campaign had been aimed at dispelling public reproaches of monopolization, its photographic evidence instead cemented the involvement of petro-corporations such as SONJ in daily life as inescapable.

Despite these photographic efforts, according to a public poll, SONJ's reputation had not changed sufficiently by 1948. Moreover, because the effect of the photographic campaign could not be measured, the project was cut back and eventually stopped in 1950. Another reason for the discontinuance was that although the SONJ photographs had been made freely available on the condition that the SONJ credit line was included, magazines and newspapers did not show the expected interest in using the photographs and thereby popularizing the oil company's photographic framing of the world.[15] Nevertheless, SONJ's

[12] Douglas A. Harper, *Changing Works: Visions of a Lost Agriculture* (Chicago: University of Chicago Press, 2001), 10.

[13] Plattner, *The Standard Oil (New Jersey) Photography Project*, 11. Numbers taken from Harper, *Changing Works*, 12.

[14] Hurley, *Industry and the Photographic Image*, 101–2.

[15] A small number of photographs from the project were printed in magazines like *Life*, *Look*, and *Fortune*. For example, see "A Portrait of Oil—Unretouched," *Fortune*, September 1948, accessed January 30, 2021, http://fortune.com/1948/09/01/standard-oil-photos-1948/. The main benefactors, however, were the company's in-house publication *The Lamp* and school textbooks. See Harper, *Changing Works*, 12; Hurley, *Industry and the Photographic Image*, 102. The impact of SONJ's photographs in official learning material on American society is yet to be comprehensively researched.

Photographic Project demonstrated that, as early as the 1940s, visually representing the oil industry meant shooting "almost everything *except* the product."[16]

The Kuwait Oil Company launched its photographic campaign six years after that of SONJ ended. Given a lack of archival evidence, it remains unclear whether and to what extent the KOC was informed or influenced by the American oil company's program. Considering the long duration and scope of the campaign and the interconnectedness of the global oil sector (the KOC was half-British, half-US owned at the time), officials at the KOC were most likely aware of the project. Besides, since 1948, Standard Oil of New Jersey (today ExxonMobil) owned 30 percent of the Arabian-American Oil Company (ARAMCO) in Saudi Arabia and hence held a foothold in one of Kuwait's neighboring countries. Members of SONJ's Public Relations Department also visited Kuwait and the KOC in spring 1958.[17] Irrespective of whether a direct connection existed, the KOC's photographic scope turned out to be equally all-encompassing and yet also much more specific, given its focus on a single country.

If "almost everything *except* the product" was used by oil companies to campaign for a (positive) public image, what creative choices did the Kuwait Oil Company make in the 1950s? The booklet *The Story of Kuwait* was the first thing the KOC published to introduce a larger readership to (its operations in) Kuwait; it was made available even before the first shipment of Kuwaiti oil had left the country.[18] Here, the KOC framed Kuwait's history and its own operations through text and, later, especially through photographic representations of Kuwait City that can be summarized and characterized by the metaphor of "making the desert bloom."

4.2 *The Story of Kuwait*: Making the Desert Bloom

Published between circa 1945 and 1963, *The Story of Kuwait* was the prime print publication that communicated the KOC's narrative of Kuwait's past and present in text and images, which initially addressed an English-speaking audience only. In *The Story of Kuwait*, textual material and visual images played a crucial role in presenting the oil company's operations and the country's transformation as interdependent success stories of petro-modernity.

16 Langford, "Photography in Industry and Commerce," 666 (italics in the original).

17 Kuwait Oil Company, Town Office monthly report, March 1958, Town Office, 1957–1958.

18 For a discussion on the iconography of oil in popular science books titled *The Story of Oil* and often published by oil companies, see Laura Hindelang, "Oil Media: Changing Portraits of Petroleum in Visual Culture Between the US, Kuwait, and Switzerland," *Centaurus* 63, no. 4 (2021), doi:10.1111/1600-0498.12418.

The Petroleum Promise

To shape the way in which oil (production) was perceived, the KOC thought it useful to provide information about Kuwait at least one year before the first oil shipment in 1946. But rather than including primarily information on the oil company, the booklet presented a short account of Kuwait's (pre-)oil history with hardly any reference to the KOC. Spread across twelve pages and without any illustrations, the content of the first small publication focused on the period from 1716, generally considered the founding date of modern Kuwait, until about 1945. As indicated on the booklet's title page, the text was based on an article by Laurence Lockhart (fig. 4.1).[19] At the time, Lockhart, a scholar of Iran, was working for the Anglo-Iranian Oil Company (AIOC), one of the KOC's 50-percent-shareholders. Lockhart was not only a knowledgeable scholar and oilman but also experienced in writing the company history of the AIOC.[20] Hence, he likely appeared as the perfect man for developing a (hi)story of Kuwait in accordance with the oil company's interests.

The resulting first issue of *The Story of Kuwait* appeared in most parts as a brief and somewhat factual historical overview on Kuwait for a lay audience. Without mentioning the oil company, the text affectively framed petroleum as a harbinger of change and prosperity. This represents a classic case of evoking the petroleum promise in anticipation of oil production, and was a narrative that later issues continued to use in order to justify the oil company's operations in the country.

In the opening paragraph of the first issue, Kuwait is carefully situated within the larger geographical and historical context of the Persian Gulf:

> The present Arab Shaikhdom of Kuwait has a history of only some two hundred years. But the part of the world in which it is situated has history in every stone, going back over thousands of years to the very birth of human civilisation. The 6,500 square miles of territory that make up the modern state of Kuwait may have formed part of the Garden of Eden, if that delectable spot ever had a precise location on earth. Certainly in the days of the Babylonian and Sumerian Empires, six or seven thousand years ago, this part of the Middle East was no desert, but a fertile plain well capable

[19] Kuwait Oil Company, *The Story of Kuwait* (London: Kuwait Oil Company, [ca. 1945]). Lockhart (1890–1975) published exactly one article on Kuwait: Laurence Lockhart, "Outline of the History of Kuwait," *Journal of the Royal Central Asian Society* 34, no. 3–4 (1947). It is unclear whether Lockhart is the author of *The Story of Kuwait* or whether he only delivered the historical information, as the journal article and the KOC publication differ strongly in tone and choice of words. While the journal article mentions the first oil shipment in June 1946, the company publication does not include this historic event. Therefore, the KOC booklet was presumably published prior to June 1946. Content-wise it foreshadows Lockhart's article, which was published later, in the July–October issue in 1947, although the KOC text is much shorter, includes fewer details, and was (re)written for a non-academic audience.

[20] "One of his most engaging duties at the company was apparently his assignment to write a history of the company for private circulation. This work became the basis for several later official histories of British Petroleum." Ernest Tucker, "Lockhart, Laurence," *Encyclopædia Iranica Online*, May 24, 2013, accessed January 30, 2021, http://www.iranicaonline.org/articles/lockhart-laurence.

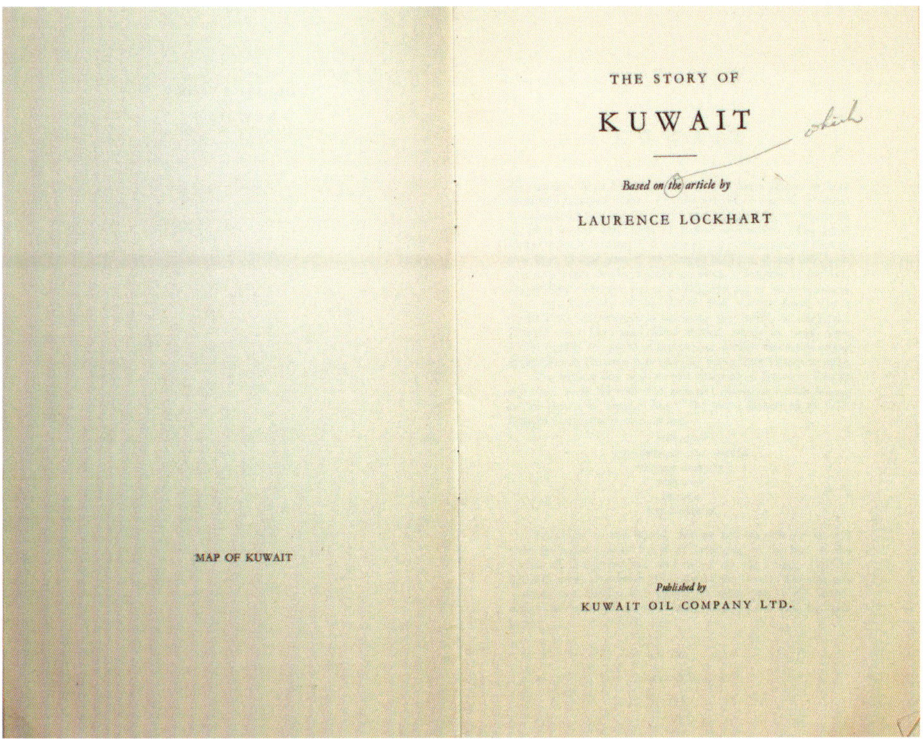

4.1 Title page of *The Story of Kuwait* (ca. 1945).

> of becoming the "cradle of mankind". Kuwait must have seen some stirring events in those days. Unfortunately no record of them exists, though excavation of the many sites in the area may one day bring their history to light.[21]

This paragraph casts Kuwait as part of the great pre-Islamic empires of the Fertile Crescent in the past simply due to its geographical location. The text triggers the reader's imagination to vividly picture this historical Kuwait as a prosperous, civilizational haven, a part of "the Garden of Eden," not a "desert, but a fertile plain." These tropes draw legitimacy from pre-modern history and ancient "golden days" in order to construct an emotionally stimulating national historiography. In this way the text resembles accounts of Iraq written at the time that similarly drew on its Mesopotamian heritage (often with a certain disregard for the present). In the case of Kuwait, the lack of archaeological evidence is conveniently overlooked. The opening paragraph of the first *Story of Kuwait* establishes a very particular tone of excitement by evoking past glories and implicitly luring the

[21] Kuwait Oil Company, *The Story of Kuwait*, 1.

reader to discover and mentally excavate Kuwait's past, all with the vague allusion to the reawakening that Kuwait could be capable of or might even be (historically) entitled to.

The text continues with a short account of Kuwait's history up until 1945 that is fairly in line with basic uncritical versions of the country's history existing today. Finally, the text ends with the promise of petroleum, which was recently discovered in the desert at Burgan. Even though the first export of oil had not yet taken place, it underscores "the new prosperity and promising future brought to the area by the oil fields."[22] The implicit message of the text is that Kuwait's alleged past glories and civilizational potency ("prosperity") will be renewed through the discovery of petroleum, the black gold of the present day. Oil therefore becomes the magically potent substance that can restore Kuwait's importance within the region and offer a life in abundance ("promising future"), an image not too far away from the idea of the Garden of Eden. *The Story of Kuwait's* authoritative voice of history distracts from its real intention of establishing high hopes and excitement toward the discovery of petroleum. Without even having to mention the KOC, this narrative served to legitimize the oil company's operations as a "petroleum promise" by planting the image of Kuwait becoming a blossoming desert in the reader's mind.

Timelessness, Emptiness, and (Flood)Lights

Apart from *The Story of Kuwait*, other articles and book publications of the 1940s and early 1950s that discussed Kuwait also established a strong dichotomy between pre-oil Kuwait and oil Kuwait in anticipation of the petroleum production. In many of these narratives, metaphors of light emerged as the symbol of transitioning from one phase to the other.

One of the first richly illustrated photojournalistic articles on Kuwait was published in *Picture Post* in July 1946, shortly before the first oil shipment commenced.[23] Titled "The Mysterious Land of Kuwait," the article characterized pre-oil Kuwait as standing still in time, both in terms of economic productivity and social progress. To the author, the coastal town represented a "timeless, mouldering East," where "everything seems sleepy."[24] In contrast, the prospect of oil production in Kuwait was heralded as a break away from pre-oil timelessness. "Now big oilfields are opening up… . The rush of modern times is about to overtake Kuwait."[25] Petroleum was portrayed as a game-changer that would connect Kuwait to an international, homogenous experience of time.

Notions of pre-oil timelessness and standstill were often paired with a narrative of emptiness; this could be framed as not having a long (urban) history or a noteworthy

[22] Ibid., 12.

[23] "The Mysterious Land of Kuwait."

[24] Ibid., 13–14.

[25] Ibid., 13.

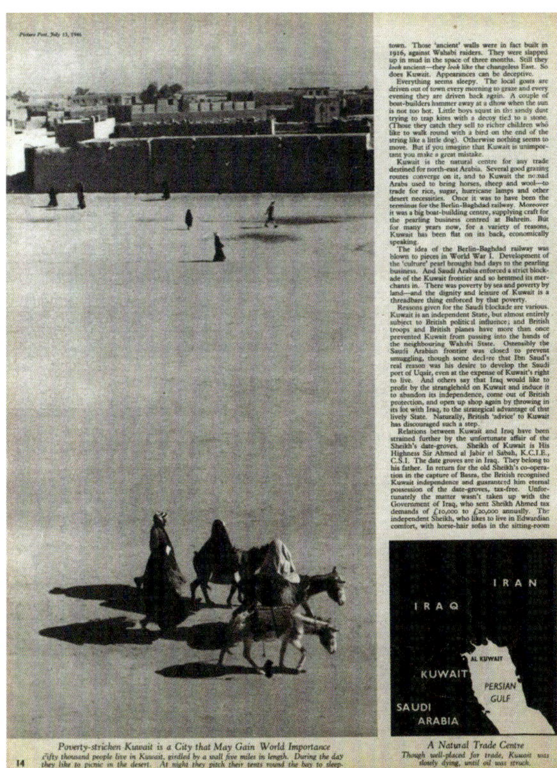
Picture Post, July 13, 1946

town. Those 'ancient' walls were in fact built in 1916, against Wahabi raiders. They were slapped up in mud in the space of three months. Still they *look* ancient—they *look* like the changeless East. So does Kuwait. Appearances can be deceptive.

Everything seems sleepy. The local goats are driven out of town every morning to graze and every evening they are driven back again. A couple of boat-builders hammer away at a dhow when the sun is not too hot. Little boys squat in the sandy dust trying to trap kites with a decoy tied to a stone. (Those they catch they sell to richer children who like to walk round with a bird on the end of the string like a little dog). Otherwise nothing seems to move. But if you imagine that Kuwait is unimportant you make a great mistake.

Kuwait is the natural centre for any trade destined for north-east Arabia. Several good grazing routes converge on it, and to Kuwait the nomad Arabs used to bring horses, sheep and wool—to trade for rice, sugar, hurricane lamps and other desert necessities. Once it was to have been the terminus for the Berlin-Baghdad railway. Moreover it was a big boat-building centre, supplying craft for the pearling business centred at Bahrein. But for many years now, for a variety of reasons, Kuwait has been flat on its back, economically speaking.

The idea of the Berlin-Baghdad railway was blown to pieces in World War I. Development of the 'culture' pearl brought bad days to the pearling business. And Saudi Arabia enforced a strict blockade of the Kuwait frontier and so hemmed its merchants in. There was poverty by sea and poverty by land—and the dignity and leisure of Kuwait is a threadbare thing enforced by that poverty.

Reasons given for the Saudi blockade are various. Kuwait is an independent State, but almost entirely subject to British political influence; and British troops and British planes have more than once prevented Kuwait from passing into the hands of the neighbouring Wahabi State. Ostensibly the Saudi Arabian frontier was closed to prevent smuggling, though some declare that Ibn Saud's real reason was his desire to develop the Saudi port of Uqair, even at the expense of Kuwait's right to live. And others say that Iraq would like to profit by the stranglehold on Kuwait and induce it to abandon its independence, come out of British protection, and open up shop again by throwing in its lot with Iraq, to the strategical advantage of that lively State. Naturally, British 'advice' to Kuwait has discouraged such a step.

Relations between Kuwait and Iraq have been strained further by the unfortunate affair of the Sheikh's date-groves. Sheikh of Kuwait is His Highness Sir Ahmed al Jabir el Sabah, K.C.I.E., C.S.I. The date groves are in Iraq. They belong to his father. In return for the old Sheikh's co-operation in the capture of Basra, the British recognised Kuwait independence and guaranteed him eternal possession of the date-groves, tax-free. Unfortunately the matter wasn't taken up with the Government of Iraq, who sent Sheikh Ahmed tax demands of £10,000 to £20,000 annually. The independent Sheikh, who likes to live in Edwardian comfort, with horse-hair sofas in the sitting-room

Poverty-stricken Kuwait is a City that May Gain World Importance
Fifty thousand people live in Kuwait, girdled by a wall five miles in length. During the day they like to picnic in the desert. At night they pitch their tents round the bay to sleep.

14

A Natural Trade Centre
Though well-placed for trade, Kuwait was slowly dying, until oil was struck.

4.2 Black-and-white photograph of Kuwait Town as published in *Picture Post*, July 1946. Photograph by N. Tim Gidal.

(architectural) appearance, or, generally, being in an unimportant location. A metaphor that was frequently applied in connection with such ascriptions was that Kuwait was "built on sand." A prominent black-and-white photograph in the *Picture Post* article encapsulated this notion of empty space (fig. 4.2). The photograph is taken from an elevated position, maybe looking from the town wall onto the coastal settlement. Open, void space, in which there are only some people walking or riding a donkey, takes up two thirds of the image. In the background, mud-brick housing emerges as a dense fortress-like entity. The picture creates a strong sense of an almost-deserted town.

Beyond such visual representations, descriptions such as "mysterious" and "obscure" also expressed and perpetuated the exoticization and othering of Kuwait. These attributions conveyed notions of Kuwait as a remote location (in relation to Europe or the US), of being unknown in the international arena, and of being hidden in darkness. In sharp contrast, as another article concluded, the impact of the oil production on this "obscure" location was like "floodlights [that] turn the desert night into day."[26] Petroleum was portrayed as vital for Kuwait to gain a new visibility. As light also stands for the sun

[26] Case, "Boom Time in Kuwait," 784.

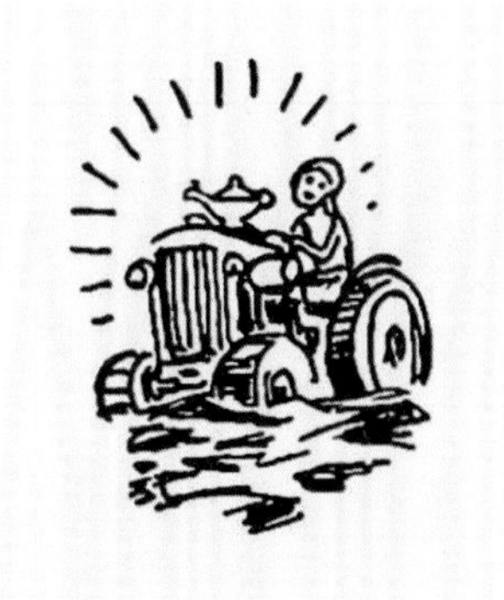

4.3 Illustration by Hakon Mielche in the margins of his *Lands of Aladdin* (1955).

and thus for the power to make things grow and change, the light metaphors not only resonate with visibility and vision but with growth, life, movement, mobility, and progress.[27] Switching on the (electric) lights, in this context, meant for this town to wake up from its timeless standstill.

Such orientalist imaginations of the Gulf region and the Middle East as "standing still in time" and awaiting awakening have a long history.[28] Against this background, petroleum's potential for radical (and positive) change became even more exaggerated and reached fantastical dimensions. For example, the oil experience was frequently metaphorized through the story of Aladdin. An excellent example of this is Danish writer Hakon Mielche's *Lands of Aladdin*, a well-researched, yet humorous travel account of the oil-producing countries of the Persian Gulf published in 1955. To give just a brief idea, in the margins the book contains an illustration that depicts Aladdin, oil lamp in hand, driving a modern tractor across the field (fig. 4.3).[29] The oil lamp, which depends on, say, kerosene to produce light, symbolizes petroleum, which in turn (as fertilizer and fuel) enables modern agriculture and the growing of crops to flourish. In this image Mielche cleverly captured the fantasies, extravagances, dreams, and hopes conjured up for Western audiences by the clichéd idea of rubbing Aladdin's lamp.

The Kuwait Oil Company drew on such already prevailing metaphors and images of how to frame soon-to-be oil-producing countries in emotionally stimulating narratives, even if *The Story of Kuwait* appeared as an almost factual account in contrast. For the second issue of the KOC publication, the Kuwait's oil-fueled transformation was demonstrated by showcasing Ahmadi and Kuwait City, and the best medium with which to do so was photography.

[27] The metaphor of light as a symbol of both vision and visibility as well as of the power to change landscapes had already played a key role in the advertisements of Hunting Aerosurveys. These advertisements showed floodlights whose beams of light panned over the landscape and transformed unbuilt areas into future settlements.

[28] Tropes such as the timelessness and emptiness of the Middle East were already present in previous centuries. They can be found in biblical pilgrimage travel writing on the Holy Land as well as, later, in Western travel accounts about the untouched nomadic desert life of the Arabian Peninsula. See Billie Melman, "The Middle East/Arabia: 'The Cradle of Islam,'" in *The Cambridge Companion to Travel Writing*, ed. Peter Hulme and Tim Youngs (Cambridge, UK: Cambridge University Press, 2002), 110.

[29] Hakon Mielche, *Lands of Aladdin* (London: William Hodge, 1955), Marginal drawings and colored photographs by the author. Mielche was an acclaimed travel writer and the book was simultaneously published in Danish (original), English, and German. It was subsequently reprinted in even more languages, testifying to its huge success in Europe.

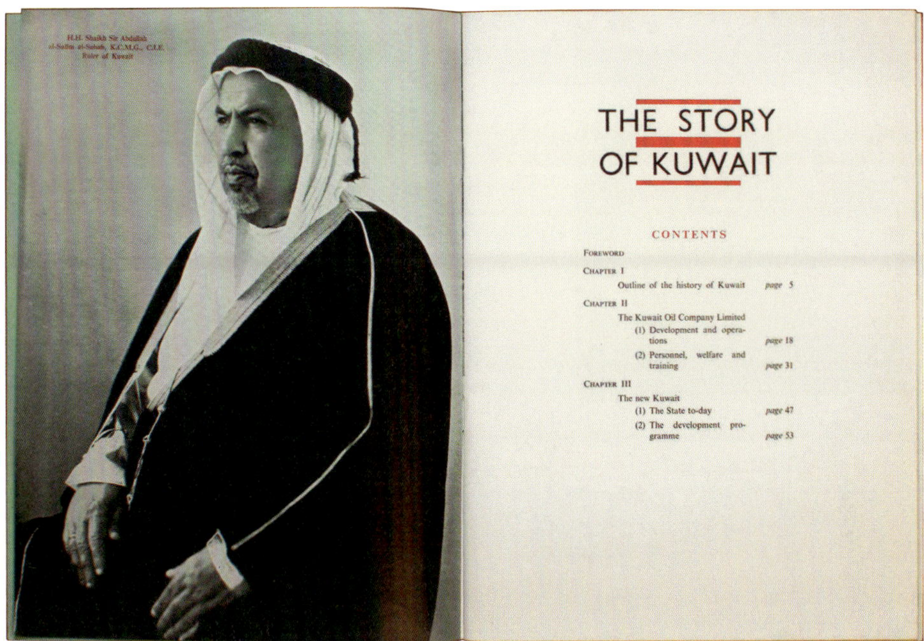

THE STORY OF KUWAIT

CONTENTS

4.4 Frontispiece with a portrait of Shaykh Abdullah and the table of contents of *The Story of Kuwait* (1955).

Ahmadi and Kuwait City as Showplaces of the Petroleum Promise

In 1955, the second issue of the KOC publication *The Story of Kuwait* appeared in a new, richly illustrated format, and with a new three-part structure (fig. 4.4).[30] Part One contained an "Outline of the History of Kuwait," which was in fact an updated version of the text of the first issue. Part Two was dedicated to a report on the ongoing activities of "The Kuwait Oil Company Ltd" in Ahmadi and its surroundings. Part Three focused on "The New Kuwait," meaning Kuwait City.

In Part One, the brief summary of the history of Kuwait was extended up to 1954. It now included historic moments like the first oil shipment in 1946, and also national political events such as the succession of Shaykh Abdullah in 1950. The section contained portrait photographs of the Al Sabah dynasty as well as black-and-white photographs and drawings of seafaring and shipbuilding and of the pre-oil town. The text used superlatives in abundance to construct a certain Kuwaiti uniqueness linking the "finest pearls" and "the finest harbor" in the pre-oil period to present-day Kuwait as "one of the principal cities in the Arab world."[31] Responsible for the latter was, according to the text, the

[30] Kuwait Oil Company, *The Story of Kuwait* (London: Kuwait Oil Company, 1955).

[31] Ibid., 14–17.

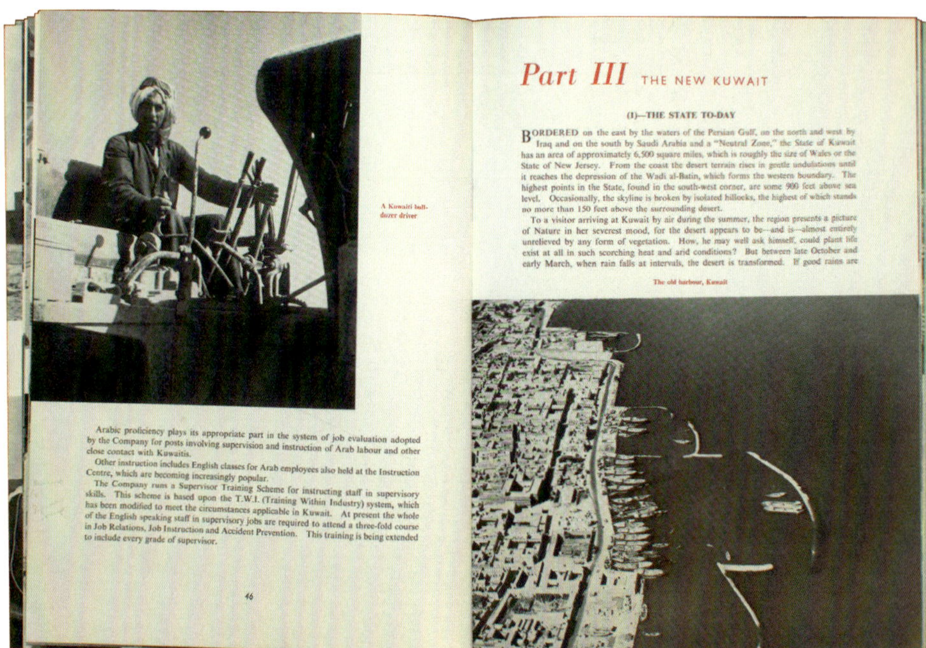

A Kuwaiti bull-dozer driver

Arabic proficiency plays its appropriate part in the system of job evaluation adopted by the Company for posts involving supervision and instruction of Arab labour and other close contact with Kuwaitis.

Other instruction includes English classes for Arab employees also held at the Instruction Centre, which are becoming increasingly popular.

The Company runs a Supervisor Training Scheme for instructing staff in supervisory skills. This scheme is based upon the T.W.I. (Training Within Industry) system, which has been modified to meet the circumstances applicable in Kuwait. At present the whole of the English speaking staff in supervisory jobs are required to attend a three-fold course in Job Relations, Job Instruction and Accident Prevention. This training is being extended to include every grade of supervisor.

46

Part III THE NEW KUWAIT

(I)—THE STATE TO-DAY

BORDERED on the east by the waters of the Persian Gulf, on the north and west by Iraq and on the south by Saudi Arabia and a "Neutral Zone," the State of Kuwait has an area of approximately 6,500 square miles, which is roughly the size of Wales or the State of New Jersey. From the coast the desert terrain rises in gentle undulations until it reaches the depression of the Wadi al-Batin, which forms the western boundary. The highest points in the State, found in the south-west corner, are some 900 feet above sea level. Occasionally, the skyline is broken by isolated hillocks, the highest of which stands no more than 150 feet above the surrounding desert.

To a visitor arriving at Kuwait by air during the summer, the region presents a picture of Nature in her severest mood, for the desert appears to be—and is—almost entirely unrelieved by any form of vegetation. How, he may well ask himself, could plant life exist at all in such scorching heat and arid conditions? But between late October and early March, when rain falls at intervals, the desert is transformed. If good rains are

The old harbour, Kuwait

4.5 Oblique of Kuwait's waterfront from the 1951 aerial survey in *The Story of Kuwait* (1955).

"enlightened policy" of the present ruler, Shaykh Abdullah, and the development program he had launched with the oil revenues, making him "a world-famed figure."[32] Together with the portrait of Abdullah as frontispiece, the booklet affirmed a close alliance between the company and the state of Kuwait through the Al Sabah rulership, a partnership that was indeed crucial for the ongoing state formation. The resulting urban transformation was framed as unique, but also as a natural continuation of Kuwait's rich history (as part of the Garden of Eden, allegedly).

Part Two of the booklet was on the KOC itself, and focused predominantly on life in Ahmadi. It presented a short history of the oil company and a report on the latest achievements, be it new oil infrastructure, the latest statistics of crude oil production, or social facilities for its employees. The accompanying photographs depicted oil derricks, pipeline construction sites, and the oil harbor—basically the whole range of typical oil infrastructure together with photos of employee accommodation and medical and educational facilities. Besides photographs taken at street level, many aerial obliques, presumably taken by the oil company itself, prominently conveyed the spatial expansion of the industry.

[32] Ibid., 17.

Part Three, on "The New Kuwait," was subdivided into two sections. The first section, entitled "The State To-Day," opened with an oblique of the Kuwaiti waterfront from the 1951 aerial survey, given that the aerial view (as shown in the previous chapter) had become the modern representative image formula of Kuwait City despite the increasing outdatedness of the actual photograph (fig. 4.5). The text addressed a reader who was imagined to be arriving in the country by airplane:

> To a visitor arriving at Kuwait by air during the summer, the region presents a picture of Nature [*sic*] in her severest mood, for the desert appears to be—and is—almost entirely unrelieved by any form of vegetation. How, he may well ask himself, could plant life exist at all in such scorching heat and arid conditions? But between late October and early March, when rain falls at intervals, the desert is transformed. If good rains are experienced, grazing of Beduin [*sic*] flocks and herds is plentiful, flowers and plants in great variety make their appearance.[33]

Apparently, the text insinuated, seeing Kuwait from above would present the viewer with the impression of a dust-dry and uninhabitable place, basically anything but welcoming. (To the urban planner, the "void" would have meant space for building, while the visitor was presented as experiencing a horror vacui.) Yet, the 1951 oblique showed a densely built coastal village and its extensive harbor front that did not resonate with the textual account of a deserted place at all. The rest of the section read much like a tourist guidebook. Kuwait's annual, partly more moderate climate, its general geographical features, and its social structure were introduced to the reader in quite favorable terms and these information were complemented by illustrations of people in traditional attire, street views of shops and vendors, an older mosque, and the Public Security headquarters at Safat Square that spoke more or less to the Western imaginary of a pre-oil Arab town.

The second section, entitled "The Development Programme," however, focused on entirely different aspects. Here, the text highlighted progress in the fields of education, medicine, industry, and urban planning in Kuwait City and suddenly the photographic language had changed. The section began by stating:

> Kuwait to-day is a prosperous and thriving territory under the wise and progressive government of its Ruler … The Ruler's policy is to use the large revenues accruing from the production of oil for the social and economic development of the territory on up-to-date lines, while at the same time preserving the traditional Arab and Moslem character of the community.[34]

The 1955 text therefore suggested that "the new prosperity and promising future brought to the area by the oil fields" foretold in the previous issue of *The Story of Kuwait* was already happening. While the oil company relied on the figure of Shaykh Abdullah to shower Kuwaiti society with oil revenues, it was clear that the KOC presented itself as responsible for producing the oil monies in the first place.

[33] Ibid., 47–48.

[34] Ibid., 53.

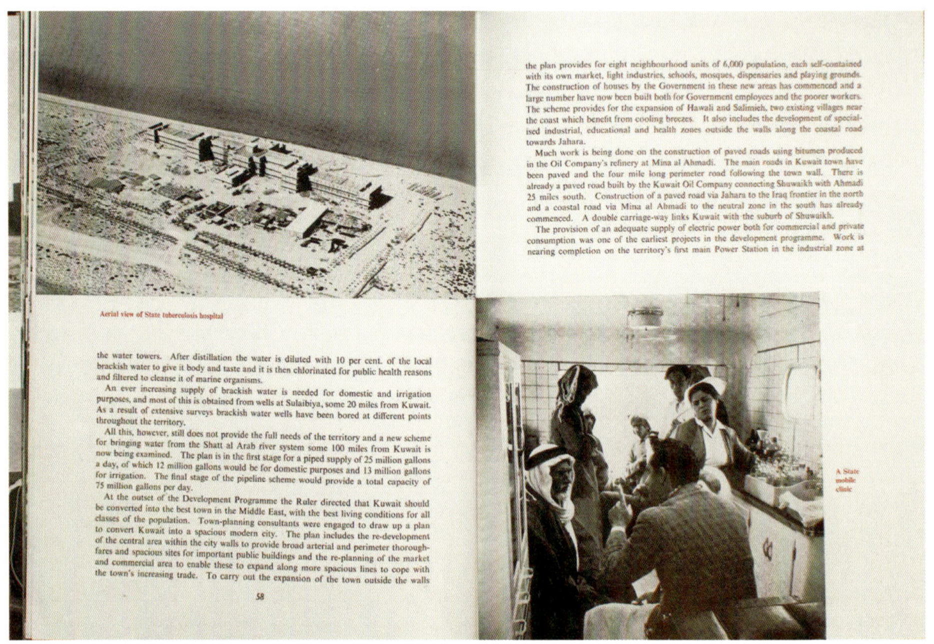

Aerial view of State tuberculosis hospital

the water towers. After distillation the water is diluted with 10 per cent. of the local brackish water to give it body and taste and it is then chlorinated for public health reasons and filtered to cleanse it of marine organisms.

An ever increasing supply of brackish water is needed for domestic and irrigation purposes, and most of this is obtained from wells at Sulaibiya, some 20 miles from Kuwait. As a result of extensive surveys brackish water wells have been bored at different points throughout the territory.

All this, however, still does not provide the full needs of the territory and a new scheme for bringing water from the Shatt al Arab river system some 100 miles from Kuwait is now being examined. The plan is in the first stage for a piped supply of 25 million gallons a day, of which 12 million gallons would be for domestic purposes and 13 million gallons for irrigation. The final stage of the pipeline scheme would provide a total capacity of 75 million gallons per day.

At the outset of the Development Programme the Ruler directed that Kuwait should be converted into the best town in the Middle East, with the best living conditions for all classes of the population. Town-planning consultants were engaged to draw up a plan to convert Kuwait into a spacious modern city. The plan includes the re-development of the central area within the city walls to provide broad arterial and perimeter thoroughfares and spacious sites for important public buildings and the re-planning of the market and commercial area to enable these to expand along more spacious lines to cope with the town's increasing trade. To carry out the expansion of the town outside the walls

58

the plan provides for eight neighbourhood units of 6,000 population, each self-contained with its own market, light industries, schools, mosques, dispensaries and playing grounds. The construction of houses by the Government in these new areas has commenced and a large number have now been built both for Government employees and the poorer workers. The scheme provides for the expansion of Hawali and Salimieh, two existing villages near the coast which benefit from cooling breezes. It also includes the development of specialised industrial, educational and health zones outside the walls along the coastal road towards Jahara.

Much work is being done on the construction of paved roads using bitumen produced in the Oil Company's refinery at Mina al Ahmadi. The main roads in Kuwait town have been paved and the four mile long perimeter road following the town wall. There is already a paved road built by the Kuwait Oil Company connecting Shuwaikh with Ahmadi 25 miles south. Construction of a paved road via Jahara to the Iraq frontier in the north and a coastal road via Mina al Ahmadi to the neutral zone in the south has already commenced. A double carriage-way links Kuwait with the suburb of Shuwaikh.

The provision of an adequate supply of electric power both for commercial and private consumption was one of the earliest projects in the development programme. Work is nearing completion on the territory's first main Power Station in the industrial zone at

A State mobile clinic

4.6 Aerial view of the state tuberculosis clinic and a state mobile clinic in *The Story of Kuwait* (1955).

In addition to a biology classroom and the inside of a mobile clinic, the selection of photographic illustrations included with the text showed large, recently erected buildings like schools, the desalination plant, hospitals as well as infrastructure like road networks that were still under construction (fig. 4.6). The preferred form of visual representation were up-to-date obliques that the KOC had photographed itself, for which the popularity of this visualization is underlined. Taken at different heights, the aerials clearly conveyed that the buildings were built somewhere in the desert, surrounded by the barren nothingness that the introductory paragraph had described for which they appeared almost monumental. These were also the photographs that would confront and thwart obliques from the by now outdated 1951 aerial survey that were still used to picture the town as "problematic" urban fabric.

In this section of Part Three, the message was that, with oil revenues, one could build even in the desert. Infused with the dominant logic of modernization theory, subsequent passages read like a modern fairy-tale miracle: "The sudden rise to fortune of Kuwait is bringing about a complete transformation of this territory."[35] While not stated explicitly in the text, the photographic illustrations clearly suggested that the oil company's

[35] Ibid., 53.

achievement in Kuwait was best measured by Ahmadi's development and Kuwait City's urban transformation.

In the third and final part of the second issue of *The Story of Kuwait*, the urban development of Kuwait City is presented as dependent on petroleum in multifold ways. The text emphasized that natural waste gas from the oil fields was used to power the massive desalination and electricity plant at low cost and that bitumen produced at the refinery in Mina al-Ahmadi was used to pave roads throughout the city. Mobility was becoming motorized, and any required products could simply be imported by plane or diesel-powered ship. However, part and parcel of modernization, the publication suggested, was not just the production but also the consumption of petroleum. The road to modernity implied total immersion in petroleum, either directly or indirectly, and with it immersion in the urban visual culture of petro-modernity.

With the 1955 issue, the KOC publication merged corporate and national narratives, portraying the history of a country through the (visual) lens of the company. The photographic showcasing of the "development" in both Ahmadi and Kuwait City served to legitimize the company's operations and the need for both oil revenues and petroleum. Up-to-date photographs of new architecture, infrastructure, and mobility delivered evidence of the change taking place under the influx of oil revenues and oil-derived products. By devoting a whole chapter to Kuwait City in the corporate publication, the KOC not only claimed authority over the oilfields and over the company town Ahmadi, but also claimed credit for the ongoing urban transformation of the city-state itself. One could say that the KOC aimed at an all-encompassing scope of motifs similar to SONJ's, yet it focused exclusively on the country of Kuwait. Just as Michael J. Langford had outlined, the KOC's (photographic) self-portrait *The Story of Kuwait* not only presented "the way of life of the local peoples" (both employees of the KOC and residents of the capital), but also showed how oil revenues were "improving social conditions" in the country. However, not everybody believed the Kuwait Oil Company to be of benefit to Kuwaiti society, as the company came to experience in the following years.

4.3 Persuasion and Ambiguity in Color

The Oil Company's Image Crisis

The 1950s in the Arab world were characterized by, among other things, rising anti-imperialism and Arab nationalism. The generally heated political atmosphere climaxed with the Suez Crisis in 1956–57. These tensions were strongly felt in Kuwait when, in late 1956, several oil wells were sabotaged and Kuwaiti social clubs pressured shop owners to stop serving British and French customers.[36] In this context, *al-Ittiḥād*, a newspaper

[36] Town Office, Incidents in Kuwait, November 21, 1956; Report on the cases of sabotage and resulting fire at well no. AH-5 on the night of the December 10, 1956, and following days, December 15, 1956, Kuwait

published by the Federation of Kuwaiti Students in Egypt, and *Ṣabāḥ al-Khayr*, an Egyptian weekly magazine founded in the 1950s and read in Kuwait, identified the Kuwait Oil Company as a harbinger of imperialism in Kuwait.

To advertise the positive impact of the KOC in Kuwait more effectively, the company decided to establish a Town Office in Kuwait City that would coordinate and expand public relation efforts toward a greater Kuwaiti and Arab public.[37] The office was situated in the Thunayan Al Ghanim Building, which was located at the Jahra Gate roundabout and was one of the most prominent and modern buildings at the time.[38] In addition to receiving responsibility for most of the KOC's corporate public relations, the department coordinated the official communication with the ruler and the government of Kuwait, and managed all issues regarding Kuwait City. The office also served as the initial point of contact with the company for visitors by providing information and photographs.

One of the new strategies of the Town Office was to place KOC-related articles in Arabic-language Middle Eastern newspapers and magazines "to indicate to the general public the good points of the Company."[39] The KOC also opened a Display Center in Ahmadi which informed visitors on the oil industry from prospecting to oil-derived products with the help of displays, dioramas, and other text-and-image material and thus served another important outlet to tailor information on petroleum (see fig. 4.19). In February 1957, on the anniversary of the accession of Shaykh Abdullah, the KOC finally released the first issue of its Arabic-language monthly *Risālat al-Nafṭ* (*Message of Oil*), which was intended to instruct, entertain, and inform the Arab employees as well as the Kuwaiti public about the company's activities.[40] The publication was received with mixed feelings: in a letter to the magazine, one reader sharply critiqued the monthly's second issue from April 1957 for its content, which he considered unsuitable, yet proudly praised

Situation in Relation to the Middle East Crisis, file 3 and 6, 1956, 106962, BP Archive, University of Warwick.

37 On the KOC's struggle in Ahmadi to challenge anti-imperialist and nationalist opposition and critique, see also Reem Alissa, "Building for Oil: Corporate Colonialism, Nationalism and Urban Modernity in Ahmadi, 1946–1992" (PhD diss., School of Architecture, University of California, 2012), chapter 3.

38 Elegantly built over a boomerang-shaped layout, the Thunayan Al Ghanim Building, or the "Rolls Royce Building," was the first multi-story building in Kuwait and allegedly the first building with an elevator that was commonly referred to as "the jumping horse." The building not only housed the KOC Town Office but, over the decades, also the famous Kuwait Bookshop, the first office of Kuwait Airways, the Sultan Gallery, and a Lebanese car wash. Information received on the walking tour "City on Display," organized by Madeenah and led by Deema Alghunaim around Fahad al-Salem Street, February 2, 2018; see also Fabbri, Saragoça and Camacho, *Modern Architecture Kuwait*, 50–51.

39 L. Y. Jordan to C. A. P. Southwell, April 16, 1957, Press and Publications 1957: Broadcasting, 106863, BP Archive, University of Warwick.

40 Arabic Magazine Meeting, April 29, 1957, ibid. Although intended as a monthly periodical, the second issue appeared two months later in April 1957.

"its printing and beautiful production, which out-classed all Arabic magazines issued by other oil companies."[41]

Indeed, the KOC was concerned that its publications "compare favourably in standard of publication and contents with those of neighbouring oil companies," such as the highly regarded Arabic and English magazines produced by ARAMCO.[42] To do so, the company realized that it needed new and up-to-date photos that would put its corporate narrative into (the right) perspective and eventually commissioned the British industrial photographer Adolf Morath to come to Kuwait in April 1956.[43] Given the turbulent times, it was no coincidence that a professional photographer who was highly experienced in helping industrial companies improve their reputation was contracted.

The Industrial Photographer Adolf Morath

Differently than the permanently-employed staff photographer, Adolf Morath (1905–1977) embodied a new type of famous, artistic, and independent photographer hired for temporary industrial assignments that emerged in the 1950s.[44] In his function as photographer for mostly British heavy industries, Adolf Morath traveled to Kuwait and other places in which British companies (that had often grown as part of an imperial network) operated with a brief and a time limit and then returned to his London studios to develop, enlarge, and color-enhance the photographs as needed.

Prior to his work in Kuwait, Morath had undertaken substantial pictorial surveys for the British Iron and Steel Federation and the British South Africa Company, which operated copper mines in Northern and Southern Rhodesia (today Zimbabwe and Zambia). He also portrayed several refineries of the AIOC (one of the KOC's shareholders) in England. On behalf of the KOC, Morath came to Kuwait to shoot in Ahmadi, in the oil fields and the refineries, and also in Kuwait City.[45]

[41] Anonymous letter to the editor of *Risālat al-Nafṭ* regarding issue no. 2 (ca. April 1957 or later), English translation by KOC employees, ibid.

[42] Arabic Magazine Meeting, April 29, 1957, ibid. Even before the publication of *Risālat al-Nafṭ*, the Iraq Petroleum Company had started issuing its Arabic-language magazine *Ahl al-Nafṭ* (*People of Oil*) and ARAMCO its *Qāfilat al-Zayt* (*Oil Caravan*), the Arabic version of the English-language magazine *ARAMCO World*.

[43] Although the KOC was owned in equal parts by American Gulf Oil and British Petroleum, initially it was BP that took the lead in steering company business, including PR. Rodney Giesler, a British filmmaker who became the director of the Kuwait Oil Company Film Unit in 1958, remembers: "The British side from BP were experienced in PR, and took command of things. There was a power struggle later on when the American interest increased, and they became responsible overall for PR." Giesler, "Memories of Kuwait 1958–1961," file 1/1.

[44] This was the case in Britain as well as in the US; see Hurley, *Industry and the Photographic Image*, 101.

[45] Practically no documentation on Morath's three Kuwait trips (besides the actual photographs of the trips, held in the oil archives at Warwick and Ahmadi) exists. The exception are three letters, in which Morath mentioned the upcoming assignment with the Kuwait Oil Company and his stay in Kuwait in April 1956

From his first visit in 1956, Morath created five color and three black-and-white photographic albums for the KOC, in which some prints existed in both color schemes. The successful execution of the first commission brought him two subsequent assignments in March 1958 and April 1960, which were then carried out entirely in color. At the time, high-quality color photography—just like multi-color printing—was not common in Kuwait. Most postcards that used photographs, for example, were hand-colored. Industrial photographer Michael J. Langford noted in the early sixties that color photography was "still very expensive" and that "its main application these days, in terms of printing, is in internal reports, in illustrations where colour must be used for technical purposes."[46] The three extensive surveys of Kuwait undertaken by Morath mostly in color therefore reflected a great financial commitment on the side of the KOC. Yet, the majority of the large-format color photographs pictured motifs for which color was not a technical necessity. Instead, color was part of an aesthetic rhetoric used to highlight the petro-fueled change of the urban environment in favor of the oil company.

A Concrete Garden Growing from the Desert

The KOC immediately used Morath's black-and-white photographs to illustrate the third issue of *The Story of Kuwait*, which was published in 1957.[47] Appearing in Part Two on the KOC and its activities in Ahmadi, Morath's photographs highlighted the relationship of the oilmen and their families with the oil company in order to give a more human touch to the industry, showing for instance workers (with family members) in front of newly built company housing, in training sessions, in class, and at the workplace (fig. 4.7).[48] Here, Morath's longstanding expertise as a portrait photographer before servicing the industry came in handy. Beneath the human element that the pictures were probably to convey, the social and racial hierarchies at play at the KOC were made apparent: Kuwaiti and Arab workers were primarily shown in situations of being provided for, of being taught and

to his former assistant Marietta Schrömbgens. Morath to Schrömbgens, January 23, February 7, and April 2, 1956, Private Collection Marietta Schrömbgens. Unfortunately, there is also no material available on who was in charge of the KOC's photography prior to Morath. A year after Morath's first visit, De Candole argued: "We need a professional photographer. It is very expensive using the services of a man like Morath, and the photographs he took for us last year are already mainly out of date." Yet despite the KOC's continuous reliance on photography for its public relations, for reasons unknown no permanent photographic unit was established and in 1958 and 1960 Adolf Morath was hired again. De Candole to General Manager, April 27, 1957, memorandum, Press and Publications 1957: Broadcasting.

[46] Langford, "Photography in Industry and Commerce," 678.

[47] Kuwait Oil Company, *The Story of Kuwait* (London: Kuwait Oil Company, 1957).

[48] Morath became famous for a style of industrial (color) photography that conveyed the "human touch" of the industries depicted. For an example of how this angle of his work was received, see for instance "The Snapshot Schoolboy Is Now a Top Photographer," *The Bulletin*, February 4, 1959, reprint.

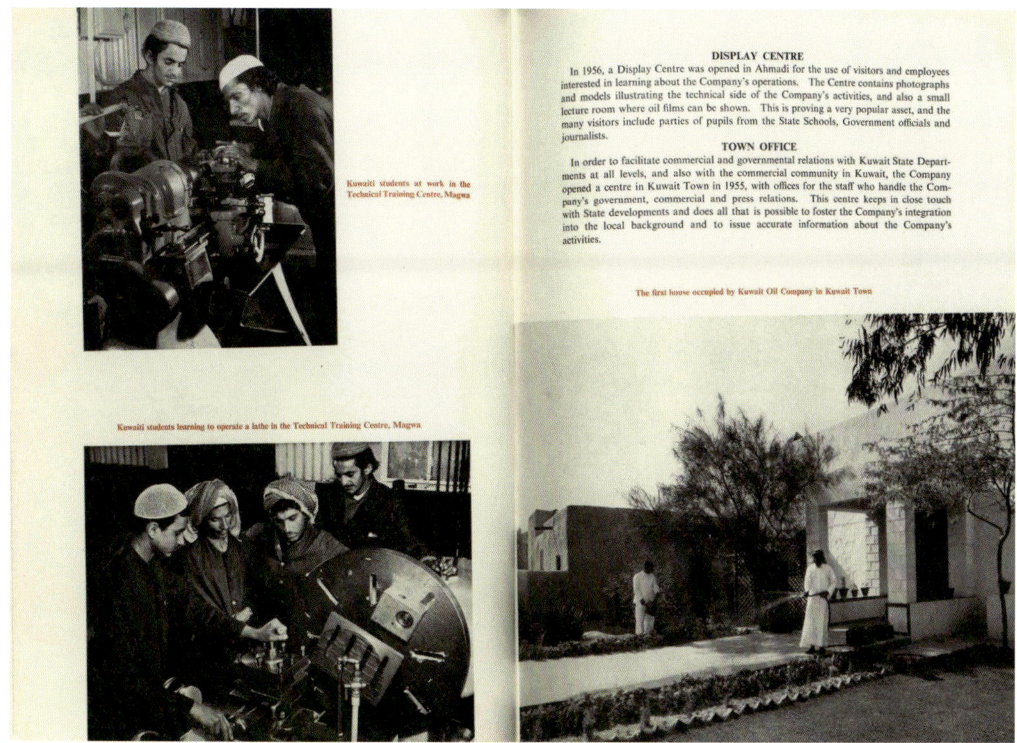

Kuwaiti students at work in the Technical Training Centre, Magwa

Kuwaiti students learning to operate a lathe in the Technical Training Centre, Magwa

DISPLAY CENTRE

In 1956, a Display Centre was opened in Ahmadi for the use of visitors and employees interested in learning about the Company's operations. The Centre contains photographs and models illustrating the technical side of the Company's activities, and also a small lecture room where oil films can be shown. This is proving a very popular asset, and the many visitors include parties of pupils from the State Schools, Government officials and journalists.

TOWN OFFICE

In order to facilitate commercial and governmental relations with Kuwait State Departments at all levels, and also with the commercial community in Kuwait, the Company opened a centre in Kuwait Town in 1955, with offices for the staff who handle the Company's government, commercial and press relations. This centre keeps in close touch with State developments and does all that is possible to foster the Company's integration into the local background and to issue accurate information about the Company's activities.

The first house occupied by Kuwait Oil Company in Kuwait Town

4.7 KOC workers in training and in front of newly built housing, photographed by Adolf Morath and printed in *The Story of Kuwait* (1957).

trained, often with white, probably British or American instructors, doctors, and teachers there to direct them.[49]

Morath's photographs had also a strong impact in the final part of *The Story of Kuwait*, the section on the development program of Kuwait City. Here, they replaced two thirds of the previously used photographs.[50] Technically, the pictures substantiate Morath's excellent knowledge of architectural photography. Set against a wide and cloudless sky, the buildings of Shuwaikh Secondary School, for example, are shot in sharp early morning light (fig. 4.8). Taken slightly from below in order to encompass the entire length of the façade, the photographer portrayed the buildings with enormous horizontal and vertical presence through the use of sidelight. People as "staffage" entering the building increases the impression of massive architectural volume.

[49] On structural hierarchies engrained in the employment and housing policies of the KOC, see Alissa, "Building for Oil," 42–44.

[50] This section contained ten images in the 1955 edition and fourteen in the 1957 edition; ten of the images in the 1957 edition were new additions.

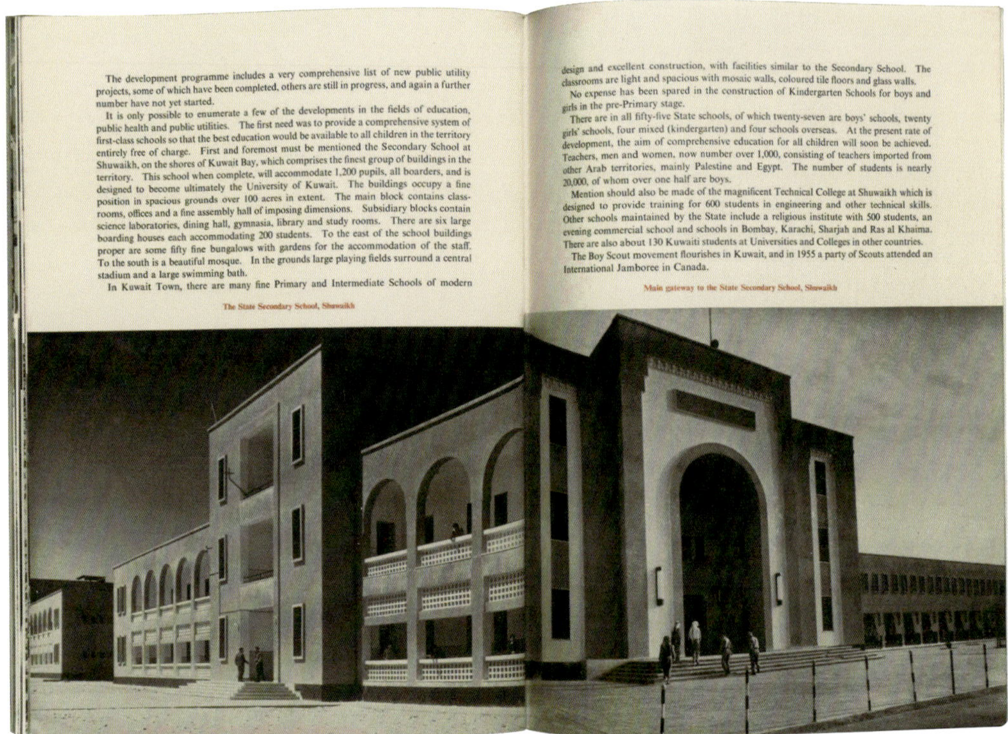

The development programme includes a very comprehensive list of new public utility projects, some of which have been completed, others are still in progress, and again a further number have not yet started.

It is only possible to enumerate a few of the developments in the fields of education, public health and public utilities. The first need was to provide a comprehensive system of first-class schools so that the best education would be available to all children in the territory entirely free of charge. First and foremost must be mentioned the Secondary School at Shuwaikh, on the shores of Kuwait Bay, which comprises the finest group of buildings in the territory. This school when complete, will accommodate 1,200 pupils, all boarders, and is designed to become ultimately the University of Kuwait. The buildings occupy a fine position in spacious grounds over 100 acres in extent. The main block contains classrooms, offices and a fine assembly hall of imposing dimensions. Subsidiary blocks contain science laboratories, dining hall, gymnasia, library and study rooms. There are six large boarding houses each accommodating 200 students. To the east of the school buildings proper are some fifty fine bungalows with gardens for the accommodation of the staff. To the south is a beautiful mosque. In the grounds large playing fields surround a central stadium and a large swimming bath.

In Kuwait Town, there are many fine Primary and Intermediate Schools of modern design and excellent construction, with facilities similar to the Secondary School. The classrooms are light and spacious with mosaic walls, coloured tile floors and glass walls.

No expense has been spared in the construction of Kindergarten Schools for boys and girls in the pre-Primary stage.

There are in all fifty-five State schools, of which twenty-seven are boys' schools, twenty girls' schools, four mixed (kindergarten) and four schools overseas. At the present rate of development, the aim of comprehensive education for all children will soon be achieved. Teachers, men and women, now number over 1,000, consisting of teachers imported from other Arab territories, mainly Palestine and Egypt. The number of students is nearly 20,000, of whom over one half are boys.

Mention should also be made of the magnificent Technical College at Shuwaikh which is designed to provide training for 600 students in engineering and other technical skills. Other schools maintained by the State include a religious institute with 500 students, an evening commercial school and schools in Bombay, Karachi, Sharjah and Ras al Khaima. There are also about 130 Kuwaiti students at Universities and Colleges in other countries.

The Boy Scout movement flourishes in Kuwait, and in 1955 a party of Scouts attended an International Jamboree in Canada.

The State Secondary School, Shuwaikh

Main gateway to the State Secondary School, Shuwaikh

4.8 Shuwaikh Secondary School, photographed by Adolf Morath and printed in *The Story of Kuwait* (1957).

Other photographs by Morath that were used in this section showed, for example, a new Kuwaiti villa and a new housing estate for middle or lower-income families in Kuwait City (fig. 4.9). The images manifest a similar tension between the horizontal wide-angle perspective, which is able to bring more of the surrounding environment into the foreground and background of the image, and the isolation of the buildings through the photographic exclusion of any architectural or urban context. In these pictures, sharp sunlight, a cloudless sky, and a foreground that often consists of loose gravel are strongly evocative of the desert and act as a void against which the new architecture (representing Kuwait City) rises. Resonating with *The Story of Oil's* foundational metaphor of making the desert bloom, Morath's photographic compositions present the newly built constructions all over Kuwait City as a concrete garden growing from the desert after being watered with petroleum. Depicted mostly at eye level, the photographs taken by Morath delivered visual proof of the petroleum promise on the ground as it happened.

Not only did the KOC meet Morath's photographic approach with approval—a much wider readership also appreciated the third edition of *The Story of Kuwait*. As an internal report from May 1957 documented, this issue received numerous press reviews

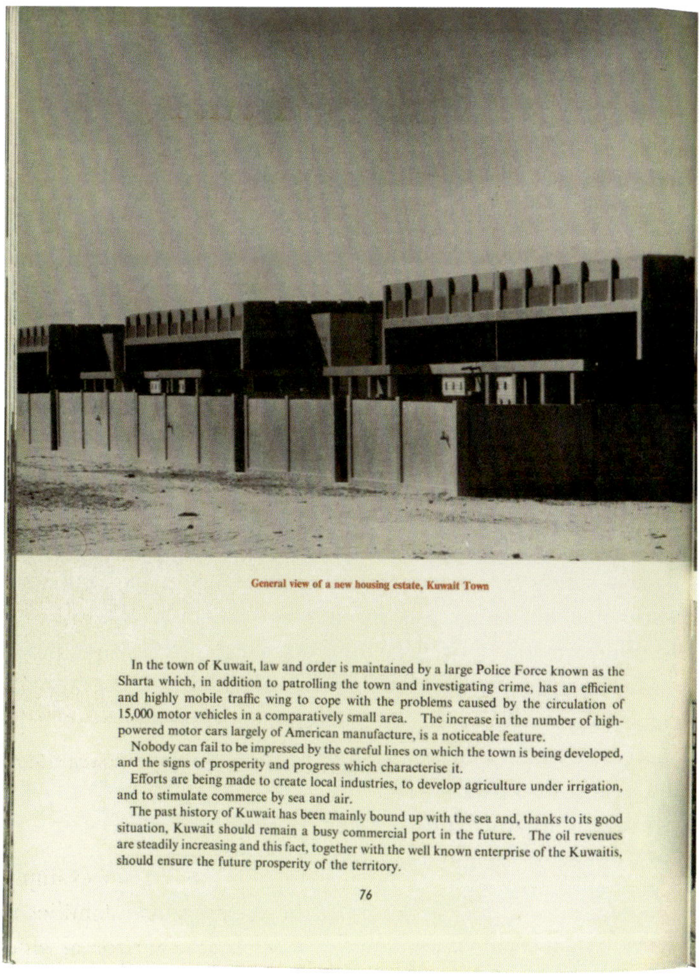

General view of a new housing estate, Kuwait Town

In the town of Kuwait, law and order is maintained by a large Police Force known as the Sharta which, in addition to patrolling the town and investigating crime, has an efficient and highly mobile traffic wing to cope with the problems caused by the circulation of 15,000 motor vehicles in a comparatively small area. The increase in the number of high-powered motor cars largely of American manufacture, is a noticeable feature.

Nobody can fail to be impressed by the careful lines on which the town is being developed, and the signs of prosperity and progress which characterise it.

Efforts are being made to create local industries, to develop agriculture under irrigation, and to stimulate commerce by sea and air.

The past history of Kuwait has been mainly bound up with the sea and, thanks to its good situation, Kuwait should remain a busy commercial port in the future. The oil revenues are steadily increasing and this fact, together with the well known enterprise of the Kuwaitis, should ensure the future prosperity of the territory.

76

4.9 Housing estate for middle- or lower-income families in Kuwait City, photographed by Adolf Morath and printed in *The Story of Kuwait* (1957).

that praised the new photographic illustrations.[51] Among the quoted reviewers were not only specialized journals like the *Institute of Petroleum Review* and *The Oil Engine and Gas Turbine*, but also the *Financial Times*, *The Times*, and *The Iraq Times*, which suggests that *The Story of Kuwait* had a broad circle of notable—English-language—recipients. Moreover, the internal report considered the reproduction of phrases and information

[51] Press review of *The Story of Kuwait* (1957), May 20, 1957, Press, Broadcasting, papers, 1958–59, 106988, BP Archive, University of Warwick.

taken from the booklet by other press outlets, such as Kuwait's oil history described as a "unique" experience, as a sign of the publication's persuasiveness and success.[52]

In line with the pressing demand to create more communication with Arabic-speaking audiences, an Arabic version was finally also produced. In March 1958, E. A. V. de Candole, public relations officer and head of the Town Office, reported that

> our booklet "The Story of Kuwait" (Arabic and English) has a very wide circulation among Government Departments and Arab visitors to our Display Centre, and we have issued over 1000 copies of the smaller Arabic booklet "Al Naft fi al Kuwait" [Oil in Kuwait] for use in Government schools. I have been complimented by the Ruler and the Director of Education on the suitability of these booklets for educational purposes.[53]

By mid-1958, 5,000 copies of the latest Arabic version of *The Story of Kuwait* had been ordered, attesting to its success and growing influence.[54]

The illustrated booklet *The Story of Kuwait* gave the KOC credit as a popular knowledge authority on Kuwait among English- and Arabic-speaking audiences alike. Its textual version of the (hi)story of Kuwait was influential, and the Kuwaiti government even relied on its Arabic material about Kuwait's oil production for educational purposes. The booklet's visual language subtly but effectively insinuated that the oil company's product was not merely crude oil, but rather that the company should be credited with (assisting) Kuwait's urban transformation and social progress, which itself was presented as a unique miracle to make the achievement seem even bigger and somewhat magical. Similarly, Reem Alissa concludes that the KOC's PR campaign directed toward its employees in Ahmadi "successfully used architecture and urban development as a means to legitime itself in order to secure its continued presence."[55] Morath's color photography, however, was the most persuasive in visualizing the KOC's favorite narratives and they reveal what it meant for the company agents in the mid-twentieth century to engage in petro-modernity.

Kuwait Illuminated

The color photographs Morath took of Kuwait City and that are today in the company archives conjured up petro-modernity as a colorful, progressive, and dynamic atmosphere, an iridescence that black-and-white photos were simply not able to

[52] Ibid.

[53] De Candole to Bernard Burrows, Political Resident, Bahrain, March 23, 1958, Town Office, 1957–1958.

[54] Kuwait Oil Company, Town Office monthly report, August 1958, ibid.

[55] Alissa also observed that *The Kuwaiti*, the English-language bi-weekly company magazine, "shifted its focus from international, British and Ahmadi news to articles which highlighted its contributing role to the architectural, urban and social development [of] Kuwait City, with particular attention to oil wealth's contribution to modern state projects" from 1957 onward. Alissa, "Building for Oil," 84.

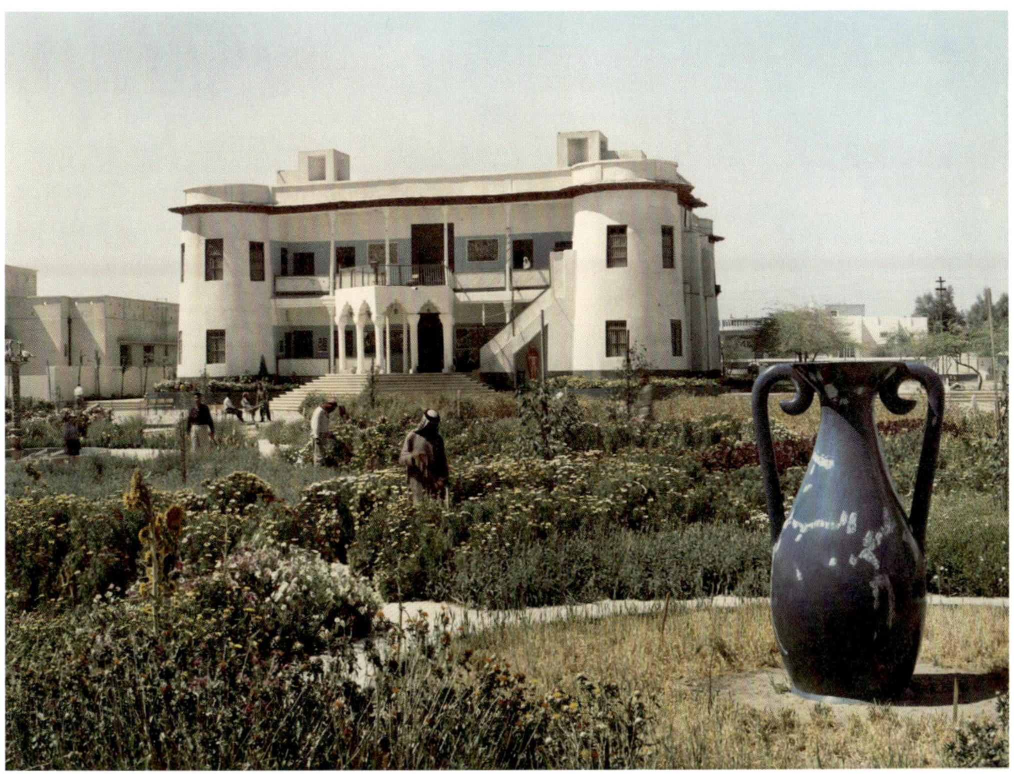

4.10 Adolf Morath, *The Museum—Kuwait Town*, March 1958. Color photograph.

communicate. Color was undisputedly better equipped to capture the blooming garden that surrounded the recently opened National Museum of Kuwait (fig. 4.10), which was housed in the abandoned diwan of Shaykh Khazʿal of al-Muḥammara (today Khorramshahr).[56] A view of the new petrol station just outside the former town wall also projected colorful scenery (fig. 4.11): the steel structure of the petrol station painted with blue and white varnish (almost certainly based on a petroleum derivative); the shiny surfaces of the freshly polished mint-green and red-and-white cars and red lorries that ran on petrol and whose industrial production depended on fossil fuels; and the blue-and-white gasoline pumps with their plastic tank hoses. To better showcase

[56] Shaykh Abdullah initiated the first National Museum in the diwan of Shaykh Khazʿal (1863–1936) in 1957, the former ruler of al-Muḥammara, in what is today Khuzestan, Iran. Khazʿal was a close friend of Shaykh Mubarak the Great and frequently stayed in Kuwait in the early twentieth century. See Noura Alsager, ed., *Acquiring Modernity* (Kuwait: National Council for Culture, Arts and Letters, 2014); Exhibition booklet of the Kuwait Pavilion curated by Alia Farid, published for the 14th International Architecture Exhibition of the Venice Biennale, 5.

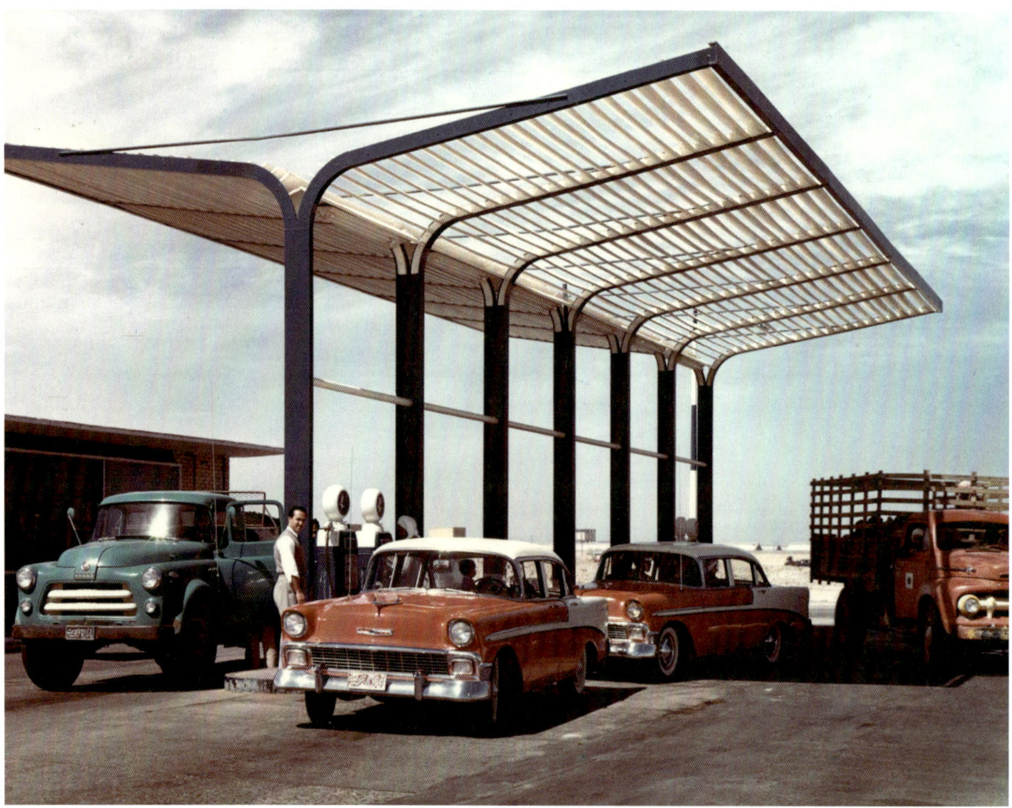

4.11 Adolf Morath, *General View of the Petrol Station Outside the Lizard Gate, Kuwait,* April 1956. Color photograph.

the petrol station, Morath also relied on a wide foreground (asphalted pavement) and a wide, empty background (desert-like space set against the blue sky) in combination with sidelights. Furthermore, Morath tended to elaborate his compositions not only with human staffage but also with cars. With their bright varnishes and beaming (metal) surfaces that contrasted starkly with the subtle color palette of the bricks, coral stone, and sand of Kuwait's pre-oil habitat, the brand-new cars stood out as both motifs and accessories. For example, a row of parked cars became the visually competing point of contrast in a photograph of the ruler's Seif Palace (fig. 4.12).

The richly saturated colors in the photographic images were vital to highlighting the arrival of petroleum-derived materials and textures previously unknown in such abundance (if at all) in Kuwait. Color allowed the images to create visibility for petroleum-derived, chemically enhanced products like varnish, paint, plastics, and rubber as well as for cues of petro-modernity in the Gulf like motorized mobility (fossil fuels), neon signs (electricity), and lush gardens (desalinated water). Kuwait City

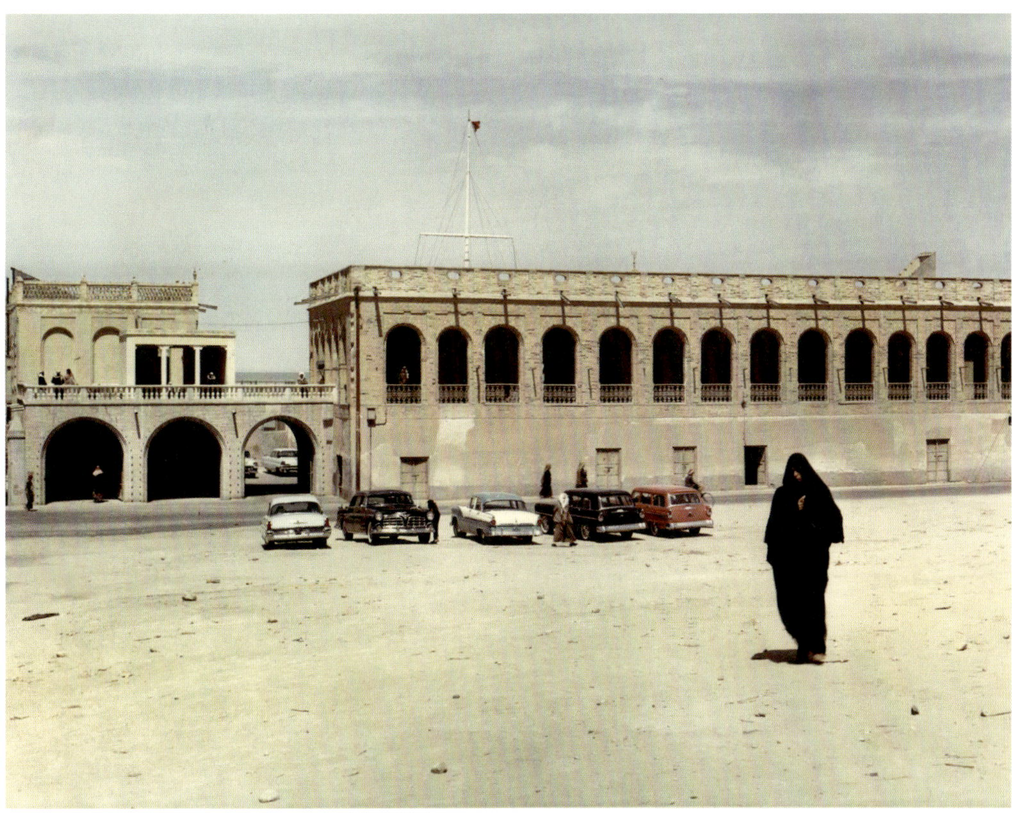

4.12 Adolf Morath, *The "Sif" Palace, on the Kuwait Waterfront*, April 1956. Color photograph.

emerged as a colorful coral reef from the sandbanks of the Persian Gulf: mesmerizing, constantly growing, and with a swirling dynamic—a grand pearl of intriguing sheen rising amid the sandy dunes. In the context of the medium of photography itself, the color photographs became novel but "authentic" and "realistic" representations of 1950s Kuwait City due to the rather factual, documentary character attributed to the medium at the time.

Of course, Morath's photographic representation of Kuwait City might have exaggerated the positive impression. Yet, accounts of the oil city given in the transregional cultural magazine *al-ʿArabī* also described the urban transformation of Kuwait by the proliferation of color in the previously sand-colored coastal town. In an article titled "Architecture in Kuwait" published in December 1959, the reader was presented with the fact that many façades of newly erected apartment blocks, private villas, and even governmental buildings, like the new municipality, made use of color in combination with pillars, railings, and window mounts in contrasting shades (fig. 4.13). As such they

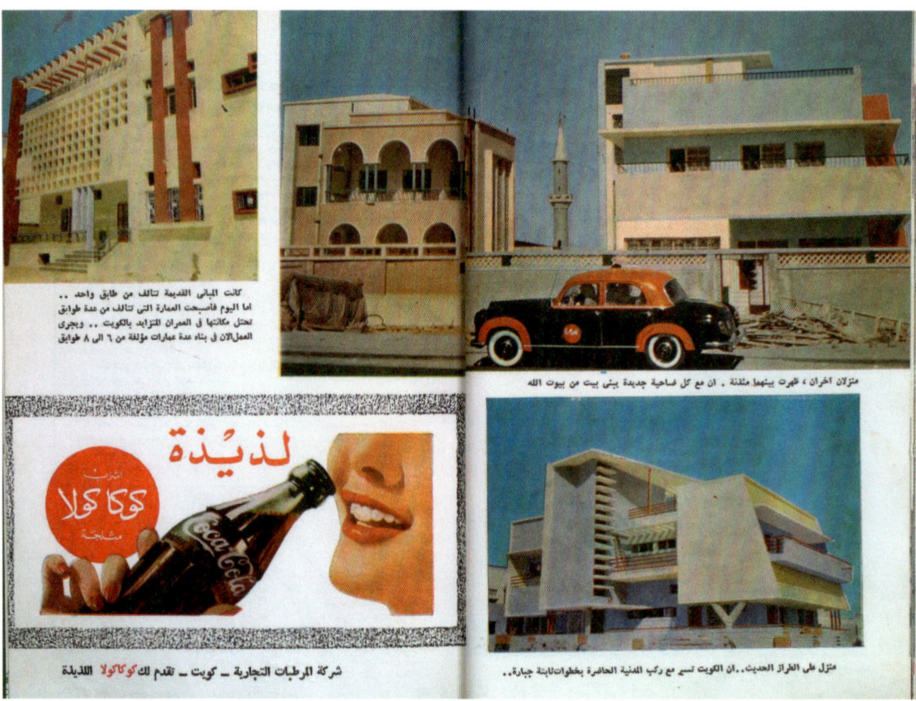

4.13 Spread from *al-'Arabī*, December 1959, showing new construction and housing projects in Kuwait City in bright colors.

appeared in the color photography of Oscar Mitri, an Egyptian photographer (*1927) who had worked for the renown magazines *Akhir Sā'a* and *al-Muṣṣawar* before moving to Kuwait to join *al-'Arabī* as its first lead in-house photographer.[57] This new appearance of the city in color was amplified by photographs of ample green space, in form of public and private gardens and of tree-lined avenues, such as the first ring road (fig. 4.14). Here, the article noted: "Having sorted out the water issue, starting gardens in Kuwait has begun, and by doing so, the yellow color of sands will be replaced with green."[58] However, the article made clear that only at nighttime Kuwait City showed its full potential, when the capital became a "river of lights on the Gulf shore":

[57] On the history of *al-'Arabī* and in its role in promoting Pan-Arabism, magazine photography, and women, see Bettina Gräf and Laura Hindelang, "The Transregional Illustrated Magazine *al-'Arabi*: Knowledge Production and Cultural Imaginations in the 1950s and 1960s," *Middle East Journal of Culture and Communication* (forthcoming 2022).

[58] "Al-'Imāra bi-l-Kuwayt [Architecture in Kuwait]," 69–70, including images on 68–69.

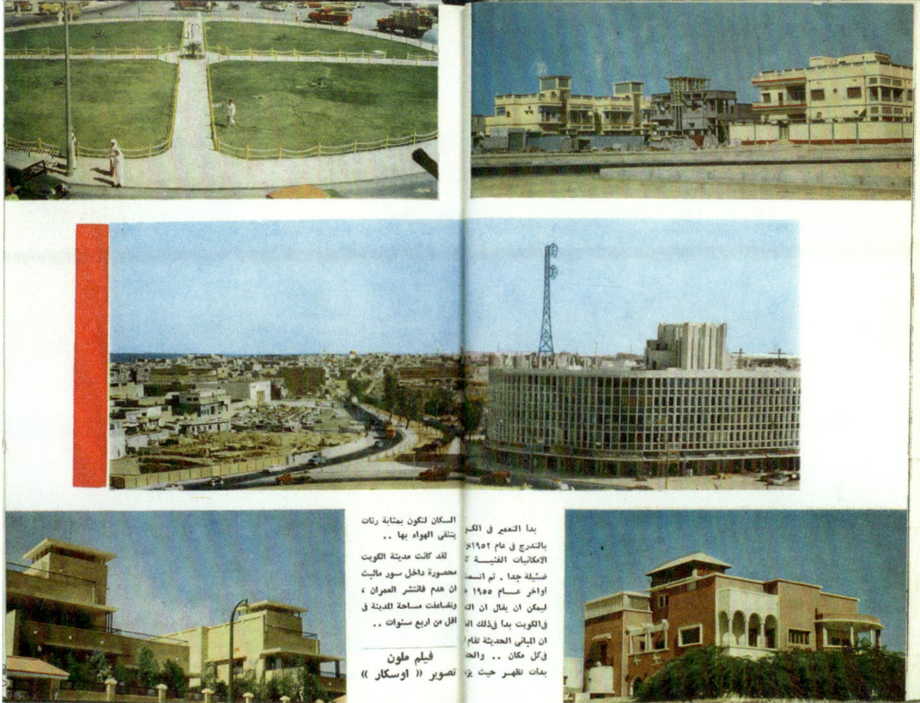

4.14 Spread from *al-'Arabī*, December 1959, showing new construction projects and green spaces in Kuwait City.

> Have you seen Kuwait at night …?
>
> The most beautiful view of the city is the one you witness out of the window of your airplane while landing at night-time at Kuwait airport.
>
> Beneath you, you will see a glittering block of lights. In the darkness of the night it reflects on the beautiful calm water of the Gulf that embraces this modern, developed city, which moves her inhabitants in thousands of cars on wide well-lit streets, not to mention that cutting-edge lighting system which uses mercury, sodium and fluorescent vapor lamps to reflect white and yellow in order to illuminate all the streets and roads.
>
> While in the big city squares there grow millions of huge colored "neon" billboards that fill the city with beauty and joy; it is impossible against this background for a person to imagine that this region was a few years ago arid desert; the fast development has turned it upside down.[59]

The by-then abundant electrification of the city changed its image lastingly. In Kuwait, natural gas was the main source to generate electricity (and desalinate water) and the almost exclusive reliance on fossil energy characterizes Kuwait's energy landscape to this

[59] "Al-Kuwayt fī l-layl [Kuwait at Night]," *al-'Arabī*, no. 25 (December 1960): 140 (author's translation).

day.[60] In regard to the color photography created of Kuwait, both the examples of KOC photographs and of *al-'Arabī's* images indicate that the unfolding of petro-modernity turned the city into an iridescence environment of color.

Color photography stood for change, for a modern Kuwait as it marked a departure from the historical black-and-white anthropo-orientalist glass plate shots of romanticized scenes of Bedouin life, pearl divers, and markets that characterized Kuwait's photographic representation in the first half of the twentieth century.[61] The new images functioned as transmitters of the iridescent effect, that demonstrated petroleum's powerful *aesthetic* and *visual* presence or resonance in images, in media, in objects, in the built environment, and in space in general. In strong contrast with the deep black and greasy crude oil—the oil companies' actual product—these images demonstrated what petroleum's chemical transformation was able to bring to life: a colorful lifestyle, an illuminated city, and a prospering society. It is not difficult to believe that such images created an affectionate relationship with petro-modernity.

For the KOC, Morath had been on several levels the perfect man to do the job. He was quite progressive in offering color photography for industrial customers this early on. Furthermore, for him color photography was not only the latest technological advance, but was crucial in constituting an atmosphere, an appeal that related to the equally transforming offices, homes, and lifestyles of the companies' clients and customers or at least stimulated such aspirations. Morath's determination to make such atmospheric immersion happen is captured in this anecdote by Riri Girardon, one of his last assistants in London before his death in 1977. She recalled how "he had to photograph an enormous working area with boilers, furnaces, stairways etc. all very dirty and not photogenic at all [for an industrial commission]. He simply said: 'I want this blue, that yellow, the stairs green! … When can I come back to take the picture?'"[62] It is unlikely that Morath resorted to such drastic means for his Kuwait commissions. Still, the anecdote shows the importance of color for corporative photography in the eyes of this photographer. And it relates to the conscious selection of motifs and frames that Morath made of the urban space of Kuwait.

The Hidden Views

How did Morath's color photography operate to convey Kuwait City as the picture-perfect materialized promise of petro-modernity? Besides contrasting architectural forms against their flat surroundings and dipping the scene in rich colors (which were technically enhanced during the development process), constructing deliberate absences was a vital

[60] Hannah Ritchie, "Kuwait: Energy Country Profile," Our World in Data, accessed January30, 2021, https://ourworldindata.org/energy/country/kuwait?country=~KWT#citation.

[61] See for example Facey and Grant, *Kuwait by the First Photographers.*

[62] Email to the author, July 24, 2020.

aspect of the image-making process. The fact that the destruction and rebuilding of pre-oil Kuwait is missing from Morath's supervised representations is striking, especially as the transformation was ongoing and unmissable at the time of his visits. Therefore, the photographer's role was crucial to the process of carefully navigating what to show and what to hide from view, what to highlight in color and what to disguise. Such selective depiction allowed for the ongoing messy and dusty "rebuilding" of the town to be translated into sleek, controlled, tidied, and beautiful urban vistas.

The urban and architectural overhaul of the capital could not have been overlooked by anyone who visited Kuwait in the 1950s. An employee from the BP office in London, Mr. Pattinson, who stopped by a few months prior to Morath in 1956, complained in internal communication in much detail that Kuwait was a large construction side:

> While there is a fair amount of new building going on in the Town itself, particularly building of residences and of new roads, there is still a vast amount to be done and little attempt, if any, seems to have been made to clean up and modernize the actual small streets and decrepit houses, of which the Town has always largely consisted. One can see from the two or three main boulevards which have been driven through the Town the same welter of miserable hovels and water flooded streets (it rained heavily yesterday) as always and one wonders whether there is not more window dressing going on than real improvement.[63]

This view of Kuwait City as heterogeneous, untidy, and only partly modernized was an impression one would have never received from seeing only Morath's images. His photographs showed almost exclusively the already modernized side of Kuwait City that fit with the oil company's public agenda of linking its own operations with fortune and progress of modern Kuwait (City); everything else was cast outside of the frame. In contrast, photographs of construction sites and scaffolded buildings in the making were frequently and matter-of-factly printed in *al-'Arabī*.[64]

The intact and vibrant vernacular townscape of Kuwait that still existed surrounding the patches of cleared and developed urban space remained largely omitted from the KOC photographic commission. Moreover, the destruction of the town's pre-oil architecture was rather deliberately hidden from view when compared with color photography that was taken around that time by other photographers working independently.

The recently published photographic work of Tareq Sayid Rajab (1937–2017) encompasses tranquil scenes of work in the local shipyard, observations of everyday street life, and of the archaeological excavations at Failaka Island, but especially photographs over photographs of individual buildings in the historic neighborhoods of Kuwait City

[63] J. M. Pattinson's Visit to Kuwait, Abu Dhabi, Persia and Iraq, January 14 to February 6, 1956, Diary No. 1, 49842, BP Archive, University of Warwick, 7–8.

[64] See, for instance, "Mawlid shāri' fī l-Kuwayt [Birth of a Street in Kuwait]," *al-'Arabī*, no. 21 (August 1960): 79–84.

intra muros.[65] Taken between the 1960s and the early 2000s, the photographs included in the three comprehensive and self-published photobooks substantiate a poetic and passionate long-term study of Kuwait, where time has become a salient ingredient, not only tangible in the atmospheric tranquility that Rajab captured, but also in his own long-spanning perseverance and dedication to revisiting places time after time.[66] Rajab never pursued a professional photographic or artistic career, working in education instead, but his lifelong productivity and the quality of his photographs, drawings, and painting speak to his artistry. In the photobooks, several scenes of urban destruction during the early 1960s are captured that are illuminating in the context discussed here, one of which is the demolition and rebuilding of New Street (*al-Shāriʿ al-Jadīd*, today Abdullah al-Salem Street).

In 1947, the *baladiyya* created New Street, a new thoroughfare linking Safat Square to Sief Street and thus with the waterfront. New Street was one of the first electrified, paved, straight, and wide streets in Kuwait, for which Asseel Al-Ragam describes it as "one of the first novel explorations of urban form" by the municipality prior to the 1952 Master Plan.[67] Ironically, New Street also—not old and decaying at all—fell prey to the redevelopment of the main square and its surrounding neighborhoods as part of the plan's implementation. A photograph taken by Rajab shot in 1962 presents the remaining walls of some of the buildings that had aligned New Street (fig. 4.15). The walls of former interior spaces painted in subtle tones of light yellow, green and white, are cracked open and also reveal their steel skeleton of reinforced concrete structures in the sharp morning light. At the center of the photo, the view opens onto a mural of a world map and the scene of a man and a woman, probably illustrations to entertain children. Besides, three dark clothed human figures stumble through the debris, obviously looking for treasures amid the rubble. The photograph discloses that the houses under demolition are lived spaces, for which their vanishing also erases the social memories of living in Kuwait. Moreover,

[65] Born in 1937 in Kuwait, Rajab received one of the first government scholarships to study art (education) in England in 1953. Upon his return to Kuwait five years later, he was already married to Jehan Wellborne (1934–2015) and father of two. In Kuwait, he first worked as a teacher, then became supervisor of the archaeological excavations at Failaka, later director of Antiquities and Museums, then manager of the KOC Display Center, and finally founder and manager of the New English School together with Jehan in 1969. In addition, the couple opened the Tareq Rajab Museum in 1980 to present their ethnographic and Islamic art collection to the public, followed by a second museum specialized in calligraphy that was opened in 2007. Besides the self-published books, Rajab's private photographic archives now await being turned into a publicly accessible collection and will hopefully receive substantial research to integrate his oeuvre into a larger visual history of the region.

[66] Tareq Sayid Rajab, *Glimpses from the Recent Past, Kuwait 1960–65* (Kuwait: Tareq Rajab Museum, 1999); Tareq Sayid Rajab, *Glimpses from the Recent Past: Kuwait 1960–1980* (Kuwait: Tareq Rajab Museum, 2005); Tareq Sayid Rajab, *Glimpses from Kuwait 60–06* (Kuwait: Tareq Rajab Museum, 2007).

[67] Al-Ragam, "Towards a Critique of an Architectural Nahdha," 41. The road gathered many important shops and agencies on both sides that demonstratively advertised their goods under the street's columnated arcades, which also got it the name "Pillar Street."

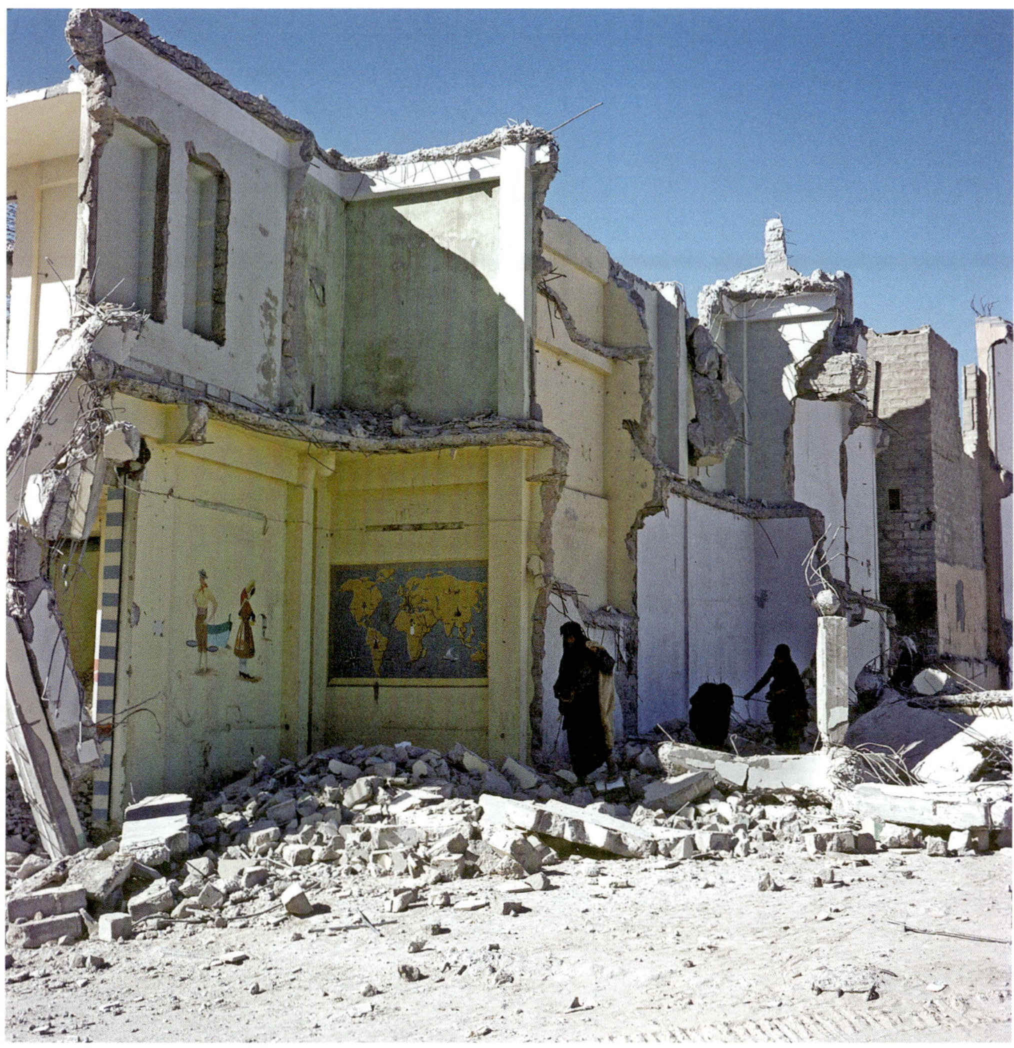

4.15 Tareq S. Rajab, *Demolition of New Street*, 1962. Color photograph.

it demonstrates that not only pre-oil traditional architecture was discarded, but modern architecture was too if it did not fit the overall urban concept.

Tareq Rajab's photographs allow not only to critically revisit Adolf Morath's photographic practice for the KOC, but it also offers a completely new view onto Kuwait's urban fabric during the early 1960s and therefore onto the early results of the petro-fueled urban transformation. The absence of such motifs in Morath's color photographs reveal deliberate decisions of what to select and what (not) to show. Moreover, Rajab's photos

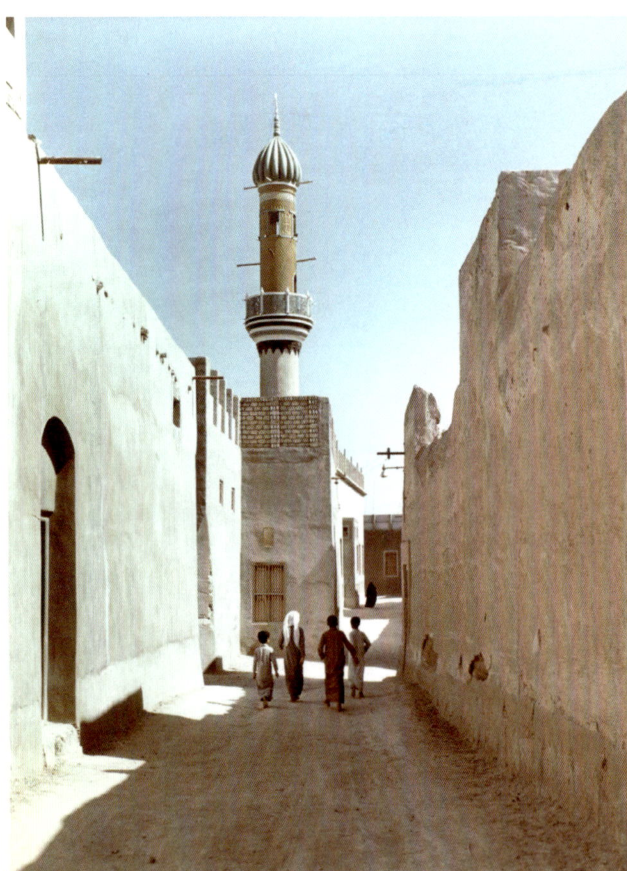

4.16 Adolf Morath, *Street Scene in Kuwait Town, Showing the Minaret of a Mosque*, April 1956. Color photograph.

evidence that the new commercial and administrative center of Kuwait City *intra muros* was not built "on sand" but on debris of the former town of Kuwait.[68]

The vernacular urban fabric of Kuwait's *intra muros* only featured in Morath's albums when it fit established notions of the decontextualized orientalist pre-oil picturesque. Typical motifs of the Kuwaiti picturesque that formed in early twentieth-century black-and-white photography included, for instance, the souk, the Bedouin market at Safat Square, mosques, or winding mud-plastered alleyways. Architectural motifs of this kind also featured in Morath's photography when it corresponded with Western expectations of an Arab Islamic city (such as mosques) or when he depicted structures that the urban planning had been singled out as worth preserving as part of the new Kuwait City (fig. 4.16).

[68] Ironically, the situation might not have differed so much from European postwar "rebuilding," which might explain why the British town planners kept referring to Kuwait's urban transformation as such.

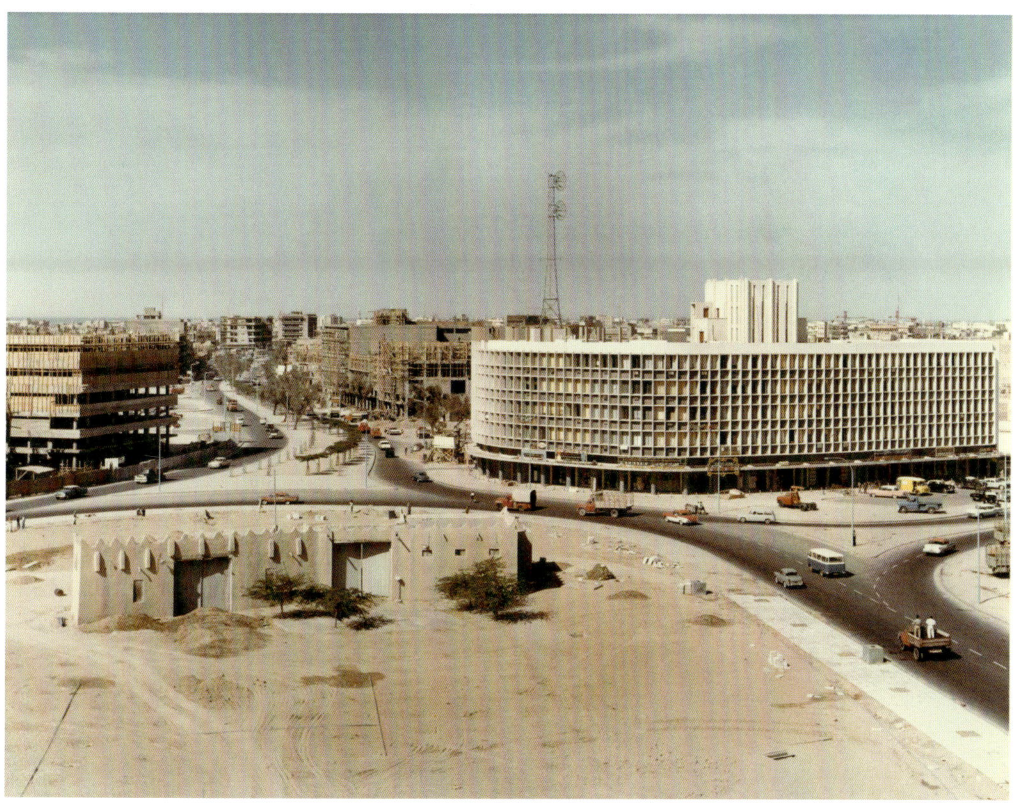

4.17 Adolf Morath, *A New Office Building in Kuwait Town*, April 1960. Color photograph.

The piecemeal preservation of built elements of the pre-oil urban settlement was integral to the first master plan's vision of new Kuwait and can be seen as an early attempt to create cultural heritage by decontextualizing preservation. In addition to some mosques and the royal palaces, the four town wall gates had been selected worthy of preservation. The gates were therefore not destroyed, but partly renovated and displayed in a new urban setting. Formerly integrated into the wall that had been built in 1921 and demolished in 1957, the gates now remained as fragments and thus traces of the historical urban boundary. Subsequently isolated on various roundabouts amid a sea of motorized traffic, the gates were no longer structures controlling access to Kuwait—their function had changed to open-air musealized objects. A rare color photograph taken by Morath in 1960 brings forth this process of de- and recontextualization, which brutally pitted the static old (Jahra Gate) against the dynamic new (construction sites, Fahad al-Salem Street, shiny cars) (fig. 4.17).

In relation to the built environment, photography has long had a crucial role in playing the old off against the new, as Elizabeth Anne McCauley exemplifies using the case of Paris' radical transformation during the nineteenth century:

> Haussmann's makeover, in effect decking out grandma in new, white false teeth and a blond wig, jarringly pitted old against new and changed residents' perception of both: the faded, crumbling medieval and renaissance looking city looked even shabbier, dirtier, and smaller, whereas the pristinely white cut stone and iron trusses of modern Paris sparkled aridly—characterless, bearing the stamp of their mechanical creation.[69]

In the Parisian context, McCauley outlines, the overhaul resulted in photographers' preference for or increased assignments on "the new," which in turn propelled the rejection of historical buildings, vistas, and materials. In the case of Kuwait, the musealized town wall gates became, literally, a popular frame of looking at the materializing future of Kuwait. For example, *al-ʿArabī* printed a photograph showing the development of Fahad al-Salem Street as seen through the old city gate (fig. 4.18).[70] Color photography fueled the pitting of old against new even more so. It drove an aesthetic wedge between the different urban layers of time and materiality, as the rather pale palette of natural materials such as sand, mud, and coral stone were not granted a strong, colorful impression within Morath's photos. The resulting selective color images of a place where everything was new, shiny, clean, dynamic, awaiting consumption, and facilitating comfort also visually disciplined the viewer in terms of how to perceive (and in turn imagine and remember) Kuwait City.

The photography of the KOC still ran under the heading of "industrial photography" and Morath was primarily an industrial photographer. In the industrial context, the use of photography has been theorized as a form of disciplining, not only by means of the controlling presence of the photographer and the situation of freezing or posing for the shoot; rather, the photograph unfolds most power when projecting the image of an ideal working process that, simply by being depicted repeatedly, triggers the internalization of the model situation by the viewer and their subsequent self-disciplining for the purpose of fitting in.[71] By analogy, Morath's photographs of a picture-perfect Kuwait City visually disciplined urban space through the careful selection of suitable motifs, the invisibility of the destruction of the already existing urban environment, and the implicit negation of the pre-oil town. Furthermore, by means of highly-curated color images the photographs showed their audiences how all of Kuwait City *should* look, and, over time, how their viewers were led to think that Kuwait City *had* in fact looked.

Morath's color photography almost invented this controlled, tidy, and colorful modern city. The more these images—and the corporate lens and seductive iridescent effect they

[69] Elizabeth Anne McCauley, *Industrial Madness: Commercial Photography in Paris, 1848–1871*, Yale Publications in the History of Art (New Haven: Yale University Press, 1994), 196.

[70] "Mawlid shāriʿ fī l-Kuwayt [Birth of a Street in Kuwait]," 79.

[71] Reinhard Matz, *Industriefotografie: Aus Firmenarchiven des Ruhrgebiets*, Schriftreihe der Kulturstiftung Ruhr 2 (Essen: Kulturstiftung Ruhr, 1987), 112.

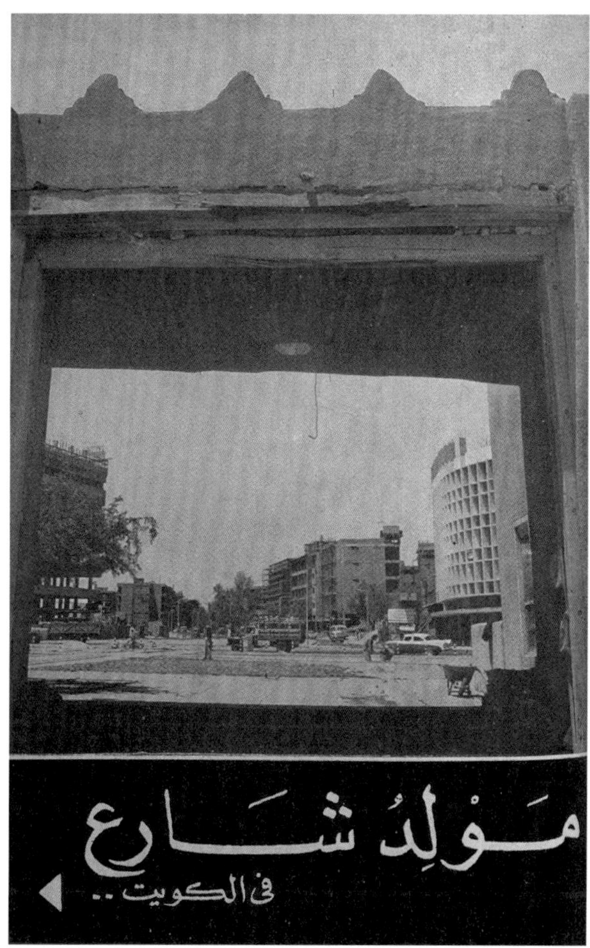

4.18 Opening page of an article on the development of Fahad al-Salem Street in *al-'Arabī*, August 1960, with a view onto the street under construction through the old city wall gates.

embodied—began circulating in glossy magazines, exhibition displays, and other outlets in Kuwait and beyond, the more this particular, one-sided image of 1950s Kuwait City solidified itself in popular perception as symbolic of Kuwait's mid-twentieth-century oil period. The broad dissemination and public exhibition of the oil company's photography was crucial for the proliferation of this image of Kuwait and pursued it in various ways.

4.4 Exhibiting Kuwait Beyond the Oil Company's Sphere

The KOC recognized the powerful role of photography "to maintain and develop relations with the Kuwaitis" and with the home audiences of KOC shareholders for which new modes of how to distribute the pictures were necessary.[72] One approach was to create public displays and soon Morath's color prints, as captured in a shot by the photographer himself, were hung as part of a permanent exhibition at the KOC Display Center in Ahmadi (fig. 4.19). Moreover, the KOC's interest resonated with the government of Kuwait's wish that the company would like to do more to publicize its activities.

In several meetings with KOC officials in summer 1957, Abdulla Mulla Saleh, the Kuwaiti ruler's official representative to the KOC, discussed the possibility of more prominent and public presentations of the photographs outside the company's sphere of direct influence, such as large-scale displays at the refreshments room of Kuwait Airport. Saleh also suggested a KOC calendar in Arabic, the sale of colored postcards based on Morath's photographs, and offering Morath photographs to "Trade Agents and Airline Agents for display here and in Beirut."[73] Morath's color photographs were also included in the oil section presented in Kuwait's National Museum.[74] At the time, the government obviously agreed with the visual representation of Kuwait City in Morath's photography. It can only be speculated what the motivation was, but the government obviously considered the pictures to be good publicity not just for the firm but for Kuwait in general—or at least the most professional and up-to-date photos currently available in such quantity and in color.

Following Morath's second assignment in March 1958, the KOC supplied the Department of Education with the new color photos, and "pictures, models and [a] supply of publications" also went to the Social Affairs Department.[75] The 1958 photo albums show even more brand-new architectural structures rising in and around Kuwait City: cinemas, new villas, schools, medical facilities, and so on, besides, of course, the company's general operations in Ahmadi, and, the inauguration of the Refinery Extension.[76] Using Morath's photographs, with their inherent corporate perspective on Kuwait's transformation, the government assisted in establishing the KOC's image of Kuwait City as the representative image of 1950s Kuwait in non-corporate and even educational contexts as well.

In Kuwait, as in other Gulf countries, photography had not yet taken root as much as in Iran or in capitals like Istanbul and Cairo. For much of the 1950s and early 1960s, the oil company's output of professional (color) photography remained unrivaled by local studies,

[72] Meeting on PR matters with owners' representatives, July 10, July 29, and September 20, 1957, minutes, Town Office, 1957, 106846, BP Archive, University of Warwick.

[73] Meeting with Mr. Mulla, October 14, 1957, minutes, ibid.

[74] Meeting on PR matters with owners' representatives, July 10, July 29, and September 20, 1957, minutes, ibid.

[75] Town Office monthly report, March 1958, Town Office, 1957–1958.

[76] Kuwait Oil Company, Town Office monthly report, March 1958, ibid.; De Candole to General Manager, April 27, 1957, memorandum, Press and Publications 1957: Broadcasting.

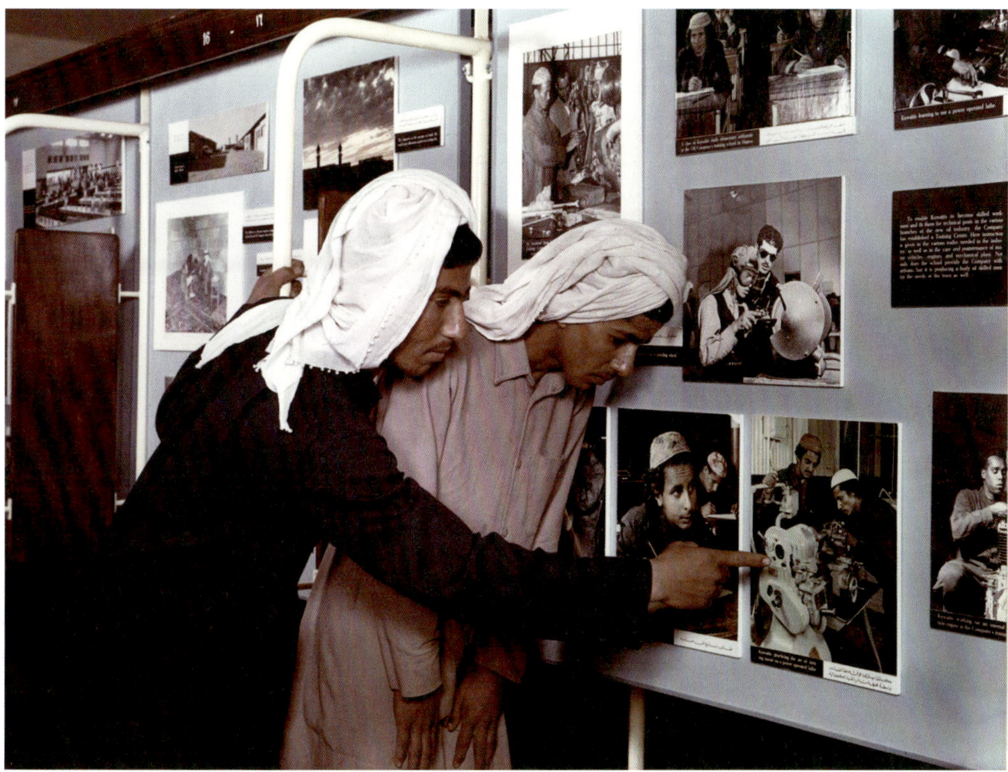

4.19 Adolf Morath, *Display Centre Interior, Photographic Display*, March 1958. Color photograph.

the government, or illustrated magazines like *al-ʿArabī*. This gave the company a leading edge as the source of photographic images. In contrast with SONJ, which competed with a myriad of other photography producers across the US and elsewhere, the KOC held a monopoly and its photographic collection covered seemingly all of the new Kuwait. Provided through the Town Office, the KOC's photographs were used by the government of Kuwait, international newspapers and magazines, as well as by independent writers.

In the 1950s, and in the following decades, many authors writing on the Arabian Peninsula cited the KOC, ARAMCO, and other oil companies as the source of their photographic illustrations, even in cases where neither the book nor the images dealt with the oil industry per se. For example, American writer Mary Louise Clifford credits eleven companies and organizations for the photographic illustrations used in her book *The Land and People of the Arabian Peninsula* (1977), six of which—including the KOC—are oil companies.[77] Yet only a minority of the book's illustrations depict obvious oil company-

[77] Mary Louise Clifford, *The Land and People of the Arabian Peninsula* (Philadelphia: J. B. Lippincott, 1977). Other examples are: George Kheirallah, *Arabia Reborn* (Albuquerque: University of New Mexico

related scenes. Instead, they show landscapes, people, and urban environments. The book is evidence that the oil companies' photography was acknowledged and utilized as a source of visual information not only on the Arabian oil industry but also on the Arabian Peninsula in general.

That much of Kuwait's 1950s color photography is in fact corporate photography with a specific political and economic agenda continues to be easily overlooked, especially because the motifs (like Kuwait City's urban space) offer no immediate clue as to their connection to the KOC and the photography was not watermarked or branded with a logo. Once the color photographs proliferated outside the corporate sphere of the Display Center and the KOC publications, and even outside Kuwait, contextualizing the production of these images became increasingly difficult. While SONJ had made the use of its photographs contingent on presenting each photo with the SONJ credit line, the KOC color photographs circulated independently of clues as to the context of their commission. Frequently displayed in (solo) shows of Adolf Morath's photography, for instance, the images became neutralized as independent photographic works and recast as authentic representations of Kuwait. This perspective in turn fostered the visual representation of Kuwait in line with the company's agenda and cemented the iridescent aesthetic of Kuwait's petro-modernity in broad popular perception. Again, color was key to the photographs speaking for petroleum and conveying that colorful iridescence that has made petro-modernity so attractive.

Viewing Kuwait Abroad

The 1957 exhibition *Industry through My Colour Camera*, held at the Ceylon Tea Centre, 22 Lower Regent Street, London, was Morath's largest solo show up to that point and took place between his first and second visit to Kuwait.[78] The venue of the exhibition was special: the Ceylon Tea Centre was an initiative of several Commonwealth tea-exporting countries at a prime location in London's commercial district around Lower Regent Street, but was not only a promotional showroom for tea-related interests. Instead, it seems to have been a vibrant exhibition space for all kinds of art and design shows as well as cultural expositions. Having worked extensively for the Ceylon Tea Propaganda Board, Morath had connections to the tea industry and these links presumably helped him realize the exhibition; to what extent the KOC was involved remains unclear.[79] *Industry through My*

Press, 1952), Photographs courtesy of ARAMCO; Sanger, *The Arabian Peninsula*, Photographs courtesy of ARAMCO, California Texas Oil and Gulf Oil.

[78] L. E. Hallett, "Other London Exhibitions: Henri Cartier Bresson, Adolf Morath (Member)," *The Photographic Journal* 97, no. 4 (1957): 65; "Humanism in Industrial Photography: Colour, and the 'Dynamic Moment,'" *Manchester Guardian*, January 28, 1957, n.p., reprint; "Industry in Colour: An Exhibition by Adolf Morath," *British Journal of Photography*, February 15, 1957, n.p., reprint.

[79] D. M. Forrest, *A Hundred Years of Ceylon Tea, 1867–1967* (London: Chatto & Windus, 1967), photographs by Adolf Morath. This publication was edited by the Ceylon Tea Propaganda Board. Other Ceylon Tea

Colour Camera was much discussed by British newspapers and received positive reviews. It was reported that the exhibition put on show "giant colour prints" with scenes of "the British steel industry, the oil industry in Kuwait, copper mining in Northern Rhodesia, and atomic power engineering."[80] Entirely in color, all photos were developed using "the Agfa negative-positive process and made in Mr. Morath's London laboratories."[81] The images were perceived as portraying "the nations' industrial power" and as marking "a new development in colour photography."[82]

From here, Morath tried to expand the perception of his work not only as industrial commissions but as industrial photography as art. Correspondence with the Museum of Modern Art (MoMA) in New York from January 1958 reveals that Morath offered his "giant size colour photographs" for exhibition.[83] While a MoMA exhibit did not materialize, exhibitions with a similar focus as the London show did take place, for example in Glasgow in February 1959.[84] Eventually, the George Eastman House in Rochester, New York, a renowned photography museum and research institution, set up an exhibition of Morath's work from October to December 1959. Here he was introduced to the American public as "a leading British industrial photographer."[85]

Attesting to the successful reception of his Kuwait photographs, Adolf Morath developed the thematic exhibition *Kuwait and Its People* shortly thereafter, which was based on the color photographs taken on the now three trips to Kuwait on behalf of the Kuwait Oil Company and the government of Kuwait, who eventually commissioned him directly, too. In November 1960, the show premiered also at the Ceylon Tea Centre, and the following May it was shown at the Near East Foundation in New York. The Foundation's invitation reads as follows:

Centers existed in Copenhagen and Melbourne. Moreover, later that year, KOC officials decided that "a new display of Morath photos will be prepared for exhibition at schools and other centres in the UK"; but it is not verifiable whether and to what extent the oil company supported, financed, or organized this or other of Morath's exhibitions outside of Kuwait. Meeting on PR matters with owners' representatives, July 10, July 29, September 20, 1957, Town Office, 1957.

80 "Camera Captures Industrial Drama: Colour Prints on Show," *Manchester Guardian*, May 28, 1957, n.p., reprint.

81 Hallett, "Other London Exhibitions," 65.

82 "Pictures of Power," *The Birmingham Post & Gazette*, January 29, 1957, 4; "Scenes from Oil Industry in London Exhibition," *The Birmingham Post & Gazette*, January 28, 1957, 7.

83 Adolf Morath and MoMA, January 7, January 8, January 22, 1958, letters, Adolf Morath Photography Bio File, Museum of Modern Art Archives.

84 The exhibition was held at the McLellan Galleries, Glasgow, February 3–11, 1959; see M. MacDonald, "Exhibition of Industrial Photographs: Brilliance of Works," *The Glasgow Herald*, February 4, 1959, n.p., reprint; "The Snapshot Schoolboy Is Now a Top Photographer," n.p.

85 The exhibition at George Eastman House was held from October 21 to December 15, 1959; see "Noted British Industrial Photographer, Adolf Morath, Exhibits at George Eastman House," news release, October 21, 1959, George Eastman House Archives, Rochester, New York.

> The Exhibition will show by means of large colour photographs the whole fascinating *story of Kuwait.* It will stress not the old Kuwait of herdsmen that has so often been depicted, but the Kuwait which has taken shape in the last few years, hand in hand with the development of the country's oil resources: the modern houses, the mosques, the schools and hospitals, the new harbour, the people at work and at play, the oil installations, the town of Kuwait at night and from the air.[86]

That the text echoes the KOC's *The Story of Kuwait* is surely no accident. Regardless of whether the KOC supported this exhibition or not, its narrative strongly reverberated in the text, which interlinked the "development" of the oil industry with Kuwait's urban transformation. Colorful images of the rapidly growing city were key evidence to substantiate this relationship.

Through exhibitions like these, Morath's color photographs of Kuwait reached a much wider audience than that initially targeted and accessible by the oil company. Most importantly though, through the images' transfer into the sphere of art and culture in form of museum exhibitions outside of Kuwait and beyond company properties, the corporate origin (and agenda) of the photographs was diffused, even neutralized, and eventually recast as authentic artistic expressions of a British photographer who had visited Kuwait.

4.5 Color Photography Showcases Petro-Modernity as Iridescence

The (color) photography of the Kuwait Oil Company has lastingly influenced the way in which Kuwait's recent past is remembered today. It was through the exciting and still expensive medium of color photography that the electric lights of mid-twentieth-century consumerism and modernization were suddenly switched on, bringing the urban transformation of Kuwait, vibrant and pretty, to light and life for (inter)national audiences. These pictures, among other images, still circulate in current debates on the modern era or oil period of Kuwait on social media platforms and private collections. In these contexts, they are often taken as authentic visual evidence of that period, usually without knowledge of their commission and their initial agenda. The color photography shot by Adolf Morath for the KOC is a testament to the strong impact of oil companies on the region's urban visual culture.

In the Arabian Peninsula, where the institutionalization of archival facilities and the continuous maintenance of collecting and preserving (visual) material remain challenging to this day, oil companies have emerged as important producers and distributors of professional photography. Often their collections reach back more than fifty years and cover a wide scope of motifs and sites far beyond the oil compound in excellent quality. These photographic archives speak to the current renewed and often nostalgic interest in

[86] Invitation to the exhibition *Kuwait and its People* at the Near East Foundation, New York, May 25, 1961, Adolf Morath Photography Bio File, Museum of Modern Art Archives (author's emphasis).

the (early) oil period of the region and will most likely continue to gain in importance as both cherished and contested repositories of social memory.

However, the more these images circulate as digital images, as mobile phone photos taken of Xerox scans of copies of the original photographic prints, the more difficult it becomes to historically contextualize them. The KOC photographs originated from a corporate environment with a concerted political, economic, and aesthetic agenda. They are not simply photographic representations of Kuwait in the late 1950s and early 1960s, they embody the picture of Kuwait that the oil company wanted to convey for its own multifold purposes. It is therefore important to carefully re-situate the photos in the oil archive and to disclose their provenance so as not to render oneself overpowered by the iridescent persuasiveness of the colorful images that hide just as much as they convey about what life was like in Kuwait.

In the case of Kuwait, the oil company created a highly polished, clean, and controlled image of Kuwait City. The appeal of these photographs, especially at the time when they were first published, is of course due to Adolf Morath's careful curation of the motifs, which showed the modern parts of Kuwait and not the remains of the pre-oil town or its destruction. However, color photography became crucial to creating a dynamic atmosphere and to conveying the proliferation of color according to the contemporary experience of the city evolving in the context of petro-modernity. Photographic representations of Kuwait City served to turn the city into a highly visible showcase of the seemingly unlimited dimensions of growth achievable when partaking in petro-modernity, metaphorized as a colorful concrete city springing from the desert. Color photographs in particular enabled, quite literally, the display in urban space of the new materials, colors, and textures provided for by petroleum.

By including images of Kuwait City's urban transformation in KOC publications such as *The Story of Kuwait* and thus into its corporate cosmos, the company instrumentalized the photographs to position itself as a patron of modern Kuwait, as its de facto motor of transformation—and petroleum as the fuel (and money) to do so. This way the KOC intended professional photography to challenge such allegations that the extractive nature of oil industries in general and of foreign-run companies such as the KOC in particular pursued the withdrawal of petroleum (and of capital) at any cost while readily accepting the drain and destruction of landscapes, societies, and local economies. The KOC's color photography are one example of the important role of urban images of the mid-twentieth-century Gulf cities as iridescent promotors of petro-modernity and petro-capitalism with a lasting effect on the future reputation of these cities.

The new photography of modern Kuwait not only benefitted the oil company's public relations efforts, but also delivered evidence to challenge notions of timelessness and standstill connected with Kuwait. It allowed them to push a new image, a new narrative of Kuwait as dynamic, progressive, and modern that also appealed to the government of Kuwait and other audiences outside of Kuwait. The appeal of this narrative most likely also accounts for the ongoing affection for these photos.

From the mid-1950s onward, the government of Kuwait started challenging the KOC's pole position in the field of image production about and branding of Kuwait in a way that both affirmed and deviated from the promotional strategy, metaphors, and style the company had initiated. Media such as the new government gazette and the first set of Kuwaiti postage stamps strove to manifest a new visual presence and rhetoric of the state in which the visual representation of the capital city played an equally important role.

5. THE PETRO-STATE, ITS POSTAGE STAMPS, AND POLITICAL ICONOGRAPHY

Having set the political agenda of creating "the finest city in the Middle East and the happiest State," the government of Kuwait had linked its efforts of state formation and nation-building with the urban transformation of Kuwait City.[1] In this context, the state was not only interested in actual physical outcomes but also in the visual repercussions of these developments. In the process of moving toward a cradle-to-grave welfare petrostate (which became known as the "Kuwaiti model"), an increasing number of sectors of daily life became regulated, institutionalized, and eventually monitored by the state. With the expansion of the bureaucratic body, the creation of new directorates (which later became ministries), and the issuance of new decrees and laws, the state embraced alternative ways of communicating and representing itself. New possibilities of manifesting the state in public and private spheres arose once new means of communication had become available in Kuwait; these included several large printing presses, the radio (1951), and, later, television (1961).[2] To communicate recently passed decrees and laws in an official manner beyond the *dīwāniyya* talks,[3] the government gazette *al-Kuwayt al-Yawm* (*Kuwait Today*) was established as a first step in 1954.

The scenario that unfolded on the cover of *al-Kuwayt al-Yawm* not only incorporated new modes of viewing and depicting Kuwait City (such as the aerial view) that were already circulating at the time, it also foreshadowed the new political iconography of the state that, by the end of the decade, emerged and sought to position Kuwait (City) as a potent petropolis equal to other petro-states. Neither the new flag design (1961) nor the new coat of arms (1956), which later resulted in the new national emblem (1962), were the medium where this iconography was most radically expressed. Foreshadowed on the

[1] "Preliminary Report on Development of Kuwait State," February 13, 1952, Kuwait State Development Board, file 101.

[2] For an insightful analysis of Kuwait's print culture, see Khaled Al Najdi and Rosalie Smith McCrea, "The History of Advertising Design in Kuwait: Post-Oil Cultural Shifts 1947–1959," *Journal of Design History* 25, no. 1 (2012).

[3] For an in-depth analysis of the role of the social gathering spaces known as *dīwāniyyāt* in Kuwaiti socio-political life, see James C. A. Redman, "The *Diwaniyya*: Guestroom Sociability and Bureaucratic Brokerage in Kuwait" (PhD diss., University of Utah, 2014), accessed January 31, 2021, https://core.ac.uk/download/pdf/276264928.pdf.

https://doi.org/10.1515/9783110714739-007

gazette's cover, the new iconography of Kuwait the oil state unfolded fully in the first series of Kuwaiti postage stamps (1959).

This first set of internationally valid stamps was not just aesthetically and iconographically impactful, it also created substantial political momentum, because the negotiation over the postal takeover from the British marked a decisive step toward political independence. In the following, the Kuwaiti government secured full control over postal communication with all nations and over its visual representation in the form of postage stamps. Stamps are not the most important political symbols per se; rather, their political character depends on the choice of motifs and on the historical context of their issue and reception. In the case of Kuwait, the 1959 series was certainly politically charged.

The main motifs of the stamps were the portrait of Shaykh Abdullah, wooden sailing boats, several newly built architectural structures (such as a desalination plant), and oil infrastructure (such as derricks). While the Kuwait Oil Company (KOC) strove to photographically integrate Kuwait City into its corporate sphere, the government of Kuwait—who already "owned" the city—visually claimed the oil infrastructure in order to position Kuwait as a petro-state. Both the KOC and the government relied on colorful "images of urban space and urban life ... to construct a visual argument about oil as a national resource."[4] In both cases, the translation of the modern built environment into widely circulating images worked "as evidence that these nation-states were plugged into the modern world" and were actively participating in petro-modernity.[5] But the KOC and the government employed their visual narratives to different ends.

The oil company used (color) photography to highlight the benefits of petroleum for the host country and for society in general by staging Kuwait City as vibrant metropolis due to oil (industrialization), thereby legitimizing its operations. The government was concerned with gaining international visibility as a confident, modernizing, and prosperous nation-state. To achieve this, it visually claimed the oil infrastructure and, thus, the oil production taking place on Kuwaiti territory in postage stamp motifs as a symbolic gesture of "nationalization." This occurred irrespective of the fact that the government was not in charge of production, not the owner of the oil industry, and that it received only 50 percent of the revenues generated by oil extraction. In the mid-twentieth century, issuing postage stamps with oil motifs became one of the key visual strategies of oil-producing and oil-refining countries to (inter)nationally showcase their relationship with petroleum in an assertive way. When presenting the new set in 1959, Kuwait embraced this visual tactic more than any other Arab petro-state. Leading up to this bold move, designing the government gazette was a decisive step.

[4] Damluji, "Petroleum's Promise," 135.

[5] Ibid., 9.

5.1 Kuwait's Image-World on the Cover of the Government Gazette

On December 11, 1954, the Kuwaiti government initiated *al-Kuwayt al-Yawm* (*Kuwait Today*) as its official weekly newspaper (*jarīda rasmīyya usbūʿīyya)*. With its characteristic bright blue cover design (which has remained almost unchanged), the gazette makes a strong visual appearance to this day (fig. 5.1).[6]

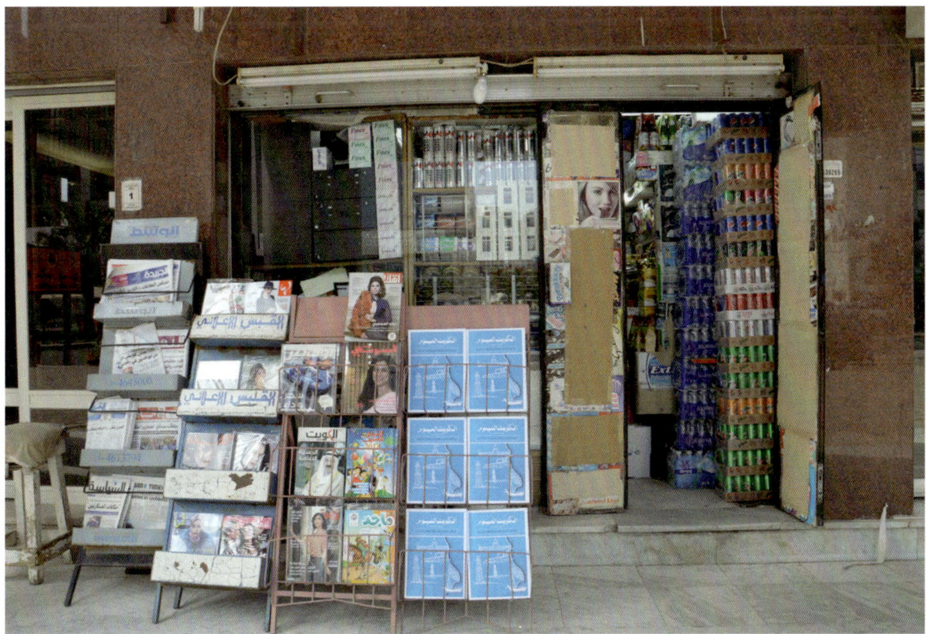

5.1 Display stand with issues of *al-Kuwayt al-Yawm* outside a *biqāla* (kiosk) in Sharq, Kuwait City.

The cover of *Kuwait Today* is divided into two sections (fig. 5.2). In the upper section, the title and subtitle are displayed. The lower, larger section consists of several white line drawings. From top to bottom, we find Shuwaikh Secondary School's main building as seen from the seaside (fig. 5.3);[7] an industrial complex consisting of three warehouses and smoking chimneys; two oil derricks viewed from different distances; and a sailing boat in

[6] See Al Najdi and Smith McCrea, "The History of Advertising Design in Kuwait," 58–60. Recent issues of the gazette no longer display the Kuwaiti coat of arms and the subtitle, but show the issue number and year instead.

[7] Shuwaikh Secondary School was first opened in 1953, although construction continued until 1957. In 1966, it became the country's first university. See Fabbri, Saragoça and Camacho, *Modern Architecture Kuwait*, 40–41.

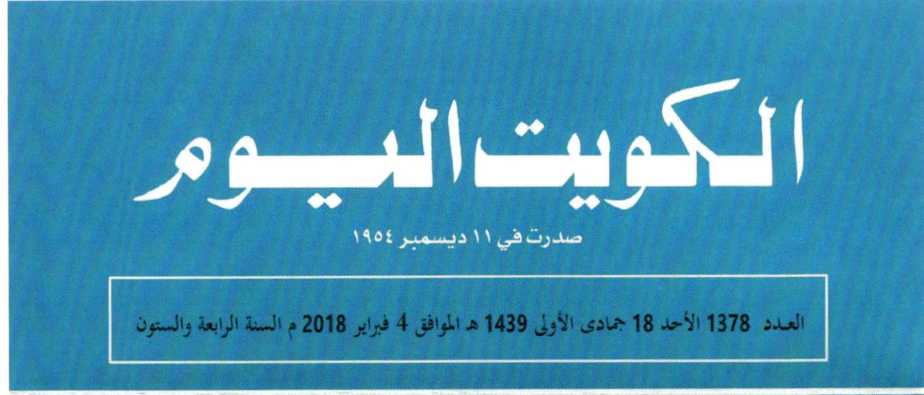

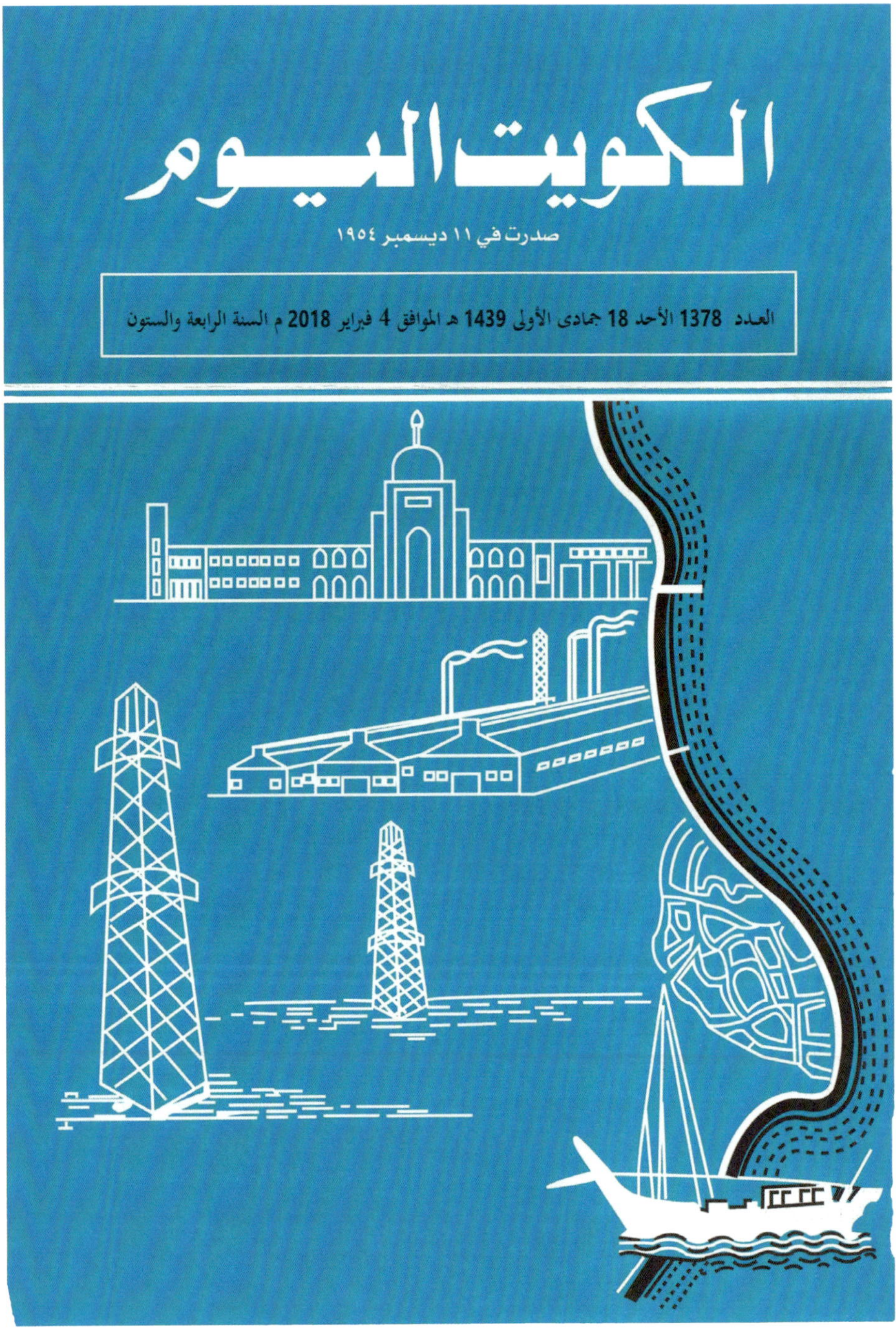

الكويت اليوم

صدرت في ١١ ديسمبر ١٩٥٤

العدد 1378 الأحد 18 جمادى الأولى 1439 هـ الموافق 4 فبراير 2018 م السنة الرابعة والستون

5.2 The cover of the government gazette *al-Kuwayt al-Yawm*, issue of February 4, 2018.

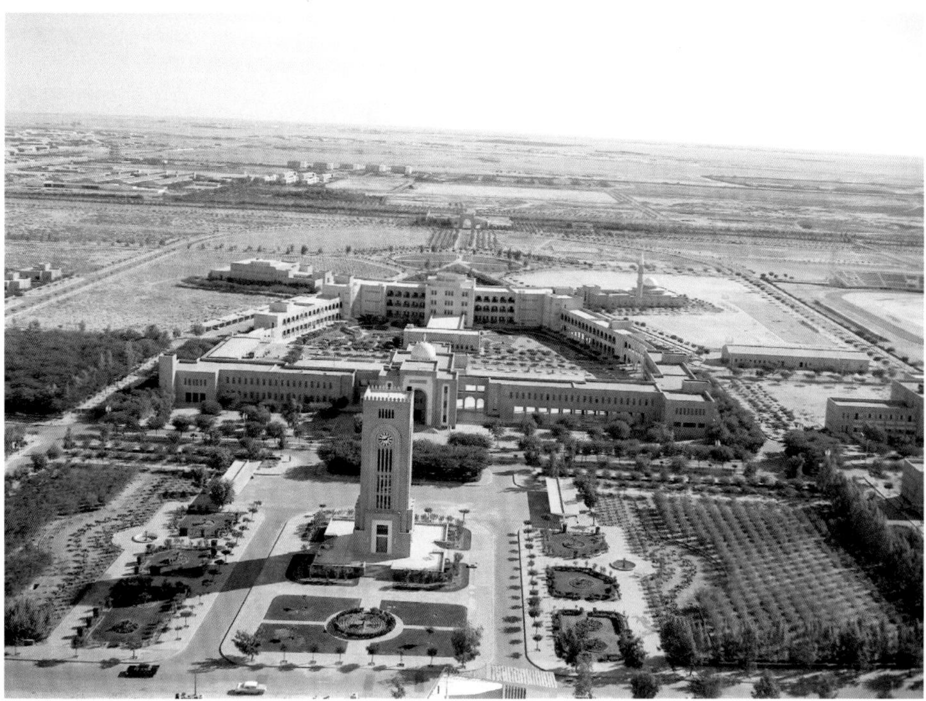

5.3 Oblique view of Shuwaikh Secondary School as seen from the sea. Undated (ca. early 1960s), photographer unknown.

the lower right corner.[8] This second section of the cover is divided into a land part and a seaside part by a curvy black-and-white line running downward to the bottom of the image. The curvy line represents the characteristically wave-shaped coastline along the spit of Kuwait Bay rotated by 90 degrees. The line divides this section into a seaside (left), where all buildings are situated, and an area afloat (right), the sea, where the dhow moors at the shore. Overall, the cover has remained the same over the decades, except for the Kuwaiti coat of arms that used to be integrated in the upper section (fig. 5.4). The coat of arms was in use between the 1940s and 1956 as both the official state symbol of Kuwait and the official coat of arms of the House of Sabah.[9]

[8] Khaled Al Najdi and Rosalie Smith McCrea claim that the building is a "simple illustration of the Al Seef [Seif] Palace"; Al Najdi and Smith McCrea, "The History of Advertising Design in Kuwait," 63. At the time, however, Seif Palace was not a symmetrical building. The drawing instead depicts Shuwaikh Secondary School, recognizable by its distinctive clock tower with a tapered cupola (see fig. 5.3).

[9] To the best of my knowledge, the government stopped issuing *al-Kuwayt al-Yawm* during the Iraqi invasion. Once publication was resumed, the cover no longer included the subtitle and the coat of arms, but the design has otherwise remained the same.

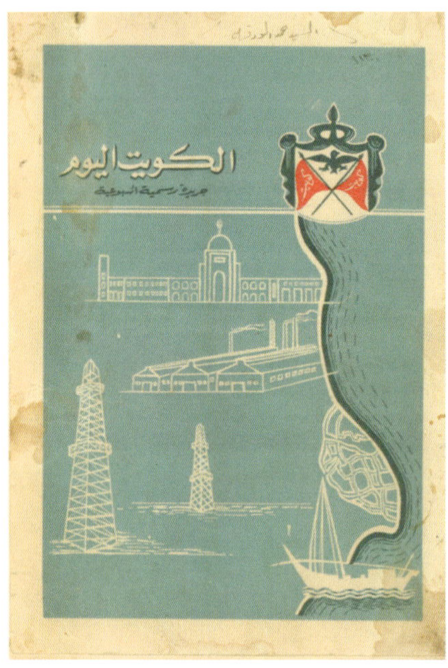

5.4 Historical cover of *al-Kuwayt al-Yawm*.

The cover clearly integrates the aerial view of the pre-oil town of Kuwait from the 1951 photomosaic and 1952 Master Plan: the black-and-white line alludes to the characteristic shape of the coastline and also references the way in which the "black" sea and the "light-gray" land appeared in the composite aerial photograph. Furthermore, the iconic form of the almond-shaped core of the pre-oil town nesting in the wave-shaped spit of Kuwait Bay is also included. However, Kuwait's road network shown here no longer follows the old alleyways; instead, it reflects the new road map proposed in the 1952 Master Plan. The cover of the gazette reproduces the iconic way of seeing and depicting Kuwait from above.

In addition, the design integrates elements that were not yet visible in the aerial survey or even the master plan. Apart from the new road network, two recent additions to the Kuwaiti (visionary) landscape were the secondary school and the industrial complex. Both of these were built in the neighborhood of Shuwaikh, which emerged on the basis of the master plan. The cover even maps these two elements with protruding bar-like piers at their approximate location along the coastline. According to this spatial location, the factory-like building could therefore be part of the developing industrial harbor or the power and desalination plant that opened in March 1953. In contrast to the accurate locations of the buildings, the oil derricks stand in a fictive proximity to the city instead of being located much further south, around the area of Ahmadi and the Burgan Oil Field. The fact that the oil derricks were the only elements not located realistically in this image foreshadows the way in which the government subsequently strove to include images of oil infrastructure within their (visual) sphere of influence irrespective of its actual affiliation, most notably in the 1959 set of postage stamps, even if this, at times, meant sacrificing the realism of such renditions.

Differently from the superimposed perpendicular aerial view, which organizes the lower section of the cover as a whole, the line drawings depict the built structures either frontally (the school) or as elevations (the factory, oil derricks)—in line with the fact that no updated photographic vertical view existed of them in 1954. Combining these different modes of viewing is highly innovative and might point to distinct photographic templates for each drawing. As a result, the cover appears like an "on-the-ground" (or, in Haraway's words, "situated") graphic update to the two seminal aerial views of Kuwait, the 1951 photomosaic and the 1952 Master Plan. The cover image both affirms the power of the aerial view as a representation of progress and petro-modernity in the early 1950s and exceeds the initial aerial survey images by updating them.

Under the headline of "Kuwait Today," these different viewpoints and elements merge to visualize Kuwait at the time of the gazette's establishment in 1954. The resulting up-to-date portrayal accords with the gazette's agenda to communicate the latest decrees and state news in its role as the official news platform of all departments and national committees. The image collage of *Kuwait Today* thematically referenced some of the most pressing issues of the time: education, industrialization, the oil industry, and the urban transformation of Kuwait City. The government's activity in these fields was expressed through recently built architecture and (oil) infrastructure as symbolic-pictorial evidence.

Subsequently, the case of producing Kuwaiti postage stamps gained political momentum because the Kuwaiti-British negotiation over the creation of original Kuwaiti stamps and over the postal handover became a catalyst for discussing Kuwaiti independence. This resulted from the fact that the new postage stamps broke with the long line of stamps previously used in Kuwait, which had been overprinted British and British-Indian stamps.

5.2 Decolonizing Postal Communication

On February 1, 1959, simultaneously with the issue of the new set of Kuwaiti stamps, the newly established Kuwaiti Administration of Posts, Telegraphs & Telephones took over the country's internal and external postal services from Britain after long and tedious negotiations.[10] This postal takeover had several important political implications.

One immediate and tangible outcome was that overprinted British stamps no longer represented Kuwait. Until 1959, overprinted British and British-Indian stamps had been

[10] If not stated otherwise, the information in this section is based on the following archival material: Transfer of Responsibility for Postal Services, Part 1, 1953–1959, Post 122/409, British Postal Agency Kuwait, The Royal Mail Archive, London; Transfer of Responsibility for Postal Services, Part 2, 1957–1959, Post 122/410, British Postal Agency Kuwait, The Royal Mail Archive, London.

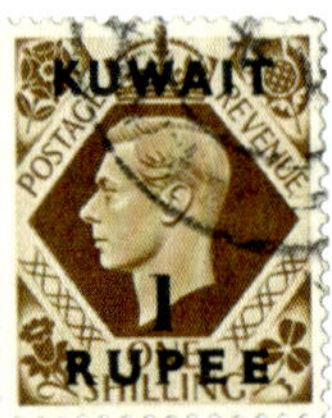

5.5 George VI definitive series, overprinted "KUWAIT" and "RUPEE," issued in 1937.

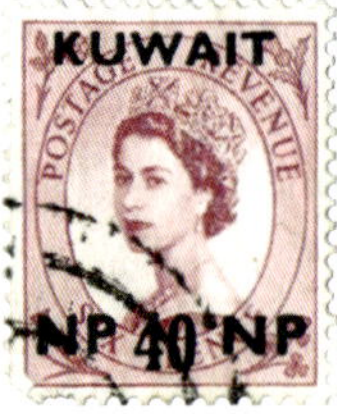

5.6 Queen Elizabeth II issue, overprinted "Kuwait" and "NP" (naye paise), ca. 1956.

used in Kuwait, indicating the respective political jurisdiction Kuwait was subjected to as a quasi-protectorate of Britain. Issued until India's independence in 1947 by the British Government of India and subsequently by the General Post Office (GPO) in London, these regular stamp sheets, for instance the George VI series and Queen Elisabeth II series, were overprinted with the word "KUWAIT" and, partly, with a different denomination and value, placing the letters and numbers carefully so as not to interfere with the monarch's head (figs. 5.5, 5.6). With the original Kuwaiti set of 1959, the word "KUWAIT" finally became an integral part of the stamp design, and it was no longer the sovereign of Britain but of Kuwait whose portrait vouched for the validity of the stamp.

Secondly, the postal takeover initiated Kuwait's independence because the handover in effect dissolved the British-Kuwaiti Agreement of 1899 that had made Kuwait a quasi-protectorate of Britain. The treaty had resulted in the additional 1904 Post Office Agreement with Britain, which had defined a British postal monopoly in Kuwait from that point onward.[11] Now, in order to run the postal services, the Kuwaiti government was obliged to apply for membership with the Universal Postal Union (UPU) as either a sovereign state or a British protectorate—legally, Kuwait was neither of them—so that negotiating the political status of Kuwait became a pressing matter.[12] Eventually, the debates surrounding the postal takeover and Kuwait's status eventually entered into a larger debate regarding British decolonization in the Gulf and Kuwait's independence in particular. However, on the Kuwaiti side, the initial incentive for discussing a postal takeover had not been anti-imperialist or national interests per se, but rather a dispute over the censorship of Israeli mail in Kuwait in 1956.

Following an appeal by the Arab League to cease mail communication with Israel in the context of the Suez Crisis, around mid-1956, Shaykh Abdullah demanded the boycott of mail to and from Israel through the British-controlled postal services in his country. The British found themselves in a dilemma: not acquiescing to the Shaykh's demand

[11] The Post Office Agreement, signed February 28, 1904, by Shaykh Mubarak, reads as follows: "As the British Government has agreed in accordance with my desire and for the benefit of traders to establish a post office at Koweit [*sic*], I on my part agree not to allow the establishment here of a post office by any other Government. I accordingly write this undertaking on behalf of myself and my successors." Reprinted in Visit [to the Gulf] by Brigadier K. S. Holmes and Mr. T. U. Meyer, January 1957, 1956–1958, Post 122/3304, British Postal Agencies, Persian Gulf Agency, The Royal Mail Archive, London.

[12] The Universal Postal Union (UPU) was founded by twenty-two states, among them Egypt and the Ottoman Empire, in 1874 in Bern, Switzerland.

would endanger their position in Kuwait, but acquiescing would strain British-Israeli relations. Eventually, it was suggested that Kuwait should take over the internal postal services, thereby transferring the responsibility (and the blame) for suspending postal services between Israel and Kuwait to the Kuwaiti government itself. By transferring the postal services only partly (internal postal services were to be managed by Kuwait, the external remained with Britain), the British would continue to run and control the delivery of mail between Britain and Kuwait but would not be held responsible for any local delivery stop or censorship of mail.[13] Rejecting the half-baked proposal, the Kuwaiti representatives successfully pressed for a complete transfer over the period of one year. The Foreign Office consented, presumably wary of adding more fuel to the fire of nationalist, Pan-Arabist but especially anti-British sentiment stirred up by the ongoing Suez Crisis that the Kuwait Oil Company also had problems fighting. In London, the Suez debacle triggered "the first serious re-assessment of the British presence in the Gulf" and, eventually, British withdrawal from the Gulf in the following decades.[14] However, losing access to oil in Kuwait, Britain's single largest supplier at the time, was not an option. The best way to safeguard economic and political stability in Kuwait, British officials argued, was therefore to foster Kuwait's independence from other countries' influence. This also implied a disconnection from Britain, as Kuwait's status as a semi-protectorate was "widely regarded as 'imperialistic and anachronistic.'"[15]

While negotiating the terms of the transfer, the British tried to secure their interests; these were listed as: "(a) the maintenance of an efficient postal service and of British advice; (b) that the Egyptians do not take over; and (c) Kuwaiti goodwill."[16] Above all, sustaining well-running postal services meant safeguarding communication between the British representatives and companies active in Kuwait and Britain, among them the Kuwait Oil Company and many construction companies. Considering the Suez Crisis, the British were anxious to keep Kuwait out of the Egyptian sphere of (anti-British) influence and to deliver the best postal service possible. The postal services had become an important political issue not only in order to maintain influence, but also to secure Britain's reputation by ensuring that, at the time of the handover, "the Kuwaitis will not be able to improve upon the service

[13] Memorandum on Kuwait Postal Censorship, June 1956, Transfer of Responsibility for Postal Services, Part 1.

[14] Simon C. Smith, "Britain's Decision to Withdraw from the Persian Gulf: A Pattern Not a Puzzle," *The Journal of Imperial and Commonwealth History* 44, no. 2 (2016): 330. On the decolonization of British-held territories in the Middle East and especially the Persian Gulf, see also David George Boyce, *Decolonisation and the British Empire, 1775–1997* (Basingstoke: Macmillan, 1999), 150–76; John Darwin, *Britain and Decolonisation: The Retreat from Empire in the Post-War World* (Basingstoke: Macmillan, 1988).

[15] Smith, "Britain's Decision to Withdraw from the Persian Gulf," 331–32.

[16] Foreign Office to Political Agency Kuwait, telegram, January 10, 1957, Transfer of Responsibility for Postal Services, Part 1

previously provided by the British Post Office."[17] To this end, hoping to prolong the process and to improve British postal performance in the meantime, the British subjected Kuwait's postal takeover to a set of conditions. These conditions were: new Kuwaiti stamps had to be ready in time, their design and printing had to be organized and paid for by Kuwait; Kuwaiti personnel had to be trained in Britain for at least one year; and an adequate building had to be provided to set up a new post office.

Between 1957 and 1959, Kuwaiti personnel were trained in Britain, Kuwaiti stamps were developed, and several new post offices were opened across town, among them the new General Post Office in Fahad al-Salem Street. On February 1, 1959, Khalid Abdullatif Al-Abdul Razzak, Director General of the Administration of Posts, Telegraphs & Telephones, officially inaugurated the General Post Office and introduced the 1959 set of stamps. In his speech, he pointed to the successful accomplishment of architectural facilities (post offices) and the design of the equipment necessary to perform postal services (stamps, cancellations) and concluded that "we have done our best to provide our dear State with the dignity and honour it deserves among our sister Arab States and the other States."[18] Razzak continued by saying that that particular day, which also coincided with the first anniversary of the United Arab Republic, marked "the start of a new regime for our existence and for the liberty of our Dear state."[19] Demonstrating Kuwait's successful takeover of the postal services was crucial to Kuwait's decolonization, to becoming a modern nation-state, and to performing as one. Postage stamps as political symbols were vital for claiming a position of being equal among others ("our sister Arab States and the other States") and for establishing a distinct (and independent) national identity ("new regime") that was to be visually communicated.[20]

5.3 The First Set of Kuwaiti Postage Pictures

The 1959 set of Kuwaiti postage stamps was a milestone (fig. 5.7).[21] It was the first set of stamps depicting motifs from Kuwait that was issued by Kuwaiti authorities and that was valid for local and international use. The stamps functioned as Kuwaiti political symbols despite the fact that the thirteen-piece set was designed and printed by the renowned

[17] Miss King, General Post Office London, to D. J. M. Lashmar, British Postal Agencies Bahrain, July 20, 1956, Post Office Accommodation, Part 3, 1953–1956, Post 122/1063, British Postal Agency Kuwait, The Royal Mail Archive, London.

[18] Khalid Abdullatif Al-Abdul Razzak's opening speech, February 1, 1959, English translation provided by British post officials, Transfer of Responsibility for Postal Services, Part 2.

[19] Ibid. The UAR's anniversary resulted in pro-Nasserist mobilization in Kuwait and many other places; see John T. Chalcraft, *Popular Politics in the Making of the Modern Middle East* (Cambridge, UK: Cambridge University Press, 2016), 345.

[20] See Anderson, *Imagined Communities*, 81.

[21] A first analysis of the Kuwaiti set and oil stamps from the MENA region was published in: Hindelang, "Oil Media: Changing Portraits of Petroleum in Visual Culture Between the US, Kuwait, and Switzerland."

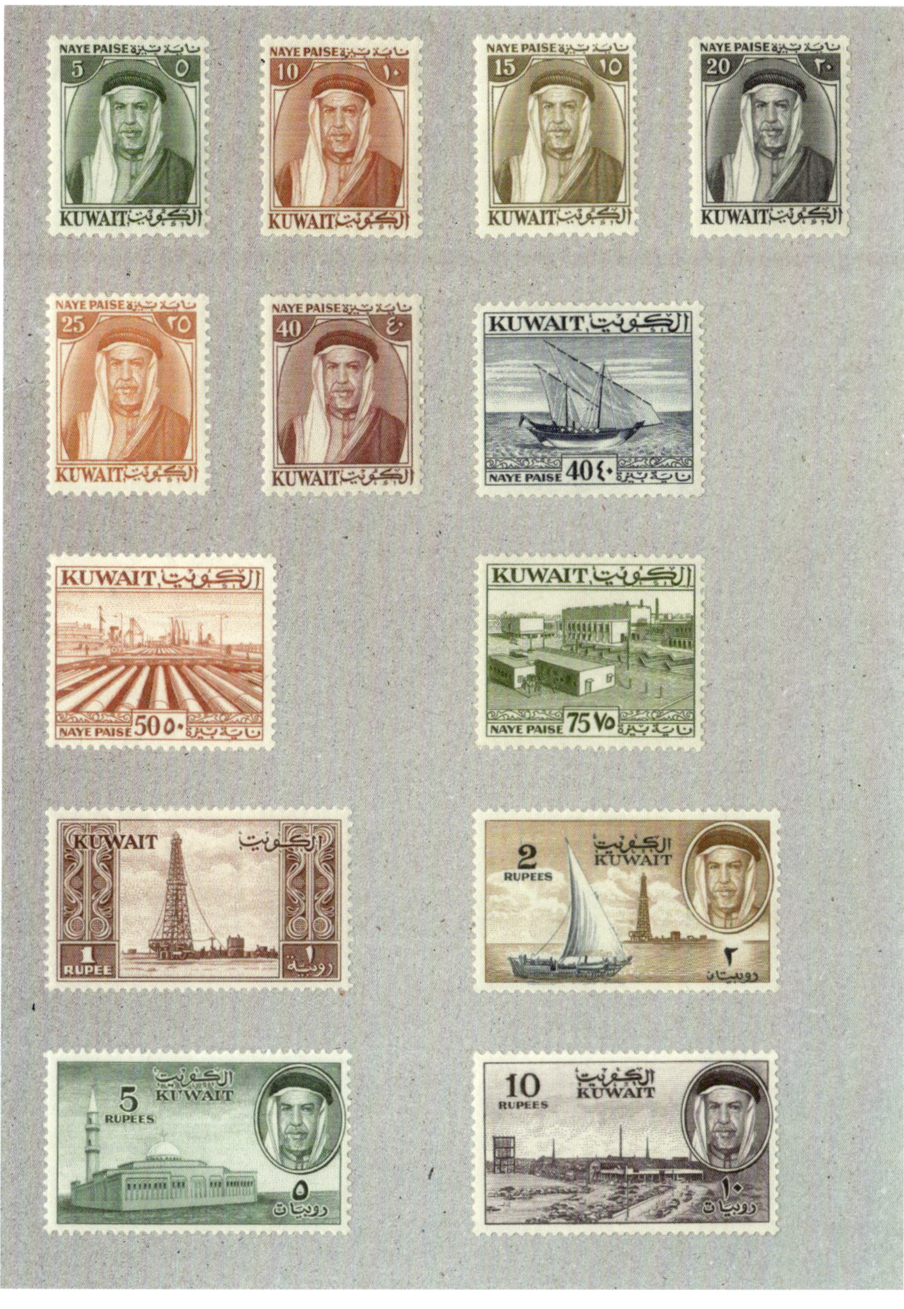

5.7 The 1959 series of Kuwaiti definitives. Shaykh Abdullah (5 to 40 naye paise); two-masted dhow (40 np); the oil harbor Mina al-Ahmadi (50 np); power and desalination plant (75 np); oil rig (1 rupee); dhow and oil rig (2 rupees); mosque of Shuwaikh Secondary School (5 rupees); Safat Square (10 rupees).

British stamp company Thomas De La Rue in London, a company that British officials had promoted in order to secure the commission for a British firm in a similar way to the commission of British urban planners for Kuwait's first master plan.[22] Given the difficulty that details and documents about the design process are extremely scarce and the names of designers and etchers are unknown, the final stamp designs are the most important material for an analysis of Kuwait's new political iconography.[23] These richly detailed postage pictures invite an analysis that considers them not merely from a semiotic point of view (as most research on stamps usually does) but regards them as aesthetic-symbolic objects.

Stamps as Aesthetic-Symbolic Objects

Since the nineteenth century and the issue of the very first stamp, the British Penny Black (1840), postage stamps have followed a more or less internationally standardized format. Perforated on all sides, the stamp's face usually displays the name of the issuing country and its value, making it a receipt of what the sender paid for transport to the issuing body. In the past, the reverse was usually gummed using dextrin, gum arabic, or, since roughly the 1960s, synthetic gums like polyvinyl alcohol (a petroleum derivative); today, most stamps are self-adhesive.[24] Stamps are of rectangular format and of very small size; they often use special typography, which in the case of a non-Roman script like Arabic is often accompanied by the same word(s) in Roman letters. Stamp designs can include ornamentation or graphics in combination with abstract, numerical, or pictorial images. They are, in effect, "miniature prints with a very high circulation."[25]

Philatelists classify stamps dominated by a picture other than a portrait, heraldic element, or number as *pictorial* stamps.[26] Due to their elaborate color printing, pictorials

[22] Gawain W. Bell, Political Agent, to D. M. H. Riches, Foreign Office, March 7, 1957, Transfer of Responsibility for Postal Services, Part 1. Thomas De La Rue, one of the oldest banknote manufacturers and stamp printing companies, started printing stamps for the United Kingdom as early as 1855. Quickly, stamp commissions for British colonies and protectorates as well as for Italy and the Confederate States of America followed. Having developed a new surface printing technique, the company continued to hold a market-leading position in the second half of the twentieth century. For a detailed history of the company see Frank Walton, *The De La Rue Collection,* 6 vols. (London: The Royal Philatelic Society London, 2014).

[23] Unfortunately, Thomas De La Rue dissolved and sold the company archives in the 1970s. Email by Paul Skinner, Lead Curator of the Philatelic Collections, British Library, to the author, October 6, 2017. Except for Ramzi Kayello, who designed an oil commemoration stamp in 1966, no artist involved in stamp designs for Kuwait for the period 1958–1985 has been recorded according to my knowledge.

[24] Jane Ormrod, "Response to 'What Is the Glue on the Back of Postage Stamps and Envelopes Made From?,'" *The Guardian*, 2011, accessed January 31, 2021, https://www.theguardian.com/notesandqueries/query/0,-1680,00.html.

[25] Gottfried Gabriel, "Ästhetik und Politische Ikonographie der Briefmarke," *Zeitschrift für Ästhetik und Allgemeine Kunstwissenschaft* 54, no.2 (2009): 190 (author's translation).

[26] Philately is the practice of collecting, systematically organizing, and studying postage stamps and other related material like stationery and cancellations.

are costly and therefore often issued as commemorative or special issues rather than as regular series, which are called *definitives*. Yet, the 1959 Kuwaiti issue was a set of pictorial definitives with eight individual designs that were extremely well executed and detailed due to the costly and sophisticated technique of etching used here. Even devoid of archival information about the design process, it is clear that the set was made with great professional care in order to deliver an excellent result according to stamp printing standards of the time.

Despite their obvious aesthetic qualities, postage stamps are hardly ever analyzed as aesthetic-symbolic objects. Almost all stamp studies that were recently published within various disciplines and fields focus on topics such as semiotics, political representation and propaganda, identity construction, and iconography.[27] The few scholars that have discussed the stamps of modern Arab countries mirror these thematic emphases.[28] Virtually no studies apply a formal or stylistic image analysis, and art-historical approaches in general are mostly absent.[29] This is especially surprising given that, in the first half of the twentieth century, influential intellectuals of art history and cultural studies like Aby Warburg, Nikolaus Pevsner, and Walter Benjamin recognized stamps as aesthetic objects with political-iconographical and historical relevance, and appreciated them as such.[30] Their writings have recently received renewed attention.

[27] Recent studies that also provide valuable general reflections on stamps include: Pierre Smolarski, René Smolarski, and Silke Vetter-Schultheiss, eds., *Gezähnte Geschichte: Die Briefmarke als historische Quelle*, Post-Wert-Zeichen 1 (Göttingen: V&R Unipress, 2019); Stanley D. Brunn, "Stamps as Messengers of Political Transition," *Geographical Review* 101, no. 1 (2011); Daniel Hammett, "Envisaging the Nation: The Philatelic Iconography of Transforming South African National Narratives," *Geopolitics* 17, no. 3 (2012); Alexander Hanisch-Wolfram, *Postalische Identitätskonstruktionen: Briefmarken als Medien totalitärer Propaganda*, Kommunikationswissenschaft und Publizistik 95 (Frankfurt: Peter Lang, 2006); Peter Jones, "Posting the Future: British Stamp Design and the 'White Heat' of a Technological Revolution," *Journal of Design History* 17, no. 2 (2004); Hans-Jürgen Köppel, *Politik auf Briefmarken: 130 Jahre Propaganda auf Postwertzeichen* (Düsseldorf: Droste, 1971).

[28] See Roswitha Badry, "Posta," in *Encyclopaedia of Islam: Second Online Edition*, ed. Peri J. Bearman et al. (Leiden: Brill, 2012), accessed April 17, 2020, https://doi.org/10.1163/1573-3912_islam_SIM_6138; Yuka Kadoi, "Postage Stamps in Islamic Art," *Grove Art Online*, July 2, 2009, accessed January 31, 2021, https://doi.org/10.1093/gao/9781884446054.article.T2082293; Donald M. Reid, "The Postage Stamp: A Window on Saddam Hussein's Iraq," *Middle East Journal* 47, no. 1 (1993); Roswitha Badry and Johannes Niehoff, *Die ideologische Botschaft von Briefmarken: Dargestellt am Beispiel Libyens und des Iran* (Tübingen: Niehoff, 1988); Emmanuel Sivan, "The Arab Nation-State: In Search of a Usable Past," *Middle East Review* 19, no. 3 (1987); Donald M. Reid, "The Symbolism of Postage Stamps: A Source for the Historian," *Journal of Contemporary History* 19, no. 2 (April 1984); Harry W. Hazard, "Islamic Philately as an Ancillary Discipline," in *The World of Islam: Studies in Honour of Philip K. Hitti*, ed. James Kritzeck and Richard B. Winder, repr. ed. (London: Macmillan, [1959] 1960).

[29] Gottfried Gabriel also notes the scarcity of art historical research on stamps and discusses the few existing ones in detail; see Gabriel, "Ästhetik und Politische Ikonographie der Briefmarke," 186, fn. 19.

[30] Ibid., 184–85; Nikolaus Pevsner, "Style in Stamps: A Century of Postal Design," *Country Life*, May 4, 1940, as quoted in Keith Jeffery, "Crown, Communication and the Colonial Post: Stamps, the Monarchy and the

Art historian Frank Zöllner, for example, traces the historical relationship between postage stamps and art historiography by examining the writing, thinking, and stamp collecting activities of Aby Warburg, an ardent philatelist.[31] Warburg's logic of organizing postage stamps correlates strongly with his concept of "pictorial argumentation" (*Bildargumentation*) and with the organizational system of his most famous project, the *Mnemosyne Atlas*. In both cases Warburg focused on classically inspired allegorical, symbolical, and heraldic imagery, state iconography and portraits of rulers—in other words, classical stamp motifs. Warburg described postage stamps as the "pictorial language of world traffic" (*Bildersprache des Weltverkehrs*), which clearly shows the importance he attributed to their mobilized visual expression.[32] Apart from Warburg, another prominent philatelist and influential intellectual in this field was none other than Walter Benjamin, who called stamps the "business cards of states," thereby highlighting their self-representative value for communication with other (nation-)states.[33]

Reconnecting with these early efforts of recognizing postage stamps as aesthetic-symbolic objects with a political iconography, the following detailed description of the 1959 Kuwaiti set of stamps provides the necessary foundation for analyzing their potential as symbols of a new political aesthetic of Kuwait's petro-modernity and as a pictorial language of communication with other petro-states, and, generally, people.

The 1959 Kuwaiti Stamps and Their Templates

Each of the thirteen definitives which comprise the 1959 set displays the country name (Kuwait) and the denomination (rupee and naye paise) in Roman (English) and Arabic script (see fig. 5.7);[34] the value of each stamp is given in (Hindu-)Arabic and Eastern Arabic numerals. Following the respective reading direction, the English is always located

British Empire," *The Journal of Imperial and Commonwealth History* 34, no. 1 (2006): 46.

[31] Frank Zöllner, "Philatelie, politische Philatelie," *Frankfurter Allgemeine Zeitung*, June 27, 2012, 4; Frank Zöllner, "'Im Geistesverkehr der Welt': Aby Warburg und die Philatelie," *Das Archiv*, no. 3 (2016): 14–21. On Aby Warburg and stamps, see Aby Warburg, "Die Funktion des Briefmarkenbildes im Geistesverkehr der Welt (1927)," in *Aby Warburg: Bilderreihen und Ausstellungen*, ed. Uwe Fleckner and Isabella Woldt, Aby Warburg Gesammelte Schriften vol. 2.2 (Berlin: Akademie Verlag, 2011); Ulrich Raulff, "Der aufhaltsame Aufstieg einer Idee: Warburg und die Vernuft der Republik," in *Wilde Energien: Vier Versuche zu Aby Warburg*, ed. Ulrich Raulff, Göttinger Gespräche zur Geschichtswissenschaft 19 (Göttingen: Wallstein, 2003).

[32] Aby Warburg and Edwin Redslob, "Die Briefmarke als Kulturdokument," essay published in *Hamburger Nachrichten*, August 15, 1927, and reprinted in Gabriel, "Ästhetik und Politische Ikonographie der Briefmarke," 200–01. Warburg even intended to write a book on the cultural history of the stamp and designed an air mail stamp for Germany in 1926. See Zöllner, "Philatelie, politische Philatelie," 4.

[33] Walter Benjamin, "Briefmarken-Handlungen," in *Walter Benjamin: Werke und Nachlaß, Kritische Gesamtausgabe: Einbahnstraße (1928)*, vol. 8, ed. Detlev Schöttker and Steffen Haug (Frankfurt: Suhrkamp, 2009), 186.

[34] On the use of different Arabic calligraphies for later issues of Kuwaiti postage stamps, see Neil Donaldson, "Arabica Bracadabra," *Gibbons Stamp Monthly* 1 (January 1970).

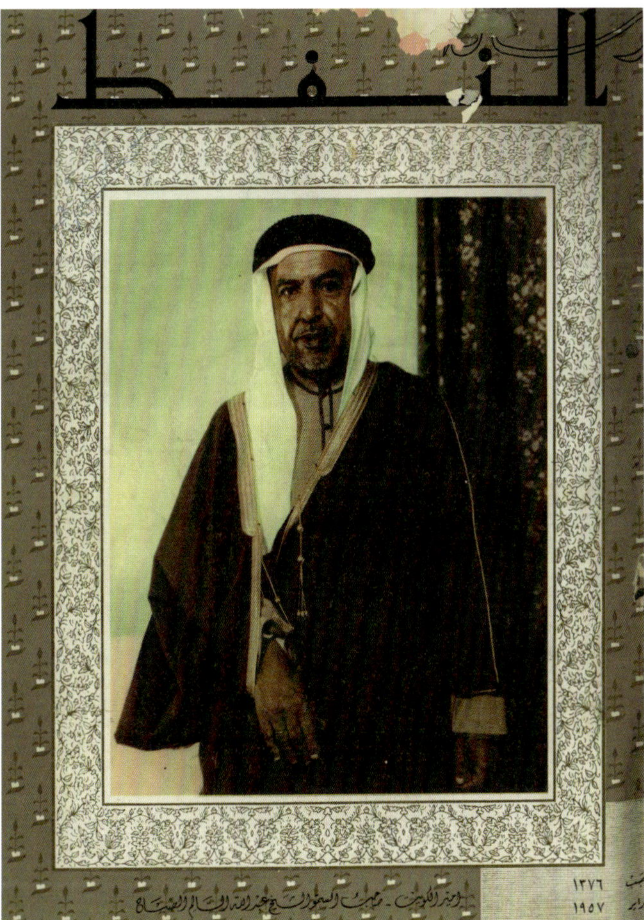

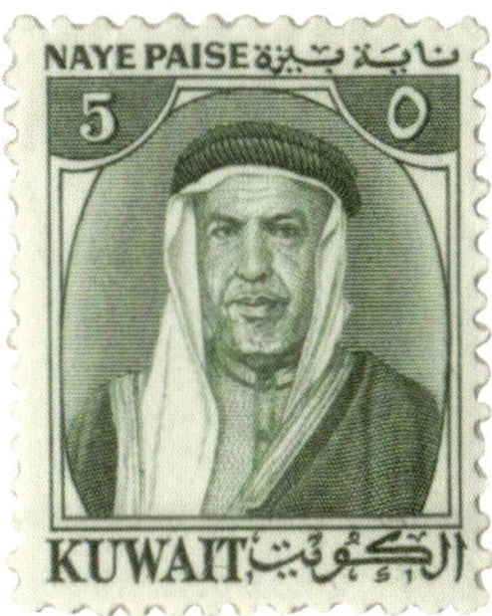

5.8 Green five naye paise stamp in comparison with the cover of the first issue of the Kuwait Oil Company's Arabic-language monthly *Risālat al-Nafṭ* (*Message of Oil*), February 1957, with the portrait of Shaykh Abdullah photographed by Adolf Morath.

on the left-hand side and the Arabic on the right-hand side. Before the introduction of the national currency (dinar and fils) in 1960, Kuwait used the Indian rupee and its smaller denomination, the naye paise.[35] The 1959 Kuwaiti set shows a portrait of Shaykh Abdullah on the six smallest values, while each of the remaining seven stamps have a different motif.[36] Overall, the set features four compositional schemes: in the first group, the five,

[35] Most of the Persian Gulf used the Indian rupee until, in May 1959, an amended version of the Indian rupee especially for the Persian Gulf region that was equivalent in value to the regular Indian rupee was issued. The new rupee was implemented as part of a strategy to stop illegal trading. See for example Peter Symes, "Gulf Rupees: A History," Reference Site for Islamic Banknotes (website), accessed January 31, 2021, https://web.archive.org/web/20030630072004/http://www.islamicbanknotes.com/gulfrupees%20(article).htm.

[36] The rose claret forty naye paise portrait stamp was withdrawn two weeks after the set was issued, apparently because its color was too similar to the red ten naye paise stamp and because the set should not contain

ten, fifteen, twenty, twenty-five, and forty naye paise stamps depict the full-face portrait of Shaykh Abdullah, Kuwait's ruler (fig. 5.8).[37] The oval-shaped portrait of his head and shoulders shows him wearing the official formal dress in which he was photographed on many occasions, including by Adolf Morath. Most likely it was a portrait of the Shaykh that Morath took for the cover of the KOC's Arabic-language monthly *Risālat al-Nafṭ* (*Message of Oil*) that served as template for the stamp, which was first released in February 1957 on the anniversary of the ruler's accession.[38] This formal dress consists of a dark robe with golden embroidery along the seams and golden piping (*bisht dhahabī*) above a lighter colored *thawb* with a banded collar and button facing, and a headdress of light cloth (*ghutra*) with a dark headrope (*ʿiqāl*).[39] Abdullah's formal appearance is furthermore strengthened by his austere look and the presentation of the image: the oval portrait is overlayered by a rectangular frame, with quarter-circles in the upper corners carrying the denomination in white numbers against a dark background. In a similar way to photographs, the posture and double framing "distinguish relations between photographic space and the viewer's space."[40] The portrait thereby creates a timeless distance from the viewer that seemingly observes the rules of protocol of how to encounter the ruler. Below the image, the writing *Kuwait* and *al-Kuwayt* acts as the title of the stamp. It is through this combination of words and image that Shaykh Abdullah came to personify Kuwait on the first official Kuwaiti stamp.

The forty, fifty, and seventy-five naye paise stamps form the second compositional group. Each of them contains a framed image in landscape format. At the top, a bar displays the country name in Arabic and English and the prominent typographies visually link the writing with the illustrations. Below the picture, two smaller bars contain ornamentations (upper bar) and the denomination in words (lower bar). The numerical denomination is stated centrally across both bars.

The dark blue forty naye paise stamp shows a traditional two-masted dhow sailing on the open sea, with thin lines indicating the movement of the waves (fig. 5.9). The ship is depicted as if viewed from another boat beside it. The image of this wooden sailing vessel, a type called *būm*, references the pre-oil economy and maritime lifeworld of Kuwait. Khaled Alabdulmughni, a Kuwaiti philatelist, suggests that the design template for this stamp was a photograph of a miniature boat, a type called *sambūk*, on display in

two forty naye paise stamps.

[37] A year earlier, a first set of three stamps with the ruler's portrait that were identical in design to the 1959 ones and also printed by De La Rue had been issued. The 1958 set was valid for local use only and served as a pre-stage to the full set that was issued a year later.

[38] I thank Khaled Alabdulmughni for pointing this out and for providing the historical visual material.

[39] This formal combination was already more "simplified and standardized" in its decoration than outfits still worn a decade earlier, even though the basic elements were the same. Bruce Ingham, "Men's Dress in the Arabian Peninsula: Historical and Present Perspectives," in *Languages of Dress in the Middle East*, ed. Nancy Lindisfarne-Tapper and Bruce Ingham (Richmond: Curzon, 1997), 50–51.

[40] Edwards, "Material Beings," 68.

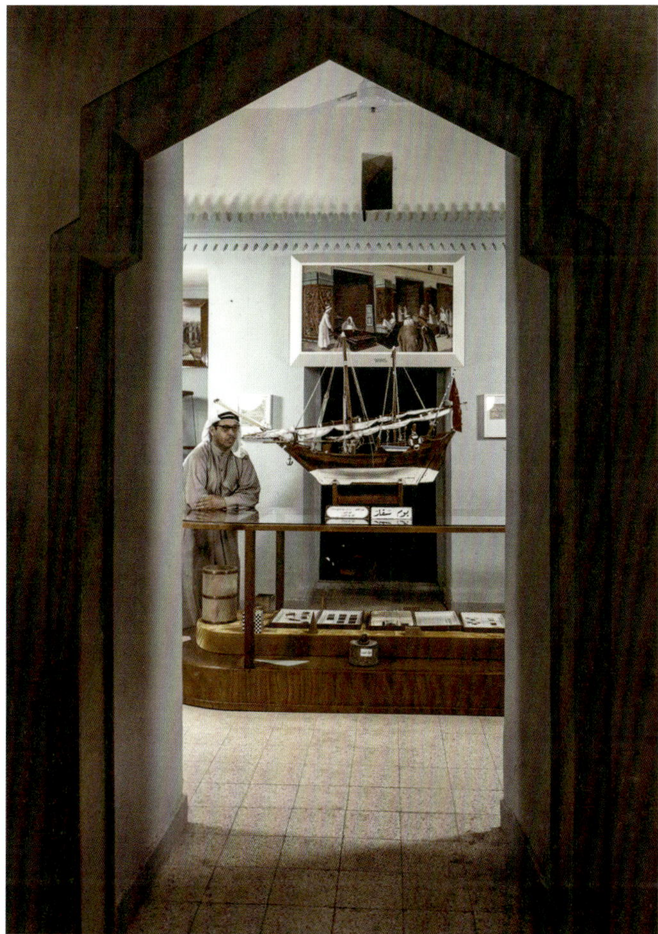

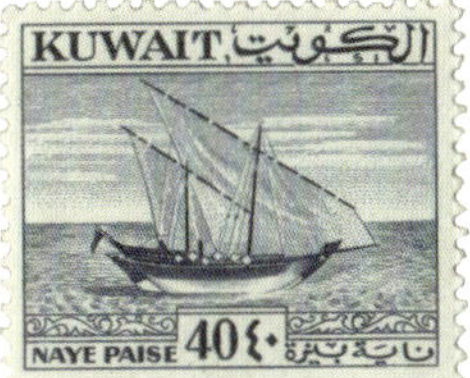

5.9 Forty naye paise stamp in comparison with an Adolf Morath photograph from the KOC archive that shows a wooden boat model on display in the National Museum in Kuwait City.

the National Museum, probably similar to the model boat that Morath photographed at the museum.[41] Like the heritagization process of photographic and urban isolation that turned the town wall gates into heritage vistas, the dhow, both as model and as stamp, is also pictorially decontextualized and severed from its former socioeconomic function.

While the forty naye paise stamp highlights the sea, the dark red fifty naye paise is dedicated to petroleum (fig. 5.10). The stamp shows a very detailed view of the oil-loading

[41] Khaled Alabdulmughni describes the model boat as a boat type called *sambūk* rather than *būm*, but Alan Villier notes that the term *sambūk* was often used to refer to all kinds of sailing vessels, therefore serving as an umbrella term. Khaled Alabdulmughni, "60 Years Since Issuing the Shaykh Abdullah Al-Salem Stamp: Boycotting Israel—Postal Service Nationalization," *al-Būsṭa (al-Posta)*, no. 40 (May 2018): 45; Villiers, *Sons of Sindbad*, 365 (appendix 1: Types of Arab Dhows).

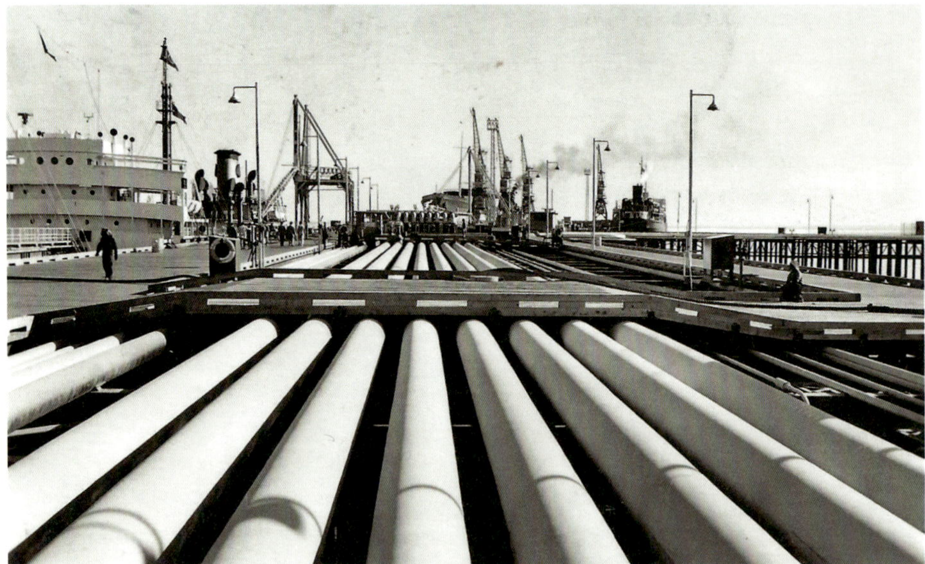

5.10 Fifty naye paise stamp in comparison with undated postcard showing Abdel Razzaq Badran's black-and-white photograph *View of Mina al-Ahmadi, the Kuwait Oil Port at Ahmadi*, 1952.

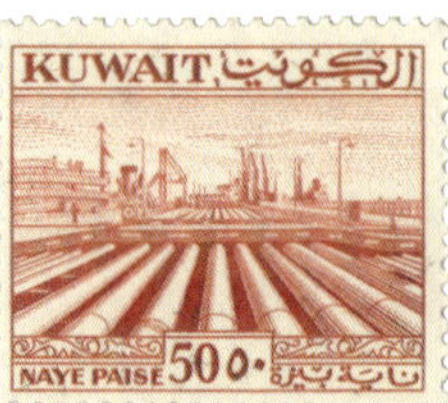

pier at Mina al-Ahmadi, the oil harbor of Kuwait located around forty kilometers south of Kuwait City. Along the jetty, oil tankers are berthed for loading and several cranes rise in the background. The linear perspective of pipelines running along the mile-long pier into the Gulf draws the viewer into the image and toward the vanishing point. Compared with historical photographs, however, the viewpoint indicates that the picture was taken while standing on one of the pedestrian bridges crossing the pipelines and looking landward. Photographs of the oil-loading jetty, often referred to as "the largest oil terminal in the world," appeared in almost every publication and every article on Kuwait and its oil industry at the time.[42] Kuwaiti collector Ali AlRais and others have established proof that the stamp's photographic template was based on a picture taken by Palestinian photographer Abdel Razzaq Badran, the owner of the famous Studio Badran in Kuwait City, in 1952.[43] Prior to proliferating as a stamp motif, the image appeared on the cover

[42] C. A. Philip Southwell, "Kuwait," *Journal of the Royal Society of Arts* 102, no. 4914 (1953): 35.

[43] Abdel Razzaq Badran (1917–2003) was born in Haifa, Palestine, and studied at the Faculty of Applied Arts in Cairo, where he graduated in 1940. Upon moving to Kuwait, he opened a photography studio, Studio

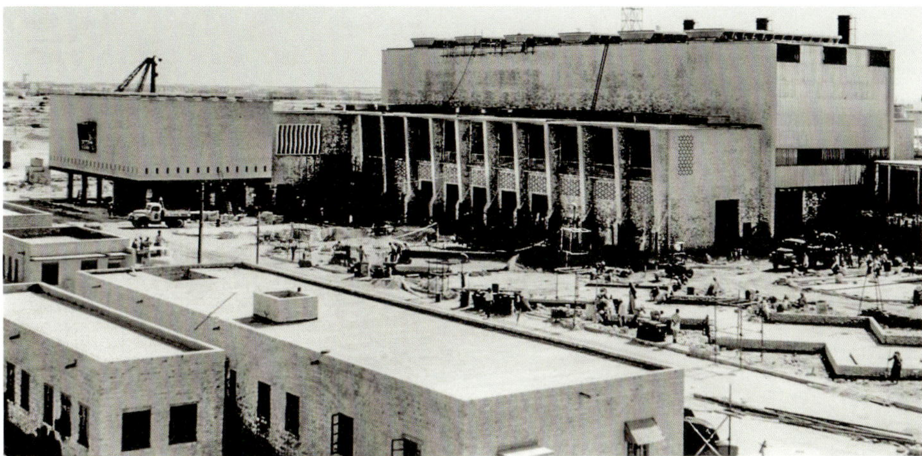

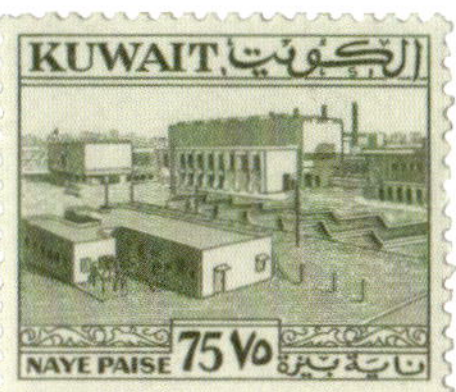

5.11 Seventy-five naye paise stamp in comparison with black-and-white photograph of the power and desalination plant in Shuwaikh, Kuwait City. Undated, photographer unknown.

of the Kuwaiti literary monthly *al-Baḥth* (est. 1950) and eventually postcards with this image also circulated. The stamp's level of detail is rare, as stamp designs of that period usually adhered to simplicity and reduction to ensure printing quality and legibility in the miniature format.[44]

Another site of technical progress and infrastructural prowess is celebrated in the green seventy-five naye paise stamp (fig. 5.11). This stamp depicts the compound of the power and desalination plant in the neighborhood of Shuwaikh, a new industrial area southwest of the former Kuwait town wall. As historical photographs show, the plant was directly situated at the seashore (fig. 5.12).[45] Inaugurated in 1953, the power and

Badran, in Amir Street, which became the first commercial studio for photography in Kuwait. ʿAlī G. al-Raʾīs, "al-Muṣṣawir al-futūghrāfī ʿAbd al-Razzāk Badrān rāʾid ṣuwar al-biṭāqāt al-barīdiyya fī l-Kuwayt [The Photographer Abdel Razzaq Badran Is the Pioneer of Postage Stamps Images in Kuwait]," *al-Būsṭa (al-Posta)*, no. 28 (April 2013); Alabdulmughni, "60 Years Since Issuing the Shaykh Abdullah Al-Salem Stamp," 44.

[44] For mid-twentieth-century discussions on the importance of simplicity in stamp design, see B. G. Harrison, "The Postage Stamp," *Journal of the Royal Society of Arts* 88, no. 4562 (May 1940): 652; John Easton, "The Design and Manufacture of Postage Stamps in the Commonwealth," *Journal of the Royal Society of Arts* 110, no. 5066 (January 1962): 116.

[45] In 1951, Ewbank & Partners—along with the subcontractor John Taylor & Sons and architects Farmer & Dark, both of which were also British companies—was appointed to design one of the world's largest power and desalination plants for Kuwait City. On the entangled visual and architectural histories of water

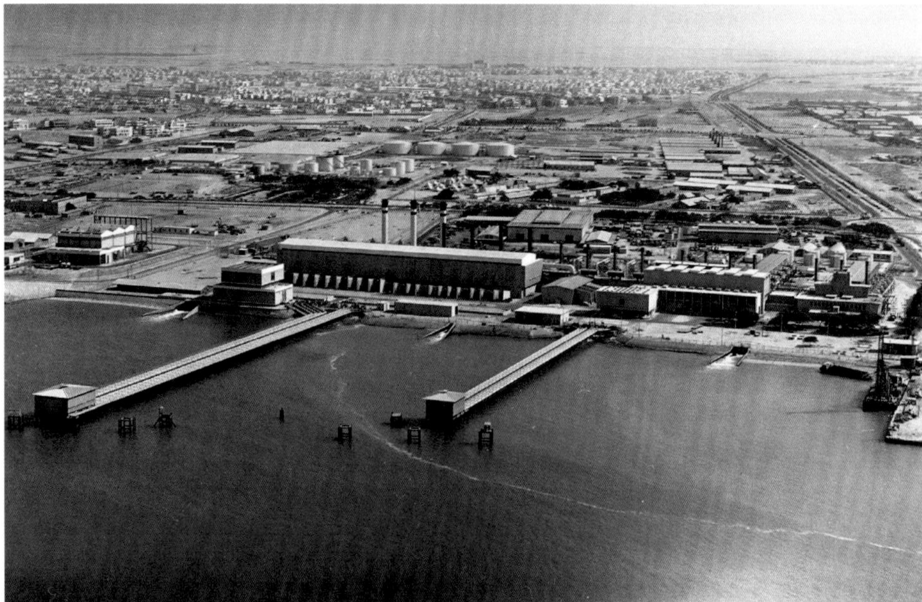

5.12 Black-and-white oblique photograph of the power and desalination plant in Shuwaikh, Kuwait City. Undated, photographer unknown.

desalination plant complex was frequently described as being among the largest plants of its kind in the world and praised for making Kuwait independent of potable water shipments from the Iraqi river of Shatt al Arab for the first time in history.[46] Photographs of the plant regularly featured in national and international newspapers, publications, and reports on Kuwait.[47] The stamp's picture shows the turbine hall of the power station with its chimneys in the center and the adjoined cubic main administration building to its left. Extending from the center to the right, the zig-zag lines indicate the water fountain and pond, which was possibly the first pool in Kuwait. The perspective of this image is also noteworthy. The viewer sees the buildings in profile from somewhere high up, almost like a close-up oblique; perhaps the photograph was taken from aboard a big ship docked at

and petroleum in Kuwait, see Laura Hindelang, "Precious Property: Oil and Water in Twentieth-Century Kuwait." In *Oil Spaces: Exploring the Global Petroleumscape*, ed. Carola Hein (New York: Routledge, 2021), https://doi.org/10.4324/9780367816049-12.

46 Monroe, "The Shaikhdom of Kuwait," 279.

47 See, for example, A Special Correspondent, "Town Planning in Kuwait: Rebuilding a Middle East Capital," *The Times Review of Industry* 5, no. 57 (October 1951); William Kitson, "Kuwait's Distillation Plant for Domestic Water," *The Times Review of Industry and Technology*, December 1951; Southwell, "Kuwait," 36; Monroe, "The Shaikhdom of Kuwait," 278–81.

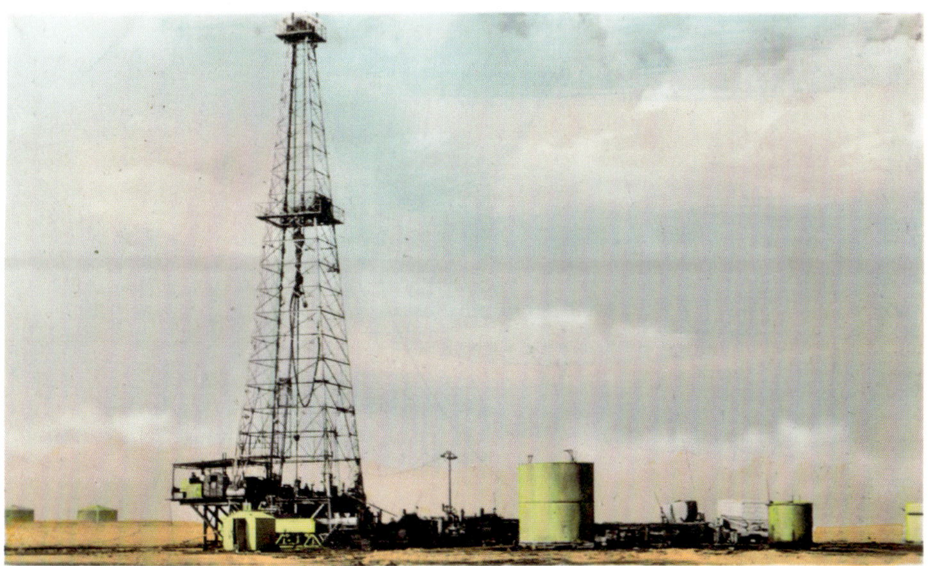

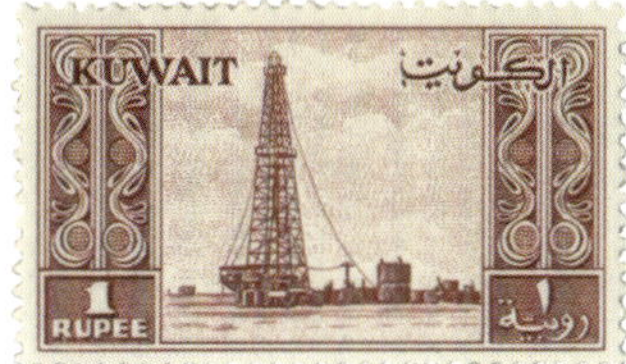

5.13 One rupee stamp in comparison with an undated and hand-colored postcard showing an oil drilling rig in the Burgan Oil Field.

one of the piers close by. Located directly at the shore, the plant was often photographed from the sea to achieve a comprehensive view of the extensive complex.

Next in line, the one rupee stamp forms a group of its own due to the vertical format of its picture: an oil tower in the desert with a small camp next to it (fig. 5.13). While the vertical picture makes up the central part of the stamp, ornamentally decorated fields frame it laterally. The denomination is inserted as pedestals below the ornaments, whereas the country name in Arabic and English hovers in the foreground in the upper part of the stamp, connecting ornament and picture. In general, oil towers such as this one indicated an ongoing prospecting and drilling process that often took months before oil was struck, if the location proved successful at all. Rising many meters above ground, these structures—mobile infrastructures towering over the flat desert—were an impressive sight. According to Khaled Alabdulmughni, the template of this stamp design could have been an undated postcard of a drilling rig in Burgan printed in England.[48]

The fourth and final compositional group comprises the two, five, and ten rupee stamps. Consisting of a framed landscape format without any ornamentation, these

[48] Alabdulmughni, "60 Years Since Issuing the Shaykh Abdullah Al-Salem Stamp," 44.

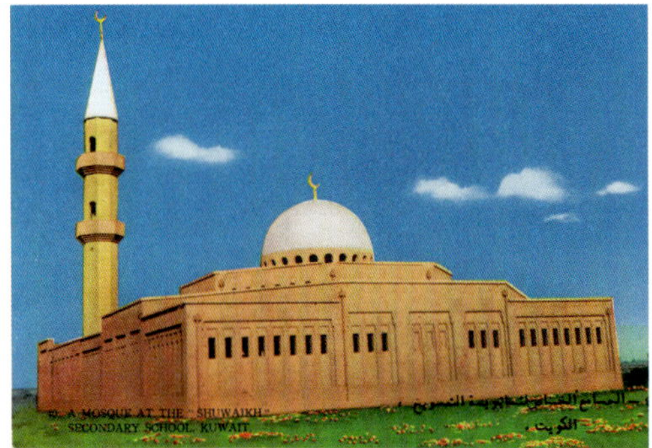

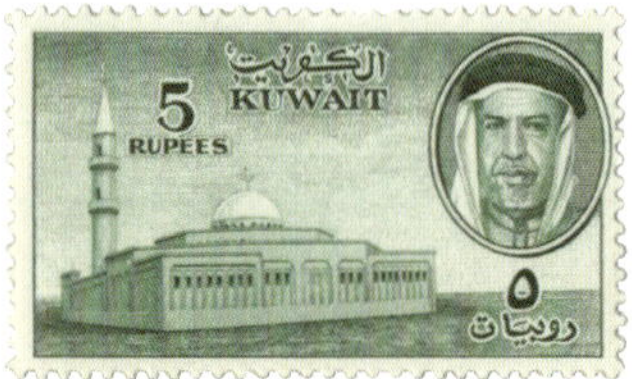

5.14 Five rupee stamp in comparison with undated postcard showing Abdul Redha Salmeen's colored photograph *The Mosque at the Shuwaikh Secondary School, Kuwait.*

stamps feature a small portrait vignette of Shaykh Abdullah in the upper right corner. The portrait is identical to the portrait of Abdullah used in other stamps in this issue, and the vignettes are set apart from the main picture by a white band. The country name is centered just below the upper edge, and the denominations are located in the upper left corner and the bottom right corner in English and Arabic respectively.

Among all of the stamps in this issue, the two rupee stamp stands out for its bicolored design (see fig. 5.7). A blue and very detailed one-master dhow (a wooden deep-sea vessel called baggala) sails in the foreground. The motif and the color clearly reference the forty naye paise stamp. The rest of the stamp has a sandy color. Here, in the background, are an oil tower and some camp structures, which connect this stamp with the motif of the one rupee stamp and make the two rupee stamp a combination of the forty naye paise and the one rupee stamps. Admired for its usually elaborately carved stern and its long-standing importance for deep-sea trade, the type of vessel presented here was already rare in Kuwait when Alan Villiers visited in 1939 and practically out-of-use by the late 1950s.[49] Juxtaposing this type of ship with oil infrastructure with this stamp but also the set as a whole created a stark contrast between the historical and modern branches of the Kuwaiti economy, between pearls and petroleum, but given that this transition had taken place under the continuous rule of the Al Sabah, the stamps also demonstrated a certain political continuity.

Shuwaikh Secondary School, which had featured prominently on the government gazette's cover, was also part of the stamp cosmos. The green five rupee stamp depicts the school's mosque (fig. 5.14). The mosque is erected on a square layout and has one minaret and a central cupola capped by a crescent finial (*alīm*). Having room for up to 1,000 worshippers, it rose to fame as the largest one at the time of its completion.[50] Noteworthy is also this stamp's perspective, with a view insinuating a drive-by mode, as the building's volume blows up and shrinks simultaneously. It is not a central perspective, which the

[49] Villiers, *Sons of Sindbad*, 364 (appendix 1: Types of Arab Dhows).

[50] Alabdulmughni, "60 Years Since Issuing the Shaykh Abdullah Al-Salem Stamp," 44.

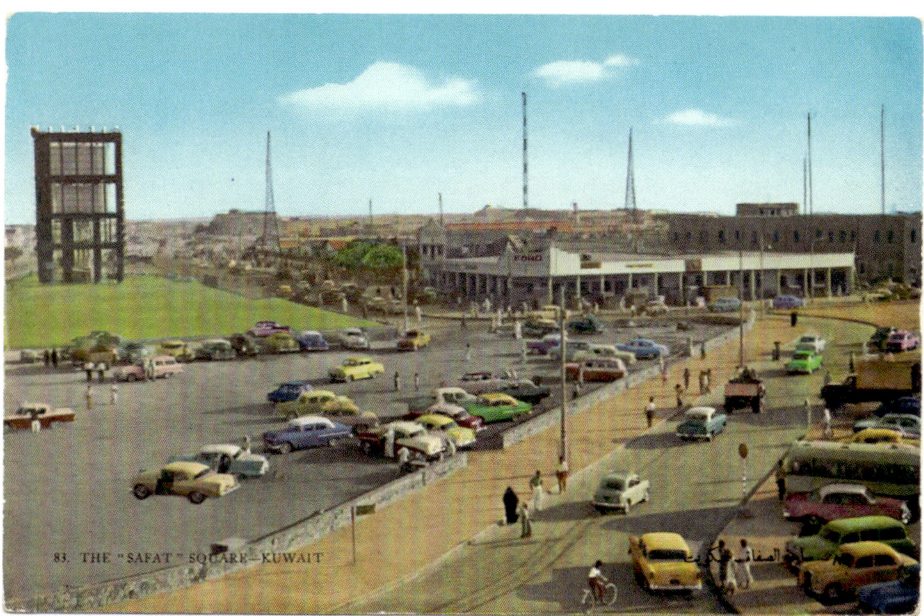

5.15 Ten rupee stamp in comparison with undated postcard showing Abdul Redha Salmeen's colored and retouched photograph *The "Safat" Square, Kuwait*.

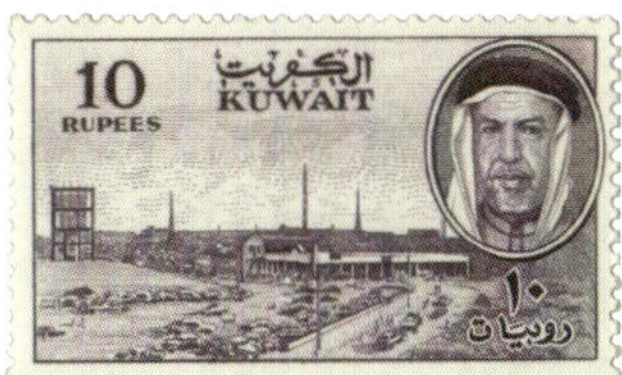

landscape format usually favors, but a little bit off. Despite its peculiarity, the photograph that the stamp was based on circulated also as a color postcard that was published either prior to or after the set of stamps; the postcard names Abdul Redha Salmeen from Basra, who also owned a photo studio in Kuwait, as the photographer.[51]

The last stamp, a purple ten rupee stamp, provides a view of Safat Square (fig. 5.15). Although it recalls the aerial view of Safat Square and its makeshift market stalls that the town planners had frequently published throughout the 1950s, the stamp presents a different image of the square altogether. In the foreground, many cars are either parked or in motion. In the center, at the corner of Safat Square and Fahad al-Salem Street (Jahra Road) and the entrance of Pillar Street, the Ford showcase room, a well-known and often photographed building in the urban landscape of Kuwait, is depicted prominently

[51] Ibid. Alabdulmughni added in a personal conversation that Abdul Redha Salmeen was an Iraqi from Basra who had photo studios there and in Kuwait. He sometimes collaborated with Studio Badran, creating hand-colored postcards from Badran's black-and-white photographs. Email to the author, May 11, 2018.

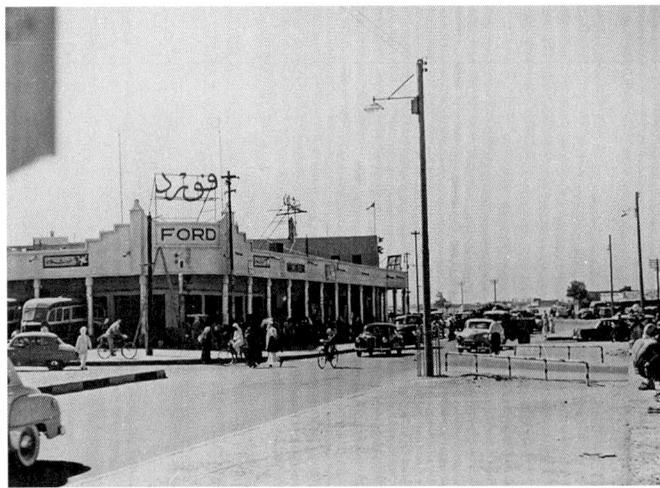

5.16 Black-and-white photograph of Safat Square with the famous Ford showroom. Undated, photographer unknown.

(fig. 5.16). An elevated water tank together with telecommunications antennae also features, forming a dominant vertical element in the urban landscape and highlighting the technological services now available in Kuwait.[52] An undated postcard with an identical photograph by Abdul Redha Salmeen exists for this stamp (fig. 5.15).[53] In close comparison, the hand-colored postcard depicts Safat Square with a central green area. The idea of turning the square into lush greens had been stimulated by the new water desalination scheme, but the development project never materialized.[54] Still, since the beginning of the decade, Safat Square had developed quickly in conjunction with the expansion of Fahad al-Salem Street, which flowed into the square, and had fast become an urban nexus of Kuwait's modernization. Called "Kuwait's Piccadilly Circus" in articles of the time, it was one of the most sought-after locations in Kuwait to open a shop, a showroom, or an office. Safat Square owed its popularity to its historical legacy as a trading locality, to its centrality, and to the availability of parking spaces.[55] Viewed at street level, Safat no longer looked anything like the obliques that had been taken only a few years earlier as part of the extensive aerial survey.

Characteristic of this 1959 set of stamps overall is the enormous attention to detail and the close similarity of its imagery to existing photographs and photo-postcards.

[52] The water tank belonged to the new water distribution scheme that connected the town to the power and desalination plant in Shuwaikh at four central points. From the tank, potable water was then distributed across town. The British telecommunications company had been one of the first foreign firms to open in Kuwait.

[53] Alabdulmughni, "60 Years Since Issuing the Shaykh Abdullah Al-Salem Stamp," 43–44.

[54] The proposed development of Safat Square is mentioned by Macfarlane, "Planning an Arab Town," 113; John Midgley, "Kuwait," *The Sphere*, June 16, 1956, 409.

[55] Banks, "Notes on a Visit to Kuwait," 49.

Given that these photographs and postcards cannot be dated precisely and there is not sufficient Arabic or English archival information on the design process of the stamps, it is not possible to conclude whether it was the stamps or the photographs that popularized the respective Kuwaiti motif. Be that as it may, assuming that the photographs existed prior to the stamp design process, specific photographs of the Kuwaiti built environment (and of Shaykh Abdullah), many of which were taken by local photo studios and also existed as postcard motifs, did serve as templates for a realistic depiction of Kuwait. This shows that the government chose already popularized but very up-to-date photographs of Kuwait. Conversely, considering that the photographs and photo-based postcards were taken (or at least gained in popularity) after the postage stamps were released, it is clear that the stamp designs also promoted certain Kuwaiti vistas and their proliferation in other visual media. Either way (or even both ways), the motifs selected for the stamps circulated in different media as part of a wider visual culture of Kuwait that emerged in the mid-twentieth century in relation to Kuwait's urban transformation and were extremely popular. Consequently, selected elements of Kuwait's recently built environment gained representative status in both popular and political cultures that mutually reinforced each other.

5.4 Oil Stamps for Petro-States

During the 1950s, the government of Kuwait developed a new communication infrastructure. Besides the government gazette *al-Kuwayt al-Yawm* as a mono-directional medium from state to citizen, among the main means of communication were the postal services, which not only connected Kuwaitis locally but also Kuwait with the world.

Given the proliferation of postal communication in the mid-twentieth century, stamps were familiar objects of everyday use and of a widespread visual culture. Firmly glued to a postcard, an envelope, or a parcel, stamps circulated widely in social, spatial, and geographical terms. Especially because of their visual quotidian presence, stamps could "touch the everyday lives (and reflect the attitudes) of both governments and ordinary citizens more readily than grand political rhetoric or state ceremonial" and could become significant political symbols.[56] The 1959 set of stamps initiated the grand visual infiltration of private space by political symbols and were thus emblematic of the expanding influence of the Kuwaiti government on everyday life and visual culture, as well as on how Kuwait was promoted (inter)nationally. This demonstrates that the state did not only rely on the physical presence of state-initiated infrastructure projects. Rather, the government's negotiation of the distribution of color photographs by the Kuwait Oil Company and its substantial efforts to produce postage stamps with Kuwait (City) motifs underscore the political importance attached to the circulation of updated urban images to Kuwait's visual representations.

[56] Jeffery, "Crown, Communication and the Colonial Post," 46.

A Pictorial Travel Guide to the Petropolis Kuwait

To reconstruct the way in which the Kuwaiti stamps circulated, the 1959 *Post Office Guide* for Kuwait provides details on all the postage rates for internal and international surface and air mail.[57] Sending a postcard or a normal letter within Kuwait cost five naye paise and ten naye paise respectively; hence, one or several Shaykh Abdullah stamps were needed. Via airmail, letters to Europe cost sixty naye paise; to Arab countries included in category A, postage started at forty naye paise, a rate that apparently popularized the blue dhow stamp.[58] However, sending a standard letter to Venezuela, another oil producer, the envelope required at least the one-rupee oil derrick stamp and twenty-five naye paise worth of ruler portrait stamps in order to travel successfully.

While the most frequently used stamps were presumably the smallest denominations and thus the ruler portrait stamps, the heavier the letter or the parcel and the greater the distance the more stamps had to be used in combination to make up the exact postal rate. Postage stamps therefore did not only travel individually but also as a combined display, as preserved envelopes from the period show (fig. 5.17). It can be safely assumed that many colorful and richly illustrated envelopes and boxes left Kuwait for other countries, thereby transporting stamp collages of images of Kuwait to destinations near and far. The potential message of such pictorial postal communication can be illustrated by an example.

When Mr. Wolstencroft, director of the General Post Office in London, visited Kuwait to attend the official ceremony of the postal handover in February 1959, his itinerary listed the following stops: On February 1, Wolstencroft was to meet the acting ruler during the opening ceremony. He would then inspect the new post office at Safat Square. In the afternoon, "a drive around the town and a tour of the Distillation Plant" were planned. For the next day, "lunch at Ahmadi" and afterward visits of a post office and an oil rig were scheduled.[59] Out of a total of eight scenes or themes depicted on the 1959 set of stamps, Wolstencroft's Kuwait itinerary covered at least four: ruler, Safat Square, distillation plant, and oil rig; maybe even the oil jetty in the harbor of Ahmadi. This description is evidence that the locations and the person depicted on the 1959 set of pictorials displayed a set of officially acknowledged, representative images of Kuwait at the time. As a combined display on an envelope, as a collage of modern Kuwait, the stamps functioned as a mobile miniature travel guide that made the addressee a visitor to Kuwait through images.

In the absence of long-established tourist attractions like the pyramids (Egypt) or Roman ruins (Baalbek in Lebanon), Kuwait confidently drew on sites of current

[57] Administration of Posts, Telegraphs & Telephones, Post Office Department, *Post Office Guide* (Kuwait: Government Printing Press, 1959).

[58] Neil Donaldson, *The History of the Postal Service in Kuwait, 1775–1959* (Bombay: Jal Cooper, 1968), 12. Category A included neighboring countries (except Saudi Arabia) like Bahrain, Iraq, but also Jordan, Lebanon, and Syria.

[59] Joe W. Lee, British Postal Agency Kuwait, to Miss D. M. King, General Post Office, January 25, 1959, Transfer of Responsibility for Postal Services, Part 2.

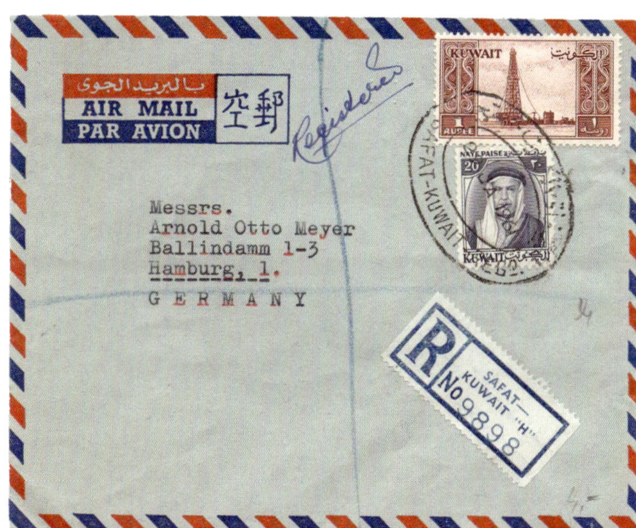

5.17 Airmail cover sent to Germany, January 29, 1961, with two stamps from the 1959 Kuwaiti set.

architectural and infrastructural development for its self-promotion. The state could have selected Seif Palace (at least early nineteenth century) or a pre-oil-era mosque; instead it showed the desalination plant and the most recently built mosque among other scenes. These choices suggest that these particular motifs were considered the most positive and attractive representations of the country for the purpose of giving a kind of "philatelic tour,"[60] which was a potential of Middle Eastern *pictorial* stamps that philatelist Robert Obojski has identified as follows:

> Such stamps offer vicarious travel through the length and breadth of the Middle East and its environs—or at least provide a kind of photo album with glimpses of those special tourist attractions that we absolutely must visit in person some day, or, if we have visited them, must never forget.[61]

Postage stamps that show richly illustrated yet realistic locations of a particular country stimulate visual familiarization but also a longing to visit, a kind of place promotion.

However, the pictorial potential of stamps, especially from the MENA region, was not without pitfalls. A large number of stamps from the decolonizing Arab world, with their rich and delicately executed motifs, meandered between confident self-representation by advertising the country in self-chosen pictures and succumbing to the "colonial picturesque." This was, as Middle East historian Donald Reid has argued, "a genre that became popular in other colonial settings throughout the Middle East and beyond" as it drew on orientalist painting and illustrations by displaying "a quaint 'Oriental' land as viewed by

[60] Robert Obojski, "A Philatelic Tour," *Saudi Aramco World* 34, no. 1 (1983), accessed January 31, 2021, https://archive.aramcoworld.com/issue/198301/a.philatelic.tour.htm.

[61] Ibid.

Western romantics and travelers."[62] By relying on the motif of the "colonial picturesque," such stamp sets turned countries with a long and rich history—like Lebanon, Syria, and Iraq—into "open-air antiquities museums."[63] Using the 1914 Ottoman set as an example, Reid described characteristics he considered typical for this type of stamp: "it has elaborate Arabesque frames, scenic landmarks as subjects, was printed in London, and revives the prominent use of a second language."[64] Reid's description clearly fits the 1959 Kuwaiti set. This might explain why an influential philatelic magazine even described the 1959 Kuwaiti series as "British Colonial pictorials."[65] To a certain extent, the extremely detailed, decorated, and colorful Kuwaiti stamps printed in London were also perceived as following the aesthetic of the "colonial picturesque" in a similar way as many other Middle Eastern series.

On closer inspection, however, the Kuwaiti stamps also defy such a categorization. Most motifs display modern, universal infrastructure that strongly distance the stamps from orientalist tropes or the ethnographically inspired black-and-white photography of Bedouins and coral-stone towns of the Arabian Peninsula, which were the historical traveler or tourist motifs emblematic of the region that would soon materialize in open-air heritage villages. In turn, the motifs resonated with modernization and development discourse that were fueling the demand for images of progressive infrastructures as symbols of industrial production, mass-consumption, progress, and so on.[66] Moreover, the pervasiveness of development and modernization could be seen in the power to project future progress and change through representations and visualizations that functioned irrespectively of local conditions, representations that embraced a certain international standardization and readability. Such a universal (yet site-specific) reading is present in the 1959 set of stamps, which projected the city-state of Kuwait City as a petropolis, a modern capital city participating in petro-modernity. To project such an image successfully, the photo-realistic templates of architectural-infrastructural sites in Kuwait underwent a process of aestheticization to create images-of-infrastructures that conveyed the enchantment and the petroleum promise of such structures.

Visualizing Infrastructural Stability in Postal Miniatures

Leaving the dhow and the portrait stamps aside, the remaining six stamps of the 1959 set depict utilitarian structures. These utilitarian structures facilitate the production of water and electricity, they transport crude oil, and house (religious) education systems.

62 Reid, "The Postage Stamp," 82. For a history of ideas of the "the picturesque" and its use in art and architecture, see John Macarthur, *The Picturesque: Architecture, Disgust and other Irregularities* (Abingdon: Routledge, 2008).

63 Reid, "The Symbolism of Postage Stamps," 243.

64 Ibid., 233–34.

65 "Stamp News in Brief: British Commonwealth," *Gibbons' Stamp Monthly* 32 (February 1958).

66 Escobar, *Encountering Development*, 5.

They also depend on motorized transportation and modern communication networks, and they connect humans and nonhuman matter. These structures have a defined physical form, are spatially fixed, and are, to various decrees, site-specific. They truly are "infrastructure" in the sense of recent (mostly anthropological) research loosely referred to as the "infrastructural turn" or "infrastructural studies."[67]

These structures, which exist(ed) somewhere in Kuwait, were translated into stamps as "pictures-of-infrastructure." The process at play was not only depiction but also beautification: to become images, the structures were colored, framed with abstract or arabesque ornaments and with Arabic and English script, and, partly, combined with Shaykh Abdullah's portrait vignette. The stamps were just as colorful as the KOC's color photography, but instead of color-highlighting specific surfaces and materials, the whole scenes were dipped in monochrome color. This pictorial transformation united the disparate structures and sites into one set of stamps of a similar aesthetic. On the stamps, the larger infrastructural networks (e.g., water supply) were represented through built forms—architectural or structural configurations—that stressed their site-specific material presence in visually conceivable forms. The photo-realistic style of depiction and the extremely skillful and detailed execution in the technique of etching enhanced the visual credibility of the structures' physical presence. In the absence of human users or traces of work processes, the compositions and motifs emphasized the visual representationality of the completed structures. We see here what Timothy Mitchell has described as characteristic for modernity: the making of reality as world-as-picture based on the "distinctive imagination of the real" in images.[68]

By turning infrastructure into colorful miniature pictures, the original (technological, religious, urban, infrastructural) function of the structures was discarded. The question of whether and how these infrastructures functioned, and why and how they connected to humans or non-human matter, was left "out of the frame." As images they work in a similar way to the architectural "white elephants" that Hannah Appel describes for Equatorial Guinea, where oil revenues help finance spectacular buildings that are, site-specifically, completely dysfunctional—their prime function is to highlight that something, anything, is happening.[69]

Yet, the projects pictured were not hollow promises. All infrastructural constructions depicted on the 1959 stamps had been built and completed throughout the 1950s and

[67] Brian Larkin offers the following definition: "Infrastructures are built networks that facilitate the flow of goods, people, or ideas and allow for their exchange over space. As physical forms they shape the nature of a network, the speed and direction of its movement, its temporalities, and its vulnerability to breakdown. They comprise the architecture for circulation, literally providing the undergirding of modern societies, and they generate the ambient environment of everyday life." Brian Larkin, "The Politics and Poetics of Infrastructure," *Annual Review of Anthropology* 42 (2013): 328.

[68] See Mitchell, "The Stage of Modernity," 16.

[69] Hannah C. Appel, "Walls and White Elephants: Oil Extraction, Responsibility, and Infrastructural Violence in Equatorial Guinea," *Ethnography* 13, no. 4 (2012).

thus during Shaykh Abdullah's rule.[70] They were solid proof of Kuwait City's urban transformation and therefore of political, economic, and technological progress and success. They were part of the petroleum promise because they expressed the idea that, with more oil, even more modernization would materialize. Through their appearance on the first state-issued stamps, these projects were integrated into the pictorial imagination and visual representation of the state. This served to transfer the positive associations of the city's development onto the political system of Kuwait and the reign of Abdullah and the Al Sabah. This infrastructure-as-image functioned through an effect that anthropologists Penny Harvey and Hannah Knox have described as the "enchantments of infrastructure."[71] They argue "that it is not in spite of unruly processes that infrastructures emerge as a form of social promise, but rather that it is through the experiences of life within and alongside unstable forces that infrastructures gain their capacity to enchant."[72] In the case of Kuwait, the completed infrastructural projects materialized as soothingly stabilizing forms in an environment of the utmost transformation of all sectors of life—and first and foremost of the built environment. They gained even more stability because they were present both physically as part of the built environment and as recurring pictures (stamps, postcards, photographs). Consequently, the 1959 set of stamps was successful in encapsulating a dominant narrative of material stability that was to become associated with the political stability and national unification orchestrated under Shaykh Abdullah that climaxed in the 1961 independence. Stability was not created through historical continuity of physical space but by displaying the present (the newly rebuilt environment) as a projection of the positive future image of Kuwait in an iridescent way.

Petrophilately[73]

State sovereignty and political legitimacy are highly dependent on a convincing visual or symbolic regime.[74] For example, recent studies have focused on political visual culture as a driving force in the processes of state formation in the modern Middle East.[75] However,

[70] It is of course possible that the exact oil derricks had in fact been built prior to 1946 to facilitate the early stage of petroleum extraction. However, this does not influence the overall argument.

[71] Penny Harvey and Hannah Knox, "The Enchantments of Infrastructure," *Mobilities* 7, no. 4 (2012).

[72] Ibid., 525.

[73] In the following, MiNo. refers to the catalog number of the stamps in *Michel Gulf States Catalogue 2013*, 2nd ed. (Unterschleißheim: Schwaneberger Verlag, 2012). SG SofW No. refers to the catalog number of the stamps in Stanley Gibbons, ed. *Stamps of the World 1978*, 43rd ed. (London: Stanley Gibbons, 1977).

[74] Gabriella Elgenius, *Symbols of Nations and Nationalism: Celebrating Nationhood* (New York: Palgrave Macmillan, 2011), 4.

[75] On the role of visual culture in relation to national politics, see Lina Khatib, *Image Politics in the Middle East: The Role of the Visual in Political Struggle* (London: I. B. Tauris, 2013); Lisa Wedeen, *Ambiguities of Domination: Politics, Rhetoric, and Symbols in Contemporary Syria*, rev. ed. (Chicago: University of Chicago Press, [1999] 2015). On visual culture as tool of nation-building, see Eric Davis and Nicholas Gavrielides,

the social and political sciences still struggle to firmly incorporate visual approaches into their toolboxes.[76] In art history, the formation of certain reoccurring motifs that draw their aesthetic as well as political legitimacy from the Zeitgeist of the era has been studied as "political iconography."[77] Martin Warnke, one of the advocates of political iconography, suggested that it is ruling elites who are most dependent on some form of visual representation as self-affirmation and expression of political stability.[78] For the Kuwaiti postage stamps of 1959, the state used architectural and infrastructural motifs, as well as the portrait of Shaykh Abdullah for its pictorial self-representation toward potential visitors, its citizens, and other states. Judging from the high frequency of visual representations of oil-related motifs, which also appeared on the stamps of other oil-producing countries during the 1950s and 1960s, Kuwaiti postage stamps were a pivotal visual media for displaying Kuwait as a petro-state and for communicating this status to other (petro-)states.

The petroleum-industrial complex is explicitly referenced in three Kuwaiti stamps from 1959: the one and two rupee stamps (oil derricks) and the five naye pase stamp (the Mina al-Ahmadi oil harbor with its pipelined pier). In addition, less immediately recognizable petroleum experiences are depicted on other stamps. For example, the seventy-five naye paise stamp features the gigantic power and desalination plant, which was paid for by oil revenues and fueled by waste gas from the Burgan Oil Field, and the ten rupee stamp shows Safat Square, the traffic nexus of the city and a place to showcase cars—for example in the famous Ford showroom.[79] Cars were also indispensable for reaching the new secondary school, whose characteristic mosque can be seen on the five rupee stamp. As part of the scheme of suburbanization and private motorization initiated by the first master plan, the Shuwaikh campus lay far outside the historical town

"Statecraft, Historical Memory, and Popular Culture in Iraq and Kuwait," in *Statecraft in the Middle East: Historical Memory and Popular Culture*, ed. Eric Davis and Nicholas Gavrielides (Miami: Florida International University Press, 1991).

[76] For debates taking place in Germany, see Marion G. Müller, "Politologie und Ikonologie: Visuelle Interpretation als politologisches Verfahren," in Schwelling, *Politikwissenschaft als Kulturwissenschaft*; Klaus von Beyme, "Why Is There No Political Science of the Arts?," in *Pictorial Cultures and Political Iconographies: Approaches, Perspectives, Case Studies from Europe and America*, ed. Udo J. Hebel and Christoph Wagner (New York: De Gruyter, 2011).

[77] The concept of "political iconography" draws on Erwin Panofsky's theory of iconography and iconology of the 1930s. See Uwe Fleckner, Martin Warnke, and Hendrik Ziegler, eds., *Handbuch der politischen Ikonographie*, 2 vols. (Munich: C. H. Beck, 2011).

[78] Martin Warnke, "Politische Ikonographie: Hinweise auf eine sichtbare Politik," in *Wozu Politikwissenschaft? Über das Neue in der Politik*, ed. Claus Leggewie (Darmstadt: Wissenschaftliche Buchgesellschaft, 1994), 170. Also, Klaus von Beyme suggests that "symbolic politics—which iconology analyzes—were, from a historical point of view, most powerful as long as the ruling ones possessed extended decision-making authority." Klaus von Beyme, "Politische Ikonologie der modernen Architektur," in Schwelling, *Politikwissenschaft als Kulturwissenschaft*, 370 (author's translation).

[79] On the power and desalination plant, see A Special Correspondent, "Town Planning in Kuwait," 91.

center and at driving distances from most newly built neighborhoods. Even as dhows subsequently became symbols of the country's maritime past (for example in Kuwait's national emblem), they also reference one of the pre-industrial local uses of bitumen or tar for sealing boats given its water-repelling qualities. Therefore, most of the stamps relate either directly or indirectly to petro-modernity.

Exploring (the history of) petroleum by flipping through a stamp album or looking at the Kuwaiti set as a travel guide, viewers were able to be comfortably at home and far away from the dirty and even dangerous oil fields, yet traveling in images. Over the decades, something like a "petrophilately," the philatelic study of oil-related stamps, developed among collectors. In a 1988 article in the oil company magazine *Saudi Aramco World*, stamp collector Raymond Schuessler explained that petrophilately not only included motifs related to the modern petroleum industry and petroleum-based products but also encompassed pre-modern uses of oil for shipbuilding, religious practices, and medicine.[80] Philatelists agree that the Republic of Azerbaijan was the first country to issue postage stamps with petroleum-related motifs: first, in 1919, two stamps depicting the mystical "Temple of Eternal Flames," which referred to the Zoroastrian oil fire cults, and then, two years later, a stamp showing for the first time oil infrastructure in the form of an oil well.[81]

Throughout the 1950s and 1960s, petroleum, especially in the form of large-scale oil infrastructure, became a frequent, somewhat universal motif of postage stamps. At first, Arab countries were not prominently represented. The presumably earliest article from 1954 on what was later called "petrophilately" discusses the hierarchy of oil producers and their philatelic presence based on a survey of twenty-one oil stamps from various countries:

> The U.S.A. has been, and still is, by far the most important oil-producing country. In recent years, however, an increasing contribution has come from Venezuela and countries in the Middle

[80] Raymond Schuessler, "Petrophilately," *Saudi Aramco World* 39, no. 1 (1988), accessed January 31, 2021, https://archive.aramcoworld.com/issue/198801/petrophilately.htm. When Schuessler coined the expression "petrophilately" in the late 1980s, the Petroleum Philatelic Society International already existed. Founded in 1974, its website mentions the heightened awareness of the political and economic implications of petroleum in the 1970s as reasons for creating the study group. With "the purpose of advancing the philately of the oil, natural gas and petrochemical industries," the society is an official study unit of the American Topical Association and an affiliate of the American Philatelic Society. Today, it is the leading authority on petroleum-related philately. See the website *Petroleum Philatelic Society International*, accessed January 31, 2021, https://www.ppsi.org.uk/. This underlines that "petrophilately" resonated with a large interest group worldwide.

[81] Azerbaijan 1919, SG SofW Nos. 9–10, showing the "Temple of Eternal Flames." Two year later, the first stamp displaying modern petroleum infrastructure, here an oil well, was issued (Azerbaijan 1921, SG SofW No. 12). See "The Philatelist's Story of Oil," *Stamp Collecting*, July 23, 1954, 611; "Oil Stamps," *Saudi Aramco World* 13, no. 8 (1962), accessed January 31, 2021, https://archive.aramcoworld.com/issue/196208/oil.stamps.htm.

> East.... As far as the philatelist is concerned, however, these vast oil riches [in the Middle East] are represented by a set of two stamps, showing oil derricks in Iraq.[82]

Despite omitting the 1953 definitive issue of Iran, which showed an oil derrick set against a city's silhouette with protruding minarets, this statement is still not surprising given that many Middle Eastern states had either not yet found oil or were still using overprinted British stamps. From the 1950s onward, however, this changed rapidly: after Iraq (1941) and Iran (1953), Kuwait (1959) was the next country to issue petroleum-related stamps, quickly followed by the United Arab Republic (1959), Saudi Arabia (1960), Jordan (1961), Qatar (1961), Libya (1961), Abu Dhabi (1964), Dubai (1966), Syria (1969), and Muscat and Oman (1969).[83] Only a decade after the 1954 article on petrophilately, a substantial body of oil stamps had been issued in the MENA region. This dissemination of oil stamps reflected the rise of Arab oil producers on an international level, irrespective, in a way, of whether it was an "oil rich" or "oil poor" Arab state, or whether a state was fully or only partially dependent on oil revenues, or in fact in charge of oil operations. This proliferation of oil stamps resonated with the fact that "the oil phenomenon has cut across the whole of the Arab world.... Oil as the primary source of rent in the Arab region has generated various secondary rent sources [like pipeline royalties] to other non-oil Arab states."[84] This meant that most Arab states were involved in the oil economy in one way or another.

A comparative analysis of these oil stamps shows that, when only one petroleum-related stamp was part of a country's regular set of definitives, the oil derrick was the

[82] "The Philatelist's Story of Oil," 613. The Iraqi stamps referred to are: Iraq 1941, MiNo. 115 (derricks) and Iraq 1955, MiNos. 188–90 (King Faisal II, industry and technology [derricks]). This article was also reprinted as a small booklet: Petroleum Information Bureau, *The Philatelist's Story of Oil* (London: Petroleum Information Bureau, 1960).

[83] This list is intended to be illustrative rather than exhaustive. It indicates the issue of the first stamp depicting an image of oil infrastructure by a (colonized or independent) country. Iraq 1941, definitives, MiNos. 115–16 (oil derricks); Iran 1953, definitives, SG SotW Nos. 999–1002 (oil derrick and mosque); Iran 1953, air mail, SG SotW Nos. 1003–06 (oil well and mosque); Iran 1953, commem., SG SotW Nos. 1007–11 (2nd anniv. of nationalization of oil industry; crude oil stabilizer, pipelines, view of Abadan, super fractionators); Kuwait 1959, definitives, MiNos. 137, 139 and 140; U.A.R. (Syria) 1959, commem., SG SotW No. 697 (inaug. of oil refinery); Saudi Arabia 1960–62, definitives, MiNos. 87–102 (oil refinery, Ain Dair); Jordan 1961, commem., SG SotW Nos. 502–03 (inaug. of Jordanian petroleum refinery); Qatar 1961, definitives, MiNos. 33–34 (derrick); Libya 1961, commem., SG SotW Nos. 263–65 (inaug. of first Libyan petrol pipeline [Zelten Field and Marsa Brega Port]; Abu Dhabi 1964, definitives, MiNos. 10–11 (derrick with camels); Dubai 1966, air mail, MiNos. 193–207 (anniv. of oil exploration in the Persian Gulf on March 15, 1964; various steps in the oil prospecting and production process); Syria 1968, commem., SG SotW Nos. 987–88 (pipeline); Syria 1968, definitives, SG SotW Nos. 1009–1015 (oil derrick); Muscat and Oman 1969, commem., MiNos. 107–09 (1st mineral oil shipment in July 1967; oil port and oil tanks in Mina Fahal, derrick in the desert). Surprisingly, Bahrain did not issue a single oil-related stamp, despite being the first of the Arabian Gulf countries to strike oil in 1932.

[84] Hazem Beblawi, "The Rentier State in the Arab World," in Beblawi; Luciani, *The Rentier State*, 59–62, here 62.

favorite motif. When several stamps illustrating different petro-industrial aspects were issued, these were usually issued as part of a commemorative set, and not a definitive one—for example, to mark the anniversary of an important oil exploration or the inauguration of an oil port. Motifs of oil infrastructure and petroleum-related events on Arab countries' stamps became so common that the power of writing a country into the global history of oil through these forms of visual references—Walter Benjamin called them "business cards" of states—cannot be underestimated.

Oil stamps certainly became a pictorial currency in the Arab world, but not only there. By 1962, in light of rapidly increasing successful oil explorations worldwide, forty-six oil-producing and oil-refining countries (like Curaçao in the Dutch West Indies) across the world had issued a total of 451 "oil stamps."[85] Many of these states relied on such typical oil infrastructure motifs as the oil derrick in order to highlight their relationship with petroleum on stamps. The oil derrick thereby became emblematic of petro-states globally.

The Oil Derrick as Political Iconography

As the preferred iconography of oil, the symbol of the oil derrick was not just a convenient icon. When one considers other fossil energy landscapes, like the former coal-mining region of the Ruhr area in western Germany, one notices that the hidden or invisible presence of subterranean deposits of coal (or oil) is indicated and made visible by vertical infrastructures, even after the coal (or oil) itself is long gone.[86] Headframes, oil derricks, and pumpjacks spatially locate and physically indicate the (former) availability of the fossil materials while towering over the landscape and are clearly visible for miles—for instance set against the flat desert of Kuwait, as historical photographs show (fig. 5.18). Apart from their indicator function, such structures are of course crucial for the extraction process that targets the precious subterranean riches. The oil derrick is therefore complicit in forms of vertically materialized dominance and power in a similar way to other structures with a heightened vertical presence, such as towers, minarets, bell and church towers, and of course skyscrapers.

Both Iran and Qatar even explored the analogy of the slender oil derrick (or tower) and the minaret of a mosque by combining the two motifs in one stamp design. While the Iranian stamp from 1953 places the oil tower in the foreground, framed and echoed by domes and minarets in the background (fig. 5.19), the first definitive Qatari issue includes one stamp with an oil derrick and another one with a one-minaret mosque (figs. 5.20a, 5.20b). The two Qatari compositions look so alike that one needs to look

[85] See "Oil Stamps." In 2011, there were ninety-eight oil-producing countries; see Reyna and Behrends, "The Crazy Curse and Crude Domination," 4.

[86] See Roland Günter, "Die politische Ikonographie des Ruhrgebietes in der Epoche der Industrialisierung," in *Architektur als politische Kultur: Philosophia practica*, ed. Hermann Hipp and Ernst Seidl (Berlin: Dietrich Reimer, 1996), 215.

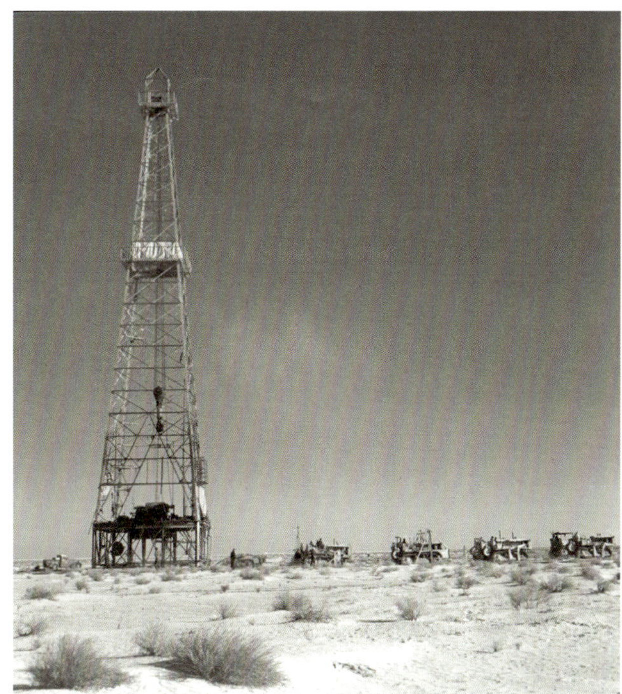

5.18 Black-and-white photograph titled *Burgan. Skidding a Rig*, 1949. Photographer unkown.

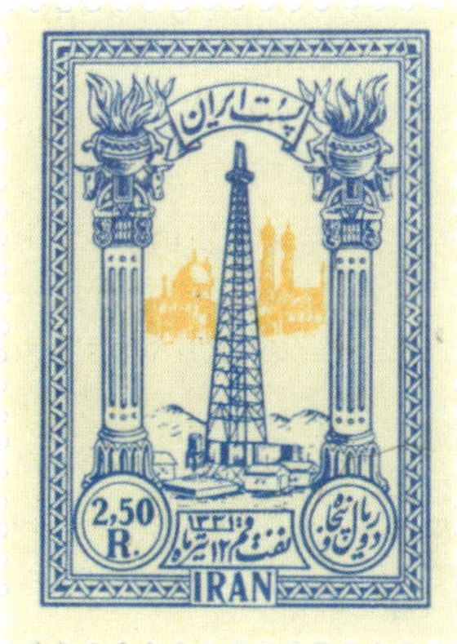

5.19 Two-and-a-half rial stamp showing an oil derrick (blue) in the foreground and a cityscape with a mosque and minarets (yellow) in the background. This stamp is part of the 1953 Iranian issue to commemorate the discovery of oil at Qom, issued February 20, 1953.

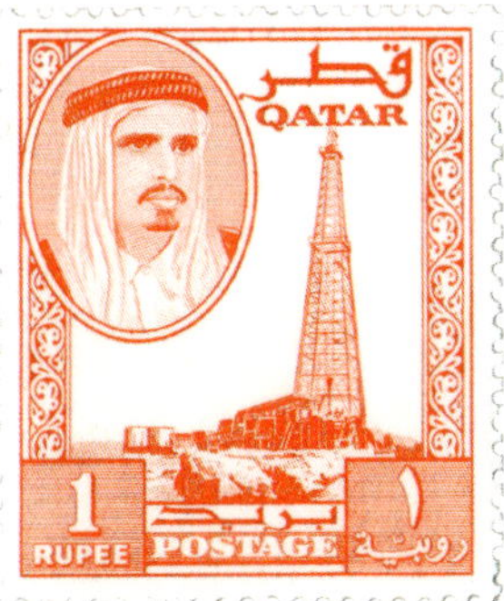

5.20a Red one rupee stamp showing an oil derrick from Qatar's first set of definitives, issued September 2, 1961.

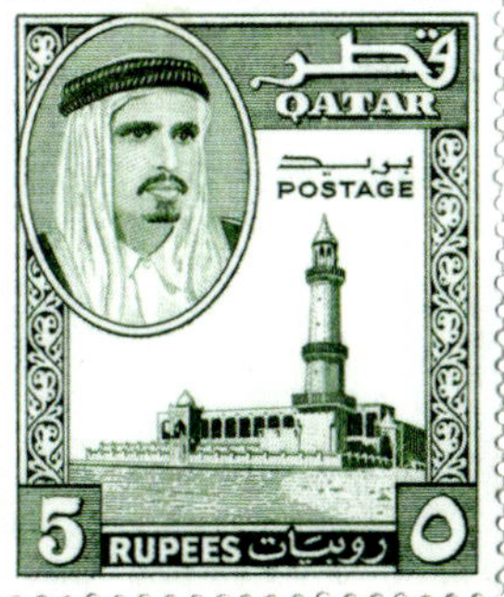

5.20b Green five rupee stamp showing a mosque from Qatar's first set of definitives, issued September 2, 1961.

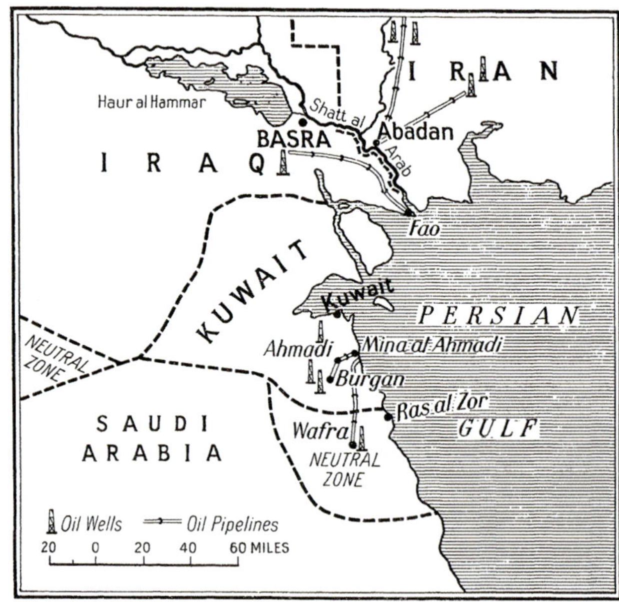

5.21 Map of Kuwait in the journal *International Affairs*, July 1954, with Kuwait's oil fields marked using an oil derrick icon.

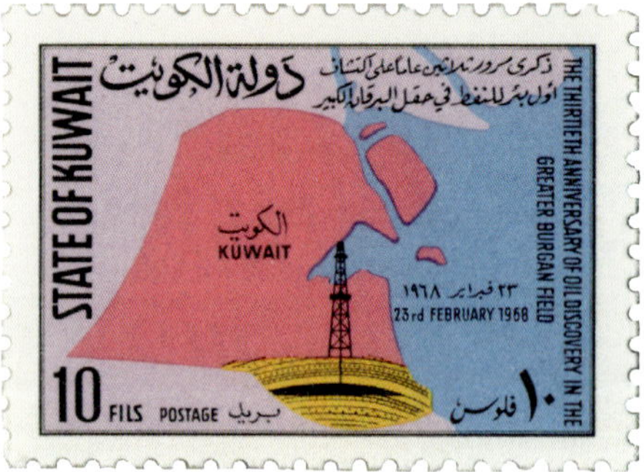

5.22 Commemorative stamp issued in set of two on the occassion of the 30th anniversary of the discovery of oil in the Greater Burgan Field, February 23, 1968.

closely to recognize the difference.[87] These typologies result, of course, from functional demands like audibility of sound (mosque) or the length of drill bits (oil derrick), yet the outstanding vertical visibility conveys more than just its functionality.

[87] Iran 1953, definitives, SG SotW Nos. 999–1002 (oil derrick and mosque); Qatar 1961, definitives, MiNos. 33–34 (derrick) and 35–36 (mosque). Interestingly, the visual juxtaposition and comparison of an oil rig and a mosque also features prominently in *The Third River*, an Iraq Petroleum Company documentary from 1951; see Damluji, "Petroleum's Promise," 141. The iconography of the infrastructural tower encountering the religious tower (minaret or church tower) is also relevant to the political iconography of the coal mine area of the Ruhrgebiet in the West of Germany. See Günter, "Die politische Ikonographie des Ruhrgebietes in der Epoche der Industrialisierung," 213–15.

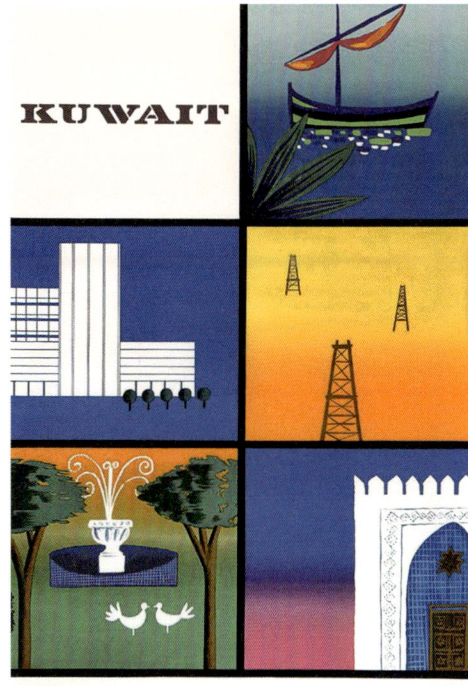

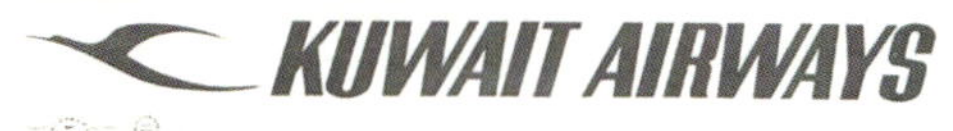

5.23 Kuwait Airways poster of Kuwait, ca. 1960, designed by Alan Gauthier, printed by La Vasselais, Paris. 90 × 60 cm, poster on linen.

In search of other visual outlets in which the iconography of the oil derrick plays a role, cartographic representations are of relevance. Since the mid-twentieth century the oil derrick has often appeared as a pictogram, a simplified graphic picture, that, according to most map keys, indicates the same universal message: that a country (or a foreign company) is tapping oil deposits in a particular location (fig. 5.21). This combination of motifs, of Kuwait's map and the oil derrick, eventually even emerged as stamp design, commemorating in 1968 the discovery of oil at Burgan (fig. 5.22).[88] Integrated into both postage stamps and country maps, the oil derrick became an essential element of the "pictorial language of world traffic" (Aby Warburg) and the political iconography of petro-states.

In the 1970s, during the so-called oil crisis, even Arab Homeland maps contained oil infrastructures "for the celebration of oil as a sign of modernization and prosperity."[89] Although many oil industries were not yet nationalized, OPEC's oil embargo had

[88] Kuwait 1968, commem., MiNos. 372–73.

[89] The map that Zayde Antrim discusses was published in *al-ʿArabī* in 1974. Zayde Antrim, *Mapping the Middle East* (London: Reaktion, 2018), 246–48 and fig. 76.

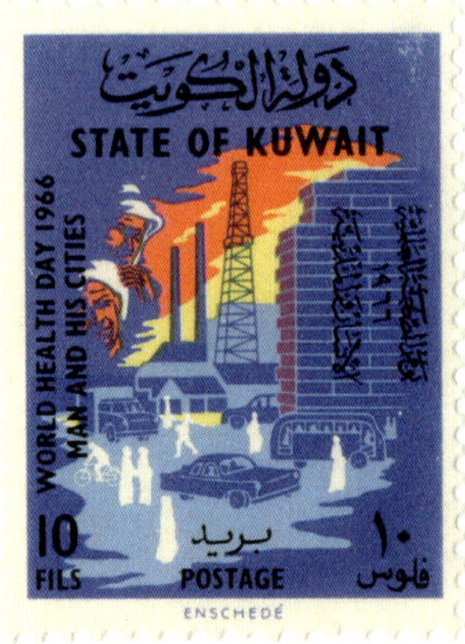

5.24 Commemorative stamp of the 1966 World Health Day with an oil derrick immersed in the industrial cityscape, issued April 7, 1966.

demonstrated the ultimate power these oil-producing countries nevertheless held over the petroleum-dependent world by turning the tap off. To incorporate petroleum icons into cartographic representations of Kuwait equally projected the country within a world interconnected by flows of petroleum.

During the state formation process of the 1950s, the government of Kuwait began using the oil derrick in various visual material issued by the state. Apart from the 1959 stamps, it was used as part of the cover design of the government gazette, and for posters of the state-owned Kuwait Airways, which advertised the country as a travel destination in the 1960s (fig. 5.23). Again and again, the oil derrick appeared in combination with other large modern architecture and infrastructure. It even appeared prominently—and somewhat ironically from today's perspective—on the 1966 World Health Day stamp issued by Kuwait that, which was themed "Man and His Cities," as integral part of the urban landscape (fig. 5.24).[90] While the symbol of the oil derrick in combination with maps and aerial views also indicated the geospatial location of oil production, in visual outlets like the poster and the gazette, the oil derrick manifested as the central element of the new political iconography of the petropolis of Kuwait that symbolically "nationalized" petroleum.

Through its oil-themed stamps, Kuwait aligned itself firmly with the growing number of oil-producing countries worldwide, other petro-states. Their usually affluent image and status was expressed in the visual business cards of oil-themed stamps. Given that Kuwait was the third Middle Eastern country to produce oil stamps and given that the 1959 definitive (pictorial but not commemorative) set included three different oil-infrastructure stamps, it is clear that the government of Kuwait fully and proudly indulged in the image of the petro-state that many other (Arab) oil producers subsequently followed, or even copied, although in an attenuated style. In particular, the 1959 Kuwaiti set's influence is

[90] Kuwait 1966, commem., MiNos. 315–16.

visible in Qatar's 1968 definitive issue, which used almost identical motifs: the ruler, a dhow, a desalination plant, an oil port, a mosque, and the town square.[91]

5.5 Absences in the Pictures of Development

In a paradoxical way, in the mid-twentieth century, while lived petro-modernity was gradually becoming inevitable, crude oil was increasingly absent from visual representations, almost becoming conspicuous in its invisibility. Natural phenomena like gushers (sudden eruptions of raw oil) and oil fires were sometimes captured on photographs, but such iconographies of oil quickly ceased to be shown as they came to signify inefficiency in oil production.[92]

The early political iconography of Kuwait was marked by other, even more decisive absences. In the 1959 set, except for the portrait of Shaykh Abdullah, none of the stamps depicted people—even though many of the sites would have normally included workers (the oil port), seafarers (the dhow), believers (the mosque), and shoppers and pedestrians (Safat Square), to name just a few. Given the extreme richness of detail in all of the 1959 pictorial stamps, it would have been easy to include a person next to the mosque or in the vicinity of the desalination plant, who would have been recognizable as such despite the small size of the postal miniatures. Only when comparing the ten rupee stamp of Safat Square with its postcard template can some small lines besides the cars extending from the foreground be identified as graphic abbreviations of people; however, only viewers who are familiar with the postcard version of the image will see them. Then again, if the postage stamps are considered as a continuation and translation of photographic images into another visual media, maybe the orientalist tradition of depopulating urban spaces and landscapes that manifested itself in the early photography of the Middle East also resonated here.[93] In any case, the 1959 set of Kuwaiti stamps renders ordinary people invisible and focuses on the representation of Shaykh Abdullah instead.

The infrastructural forms that took center stage in providing physical and visual evidence of the materialization of the emerging state (the provision of water and new educational institutions, for example) were strongly tied to the portrait of Shaykh Abdullah through the stamps' composition (country name and portrait). Such an observation almost echoes the *National Geographic* article from 1952, which claimed: "Behind all of

[91] Qatar 1961, definitives, MiNos. 341–54.

[92] Rare stamp examples are, for instance, a 1936–37 stamp from Peru depicting an oil gusher as a motif; also a Canadian stamp from 1950 presenting two oil derricks and an oil gusher.

[93] Ali Behdad and others have analyzed how "locals" were often staged in early photographs. Sometimes, however, "the Orientalist photograph depopulates the Orient of its inhabitants, for their presence robs the image of its quest for visual monumentalism and circumvent the possibility of visual appropriation." Ali Behdad, "The Orientalist Photograph," in *Photography's Orientalism: New Essays on Colonial Representation*, ed. Ali Behdad and Luke Gartlan (Los Angeles: Getty Research Institute, 2013), 22–24, here 24.

the modernization and breathless expansion is Kuwait's ruler, Sheik Abdullah Salim."[94] By contrast, the stamps seem to imply that ordinary people were supposedly not part of the image that Kuwait's multiple picturesque "business cards" should convey.

Postage stamps from socialist countries like the German Democratic Republic also celebrated infrastructures visually but—in line with socialist iconography—demonstratively placed "the workers" in front of them. Did the state of Kuwait not consider people crucial to its political and social imaginary, or did they have to be tamed and contained through visual absence from its political iconography to fit the intended state image? Can the absence of people in light of the visual dominance of infrastructure be read as a containment strategy of "unruly forces," as Penny Harvey and Hannah Knox have suggested elsewhere?[95]

When thinking about stamps as political symbols, contemporary politics in fact negotiated the conditions and political representation of Kuwaiti citizenship at the time. The same year the stamps were issued the government passed the first Kuwaiti citizenship law. For this law, a new official definition of what being "Kuwaiti" meant had to be found. With the new nationality law, as Farah Al-Nakib has shown, the state intended to create "a singular Kuwaiti national identity through citizenship subordinated to the nation-state previous loyalties to *farīj*, sect, family or tribe."[96] However, especially the "nationality law's emphasis on origin" produced a lasting differentiation between the townspeople as "original" Kuwaitis (or *ahl al-sūr*, the ones living inside the 1920 wall) and of "newcomers," the historically nomadic, later sedentarized Bedouin, despite the fact that they had equal shares in the historical formation of Kuwait, as well as people who had historically migrated from places like India, Iran, and Balochistan to Kuwait, who could also not or did not prove their presence within Kuwait Town prior to 1920.[97] Within Kuwaiti society, the law eventually stimulated a lasting estrangement between these groups, the *ḥaḍar* (settled urbanites including townspeople, merchants, sailors, pearl divers and so forth) and the Bedouin (or *badū* in local use; nomadic herdsmen and traders) in particular. Moreover, many non-Kuwaitis (like, for example, long-term residents of Iranian origin) and large numbers of incoming workers from other Arab, South Asian, and Western countries, who also lived in Kuwait City, had their hopes of gaining Kuwaiti citizenship dashed overnight by the nationality law. This strained situation relates, at least symbolically, to the absence of people in the pictures in view of the unsolved dilemma of the political representation of the various groups of people living in Kuwait as citizens.

94 Case, "Boom Time in Kuwait," 800.

95 They write, "The rhetorical narrative force of the developmental promise is thus amplified by those material engagements that reinforce the desire for infrastructural forms to contain unruly forces (human and non-human)." Harvey and Knox, "The Enchantments of Infrastructure," 534.

96 Al-Nakib, "Revisiting Ḥaḍar and Badū in Kuwait," 11 (italics in the original).

97 See ibid., 11–14.

Leading up to the country's independence in 1961, the quickly-expanding state apparatus was heavily fueled by oil revenues and became ever more focused on the persona of Shaykh Abdullah as the nexus of centralizing political power. This marked a shift from a diversified political power structure that included various social groups such as seafaring merchants, captains of pearling ships, and Bedouin traders toward a concentration of power in the House of Sabah, which was the sole receiver and distributer of oil revenues. The process of selecting recently built infrastructure and artistically translating them into pictures on Kuwaiti stamps initially decontextualized and defunctionalized them. Yet, in this new context, the images served to create a new infrastructure of political communication and to establish a new, internationally comprehensible state iconography—an iconography with links to other decolonizing nations and petro-states through the visual depiction of oil culture and the symbol of the oil derrick. The 1959 set of stamps set a precedent as an iridescent showcase of petro-modernity in urban visual culture.

5.6 Political Displays Beyond the Oil Stamps

The first issue of definitive Kuwaiti stamps not only marked the country's postal independence from Britain but also symbolized the initiation of political decolonialization that lead to Kuwait's independence on June 19, 1961. In this context, the new Kuwaiti stamps served as easily disseminated miniature travel guides that functioned as powerful visual icons of national self-representation to people abroad, entering offices, private homes, drawers and albums in Kuwait and elsewhere as a single miniature or as colorful pictorial collages.

In retrospective, the emerging political iconography of the modern petropolis had first been formulated for the cover of *al-Kuwayt al-Yawm* in 1954. The 1959 set of stamps consolidated the programmatic collage of infrastructure, modern architectural forms, maritime history, and petro-modernity that was continued and enlarged with the next set of stamps (in Kuwaiti Dinar) and the first set of Kuwaiti Dinar paper money and coins.

Kuwait's second set of definitives adopted four more or less identically stamp designs from the previous issue and was released on April 1, 1961, two months prior to independence. The 1961 set followed the imaginaries and narratives of modernization and progress through infrastructure and the representations of petro-modernity (displayed as oil derrick, oil-loading jetty, and Kuwait Airways plane), and also insofar as this set too was devoid of representations of ordinary people.[98]

98 Kuwait 1961, definitives, MiNos. 145–62.

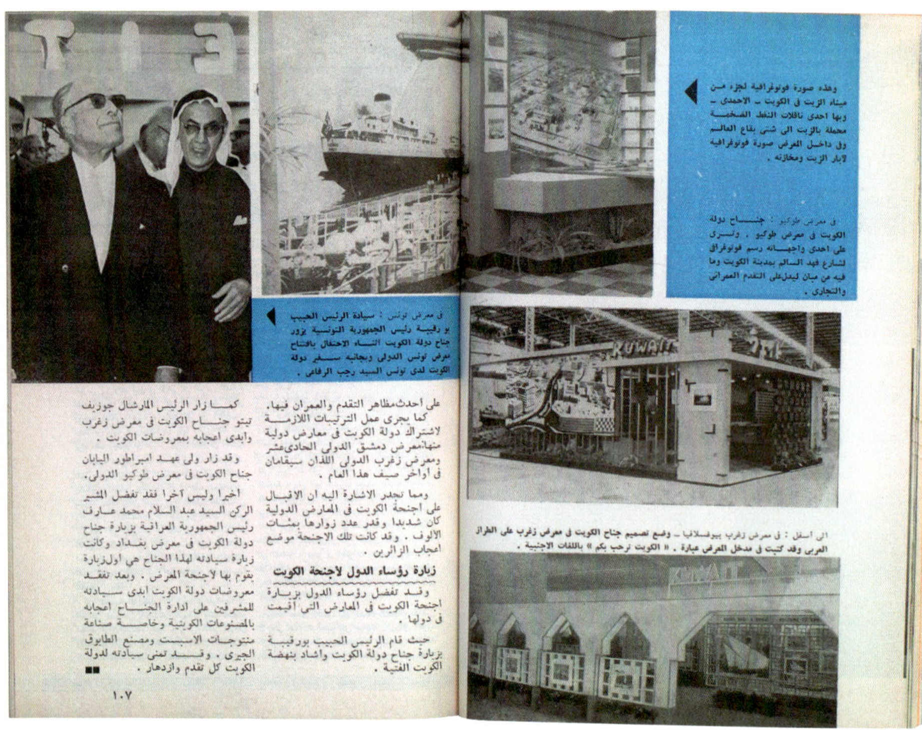

وهذه صورة فوتوغرافية لجزء من ميناء الزيت في الكويت ـ الاحمدى ـ وبها احدى ناقلات النفط الضخمة محملة بالزيت الى شتى بقاع العالم وفي داخل المعرض صورة فوتوغرافية لآبار الزيت ومخازنه .

في معرض طوكيو : جنـــاح دولة الكويت في معرض طوكيو . ونـــرى على احدى واجهـــاته رسم فوتوغرافي لشارع فهد السالم بمدينة الكويت وما فيه من مبان ليدل على التقدم العمراني والتجارى .

في معرض تونس : سيادة الرئيس الحبيب بو رقيبة رئيس الجمهورية التونسية يزور جناح دولة الكويت اثنـــاء الاحتفال بافتتاح معرض تونس الدولى وبجانبه سـفير دولة الكويت لدى تونس السيد رجب الرفاعى .

على أحدث مظاهر التقدم والعمران فيها.

كما يجرى عمل الترتيبات اللازمـــة لاشتراك دولة الكويت في معارض دولية منها معرض دمشق الدولى الحادى عشر ومعرض زغرب الدولى اللذان سيقامان في اواخر صيف هذا العام .

ومما تجدر الاشارة اليه ان الاقبـال على اجنحة الكويت في المعارض الدولية كان شديدا وقدر عدد زوارها بمئـات الالوف . وقد كانت تلك الاجنحة موضع اعجاب الزائرين .

زيارة رؤساء الدول لاجنحة الكويت

وقـــد تفضل رؤساء الدول بزيـارة اجنحة الكويت في المعارض التى اقيمت في دولها .

حيث قام الرئيس الحبيب بورقيبـة بزيارة جناح دولة الكويت واشاد بنهضة الكويت الفنية .

كمـــا زار الرئيس المارشال جوزيف تيتو جنـــاح الكويت في معرض زغرب وابدى اعجابه بمعروضات الكويت .

وقد زار ولى عهـد امبراطور اليابان جناح الكويت في معرض طوكيو الدولى.

اخيرا وليس آخرا فقد تفضل المشير الركن السيد عبد السلام محمد عـارف رئيس الجمهورية العراقية بزيارة جناح دولة الكويت في معرض بغـداد وكانت زيارة سيادته لهذا الجناح هي اول زيارة يقوم بها لاجنحة المعرض . وبعد تفقـد معروضات دولة الكويت ابدى سـيادته للمشرفين على ادارة الجنـــاح اعجابه بالمصنوعات الكويتية وخاصـــة صناعة منتوجـات الاسبـست ومصنع الطابوق الجيرى . وقـــد تمنى سيادته لدولة الكويت كل تقدم وازدهار . ■■

الى أسفل : في معرض زغرب بيوغسلافيا ـ وضع تصميم جناح الكويت في معرض زغرب على الطراز العربي وقد كتب في مدخل المعرض عبارة . « الكويت ترحب بكم » باللغات الاجنبية .

١٠٧

5.25 Spread from *al-'Arabī*, April 1964, reporting on Kuwaiti pavilions at international exhibitions in Tunis, Tokyo, and Zagreb (clockwise).

Also on April 1, 1961, the Kuwaiti Dinar, as the country's new currency, was put into circulation for the first time.[99] While displaying a profile portrait of Shaykh Abdullah on the front, the paper money's reverse offered five different designs with motifs of the port of Kuwait in Shuwaikh (quarter dinar); Shuwaikh Secondary School (half dinar); a cement factory (one dinar); a street view of modern-looking middle-income housing (five dinar); and a two-masted dhow (ten dinar). Clearly, the national currency also engaged with the political iconography established by the government gazette and the postage stamps, although it did not refer to petroleum infrastructures as such. Maybe it was too suggestive and thus politically problematic to reference the petroleum industry on the paper version of the oil monies that Shaykh Abdullah received from the Anglo-American oil company.

The influence of this visual program of political representation was lasting and manifested in other forms of political display, too. During the 1960s, the Kuwaiti government frequently showcased the country on an international stage by participating

[99] To view the first issue of Kuwaiti banknotes, see Central Bank of Kuwait, Banknotes of the First Issue, accessed January 31, 2021, https://www.cbk.gov.kw/en/banknotes-and-coins/banknotes/first-issue.

in various international exhibitions. As one article in *al-ʿArabī* magazine reported, Kuwaiti pavilions were shown at exhibitions in Tripoli, Tokyo, Damascus, Zagreb, Tunis, and Milan (fig. 5.25).[100] Judging from the report and the photographs presented in the article, the Kuwaiti pavilion at Tokyo featured the display of the oil terminal in Ahmadi (infrastructure) and a large-scale photograph of Fahad al-Salem Street (architecture). Oil installations and newly built architecture were also a topic at Tripoli. Photographs of the installations at Tunis and Zagreb document displays of pre-oil maritime culture that, according to the article, were well-received. This indicates that even in the following decade, architecture and large-scale (oil) infrastructures functioned as markers of modernization and petro-modernity with which Kuwait was internationally represented. Yet, its maritime history also played a role in creating the image of Kuwait to audiences abroad, similar to the pictures of traditional boat types included in the 1959 set of stamps and the cover of *al-Kuwayt al-Yawm*. Moreover, it is noticeable that for Kuwaiti artists such as Abdullah Al Qasser, Tareq Sayid Rajab, and Ibrahim Ismail, the country's maritime past of pearling, fishing, and boat building emerged as important themes in visual arts production during the second half of the twentieth century that equally acknowledged and challenged Kuwait's rapid urban transformation. Then, in August 1990, the country unwillingly experienced a second rupture, a second transformation that, triggered by petroleum, brought the dark side of petroleum to the fore.

[100] "Al-Kuwayt fī l maʿāriḍ al-duwaliyya. Baʿḍa āyām tashtariku fī maʿriḍ mīlānū al-ʿālamī [Kuwait at the International Exhibitions: In a Few Days It Is Participating in Milan's International Exhibition]," *al-ʿArabī*, no. 65 (April 1964): 103–7.

6. THE 1990–91 GULF WAR: OIL FIRES, ECOLOGICAL CATASTROPHE, AND A SECOND RUPTURE

Kuwait maintained its position as the role model of the oil welfare state until that moment when the 1990–91 Gulf War made the firm belief in petroleum as harbinger of a prosperous future vanish into thin air. Leading up to it, the 1980s were a turbulent decade: in 1982, the country experienced the crash of its unofficial stock market Souq al-Manakh, subsequently a rapid decline of petro-welfare that had been created with the "Kuwaiti model," and the temporary suspension of the constitution and the National Assembly in 1986. In August 1990, the Iraqi army under Saddam Hussein invaded Kuwait and annexed the city-state. Especially for Kuwaitis, but by default for the Gulf region at large, the resulting Gulf War and the images of burning oil wells and massive oil spills unfolded a destructive side of petroleum on a scale hitherto unknown that sedimented in the collective memory of the region.

The Gulf War, which was effectively a war about petroleum, played out in a calamitous stroke against Kuwait's political, social, and financial viability as well as in a devastating ecological catastrophe caused by military warfare, oil fires, and oil spills. Consequently, a shift in the ways in which petroleum was seen and valued happened. Following the oil industrialization in the mid-twentieth century, petroleum had predominantly represented political stability, prosperity, and sociocultural modernization on the Arabian side of the Gulf in accordance with the interests of various stakeholders as the discussion in the previous chapters has shown. Now, around forty years later, petroleum had triggered a hitherto unimaginable nightmare that left Kuwait and the Gulf in limbo. Kuwait's personal "oil curse" became the Gulf War, from the Iraqi invasion, Operation Desert Storm, to the fight against oil spills and fires in the months after the war had ended. Therefore, as a historic case study, Kuwait and its twentieth-century relationship with oil not only represent the extraordinary and sudden abundance of petro-pleasures, but also the confrontation with petro-modernity's worst nightmares, for which the history of petroleum in Kuwait puts the whole spectrum of iridescence on display. Looking back, Kuwait's "golden era" came to an end with the Iraqi invasion and the Gulf War.

https://doi.org/10.1515/9783110714739-008

A War About Petroleum

On August 2, 1990, the Iraqi army invaded Kuwait crossing their shared northern border and occupied Kuwait City. Iraq had just emerged defeated from the draining Iran-Iraq War (1980–88) and the military maneuver hit Kuwait rather unprepared.[1] Yet, Iraqi threats to Kuwait's sovereignty were nothing new. Already in 1961 shortly after Kuwait's independence from Britain, Iraq had questioned its neighbor's political status and claimed to incorporate Kuwait's territory into its realms as a "19th province."[2] These were not just empty words, as the newly-independent Iraqi state under Abd al-Karim Qasim mobilized its forces along the shared Kuwaiti-Iraqi border to underline its claims. At the time, British troops were moved to Kuwait and were later superseded by troops of the United Arab Republic, Jordan, Saudi Arabia, Sudan, and Tunis to prevent a military conflict. Although the insecurity that a bigger (neighboring) country would invade the city-state had remained ever since, the threatening feeling had been more or less successfully suppressed during the following peaceful and prosperous decades.[3] Yet, Iraq's motivation to claim the rich oil reserves and the sophisticated infrastructure that Kuwait had built and showcased in a myriad of circulating images resurfaced abruptly in the early nineties.[4]

What unfolded over the following seven months was a political, social, ecological, and economic catastrophe with petroleum as the decisive factor in it. Prior to the invasion, Kuwait's oil industry had produced around 2 million barrels of crude oil per day and refined around 750,000 barrels daily in high-tech refineries.[5] By the time the Iraqi army had left, according to the KOC, at least 613 oil wells were ignited, an additional 76 wells

[1] Although the invasion of the Iraqi army surprised Kuwait's citizens and residents overnight, it did not come totally out of the blue in the summer of 1990. The invasion preceded debates among Iraq, Kuwait, and other OPEC members regarding the oil price and the production volume. Iraq had argued in favor of a substantial oil price raise and had accused Kuwait of putting too much oil on the market. Negotiations between Iraq and Kuwait held in Jeddah on August 1 failed. At the time, Iraqi troops were already stationed along Kuwait's northern border. Shortly after the Iraqi army had occupied Kuwait, the United Nations ratified several resolutions that Iraq should retreat peacefully, arguing that its claims were unjustified and imposed various international sanctions against Iraq. Many countries decided on oil embargos against Kuwaiti and Iraqi oil. Iraq's oil pipelines, such as the al-Muajjiz Pipeline across Saudi Arabia and the Kirkuk–Ceyhan Pipeline to the Mediterranean crossing Turkey, were consequently closed, while imports into Iraq and Kuwait were sanctioned and aviation was blocked.

[2] For a detailed discussion, see Miriam Joyce, *Kuwait, 1945–1996: An Anglo-American Perspective* (London: Frank Cass, 1998). For contemporary newspaper reports, see "The News in Pictures," *The Sphere* July 8, 1961, 43; "The Allure of Oil and the Threat to Independence: Tension in Kuwait," *Illustrated London News*, July 8, 1961, 40–41.

[3] Kuwaiti historian Hassan Ali al-Ebraheem described Kuwait's feeling of geopolitical insecurity as that of a "small state living in a bad neighborhood." Quoted after Mary A. Tétreault, "Kuwait: The Morning After," *Current History* 91, no. 561 (1992): 6.

[4] Ibid.

[5] Ibid.

were gushing only, and 99 were damaged.[6] Considering that Kuwait had 1,135 operating oil wells prior to the invasion, this was a substantial blow to its oil industry and thus its national economy.[7] Tellingly, never before in the history of Kuwait or the Gulf had petroleum as raw material become so visible and visual as when the oil fields started burning and massive oil spills stained the desert, coastlines, and the Gulf waters. Kuwait's petro-modernity culminated in this dramatic upsurge that openly revealed not only what greed for oil and petro-capitalism could do but petroleum's toxicity as it destroyed Kuwait's and the Gulf's flora and fauna and caused heavy air pollution that people were immediately affected by.

During and immediately after the Gulf War, scientists were afraid that the oil spills and oil fires in Kuwait and Saudi Arabia (where most of the sea-carried oil arrived) would cause globally devastating scenarios such as "a global climate chill, intense acid rain, or a failure of the monsoons in Asia."[8] It quickly amounted to a potentially global threat revealing the strategic importance of Kuwaiti oil to the global economy as well as the unknown hazardous potential of the gigantic amounts of oil that escaped out into the open; something that Gulf oil states and oil companies operating there had tried to prevent all along. Moreover, for people living in Kuwait, citizens and residents alike, petroleum, prior to August 1990, had come to signify Kuwait's national identity and its prosperous future perspective (as wealthy, sovereign state). The Iraqi invasion not only destroyed the material and economic base, but also hollowed out these components of identity. Overall, the Gulf War disclosed the fragility of the Kuwaiti oil welfare state and of a global economy that essentially depended on oil and was willing to wage war for it.

Early in the Gulf War, Saddam Hussein announced that petroleum would be used as a weapon of war and Kuwait's oil reserves would be destroyed. Given Kuwaiti oil's strategic importance but also the alleged fear that Iraq would build an atomic bomb or use chemical weapons, the United States, together with Canada, Great Britain, and France, initiated the Operation Desert Shield, gathering air and ground forces in the region, especially in Saudi Arabia, in preparation of a strike against the occupying Iraqi forces in Kuwait.[9] Mary Ann Tétreault has highlighted that Kuwait's government-in-exile paid substantial amounts to the US and other partners in the allied coalition for the invasion.[10] After Saddam Hussein ignored the final ultimatum set by the United Nations to leave Kuwait by January 15,

[6] Muhammad Sadiq and John C. McCain, *The Gulf War Aftermath*: An Environmental Tragedy, Environment & Assessment 4 (Dordrecht: Kluwer Academic, 1993), 59. Overall, estimations vary greatly, see the tabular overview in Sadiq and McCain, *The Gulf War Aftermath*, 67, table 3.1.

[7] Sadiq and McCain, *The Gulf War Aftermath*, 68, table 3.2. Tétreault, however, mentions 1,330 active oil wells, Tétreault, "Kuwait," 6.

[8] Faye Flam, "A Brighter Forecast from Kuwait," *Science* 253, no. 5015 (1991): 28.

[9] However, no evidence for chemical weapons nor an immediate nuclear threat could be found, Marie Gottschalk, "Operation Desert Cloud: The Media and the Gulf War," *World Policy Journal* 9, no. 3 (1992): 452, 463.

[10] Tétreault, "Kuwait," 9.

1991, the coalition started its aerial attack on January 16. In what is known as Operation Desert Storm, allied ground and aerial attacks on the Iraqi army continued over the next forty-three days. On February 28, Kuwait was liberated, but many human lives had been lost and much petroleum spilled.

It was not only a war about petroleum, it became a war with petroleum; not only a fossil-fueled war, but a crude war. The Iraqi army under Saddam Hussein occupied and annexed the Gulf monarchy; it then looted the country, especially its oil fields. During December 1990 to late February 1991, Iraqi troops set over 600 oil wells on fire and damaged oil terminals, pipelines, refineries, and berthing tankers. Yet, it is now believed that US-led bombing also caused severe damage to the oil facilities and contributed to the known oil spills.[11] As a result of the escaping crude, as one study published in the journal *Science* noted, "close to the fires the smoke rained oil drops… . This oil, together with soot fallout, coated large areas of the desert with a black, tar-like covering."[12] In addition, as the study reported, "oil spewing out from uncapped wells formed large pools of oil on the desert, some of which were alight."[13] The oil that emerged from the oil wells now built its own tarred roads in the desert and constructed its own pools, not swimming pools, but pools filled with tar.[14] Once the Iraqi army had withdrawn, Kuwait became the scene of an international battle against the burning oil wells and the seeping of oil into the Persian Gulf, until, on November 6, 1991, the last oil well fire was finally extinguished. In this short period between August 1990 and then, some of the most iridescent images of oil emerged that are emblematic of the ambivalence of petro-modernity overall.

The Ecological Catastrophe as an Aerial View

An aerial photograph taken by the National Aeronautics and Space Administration (NASA) from their space shuttle *Atlantis* on April 7, 1991, shows the oil well fires and the smoke plumes north and south of Kuwait City (fig. 6.1).[15] From an altitude of 457 kilometers, the characteristic spit of Kuwait Bay with its densely built-up urban area contrasts with the hinterland and the Gulf. Several hundred burning oil wells cast their lengthy pitch-black smoke plumes that drift from north to south over the region,

[11] Gottschalk, "Operation Desert Cloud," 453.

[12] Peter V. Hobbs and Lawrence F. Radke, "Airborne Studies of the Smoke From the Kuwait Oil Fires," *Science* 256, no. 5059 (1992): 987. See also Sadiq and McCain, *The Gulf War Aftermath*.

[13] Hobbs and Radke, "Airborne Studies of the Smoke From the Kuwait Oil Fires," 987.

[14] In the early 2000s, a project was proposed to pave "roughly 5,000 kilometers worth of roads" using high-petroleum concentrations in the sand that remained from the war. The reporting journalist commented sarcastically, "When life gives you asphalt, make a highway." See Ben Shouse, "Kuwait Unveils Plan to Treat Festering Desert Wound," *Science* 293, no. 5534 (2001): 1410.

[15] "Smoke from a Distant Fire," *Nasa Earth Observatory*, July 8, 2011, accessed January 18, 2021, https://earthobservatory.nasa.gov/features/ShuttleRetrospective/page8.php.

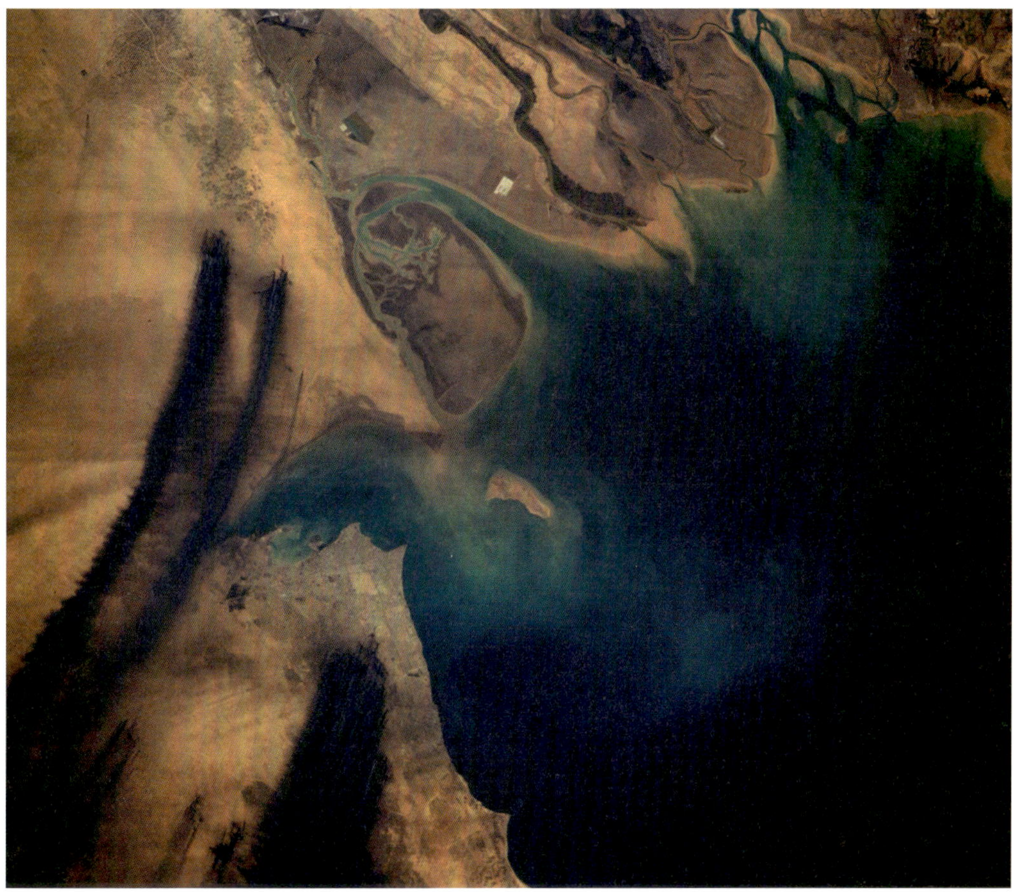

6.1 Aerial photograph taken by the NASA from the space shuttle *Atlantis* on April 7, 1991, that shows the oil well fires and the smoke plumes on Kuwaiti territory.

enveloping it for hundreds of kilometers in darkness. By the late 1980s, lifestyles across the globe had become reliant on the burning of fossil fuels, but in 1991, the downside of oil cultures materialized as geographically condensed form in Kuwait, as the earth was bleeding black tears across the sand and sea for hundreds of kilometers. Therefore, the aerial images of this oil catastrophe encapsulated the age of fossil energy and the high costs of its anthropogenic deployment.

Aerial imagery provided by agencies like NASA, the Système Probatoire d'Observation de la Terre (SPOT), and LANDSAT Thematic Mapper (LANDSAT TM), was crucial in determining whether and where oil wells were burning as well as the quantity of oil fired up at each side. It has been estimated that the approximate 6 million barrels which burned per day would have fueled 7,312,500 tanks of a regular car or a jet for 193 trips around the globe.[16] In addition, once the war had ceased, various scientific initiatives flew aerial surveys to examine the smoke dispersion and to describe the morphology of fire flames and smoke plumes.[17] Like crude's iridescence and pearls' luster and shapes, the flames and the smoke emitted by the oil fires were not only of different shapes, but they also displayed a "color" spectrum, so to speak, varying from "gray-white to dense dark in color," depending on the exact chemical characteristics of the burning matter.[18]

Shortly thereafter, cultural analyst Andrew Ross argued that "if the oil slick became the leading ecological actor during the war itself, the spectacle of the burning Kuwaiti oil wells played the starring role in the media war's denouement… . The oil slick and the burning wells were the only images of ecological spoliation the public did get to see, and the ones that the public remembers."[19] These images also came to stand in place of the human beings who died and the several hundred prisoners of war on both sides, many of which never returned. Ross added that the circulating aerial images of the ecological catastrophe helped to distract from the military complex (allied and Iraqi) as probably the biggest pollutant in the conflict.[20] The disembodied aerial view as cast from an unmanned satellite or a detached space shuttle again unfolded its play of miniaturization and sublime minimization of the violent social actions taking place on the ground.

In light of the decades-old debate about the peak of fossil deposits and their finiteness, the Kuwaiti oil fires and oil spills sarcastically testified to the substantial availability of the fossil raw material in the Gulf region. The question that oil companies, nation-states, scientists, citizens, activists, and journalists have always asked and have since continued to ask—how long will oil last?—was answered in smoke and fire, loud and clear: for a long time. And for once, this response was met with ambivalence, at least as long as the region suffered under the smoke, the fires, and the loss of its resources. The ecological catastrophe as it spilled out on site and emerged in imagery did not lead to a serious consideration of stopping the oil production in Kuwait or the region. Rather, the visual representations of oil spills played favorably into the hands of the controlled corporate exploitation of petroleum, given that the KOC represented a (also visual) history of uninterrupted, efficient oil production with hardly any ecological calamities until 1990. Even the nationalization of the industry in 1976 had been a peaceful takeover. It is therefore not surprising that there was an overall agreement on reopening industrial production in Kuwait once the oil spills were brought under control.

[16] Christ Paine and John Quigley, "Gulf War Oil Disaster," *Counterspill*, accessed February 5, 2021, https://www.counterspill.org/disaster/gulf-war-oil-disaster#timeline.

[17] Sadiq and McCain, *The Gulf War Aftermath*, 76–80, 86–90.

[18] Ibid., 60.

[19] Andrew Ross, "The Ecology of Images," in *Visual Culture: Images and Interpretations*, ed. Norman Bryson, Michael A. Holly, and Keith P. F. Moxey (Hanover: Wesleyan University Press, 1994), 327.

[20] Ibid., 327–28.

With the Gulf War, Kuwait's existence was revealed to be tied to petroleum for good. Petroleum had stimulated both Kuwait's stability during the "golden era" and the country's fragility during the 1990–91 invasion. Until today, the latter marks a historic caesura in Kuwait's history, a second rupture or transformation causing a new nomenclature of "pre-" and "post-war." Yet, how Kuwaiti citizens and residents experienced and came to view the war differs greatly. Given that the invasion happened during the hot summer months, many Kuwaitis were abroad, on holidays, business trips, or in their second homes elsewhere. Only about one third of the population experienced the invasion as "insiders" in the country itself, while the "outsiders" watched it from afar on television together with the rest of the world.[21] Even people who remained inside Kuwait often watched the warfare unfold on their TV sets, and so the Iraqi invasion became a TV experience and a mass-media spectacle for many, starring petroleum as an element with major screen time. Political scientist Marie Gottschalk and others have concluded that the Western and especially US media coverage of the Gulf War was heavily biased.[22] The sophisticated technology of media coverage "was employed primarily to transport the viewer to the big event, not to increase the viewer's understanding of the big picture."[23] Often called a "video-game war" due to its precision bombing and night-vision equipment that felt "cinematic and often sensational" underlined with "pounding new theme music," it comes hardly as a surprise that the Gulf War has been given a firm presence in video games such as *Battlefield 3* (2011) and *Call of Duty: Modern Warfare* (2019).[24]

The Gulf War and Visual Culture

The Gulf War has triggered various forms of documentary and artistic engagement with the events ever since. Providing a detailed analysis of the visual culture and subsequent artistic examination of the Gulf War would exceed the scope of this book, although its art-historical analysis would be an important undertaking especially as the historic documentation, scientific investigation, and artistic inquiry of the Gulf War appear very heterogenous with multiple, contradicting narratives and perspectives. To provide a preliminary idea of the range that spans the Gulf War's visual culture, I point to some aspects that would be worthy of further research.

[21] Philip Shenon, "A New Divide for Kuwaitis: Who Stayed and Who Fled," *The New York Times*, March 12, 1991, 13, accessed January 18, 2021, https://www.nytimes.com/1991/03/12/world/after-the-war-kuwaiti-politics-a-new-divide-for-kuwaitis-who-stayed-and-who-fled.html.

[22] Gottschalk, "Operation Desert Cloud"; Stewart Purvis, "The Media and the Gulf War," *RSA Journal* 139, no. 5423 (1991).

[23] Gottschalk, "Operation Desert Cloud," 472.

[24] Ken Burns, "The Painful, Essential Images of War," *The New York Times*, January 27, 1991, accessed February 5, 2021, https://www.nytimes.com/1991/01/27/arts/the-painful-essential-images-of-war.html.

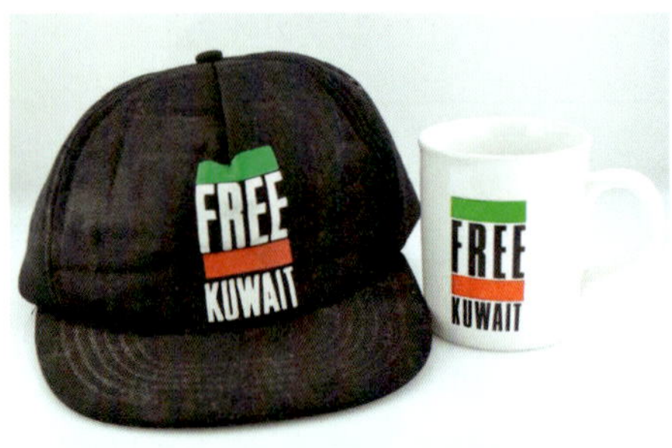

6.2 Hat and mug with the Free Kuwait logo which had been designed by Michael Lorrigan, Sam Bassan, and Ali Al-Mulaifi. Photograph taken by Adel Al-Yousifi, 2012.

Almost immediately after the country's occupation, Kuwaiti citizens and government officials, who were exiled abroad, formed the *Free Kuwait Campaign* together with sympathizing foreigners that became crucial in advocating for Kuwait's liberation and for the reinstation of the Kuwaiti government. The "Free Kuwait" logo, which consists of a horizontal green stripe, the capitalized writing "FREE", a red horizontal strip and the capitalized writing "KUWAIT" stacked below one another—in reference to the Kuwaiti flag—became crucial in promoting the movement widely and visibly (fig. 6.2). The campaign materialized and mobilized with the help of a broad variety of merchandise articles, such as caps, pins, and T-shirts, with the eye-catching logo.

A member of *Free Kuwait* in Britain, the Kuwaiti photographer Adel Al-Yousifi returned from London to Kuwait once air flights were permitted again and subsequently documented the immediate aftermath of the war in over 15,000 photographs covering not only Kuwait City but also the hinterland and coastal areas. Today, Al-Yousifi has

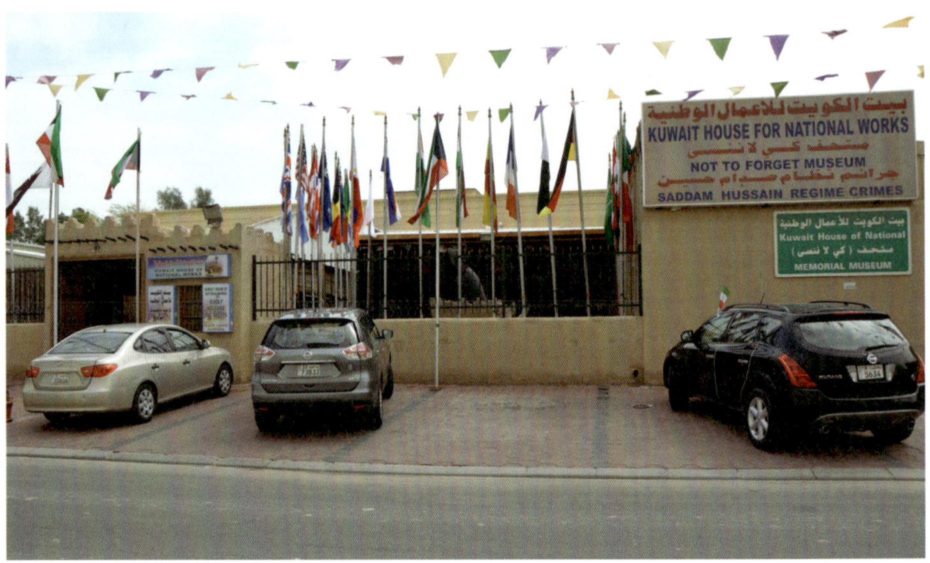

6.3 The entrance of the Kuwait House for National Works, Kuwait City. Photograph taken in February 2016.

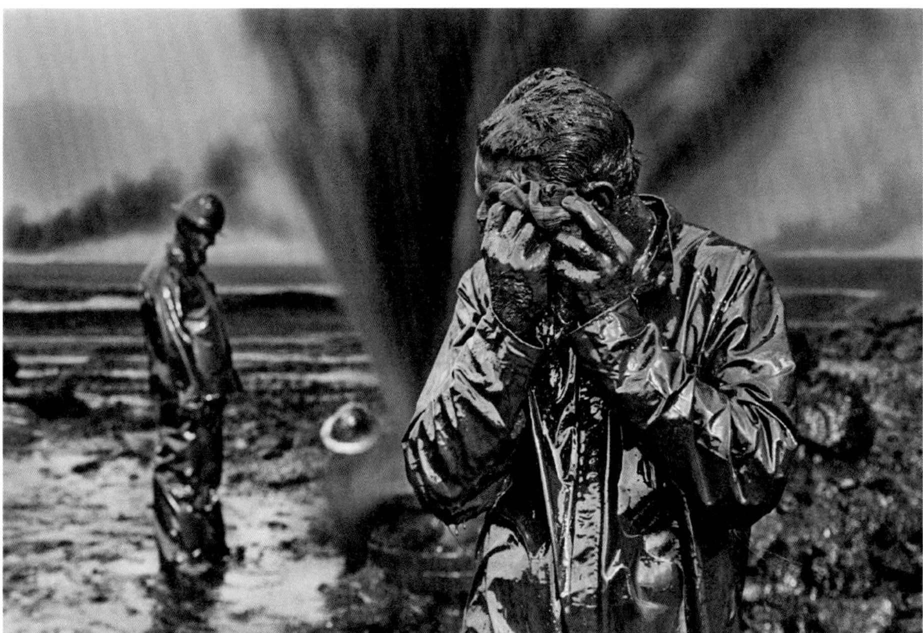

6.4 Sebastião Salgado, *Desert Hell*, Kuwait, 1991. Gelatin silver print.

published his photographs and his point-of-view online with an extensive website.[25] Moreover, his photographs became publicly accessible as part of the memorial museum *bayt al-Kuwayt li-lʿamāl al-waṭaniyya* (The Kuwait House for National Works), also called the "Not to forget Museum Saddam Hussain Regime Crimes," which is a private initiative. The museum, located in a converted warehouse, thematizes the Iraqi invasion in form of illuminated dioramas and photographic displays of the warfare and damage done to Kuwait and its society (fig. 6.3).[26]

Another extensive photographic corpus, which has already received international attention, was created by Brazilian photojournalist Sebastião Salgado (*1944, Aimorés, Brazil).[27] Salgado visited Kuwait throughout the month of April 1991 to photograph the joint efforts of Kuwaiti and international teams to extinguish the burning oil wells for a

[25] Adel Al-Yousifi, "Kuwait Invasion: The Evidence," *Evidence*, accessed February 5, 2021, http://www.evidence.org.kw.

[26] Yasser Mahgoub briefly mentions the museum, but a substantial analysis is yet missing. See Yasser Mahgoub, "The Impact of the War on the Architecture of Kuwait," *International Journal of Architectural Research* 2, no. 1 (2008): 239.

[27] Salgado first started out as an economist, shifting to photography in the early 1970s. He became an associate member of Magnum Photos in 1981 and a full member in 1984.

New York Times reportage that appeared in June.[28] The stylized portraits of fire fighters drenched in metallic shimmering mud, the oil slick, are emblematic (fig. 6.4). The iridescent oil slick, which also coated every rift of the environment, in combination with the sheer endless variations of dramatic shapes of oil fires, smoke, and clouds made the catastrophe appear both haptic and sublime. Twenty-five years later, in 2016, Salgado and his wife Lélia Wanick Salgado published the photobook *Kuwait: A Desert on Fire* that contains a large number of partly unpublished photographs taken in 1991. Asked about the reasons for publishing the shots so many years later, Salgado explained: "I felt the images had a timeless quality; they were taken in 1991, but they could be taken today or tomorrow if a similar disaster occurred."[29] Thus, in Salgado's view, the ecological catastrophe that affected Kuwait and the Arabian Peninsula stands in pars pro toto for oil disasters around the world that have since regularly occurred and will most likely continue to happen in the future.

Recently, renewed interest in artworks that thematize the Gulf War was demonstrated. MoMA PS1 showed the exhibition *Theater of Operations: The Gulf Wars 1991–2011* from November 2019 to March 2020 in New York.[30] Linking the Gulf War with the Iraq War that started in 2003 and the since then ongoing military conflict, the curators Peter Eleey and Ruba Katrib brought together "a multigenerational group of Iraqi and Kuwaiti artists, and some of Iraqi descent, who were working contemporaneously in different regions and under differing circumstances" in conjunction with Western artists, mostly from the US.[31] The show deliberately discusses the US involvement in these wars, investigating the relationship with Iraq in particular. Still, a substantial number of artworks thematize the invasion in Kuwait and the 1991 Gulf War, such as several paintings and drawings by Thuraya Al-Baqsami, the *War Diaries* of Dia al-Azzawi, Susan Crile's *Field of Fire*, video works by Monira Al Qadiri and Alia Farid, as well as photographic works by Tarek Al-Ghoussein and Jean-Luc Moulène. Taken together, they provide for divergent experiences, perspectives, and subjectivities through which to examine the atrocities as well as the role oil has played in the conflict.

[28] Wald wrote that "Salgado shoots an average of 10 to 12 rolls a day. In the Kuwaiti oilfields, he shot 200 rolls, or a little more than 7,000 pictures, of which he printed an average of six from each roll, in small work prints. From these he selected 47 to send to this magazine. (Usually, photographers send either all their film of a shoot to their editors or their selection of hundreds of prints)." Matthew L. Wald, "Sebastiao Salgado: The Eye of The Photojournalist," *The New York Times*, June 9, 1991, 72, accessed February 5, 2021, https://www.nytimes.com/1991/06/09/magazine/sebastiao-salgado-the-eye-of-the-photojournalist.html.

[29] Sebastião Salgado and Lélia Wanick Salgado, *Kuwait: A Desert on Fire* (Cologne: Taschen, 2016), 15.

[30] Peter Eleey and Ruba Katrib, eds., *Theater of Operations: The Gulf Wars 1991–2011* (New York: MoMA PS1, 2019); Exhibition catalog published in conjunction with the exhibition of the same name, shown at MoMA PS1, New York, from November 3, 2019 until March 1, 2020. Unfortunately, I was not able to visit the exhibition at the time.

[31] Peter Eleey and Ruba Katrib, "Preface and Acknowledgements," in *Theater of Operations: The Gulf Wars 1991–2011*, ed. Peter Eleey and Ruba Katrib (New York: MoMA PS1, 2019), 10.

National Oil Ceremonial Revisited

In addition, the Kuwaiti government employed state ceremonies and national symbols to subsequently integrate the experiences into official narratives. By doing so, it aimed at performing and displaying stability and continuity, and guiding an official way of reading the historic event. Moreover, these symbolic forms can be interpreted as an attempt to level out the negative upheavals of petro-modernity by showing the government in a position of control, even if it is control over ceremonial and performative forms.

Historically, the first state official oil ceremony took place on June 30, 1946. That day, then-ruling Shaykh Ahmad al-Jaber Al Sabah inaugurated the first oil shipment to Britain, officially marking Kuwait's initiation as an oil-exporting country. Now-iconic photographs show the ruler turning a silver valve to open the pipes that would fill the oil tanker

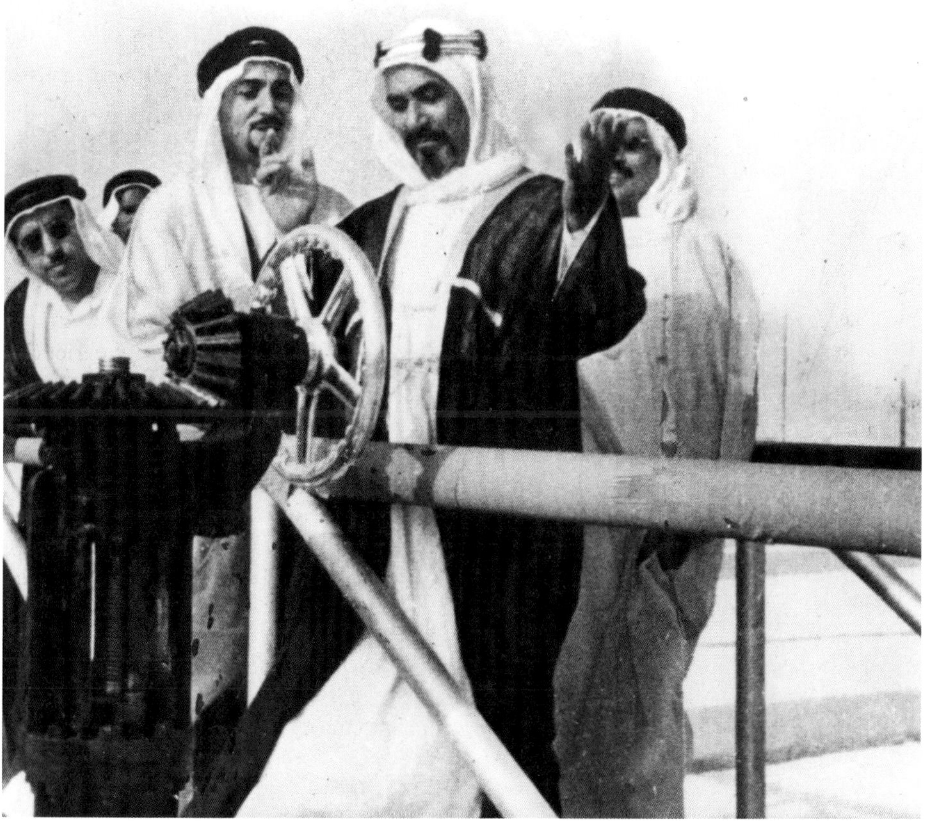

6.5 Black-and-white photograph of His Highness Shaykh Jabir Al Sabah at the ceremony to celebrate the first loading of oil in Kuwait. June 30, 1946, photographer unknown.

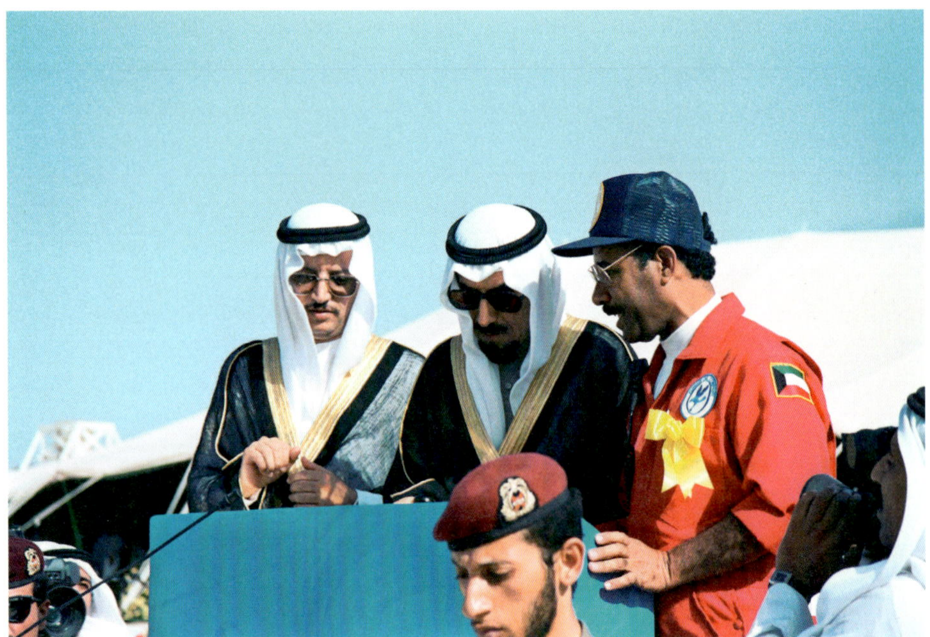

6.6 Emir Jaber al-Ahmad al-Jaber Al Sabah during the ceremony of extinguishing the last burning oil well, November 6, 1991.

British Fusilier with petroleum in less than twelve hours (fig. 6.5).[32] In the photographs documenting the ceremonial setup, Shaykh Ahmad takes center stage together with the valve allegedly made from silver, arguably to symbolize petroleum's financial value. Today, this photo marks the beginning of Kuwait's oil industrialization.[33]

While the 1946 celebrations had signaled an official opening, the related 1991 event served to symbolize closure. On November 6, 1991, Emir Jaber al-Ahmad Al Sabah (r. 1977–2006) officially closed the last burning oil well, Burgan 118. Actually, firefighters had already quenched this well some days prior, but it was reignited to turn its capping into a symbolic event by the hand of the emir. This event also took place in the desert, where a stage had been erected, embedded into a landscape of large carpets, tents, and rows of chairs for the members of the royal family, government officials, the press, and the

[32] On the 1946 photograph and the iconography and (in)visibility of oil and water in the second half of twentieth-century Kuwait, see Hindelang, "Precious Property."

[33] This ceremony was repeated, almost reenacted, on June 30, 1996, in celebration of the oil industrialization's fiftieth anniversary. Again, Emir Jaber turned a golden valve in acknowledgment of the historic opening ceremony. The photographic documentation shows the emir, the valve, and several officials accompanying the ruler. Wearing a traditional *bisht dhahabī*, their clothing matched the valve, whose materiality had shifted from silver to gold, probably not only to highlight the value of the "black gold" but also the successful longevity of the industry.

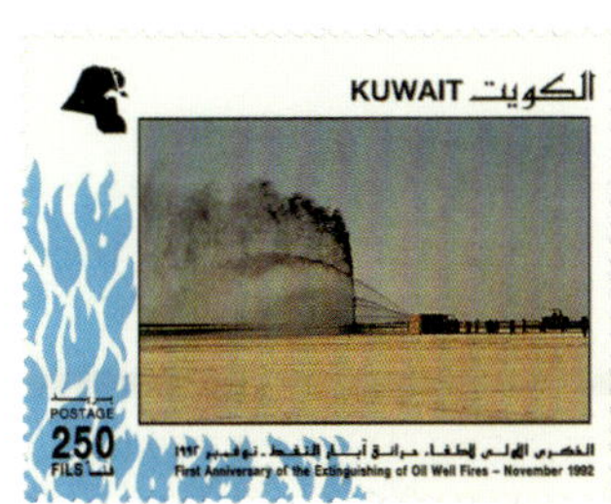

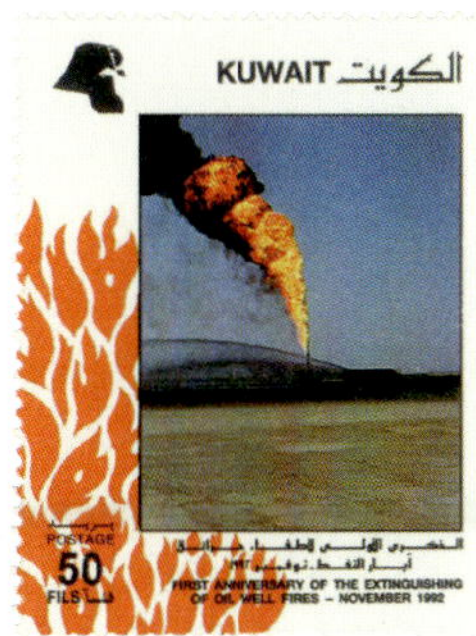

6.7 Two stamps from a set of four multicolor commemorative stamps issued on the occassion of the "First Anniversary of Extinguishing of Oil Well Fires," November 16, 1992.

firefighter teams. Standing slightly elevated on a blue platform, the ruler used a remote electronic device to push the button that closed the well instead of turning a silver valve (fig. 6.6). Both the 1946 and the 1991 ceremony are decisive, orchestrated moments of national petroleum choreography that bind the state and the infrastructural flows of petroleum together in a lasting union. One year later, a commemorative Kuwaiti series was issued on the occasion of the first anniversary of extinguishing the invasion's oil well fires (fig. 6.7), honoring petroleum's long-standing relationship with stamp culture.[34] It is striking that these three stamps mark one of the rare occasions that oil was visualized as a material substance and—in the form of a gusher—as a natural phenomenon on a Kuwaiti stamp.

Subsequently, Operation Desert Storm and the quenching of the oil spills and fires have become officially remembered and celebrated as "liberation." In 2011, the state of Kuwait celebrated a fifty/twenty anniversary: fifty years of independence and twenty years of liberation. Despite being framed as a national achievement and although Kuwaitis were important in organizing resistance inside and outside of the country during the Gulf War, the "liberation" was successful thanks to the US-led allied forces, as Kuwaiti curator and artist Barrak Alzaid analyzing the 2011 festivities in the magazine *Ibraaz* emphasized: "This spectacle, replete with images that manipulate nostalgia and assert a particular narrative of the Gulf War, ends in a reclamation of the country by and for the people."[35] He attests "society's alienation from its legacy of war," for which the national celebrations are intended to provide "an identity that could be consumed and interpellated as the legitimate Kuwait."[36] Alzaid thus analyzed the experience of the Gulf War, the vulnerability and the violence experienced as a lasting social trauma for the country that has not been fully overcome.

[34] Kuwait 1992, commem., MiNos. 1333–36.

[35] Barrak Alzaid, "Staging the Nation," *Ibraaz*, May 6, 2016, accessed July 8, 2020, https://www.ibraaz.org/essays/149.

[36] Ibid.

Ever since the Gulf War, the petroleum promise's iridescent spell on the region has begun to lift and petroleum's stranglehold on the future imaginary has begun to dwindle. The experience of a second rupture—caused by the Iraqi invasion, the oil spills, and Operation Desert Shield, as well as the subsequent loss of control over oil production and revenues—has created long-lasting effects. Some have come to see the first rupture—the rapid transformation from the pre-oil to the oil period—in a more subtle, at times even nostalgic light. Today, a growing awareness of climate change, the towering finitude of conventional oil, the sharply declined demand during COVID-19 lockdowns as well as the expansion of authoritarian control by national governments has led many in the Gulf to feel that past, present, and future no longer form a straight and fairly unobstructed path. There is a feeling that past and present do not align, and in fact may have never aligned, at least not in the way in which official narratives have suggested. As a result, doubt has proliferated: doubt about the state's image, but also doubt about the images that have typically showcased the oil period and Kuwait as petropolis. Today, contemporary art provides for a crucial arena where Kuwait's and the Gulf's mid-twentieth century oil history as well as the legacy of its urban visual culture can be critically investigated.

7. THE PETROLEUM PROMISE, NOSTALGIA, AND FUTURISM

With the full disclosure of petroleum's dark side during the Gulf War, the image-world from times prior to that is now also under scrutiny. For some, these historical images are a nostalgic retreat and refuge; for others they are a point of access from which to challenge the official (hi)stories of Kuwait and other Gulf states and from which to imagine alternative future scenarios and imaginaries. It is this spectrum that is currently negotiated in the contemporary art scene in the Gulf region through artworks that deal with petroleum and notions of past, present, and future.

For a long time, the petroleum promise fueled the imaginaries of the future. Dipesh Chakrabarty has outlined the project of history insofar as "the discipline of history exists on the assumption that our past, present, and future are connected by a certain continuity of human experience. We normally envisage the future with the help of the same faculty that allows us to picture the past."[1] The infinitely perpetuating petro-modernity that has been the dominant global expectation of our time is especially contingent in the oil-producing Gulf. Here, petro-modernity and its iridescent urban visual culture not only constituted the experience of "modernity," but also coincided with and even partially determined the crafting of state images, national identities, and (physical) nation building, as the case of Kuwait has demonstrated.

In Kuwait, the oil period began with the first shipment of petroleum in 1946. In the following decades, oil unfolded its iridescent power in a multitude of images. The highly successful and internationally visible city-state of Kuwait was the forerunner of other Gulf states like Qatar, Abu Dhabi, and Dubai, which subsequently also became oil producers, rich welfare states, and independent nation-states that have been as deeply invested in curating their image.

The image-world of petro-modernity that emerged and proliferated in Kuwait from the 1950s onwards, a time when petro-modernity disseminated around the globe, promoted a belief in the unlimited alteration of urban space and supported the integral role that the aerial view could play in this transformation. It was thought that "making the desert bloom" through the power of petroleum was a benefit bestowed on oil-producing

[1] Chakrabarty used this explanation to reflect on the idea of what a planet Earth would look like without human beings. Chakrabarty, "The Climate of History," 197.

https://doi.org/10.1515/9783110714739-009

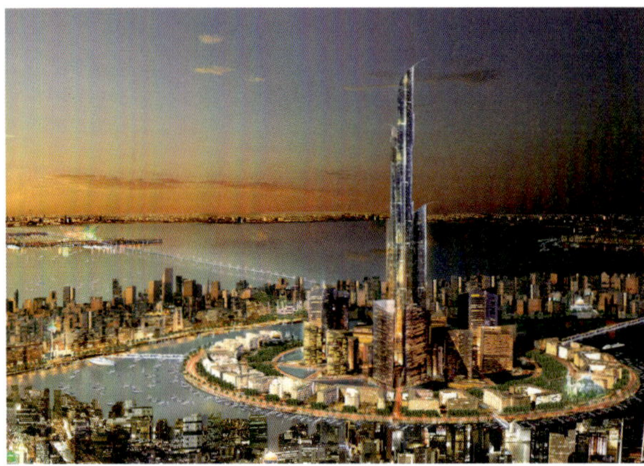

7.1 Digital rendering of Madinat al-Hareer (Silk City) with the Mubarak al-Kabir tower at the center, ca. 2018.

and oil-consuming countries by the oil companies and, ultimately, the governments. Furthermore, there was a belief that one could position oneself as a self-confident petro-state on the international stage by constructing and depicting (petroleum) infrastructure. Since the 1950s, images of transforming urban space, of the latest architectural styles, and of impressively large building projects have circulated as *the* national currency. Among other things, petro-modernity has meant experiencing (urban) space as image.

Acknowledging the historical fixation on infinite urban overhaul and on brand-new architecture as visual markers of national progress helps to explain the unbridled energy of nations in the Gulf region to destroy existing buildings and to erect previously unimaginable glass, concrete, and steel structures in their place. From the 1950s onward, even more impactful than the sky-rocketing high-rises themselves have been the images of these undertakings, which often sought to mesmerize the viewer with a futuristic aesthetic. A difference between images of today and the images proliferating in the 1950s is probably one of scale and quantity, given that a plethora of digital renderings visualize spectacular architectural projects in the Gulf today, irrespective of the fact whether they are being built or remain as images only. One current example of the contemporary architectural hubris enveloped in a digitally rendered futuristic yet generic aesthetic is the projected Silk City in the north of Kuwait (fig. 7.1), but one could equally think of NEOM (Saudi Arabia) or Burj Jumeirah (Dubai).[2] With the advance of visualization technologies and social media, the power of images to show urban transformation has

[2] Silk City (or Madinat al-Hareer) is a Kuwaiti development project in cooperation with China that is scheduled for completion in 2035. The 250-square-kilometer site is projected to encompass a self-sufficient city in Subiya, northern Kuwait, that will include tourist attractions, an Olympic stadium, and the high-rise Burj Mubarak al-Kabir, whose height of 1,001 meters will be a to reference the *Arabian Nights*. For a general critical assessment of the Gulf's urbanization, see Steffen Wippel et al., eds., *Under Construction: Logics of Urbanism in the Gulf Region* (Farnham: Ashgate, 2014).

expanded significantly. Yet, in light of the dwindling spell of the petroleum promise, the governmental and corporate projections of an accelerated ever-expanding future that materialize in such building proposals are no longer embraced by a civic majority in Kuwait—not to mention the residential majority, which has no say in this at all.[3]

In recent years, a young generation of artists from the Gulf region have developed works that question the ability and trustworthiness of governments and companies to project sustainable futures. In their artistic (research) practices, many artists re-engage with the urban visual culture that has emerged since the mid-twentieth century and the resulting artworks are of particular importance to the book's scope. Here, the artistic interest lies in the widespread circulation of shared memories, photographs, and other historical cultural artifacts on social media, private blogs, and websites, as well as in printed books. However, also the unearthing of private archives or the engagement with documents and artefacts from corporate or state collections play an important role. Current artistic practices therefore substantiate the large popular interest in revisiting the recent past and present in light of a future that seems increasingly impossible to imagine.

Petro-modernity as iridescence has been so all-encompassing and seductive that the resulting images that came to portray the recent past and present have made it difficult not to believe this version of the (hi)story of Kuwait. However, reassessing a country's prevailing imagery is currently not only taking place in the artistic practice of Kuwait and the Gulf region, but in the Middle East at large. This is because petro-modernity is not just a Kuwaiti phenomenon; rather, it has come to characterize the individual and collective experiences of the second half of the twentieth and early twenty-first century for everyone. In an article titled "Anachronistic Ambitions: Imagining the Future, Assembling the Past" published in the magazine *Ibraaz* in May 2014, writer Sheyma Buali describes current artistic practice based on a similar understanding of past and future as Chakrabarty quoted earlier:

> Despite a general inaccessibility to history, artists and writers have been there to set it fee so peoples can reassess what has brought them to where they are, and in turn, decide how they are to overcome those very positions. And it is this overcoming that is today vital. The dystopia of forgetting is not about the past, but about taking control of history and moving on with as much knowledge and imagination as possible. It is about understanding the past so as to take control of the future.[4]

Informed by artistic research, intensive archival digging, the tracking down of officially forgotten or buried memories, and the assembling of disparate and rediscovered factual

[3] According to the 2011 census, Kuwait had a total population of 3,065,850, of which almost 65 percent were non-Kuwaiti. State of Kuwait, Central Statistical Bureau, "Statistical Review 2014" (Kuwait, 2014). These numbers do not consider the large number of *bidūn* (Arabic for "without," meaning here without citizenship), who the government classifies as illegal residents, often despite decades of residence in Kuwait, and who are juristically stateless.

[4] Sheyma Buali, "Anachronistic Ambitions: Imagining the Future, Assembling the Past," *Ibraaz*, May 8, 2014, accessed June 21, 2019, https://www.ibraaz.org/essays/91#_ftn20.

and fictional material have become strong tools in countering amnesia and pervasive ideologies. This has gone a long way toward combatting the inaccessibility of history (and of archival material), and also toward unraveling the cultural complexity and (in)visibility of petroleum in everyday life.[5] Contemporary art from the Gulf states circulates not only in established and emerging spaces within one country but also regionally and even internationally.[6] The regional and global connectivity of artists, cultural practitioners, and creative entrepreneurs from the Gulf is crucial. Cultural events like conferences, exhibitions, and art fairs are usually attended by a regional instead of an exclusively national audience, and social media is of course a perfectly suitable medium for the transnational production and circulation of forms of knowledge that are increasingly thought of collectively rather than nationally. Elsewhere it has been emphasized that "the Gulf world from the earliest times has been characterized by a dense web of economic and social connections."[7] Despite another peak in nationalist thinking, current cultural and artistic collaborations show themselves to be a continuation of that network among the affluent, social media savvy, and highly mobile younger generations of the Gulf.[8]

Some contemporary artworks by Kuwaiti artists and artistic collectives based in the region have constructed, as I see it, a form of visual response to the urban visual culture that has emerged in Kuwait since the mid-twentieth century by reassessing the historical image (world) of Kuwait and the herein embedded narratives. A selection of these is discussed here and provides for a potential bottom-up counter-narrative to past and present official political and corporate narratives or at least a re-evaluation of those. These artworks can be considered pivotal in challenging the 1950s hegemonic discourse of images through images from a position of today. The—admittedly small and biased—selection of art projects from the Gulf region to be discussed in this chapter, and the theoretical discourse embedded therein, provides thought-provoking insight how the mid-twentieth-century image-world of petro-modernity is perceived and negotiated today. Contemporary art has become a progressive field where investigations into petro-modernity are currently undertaken, from which I have chosen especially such projects that address the relationship, or incommensurability, of past and future.

5 Sheena Wilson, "Energy Imaginaries: Feminist and Decolonial Futures," in *Materialism and the Critique of Energy*, ed. Brent R. Bellamy and Jeff Diamanti (Chicago: MCM, 2018), 379.

6 The term "contemporary art" is used as a temporal category to refer to artworks produced since the 2000s. In addition, the artistic language and media of the works discussed in the following section also resonate with transregional and even transcultural audiences, and are intended to circulate in both the regional and the international contemporary art scene.

7 Lawrence G. Potter, "Introduction," in Potter, *The Persian Gulf in History*, 7–8.

8 On the rise of national identities and their increasingly tribal branding, see Miriam Cooke, *Tribal Modern: Branding New Nations in the Arab Gulf* (Berkeley: University of California Press, 2014).

7.1 Deconstructing Nostalgia in Contemporary Art

Inquiring into Kuwait's petro-fueled political iconographies and national imagery is a central theme in Aseel AlYaqoub's (*1986, Kuwait) work. AlYaqoub assesses the symbolic-aesthetic narratives of the national/political by deconstructing historical postage stamps that the Kuwaiti government issued during the second half of the twentieth century. In conversations with the artist in 2018 and again 2020, AlYaqoub related how she had long felt a strong sentiment, a kind of nostalgia, for the twentieth-century oil period prior to the Iraqi invasion—a period that was known in popular parlance as the "Golden Era" (*al-ʿaṣr al-dhahabī*).[9] This was a period she had hardly experienced herself, but which felt so familiar to her from stories, historical images, and videos. Susan Sontag has pointedly described how images, especially photographs, can make the viewer feel like a participant in historical events that one merely saw in images and experienced as images.[10] Images can make the (experience of the) situation feel even more real and yet inaccessible, as the situation itself remains encapsulated in an iridescent picture. As one keeps trying in vain to access these periods, we experience nostalgia. AlYaqoub explained that she eventually decided to confront these strong affects by deconstructing historical visual material from the oil period and by using her sense of nostalgia as a seismographic device.

For the series *Cultural Fair: Yesterday* (2018), AlYaqoub dissected original Kuwaiti stamps under the microscope and reassembled them meticulously in long hours of manual labor. The resulting stamp-collages were placed on jutting stud planks of brown-stained wood and displayed under a magnifying dome (fig. 7.2). Despite the dissimilarity of the collaged elements to the original stamps and the absurdity of many of the compositions, the new stamp-images convey an astonishing homogeneity that, at first glance, makes them appear as authentic stamps. Similarly to the disguise of the photomosaic's composite nature, the viewer is able to unravel the artistic constructedness of the stamp-collages only when looking at them in close proximity. Knowing that each and every reused element had been part of an original stamp issue raises questions about Kuwait's political iconographies.

One of AlYaqoub's stamp-collages, *Stone Commandments*, depicts a dinosaur with a laser sword in a well-maintained park in front of Kuwait's gleaming white Palace of Justice; in the foreground, a man with stretched-out hands covered in white paint exits the scene (see fig. 7.2). Similarly to the first Kuwaiti stamps from 1959, this image presents a large building complex erected in Kuwait City in a photographically detailed yet color-beautified style. However, the composition ridicules this "stable" architectural image as a form of national representation ("stone commandments") by juxtaposing it with a sword-wielding dinosaur. The white color on the man's hands possibly indicates that the building was just recently painted, suggesting a newness that is mirrored by the freshly manicured

[9] Conversations between the artist and the author in January/February 2018 and August 2020.

[10] Sontag, "The Image-World," 121–26.

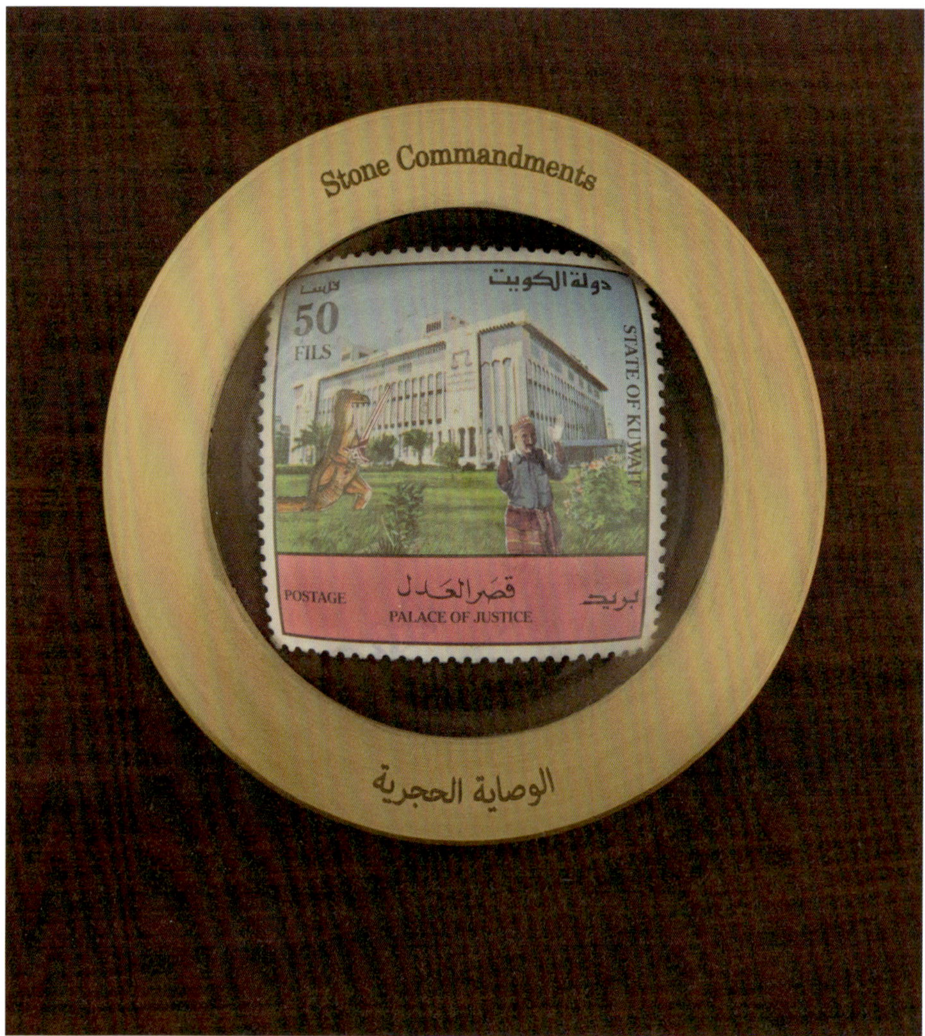

7.2 Aseel AlYaqoub, "Stone Commandments," from the series *Cultural Fair: Yesterday*, 2018. Four-layer stamp collage, magnifying dome, etched brass, stained wood, 25 × 25 × 15 cm.

garden. Having white hands, AlYaqoub has noted, also relates to the expression *aydī bayḍā'*, meaning "my hands are white," used to declare one's innocence. For viewers acquainted with current politics, the "fresh" appearance of the judicial institution—which stands for the governmental apparatus at large—clashes with the frequently felt inefficiency of the state, which has witnessed several parliamentary gridlocks over the past decade. The upkeep of the building thus equals mere window dressing. Tellingly, after several years of not issuing new stamp designs, the Kuwaiti government recently also shut down most of its postal services. Moreover, one wonders how a dinosaur ever made it onto a national stamp and what this motif is supposed to convey about Kuwait.[11]

In contrast to Kuwait's first issue, unruly forces, both humans and nonhuman matter have entered the national imaginary conjured up by the artist and have destabilized the political iconography. In the 1950s and beyond, infrastructure-as-images on stamps symbolized future stability in the form of already built structures, a promising future already tangible in the visual present. This future promise, a petroleum promise, AlYaqoub's work seems to imply, has been hollowed out, because even though it has been manifested in concrete, the commandments that the structures supposedly represented have not materialized with lasting effect for the present.

Intrinsic to Aseel AlYaqoub's work is a deep skepticism about the authenticity of the state's political iconography and about the (postal) images it has developed as national representations over the decades. "Shouldn't one understand who we are and what we have become in order to reposition ourselves within the narratives of the past?" she argued during a talk at the Abu Dhabi Art Fair in 2017. "How can one do so when there is an increasing mistrust of official history?"[12] In a subsequent conversation with the author, the artist underscored that, viewed from today's perspective, the postage stamps have projected images of the past and the future that are highly ambiguous. Nevertheless, the images presented on the postage stamps have had a strong impact on the Kuwaiti imagination, in AlYaqoub's case in the form of creating a nostalgic sentiment. Her artistic practice seeks to disclose this discrepancy by hijacking the historical visuals, their aesthetics, and medial forms and confusing them with her artistic propositions of (impossible) what-ifs, unlocalized in time.

That stamps once used to be a novel and important media for the state to reinvent itself is both revived and scrutinized by AlYaqoub's stamp-collage *The New Kuwait* (fig. 7.3). In this piece, a 1961 stamp depicting the desert landscape around the hill of Wara close to the Burgan Oil Field has been transformed into the set of a moon landing, with one astronaut having planted the Kuwaiti flag. The artwork plays with the "futuristic" aesthetic of many stamps and the belief in infinite progress, unlimited mobility, and the concept of linear history that petro-modernity has been fueling. The composition, staged amid the desert around Wara, provokes questions such as whether there might have been a Kuwaiti space mission, whether Kuwait has become impossible to live in, or perhaps whether the country has been transported elsewhere. AlYaqoub's work also relates to modern Kuwaiti

[11] However, in popular discourse on petroleum, the dinosaur is often but falsely considered the source material (the dead organic material) of coal, crude oil, and natural gas.

[12] Aseel AlYaqoub, "GCC Narratives: National Nostalgia: The Construction of Kuwaiti Identity," YouTube video, 19:43 min., uploaded by Abu Dhabi Art, January 4, 2018, presentation originally delivered at Abu Dhabi Art, November 2017, accessed February 5, 2021, https://www.youtube.com/watch?v=am2sY-ZLIwg.

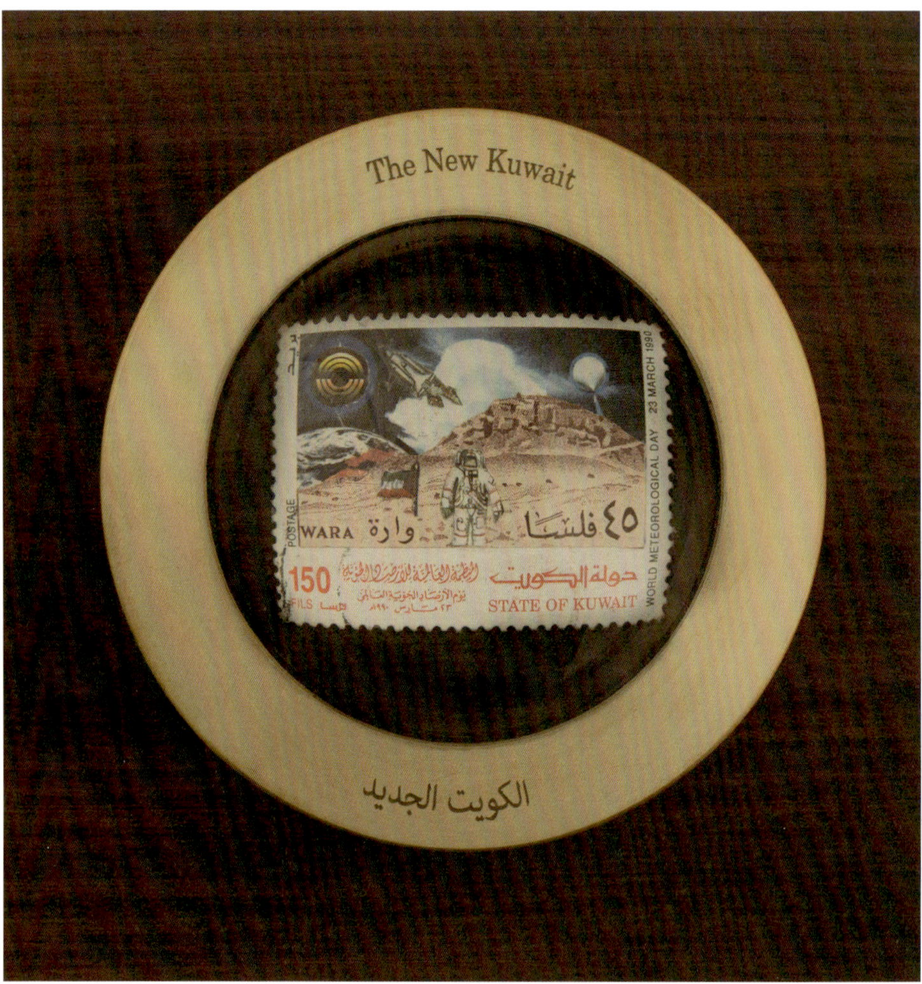

7.3 Aseel AlYaqoub, "The New Kuwait," from the series *Cultural Fair: Yesterday*, 2018. Six-layer stamp collage, magnifying dome, etched brass, stained wood, 25 × 25 × 15 cm.

art by an older generation of artists, such as Ibrahim Ismail, who created a ceramic sculpture of an astronaut in 1977.[13]

However, in contrast to the Emirates' Mars Mission that targets to build a city on Mars within a hundred years and that has successfully sent the first orbiter (called Hope or Al Amal) into space in July 2020, Kuwait's space images belong to a national imagery that

[13] Ibrahim Ismail, *Rāʾid al-Faḍāʾ (Astronaut)*, 1977, ceramic, 10 × 10 × 30 cm, Barjeel Art Foundation, accessed January 19, 2021, https://www.barjeelartfoundation.org/collection/ibrahim-ismail-raed-al-fada-astronaut/.

characterized the twentieth century, the fictional "yesterday" of the series' title.[14] *The New Kuwait* portrays an exaggerated and fanciful vision of the future but also discloses that the power of images such as those used in the Kuwaiti postage stamps is derived from conflating past and future into one dense vision—just as the 1952 Master Plan's "aerial space" vision projected a future Kuwait City on top of the existing town, which overnight came to represent Kuwait's pre-oil past.

The deconstruction and reassembling of historical imagery raise questions about the ways in which the future was depicted in the past. The artistic stamp-images provide for experimental impossible futures or futuristic past-presents around the themes of nation-building, (visual) representation, and petro-modernity, for example by being encapsulated in the (image) world of space exploration. Currently, similar themes can be seen in the work of several other artists from the MENA region, including Larissa Sansour, Joana Hadjithomas and Khalil Joreige, and Christina De Middel. For instance in the multi-media project *The Lebanese Rocket Society*, which has been ongoing since 2012, Joana Hadjithomas and Khalil Joreige revisit historical postage stamps and other artifacts to unearth Lebanon's short-lived space program, which was buried together with the Pan-Arab project after the 1967 Six-Day War. The artists understand their practice as a tactic of "overcoming the nostalgia for what used to be, the regret over what could not be achieved," a supposed certainty regarding a progressive future that, they find, was encapsulated in the 1960s utopian and modernist visions of grand architectural schemes and space traveling. The artists also admit that they feel a haunting sense of nostalgia, which they attempt to resist, for this foregone phase of petro-modernity.[15]

Nostalgia, as generally understood, develops from the idea that the past is no longer available, often springing from the sense of a rapture or discontinuity between past and present/future. It is often associated with the feeling of melancholy. In *Living Oil*, Stephanie LeMenager discusses contemporary "petromelancholia," a term she coined to capture "the grieving of conventional oil resources and the pleasures they sustained."[16] But rather than melancholy, I would argue, it is nostalgia with which the affective mourning in response to the end of the cheap fossil energies of the twentieth-century and the lifestyles they enabled is encountered, and that characterizes the mixed feelings often stirred up while recognizing and even welcoming that the spell of the petroleum promise is dwindling; it is the nostalgic feeling for the unclouded pleasure of driving a private car smoothly and speedily through the landscape without thinking about the ecological

[14] For a detailed discussion of the relationship between space science and nationalism, science fiction, and the Mars Mission, see Jörg Matthias Determann, *Islam, Science Fiction and Extraterrestrial Life: The Culture of Astrobiology in the Muslim World* (London: Bloomsbury, 2020); Jörg Matthias Determann, *Space Science and the Arab World: Astronauts, Observatories and Nationalism in the Middle East* (London: I. B. Tauris, 2018), 162.

[15] Joana Hajithomas and Khalil Joreige, "On the Lebanese Rocket Society," *e-flux journal*, no. 43 (March 2013), accessed June 24, 2019, https://www.e-flux.com/journal/43/60187/on-the-lebanese-rocket-society/.

[16] LeMenager, *Living Oil*, 102–3. On petroleum and affect see also Wilson, "Energy Imaginaries."

consequences. Clearly, the longing sentiment for Kuwait's past that AlYaqoub experienced is also a longing for the optimistic heyday of petroleum-fueled and -financed modernity, for this particular iridescent image of Kuwait as encapsulated in the image-world of the mid-twentieth century.

Nostalgia in Kuwait, it appears, has moreover arisen from the experience of a second rupture, the invasion, the Gulf War, and the oil spills. Significantly, this moment also marked a loss of control over the promising image of petroleum and the iridescent image of the state, as crude went up in smoke. The reference in popular discourse to the period between the 1950s and the early 1990s as Kuwait's "Golden Era" is a sign of the positive way it is remembered by many Kuwaitis today in contrast to what came after. The inherent nostalgic longing for this iridescent-positive era is also caused by the "stability" of the image-world of the period, especially when contrasted with the unsettling events and imagery that followed in 1990–91.

Is nostalgia an uprising against petro-modernity, an escape from petroleum's iridescent effect? Or is nostalgia complicit in petro-modernity, a way of consuming not just the future but also the past in a pervasive process of recycling petro-fueled images? In contemporary artistic practice, such as in AlYaqoub's *Cultural Fair: Yesterday*, nostalgia can be used to trigger a conscious distancing in time and/or space for the purpose of creating a void for a self-critical, self-reflective longing, when, at the same time, the government of Kuwait is presenting its current agenda in the form of the Kuwait National Development Plan "Kuwait Vision 2035 *New Kuwait*," that "stems from his Highness … conceptualized vision of a new Kuwait by 2035" as "a consolidated approach toward a prosperous and sustainable future." The path to implement this plan is described as: "to mobilize all efforts in order to achieve the objectives of the development plan across seven main pillars targeting the transforming of Kuwait into a leading regional financial, commercial, and cultural hub by 2035."[17] The idea of transforming the country by a certain date according to the vision of a ruler by means of a large-scale development plan certainly sounds—historically—very familiar and continues to be practiced all over the Gulf today.

The growing temporal distance to the "Golden Era," the accumulation of (digitally circulating) historical visuals of that period, and the crumbling of the urban fabric that once stood for the petroleum promise and the petro-state have led to a collective awareness that continuing as if nothing has happened no longer adds up. This is especially because Kuwait has not been able to reassume the avant-garde position in politics, economics, and culture that it held prior to the Iraqi invasion, particularly in comparison with the other Gulf states. In contrast to Qatar and Dubai, for example, Kuwait has still not diversified its economy and is today probably the least-known Gulf state of them all.

In *The Future of Nostalgia*, written with a view to post-communist memory and the end of the Soviet Union, Svetlana Boym perceptively noted that

[17] Government of Kuwait, "Kuwait Vision 2035 *New Kuwait*," accessed February 7, 2021, https://www.newkuwait.gov.kw/home.aspx.

> at first glance, nostalgia is a longing for a place, but actually it is a yearning for a different time—the time of our childhood, the slower rhythms of our dreams. In a broader sense, nostalgia is rebellion against the modern idea of time, the time of history and progress. The nostalgic desires to obliterate history and turn it into private or collective mythology, to revisit time like space.[18]

In view of the remnants of the oil period, the feeling of nostalgia is especially pervasive in Kuwait. *Cultural Fair: Yesterday* attempts to revisit the Golden Era from a position of today by holding on to a similar (stamp) aesthetic, the same (by now outdated) media form, and even the original artifacts of that period. The continuity this creates underscores the lasting identification with petro-modernity's mid-twentieth-century urban visual culture, which continues to linger even as it is critiqued.

Nostalgia, however, also has the potential to create alternative futures. The sentiment can be used as an access point not only for revisiting but also for changing memory and establishing alternative representations. Instead of a linear progressive path forward, it is a meandering, a flaneur-like explorative mission that challenges officially promulgated notions such as modernization and development. Svetlana Boym differentiates between "restorative" nostalgia, which "manifests itself in total reconstructions of monuments of the past," and "reflective" nostalgia, which "lingers on ruins, the patina of time and history, [and] in the dreams of another place and another time."[19] *Cultural Fair: Yesterday* shows that, when nostalgia is involved, the line between the total reconstruction and the deconstruction of petro-modernity's iridescence is fine indeed.

In relation to the built environment, the two notions of nostalgia identified by Boym find their architectural counterparts in heritage village theme parks and decaying twentieth-century modern architecture. But what happens in those cases where there are no ruins left anymore, when Kuwait (and the Gulf at large) has already "rejuvenated" itself during the next phase of national development planning? Does the photographic image suffice, or is the (photographic) image as memory replacement even more effective than a (ruinous or reconstructed) built environment? These questions are tackled by another Kuwaiti artist, Mohammed Al Kouh.

7.2 Architecture as Alternative History

The often-controversial approach with which the (historic) urban fabric of Kuwait City and other Gulf capitals is handled by governments, investors, construction companies, and the media gives insight into the way in which the urban past and the heyday of petro-modernity are currently negotiated. Photography has played a central role in visually preserving the urban fabric, but also in foreshadowing its destruction, highlighting certain vistas, and hiding other vistas from view, as the examples of the aerial photomosaic for

[18] Svetlana Boym, *The Future of Nostalgia* (New York: Basic Books, 2001), xv.

[19] Ibid., 41.

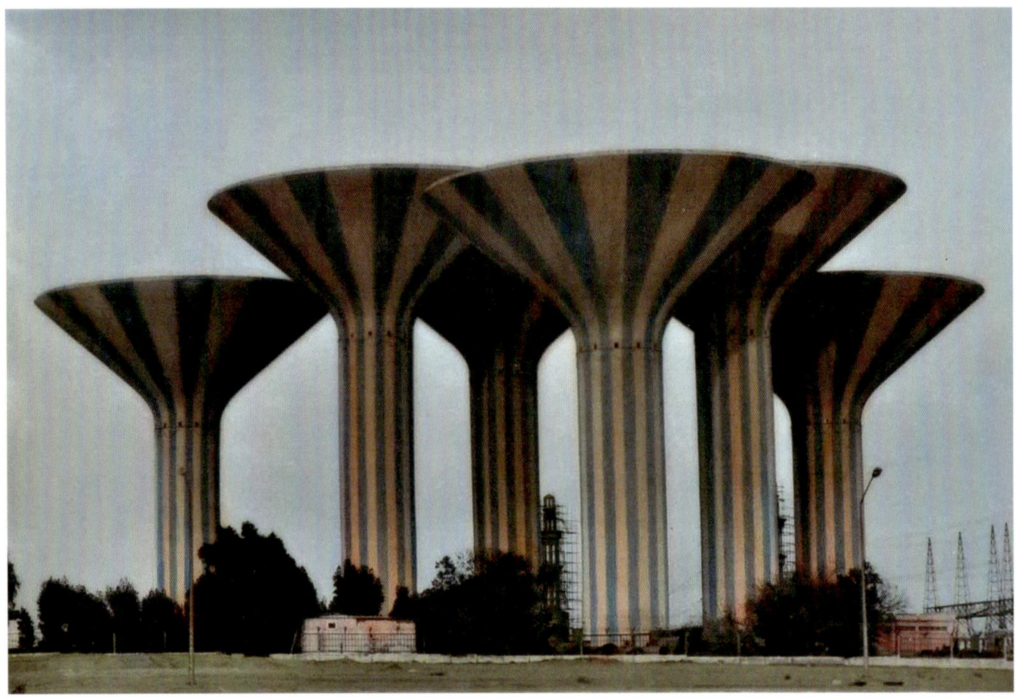

7.4 Mohammed Al Kouh, "The Kuwait Towers," from the series *Tomorrow's Past*, 2012. Hand-colored gelatin silver print, 40.6 × 50.8 cm.

Kuwait City's first master plan and Adolf Morath's photographic framing of the capital have shown. The work of visual artist Mohammed Al Kouh (*1984, Kuwait) plays with photography's representational ambiguity in relation to such historical architecture that was once showcased as being emblematic of petro-modernity. For the series *Tomorrow's Past*, Al Kouh revisited urban localities in Kuwait City over the course of the year 2012 and captured selected buildings that he considered representative of Kuwait's oil period with an analog camera. Believing that a photograph also captures a trace of the photographed object, he understands his work as a practice of preserving Kuwait's "Golden Era" architecture.[20]

While petro-modernity has not yet ended, its speed and eternally unsatisfied hunger for change triggers a kind of nostalgic longing for deceleration and stabilization or even for freezing the dilapidated buildings in time in order to provide for a critical assessment of Kuwait's urban transformation since the 1950s. What tool and visual medium is better suited for this than the Janus-faced medium of photography?

[20] Interview and conversations with the artist in January/February 2018 and September 2020.

To "preserve" an object, Al Kouh carefully prepares the composition before releasing the shutter of his analog camera while being physically face-to-face with the architecture. The practice of shooting each of the series' twelve motifs, the first step of the artistic process, contrasts starkly with today's digital renderings of yet-to-be-built skyscrapers or mobile phone snapshots taken in an SUV-drive-by mode. Instead, it reconnects with twentieth-century analog practices. The second step is also elaborate and time-consuming: it involves developing gelatin silver prints from the film and carefully hand-coloring them in pastel-colored hues. In conversations with the artist, Mohammed Al Kouh has described how, after discovering a large hand-colored photograph in a photo studio in Kuwait, he began learning the almost forgotten technique, a process that took him several years.[21]

Al Kouh's series *Tomorrow's Past* (2012) shows buildings that were erected in the second half of the twentieth century in the new modernist architectural language prevalent in Kuwait and that became prominent locations of everyday life. As such, the series' selection of motifs is reminiscent of the travel guide-like intention of the first series of Kuwaiti postage stamps, despite the fact that it spans a broader time frame and also depicts different architectural (infra)structures.

For Al Kouh, the selected architectural objects are symbolic of the bright side of petro-modernity, which the Iraqi invasion shattered overnight. However, the buildings are also localities that remind him of a childhood spent in Kuwait City. Some of the motifs depict today's official landmarks, like the stripy mushroom-shaped water towers (fig. 7.4). Most of the photographs, however, show structures that, in the year the photographs were taken, were already in dilapidated conditions, like the Thunayan Al Ghanim Building, home to both the KOC's Town Office and the Sultan Gallery (fig. 7.5). Furthermore, today, more than seven years after the series was shot in 2012, some buildings are in the process of being demolished or have already been destroyed.[22] The dereliction (or destruction) is taking place despite the buildings' and objects' undoubtedly important role for both the (historical) architectural development and the (contemporary) urban social life of Kuwait. For example, some hand-colored photographs show extremely popular cinemas, and the Thunayan Al Ghanim Building was considered the face of Kuwait's first modern avenue—Fahad al-Salem Street.[23] Through Al Kouh's artistic process, these buildings have been revived as part of Kuwait's "Golden Era" in the form of photographs.

[21] Ibid.

[22] In August 2020, Al Kouh reported that "four buildings from series had already been demolished and the fifth is on its way. It's like the past for these buildings has already begun to happen." Email to the author, August 21, 2020.

[23] The well-known Egyptian architect Sayyid Karim designed the building in the 1950s for the Kuwaiti entrepreneur Yusif Ahmed al-Ghanim. See Fabbri, Saragoça, and Camacho, *Modern Architecture Kuwait*, 50–51. It was a hotspot that over the decades also housed the famous Kuwait Bookshop, the first office of Kuwait Airways, the Sultan Gallery, Kuwait's most important art gallery, and a Lebanese car wash.

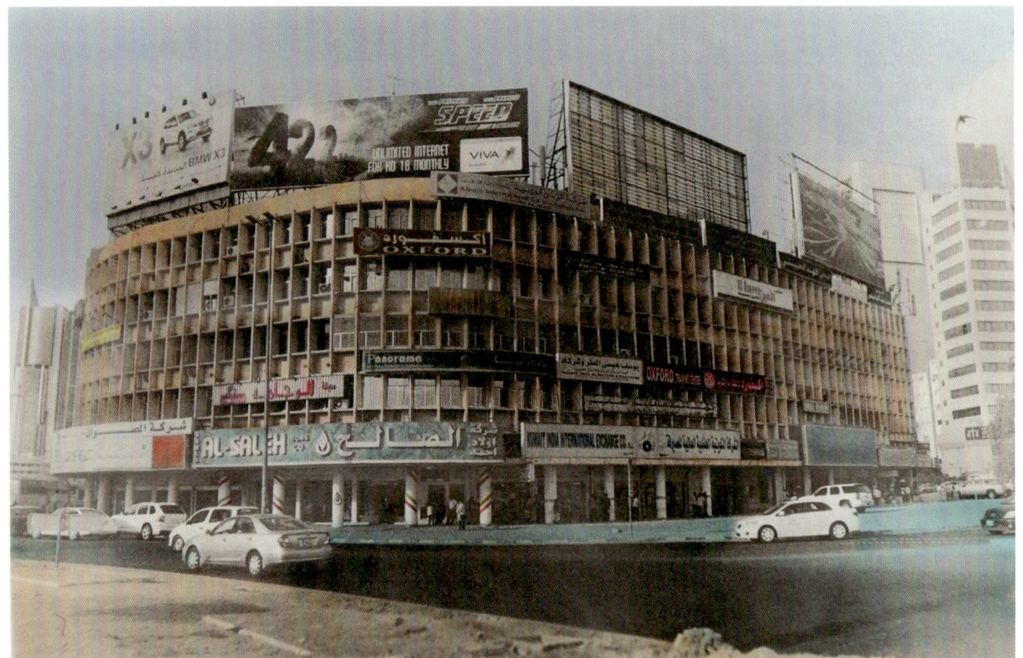

7.5 Mohammed Al Kouh, "The Rolls Royce Building," from the series *Tomorrow's Past*, 2012. Hand-colored gelatin silver print, 40.6 × 50.8 cm.

To achieve this revitalization, strokes of pastel colors are softly brushed over the marks of dilapidation and neglect: the colorful enhancement makes the buildings shine again. In a way, the series of photographs even speaks to the iridescent effect set forth most profoundly by Adolf Morath in his color photographs for the KOC. However, through the use of imperfect hand-coloring, the belated application of color communicates the photographs' artificiality and therefore concedes the impossibility of retrieving the bright, multicolored, and highly selective appearance staged in Morath's shots. Moreover, with the photographic development process of using gelatin silver prints, the photographs obtain such a blurry and grainy texture that they appear to resurface from a different century altogether. These photographs of Kuwait's modernist architecture therefore speak more to early twentieth-century photography of the Middle East and might intend to claim a similar historical—i.e., respectable and valuable—status. Consequently, *Tomorrow's Past* seems to propose imagining modern Kuwaiti architecture as an antiquated yet meaningful architectural heritage by framing it in what Al Kouh calls "a visual language of the past."[24] However, this artistic practice also creates premature death pictures of these buildings and

[24] Mohammed Al Kouh, "*Tomorrow's Past*: Artist's Statement (2012)," artist's website, accessed February 5, 2021, https://www.mohammedalkouh.com/tomorrowpast.

urban sites, in which the real architecture has already been replaced by a photograph that will, with rouge on the cheeks so to speak, remain the same even as the physical structure suffers a different fate.

However, the debate about the fate of Kuwait's and other Gulf capitals' historical urban fabric is not restricted to images only. Given that the negotiation of these (photographs of) architecture has taken place after a second rupture within Kuwait's history, and in view of the currently ongoing destruction of this historical layer of Kuwait City's built environment, *Tomorrow's Past* encourages viewers to reflect on whether a certain physical continuity of the built environment is in fact relevant; something that Arab and Kuwaiti urban professionals became convinced of when reassessing the radical urban overhaul of the pre-oil town according to the dictates of the first master plan through historical aerial photographs. With today's rapid vanishing of modernist architecture, Al Kouh and others argue, the social memory that is connected with these material testimonies is vanishing, too. In a way, artworks like *Tomorrow's Past* strive to reevaluate modernist architecture as urban heritage for people of Al Kouh's generation, people who were born during the end of the "Golden Era." Maintaining this architectural (hi)story would create a stark contrast to the typical government-run heritage village displays, with their kitsch mise-en-scène of pre-oil life, that usually pass for heritage.

The Story of Kuwait's narrative suggested that Kuwait would achieve prosperity and social progress through oil, a transformation that provoked the drastic destruction and de-urbanization of the historic town of Kuwait and that culminated in a second destruction of Kuwait City during the Iraqi invasion. *Tomorrow's Past* asks whether, this time, a conscious appreciation of existing architecture should not play a role, whether architecture should be maintained, valued, and revisited for all the stories it is able to tell. This may be especially important in light of the next historical period, a period that is approaching slowly but surely: a period "after oil."

The belief in architecture as an alternative source of history and of collective storytelling is evident in the work of Mohammed Al Kouh and others. According to Boym, this belief is infused with a "restorative" nostalgia and a desire to renovate these buildings and let them shine in their old glory. However, this is not just meant as window dressing; rather, it is wishfully seen as a way for society to reconnect with that "golden" past, a time before the image of the state and petroleum was shattered. Al Kouh's photographs, however, are also somewhat "reflective" in their negotiation of nostalgia in that they are accepting of the patina that the architecture accumulated over the decades and which the gentle hand-coloring only covers up so much. His photographs capture the traces of architecture's life stories in the form of light waves reflected by physical structures that face an even more accelerated urban transformation, another potential architectural amnesia, and even more futuristic propositions for the Gulf. It seems that the Gulf has gained a paradoxical new image that vacillates incongruously between running out of petroleum and building even grander. One provocative perspective on how to make sense of such a Gulf today is proposed by a group of artists who term their approach "Gulf futurism."

7.3 Gulf Futurism

In an interview with *Dazed* magazine in late 2012, Kuwaiti visual artist and musician Fatima Al Qadiri spelled out the motivation behind "Gulf futurism," a term that American-Qatari visual artist and writer Sophia al-Maria had coined around 2008 and the two had developed further. Al Qadiri explains:

> Huge swathes of Gulf cities are being knocked down for like, this insane skyscraper with a laser on top of it pointing to Jerusalem. Gulf futurism is really about this destruction and rebirth. We lost our architectural and cultural identity and had to start over. There's a secret, hidden history and then [there is] this horrifying, stark future.[25]

Gulf futurism takes the dystopian dis-alignment conjured up by the Gulf's contemporary image at face value: infinite skyscrapers, enormous luxury villas, 99 percent motorization, and a dependency on an endless supply of maids and other migrant workers mixed with static projections of Bedouin desert culture, pearling, and dhow seafaring. In a way this image is the contemporary continuation of the Gulf's peculiarity, its derogative othering that is ascribed not only from the outside but increasingly from the inside. The petroleum promise, orientalized as Aladdin rubbing the oil lamp and portraits of Kuwait as "the richest country in the world," were just as unbalanced as the (mental) images and tropes that are predominantly connected with the Gulf today, including preposterous new cities from scratch, the senseless race for the world's-highest skyscraper, and unimaginable decadence in pseudo-feudal settings.

The basic idea of Gulf futurism is to consider the Gulf's hyperreal presence as a microcosmic dystopian future scenario of the petro-capitalist world and the rapidly warming planet. In the logic of Gulf futurism, the Gulf has already far exceeded the modernization target, the mark set by the developmentalist logic of the 1950s. The question of where to position the Gulf on the global timeline of capitalist linear progress has become somehow irrelevant in light of the fact that, from the perspective of Gulf futurism, the Gulf has been catapulted into another time-space nexus on the way altogether.

In the 2012 interview with *Dazed*, Al-Maria and Fatima Al Qadiri essentially proposed Gulf futurism as a prism for viewing the Gulf's reality as a form of "prophecy of what's to come" for the rest of the world.[26] They suggest nothing less than that the Gulf no longer serves as a playground but that it has become the "avant-garde" of the future, a future that has already taken place. They see the Gulf as a region that, from pre-oil standstill and tropes of timelessness, skyrocketed upward with the aid of fossil fuels and ever-increasing oil revenues, only to crash-land in a dystopian future. This way of portraying the Gulf's

[25] Karen Orton, "The Desert of the Unreal: Conversation with Fatima Al Qadiri and Sophia Al-Maria," *Dazed*, November 9, 2012, accessed February 5, 2021, https://www.dazeddigital.com/artsandculture/article/15040/1/the-desert-of-the-unreal.

[26] Ibid.

present as a future already reached holds great potential because the domain of "futuring" is usually firmly in the hands of the Gulf governments, who draw political legitimacy from projecting yet another utopian "national development plan" to be realized over the next few decades. In view of the origin of this rhetoric in the 1950s, this becomes a "business-as-usual" attitude at odds with the unsustainability of the petro-capitalist system. Jonathan Crush has nicely summarized the conceptualization of "future" and "past" from the perspective of a perpetually developmentalist logic:

> Because development is prospective, forward-looking, gazing towards the achievement of as yet unrealized states, there seems little point in looking back. The technocratic language of contemporary plan writing—the models, the forecasts, the projections—all laud the idea of an unmade future which can be manipulated, with the right mix of inputs and indicators, into preordained ends.[27]

In a way, Gulf futurism suggests the complete opposite because it takes the past seriously by seeking alternative narratives to the official texts. It proposes radical alternatives to the speculative visions and future outcomes that development boards, development plans, and development theory produced in the twentieth century, because it does not view the Gulf's progress as the accomplishment of pre-set objectives (formulated by foreign and national consultants alike). Instead, it sees the status quo as something altogether different and, importantly, something already achieved. Gulf futurism plays with the idea that the future of the planet has very recently been written in the Gulf—not just written in the form of a global development plan, but actually implemented. Moreover, the plan did not go quite as outlined or projected, turning the Gulf into a prophetic dystopian hyperreality.

Initially, the breeding hub of ideas around Gulf futurism was Al-Maria's blog *The Gaze of Sci-Fi Wahabi* (since ca. 2008), which included texts and a series of experimental video works. The discourse on Gulf futurism has subsequently taken place mainly in (online) journals such as *bidoun*, *Ibraaz*, and *Dazed* and in collaboration with Fatima Al Qadiri, but also with other artists who are loosely connected around and through the Gulf-based artist collective GCC (named after the Gulf Cooperation Council).[28] Sci-Fi Wahabi is the alter ego of Al-Maria, whose father allegedly originates from the Bedouin Al-Murrah tribe, a tribe that the artist describes as "fervently Wahabi."[29] In Al-Maria's own words, Sci-Fi Wahabi "is an attempt at the leveling of a dogmatic, genderless gaze through which to view the Gulf's uncharted expanses and bizarre output after its crash landing

[27] Jonathan Crush, "Imagining Development: Introduction," in *Power of Development*, ed. Jonathan Crush (London: Routledge, 1995), 9.

[28] The GCC collective was founded in 2012 by Abdullah Al-Mutairi, Amal Khalaf, Aziz Al Qatami, Barrak Alzaid, Fatima Al Qadiri, Khalid al Gharaballi, Monira Al Qadiri, and Nanu Al-Hamad.

[29] Sophia Al-Maria, "The Way of the Ostrich: Or, How Not to Resist Modernity," *Bidoun*, no. 11 (Summer 2007), accessed February 5, 2021, https://www.bidoun.org/articles/the-way-of-the-ostrich-or-how-not-to-resist-modernity.

in the future."[30] Petroleum's role is vital for this spectacle's historical growth, which Sci-Fi Wahabi assesses in the following terms:

> The last event that went unrecorded by the jawal was the moment of collapse. The cameras weren't rolling when the colossal gravitational force of the Gulf's ancient cultural/spiritual/technological platforms bored a hole in reality. The volatile forces of a regressive Islam, foolhardy futurism and sudden wealth jettisoned the oil-states through this fresh temporal portal into a prophetic unreality at the edge of our end.[31]

When oil companies started oil exploration, the mobile phone (*jawal*) was not yet invented to record it. Oil companies' drill bits not only bored oil wells, but "a hole in reality," through which the newly appointed oil states have been sucked, time-(and space-) traveling, into "a prophetic unreality at the edge of our end," a state she refers to as being "left ahead in an elsewhere."[32] Sci-Fi Wahabi continues:

> This is why the Arabian Gulf is unique in the world as a floodlit, pressurized stage of the imaginary and birthplace of the very hole which caused its still recent conception. It is an infuriating abiogenesis which haunts all discussion around the Gulf, fueling what Jean Baudrillard called an "obscene rage" to unveil truth … . Just as Orientalists were seduced and subsequently obsessed by what lay beyond the veil/garden-wall/Mecca, now we court speculation over what lays beyond reality: an imaginary visualized easily on the brittle science fictive pulp of today's Ole [*sic*] Araby.[33]

The Gulf is conceptualized as the "floodlit" mold of petro-modernity and petro-capitalism in the form we know it today. It manifests itself not only as its poster child, but as its essentialized dystopian reality, hyper-accelerated by geopolitically concentrated fossil fuels and petro-dollars. Yet, the perpetual invisibility and unsustainability of energy emanating from nonliving fossil matter ("abiogenesis") triggers the furious speculation of what comes next, what comes after this kind of reality. For Sci-Fi Wahabi, the contemporary Gulf already projects a disturbingly real presence of the fossil-fueled hyperreality or post-reality: while the rest of the world tries to conjure suitable scenarios of peak oil, the Gulf is already living it.[34] Consequently, what makes Gulf futurism so compelling is that the speculative analysis of the Gulf's status quo allows for a look into an already-present future, a futurist imaginary that conjures up the greatest nightmares of globalization, climate change, and capitalism. Acknowledging the Gulf in this way and developing new futuristic imaginaries from here, as Gulf futurism proposes, could establish the Gulf as an innovative artistic-theoretical breeding-ground miles ahead of the unimaginative rest

[30] Sophia Al-Maria, "The Gaze of Sci-Fi Wahabi: A Theoretical Pulp Fiction and Serialized Videographic Adventure in the Arabian Gulf," artist's blog, accessed February 5, 2021, http://scifiwahabi.blogspot.com/, Sci-Fi Wahabi section, September 7, 2008.

[31] Ibid., Introduction section, September 7, 2008.

[32] Ibid., Sci-Fi Wahabi section, September 7, 2008.

[33] Ibid.

[34] The term "peak oil" describes the final climax of oil production before its rapid demise.

of the world. It relates to Chakrabarty's observation that "climate change poses for us a question of a human collectivity, an us, pointing to a figure of the universal that escapes our capacity to experience the world. It is more like a universal that arises from a shared sense of a catastrophe."[35]

Explored as an artistic entry point toward Gulf futurism, but also as the figure of thought to petro-modernity as iridescence and thus to this book, Monira Al Qadiri's *Alien Technology* shows uncanny ways of relating Kuwait's and the Gulf's experiences of petroleum to a futuristic reading of the Gulf's past-future through monumental iridescence.

7.4 Monumentalizing Petro-Modernity Through Iridescence

Alien Technology is the larger-than-life sculpture of an oil well drill bit turned upside down (fig. 7.6). Made of fiberglass and then carefully coated with layers of iridescent varnish, the smooth surface of the sculpture shimmers in an iridescent color spectrum, from orange to petrol-blue, in pearlescent white, and grayish-black in the different realizations of the artwork. Kuwaiti artist Monira Al Qadiri (*1983, Dakar) understands her work as "making fictional and formal connections between pearling and oil," working against a strongly felt rupture between lifeworlds without and with oil, a rupture that in her opinion has become an obstacle to imagining the future.[36] Trying to connect these historical episodes, Al Qadiri points out that iridescence is characteristic of both petroleum and mother-of-pearl (pearlescence) and that this particular color spectrum thus forms a powerful prism through which to challenge the apparent incommensurability of the pre-oil and the oil periods.[37]

The unfamiliar organic volume and the intensive swirling sheen of the sculpture are reminiscent of bio-morphologies, the strangely beautiful bioluminescent forms of maritime life that make up the environmental home of the Gulf pearl. Yet, these characteristics also allow for a futuristic interpretation of the sculpture as an iridescent flower rising from the sandbanks of the Persian Gulf, as Kuwait City did in *The Story of Kuwait* and Adolf Morath's color photographs. The reflective, shiny, and perfectly smooth surface of the monumental sculpture confers comforting fragility and overwhelming beauty, yet it can also trigger vertigo in the face of the constantly changing and reflecting nuances that oscillate from orange to pink to petrol-blue. The sculpture irritates the viewer

[35] Chakrabarty, "The Climate of History," 222.

[36] Melissa Gronlund, "A Tropical-Island, Dream-Land Purgatory Place: Monira Al Qadiri Lands in Abu Dhabi," *The National*, November 17, 2018, accessed February 5, 2021, https://www.thenational.ae/arts-culture/art/a-tropical-island-dream-land-purgatory-place-monira-al-qadiri-lands-in-abu-dhabi-1.792771.

[37] In the following, "Al Qadiri" refers to Monira Al Qadiri and not her sister Fatima Al Qadiri, who was mentioned earlier.

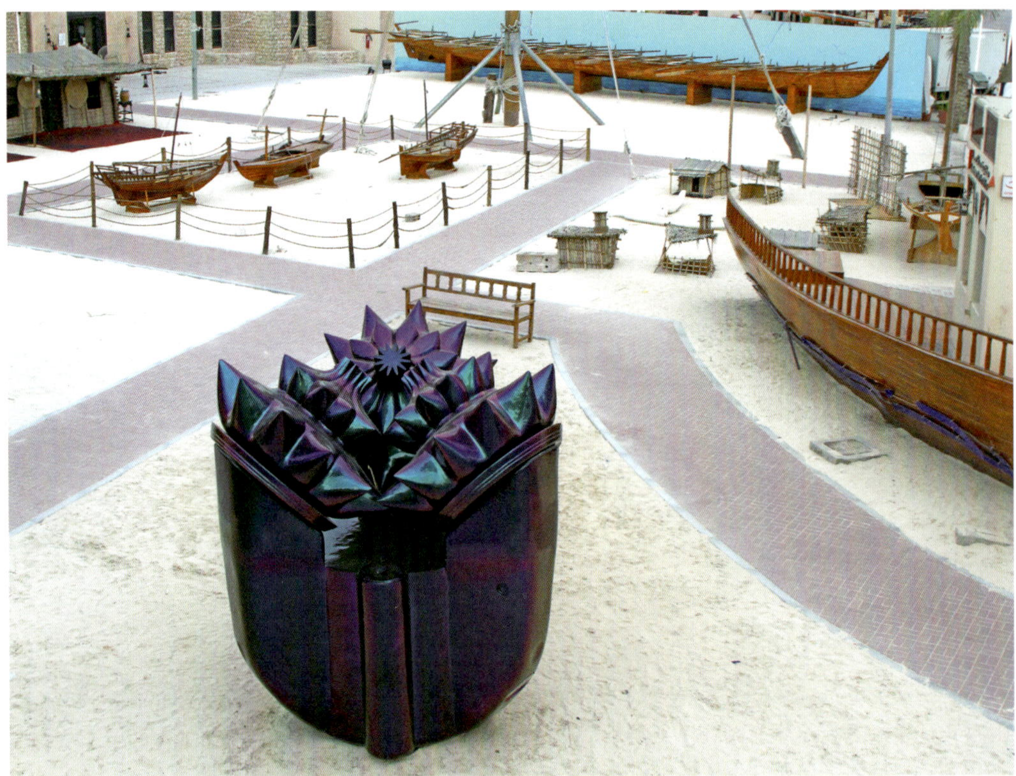

7.6 Monira Al Qadiri, *Alien Technology*, 2014–19. Fiberglass sculpture, automotive paint, 3 × 2.5 meters. Installation view at Shindagha Heritage Village, Dubai, 2014.

as its formal language and color install a sense of organic animation that crunchingly collides with the idea of the drill bit as a heavy mechanical tool.

Alien Technology intrigues with its perfectly smooth and iridescent surface; also historically, the skin of pearls was a crucial characteristic. One mid-twentieth-century account recounted that: "A first grade pearl should have a perfect 'skin,' i.e., be free from flaws and specks, and should have a fine 'orient,' that is, a delicate texture of translucent pink or cream color with an *iridescent luster*."[38] Since the first realization of *Alien Technology* for the Shindagha Heritage Village in Dubai in petrol-pink hues, Al Qadiri has developed various other versions, one of which in pearlescent white, and another in asphalt grayish-black. Gulf pearls were not only known for their nacre but to be "of all colors—white, black, gray, green, yellow, gold, and pink."[39] Yet, "luster is probably the most

[38] Bowen, "The Pearl Fisheries of the Persian Gulf," 162 (author's emphasis).

[39] Ibid., 162. Harold Dickson praised the Gulf for the "best rose-pink pearl" that even Japanese pearl producers could not imitate. Dickson, *The Arab of the Desert*, 484. Hightower suggests that "the dominant hue for

important characteristic of a first-class pearl;" and according to the same account, "other qualities can be more or less lacking if the pearl has good luster or depth."[40] Obviously, iridescence (or luster) and color reinforced each other. Likewise, also the various case studies of petro-modernity, iridescence, and visual culture discussed in this book have indicated that color has played a crucial role.

With *Alien Technology*, Al Qadiri moreover challenges the strange invisibility of petroleum production outside the oil fields and the highly-guarded oil production facilities, as well as the absence of the viscous, black-yet-iridescent crude material itself. In an interview with the UAE newspaper *The National*, the artist recalled encountering a drill bit:

> I thought, I'm from Kuwait and I don't know that the things that sustain our society look like this. Why isn't this a part of our education? These things are me—they're a representation of who I am, more than a dhow or a pearling boat or a camel. Those things represent my freak generation. The oil interval in history is a freak interval. It's not going to last long. What came before? What will happen after? It's an existential question I deal with all the time.[41]

Al Qadiri belongs to the younger generation of artists who grew up with the haunting images of the Kuwaiti oil fires that made petroleum as raw material and almost unstoppable natural force visible to many people for the first time. Never had petroleum been such a firsthand experience for such a large group of spectators; never had it been so directly visible in all its physical facets from liquid to fire to smoke. For this generation of artists, the literal burning of Kuwait's oil wells has become an unforgettable, personally relatable symbolic image of contemporary worldwide concerns about the unsustainability of fossil energy and global warming. Yet, the petroleum "freak interval" that is petro-modernity is still ongoing: our world is still visually and materially drenched in petroleum-derived products and petro-modernity's morphing visual culture.

In a way, *Alien Technology* imitates oil infrastructure's "stabilizing image of functioning production" by relating to modern refineries and other oil infrastructure in monumental size, clean and shiny surfaces, and physical presence.[42] This effect of stabilization and iridescent mesmerizing was also claimed by the first series of Kuwaiti stamps and the KOC photographs. At the same time, the artwork disrupts these infrastructurally contained notions of tranquility and security by means of its obvious dysfunctionality and its provocatively alienating and attractive sci-fi aesthetics of monumental iridescence.[43]

Gulf pearls is yellow, though other colors—pink, yellow, green, or blue—are possible." See Hightower, "Pearls and the Southern Persian/Arabian Gulf," 48.

40 Bowen, "The Pearl Fisheries of the Persian Gulf," 162.

41 Gronlund, "A Tropical-Island, Dream-Land Purgatory Place."

42 Pendakis and Wilson, "Sight, Site, Cite," 4.

43 Al Qadiri often explains this with her experience of hyper-futurist aesthetics in Japan, a country known for its futuristic craze, where she lived while studying and pursuing a PhD in inter-media art. "Sweet Talk: A Conversation with Thuraya Al-Baqsami and Monira Al Qadiri," *Bidoun*, 2018, accessed February 5, 2021,

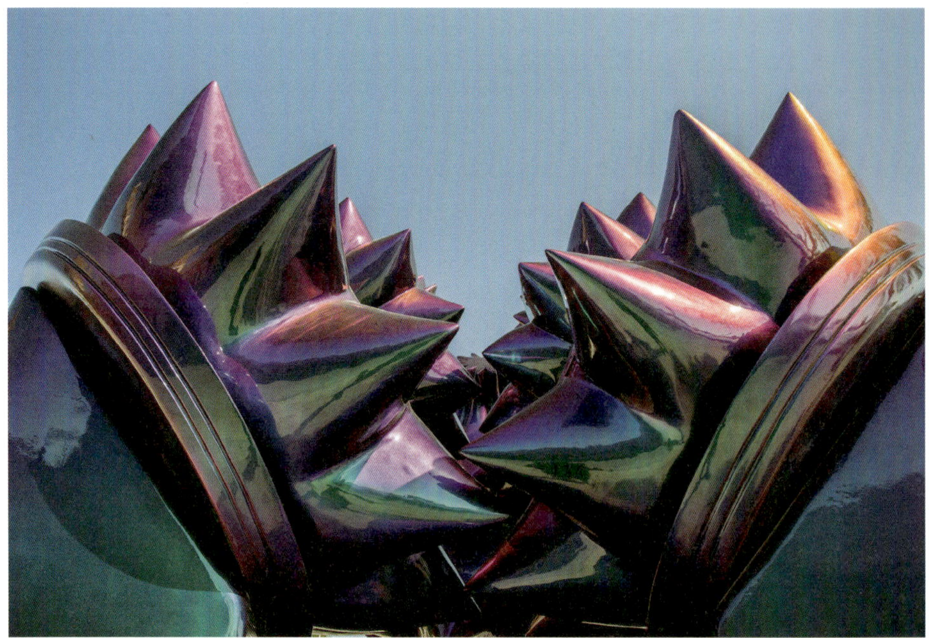

7.7 Monira Al Qadiri, *Alien Technology*, 2014–19. Detail of the sculpture's head while on display in Dubai, in 2014.

In *Alien Technology* the drill bit is positioned upside down. Instead of driving its head into the ground as an oil company would have it do, the drill bit is pointed up towards the sky (fig. 7.7). This allows for a moment of rest and contemplation to open up. Is the drill bit only temporarily at rest? Does its dysfunctional position indicate that it has already become an obsolete object of estranged yet compelling beauty, like retired headframes and oil derricks that continue to mark the former availability of the fossil material in the horizontal? Or is this object even announcing the arrival of a time "after oil"? While installed in the Shindagha Heritage Village in Dubai, the sculpture featured next to reconstructions of pre-oil housing made from coral stone, mud bricks, and palm leaves and next to displays of pearling and seafaring culture and the Bedouin nomadic lifeworld (see fig. 7.6).[44] Embedded in this context, the sculpture could be read as a premature monument to petroleum for Al Qadiri's generation: it both acknowledges oil's (continuous) influence on humankind and triggers speculative reflections on its expiration. In fact, Monira Al Qadiri has called her work a self-portrait that "[evokes] my cultural heritage as a child

https://www.bidoun.org/articles/sweet-talk; see also Robert Barry, "Remembering the Future: An Interview with Monira Al Qadiri," *The Quietus*, July 22, 2017, accessed February 5, 2021, https://thequietus.com/articles/22891-monira-al-qadiri-gcc-gasworks-london-interview.

[44] Due to reconstructions, the sculpture was removed in 2015. Interview with the artist, July 2020.

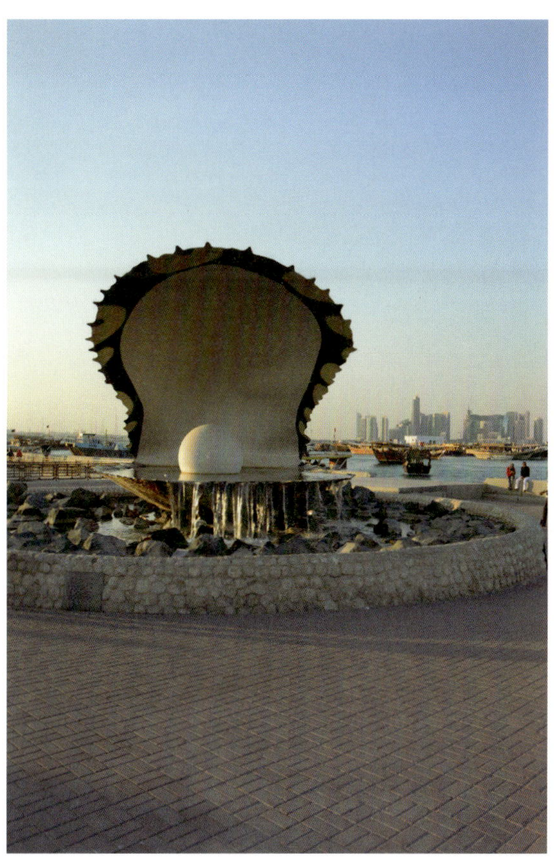

7.8 Arabic coffeepot and cup as entrance gate monument at a park in Abu Dhabi.

of oil."[45] What is exciting about this work is that, by monumentalizing iridescence in the form of *Alien Technology*, petro-modernity is given a monument in a way that recognizes the pre-oil period as an intrinsic part of Kuwait's (hi)story.

Alien Technology, as installed in Dubai, had another site-specific twist to it, namely the way in which it engages with the Gulf's shared (visual) culture. Its monumental size, figurative-objective form, and its decontextualized presence in a semi-public space makes the work reminiscent of many of the monumental sculptures placed at roundabouts and parks across the Gulf. For example, at Doha's corniche, a half-opened pearl oyster is on display, while in Abu Dhabi's city center, a giant brass-colored Arabic coffeepot welcomes visitors to a park (figs. 7.8, 7.9). Reminiscent of Robert Venturi, Denise Scott Brown, and Steven Izenour's duck theory, which describes an overtly sculptural building as a sign in urban space, the sculptures embody objects of apparent historical importance to the region, objects one would also find in heritage villages, souvenir shops, and national

45 "Sweet Talk."

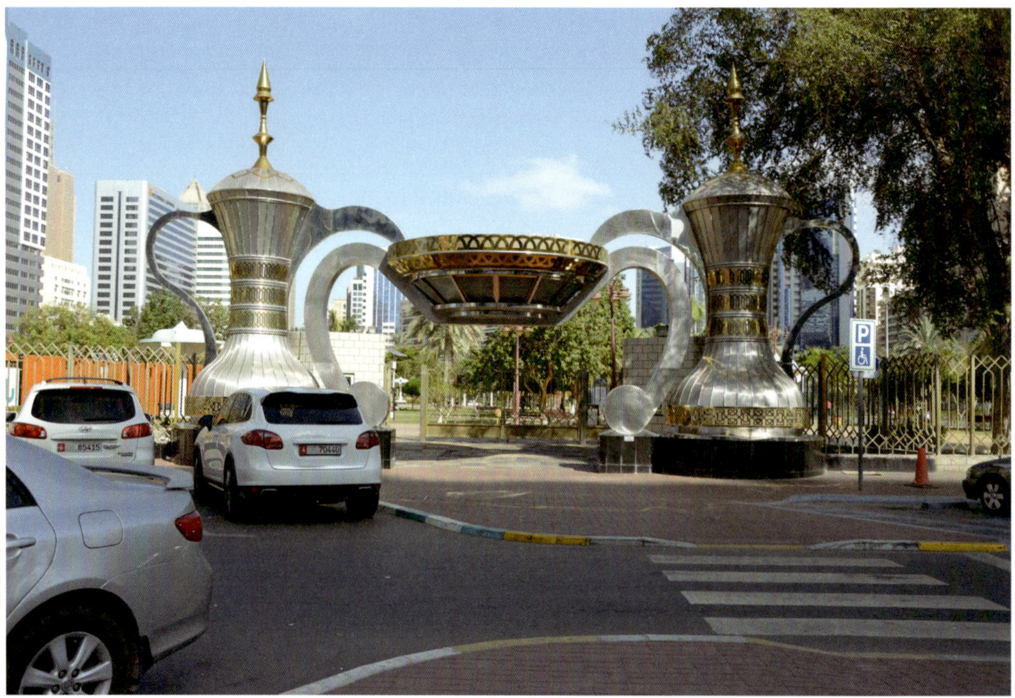

7.9 Pearl Oyster monument at Doha's Corniche.

museums, like a coffeepot or a pearl oyster shell.[46] In the Gulf, these monuments are usually unauthored and produced in a local workshop. Their immediately recognizable form speaks to their decorative and beautifying intentionality, which seemingly serves to pacify public space instead of responding to the location's (historical) specificity in a complex way. Nevertheless, over the years, many of these "maxiaturen" have become beloved local icons and important points of orientation in rapidly transforming cityscapes, and thus part of the regional urban visual culture.

Al Qadiri initially conceptualized *Alien Technology* as a sculpture on a roundabout and given the size, her work relates to these monumental sculptures spread across the Gulf region, which, for a long time, have been the only attempt at something like public art. At the same time, she challenges the acknowledged symbols of "Khaleeji" heritage, such as the teapot, the pearl oyster, and the camel, by presenting an oil drill head as addition

[46] Robert Venturi, Denise Scott Brown, and Steven Izenour, *Learning from Las Vegas* (Cambridge: MIT Press, 1972), 13–18 and fig. 15.

or, rather, alternative symbol of Gulf heritage, postulating *oil heritage* as, undoubtedly conflicted, local yet global legacy.[47]

What point of view on petro-modernity can *Alien Technology* provide? Energy humanist Sheena Wilson has cautioned that while the current energy impasse needs alternative futurist imaginaries, many proposals are a "mere repackaged/re-glossaried perpetuation of petro-capitalist relations greenwashed with tech solutions."[48] Similarly, one could claim that Al Qadiri's sculpture over-aestheticizes oil infrastructure and thus runs the risk to divert attention away from oil's disastrous implications. However, in line with this book's approach, petroleum and its system need to become aesthetically visible and thereby accountable in order to propose radically new imaginaries outside of oil. Al Qadiri's sculpture, if placed on a roundabout in a Gulf capital, would be a perfect start for a visual, artistic, and public face-to-face with the Gulf's oil period and its lasting legacy, but the heritage village proved an intriguing testbed for this encounter, too. Instead of staying in the tradition of sci-fi, which mingles the past with the future but usually omits the present, *Alien Technology* became physically embedded in the now, in an actual physical space in Dubai. This site-specificity "roots" the ideas and aesthetics it conveys in an actual existing environment. Even if the heritage village is a kind of simulacrum or fake environment, in line with Gulf futurist thinking, it is part of the Gulf's present. Monira Al Qadiri's sculpture best embodies, in an artistic way, the "iridescent effect" as a sculptural demonstration of petroleum's ability to have a powerful aesthetic and visual presence that resonates with our experience of the world. Iridescence, as monumentalized in *Alien Technology*, tries to capture the mesmerizing attractivity of the visual effects petroleum is invested in and points to petroleum's characteristic of always being in pursuit of new and more materials, surfaces, textures, and colors to create and synthesize. It monumentalizes iridescence as the elusive and endlessly mutating spectrum of blessing and curse, cure and poison that results from petroleum and its anthropogenic usage.

It is through iridescence, understood as the color of both pearls and petroleum, that the omnipresent incommensurability of the pre-oil and the oil period can be overcome. This, however, requires the viewer to connect these two periods with each other, as petro-modernity's urban images have worked extensively to dissolve one from the other. From this point of view, the prevailing tropes of pre-oil Kuwait as being static and timeless and then suddenly gone, and of modern Kuwait City as being built on sand, must be challenged. Consequently, to engage critically with Kuwait's first postage stamps, the 1951 aerial survey, the 1952 Master Plan, Adolf Morath's color photos for the KOC, and many other images that form the mid-twentieth-century urban visual culture of

47 The adjective "Khaleeji," which derives from the Arabic word *khalīj* (gulf), is used to refer to the Arabian/ Persian Gulf (states).

48 Wilson, "Energy Imaginaries," 385. Wilson defines the "energy impasse" as "the political, economic, and environmental deadlock created by the limits of Western ontologies and epistemologies that need to be newly thought." Wilson, "Energy Imaginaries," 378.

petro-modernity and in order not to be nostalgically overwhelmed, an iridescent prism such as *Alien Technology* is crucial. As a figure of thought, *Alien Technology* exposes the destruction of the pre-oil urban fabric necessary for mid-twentieth-century buildings to rise. It also acts as a site-specific access point that relates the locations depicted in pre-oil urban photographs to sites of modern Kuwait City and vice versa in an attempt to form a continuation, a connection that is worthy of the complex process that urban transformation always is.

No longer is the Gulf merely a place of petroleum extraction and cultural-technological-social-political-economic injections, no longer simply a playground of foreign interests. The Gulf is no longer a development project. The positions, in a way, have reversed. New theories and imaginaries, which reinstate the Gulf as a futuristic iridescent foil over an actual built environment, as a place from which to not only see but experience the rest of the world's dystopian development in the near future in real time, are seething and bubbling beneath the surface of the Gulf's bling. The artistic and theoretical practice put forward by artists such as Mohammed Al Kouh, Aseel AlYaqoub, Sophia Al-Maria, Fatima Al Qadiri, Monira Al Qadiri, and others allows for a provocative reflection on the local, regional, and international perception of the Gulf and our relationship with petro-modernity. It is clear that, to be really fruitful, unraveling petro-modernity visually, materially, and aesthetically can only be a collective effort across disciplinary boundaries and in close conversation with artistic practice. Investigating the image-world of petro-modernity is far from finished.

BIBLIOGRAPHY

Archival Sources

Adolf Morath and MoMA, January 7, January 8, January 22, 1958, Letters. Adolf Morath Photography Bio File, Museum of Modern Art Archives.

"Air Photographs of Kuwait and Aerial Reconnaissance," File 6/11. India Office Records and Private Papers, British Library.

"Noted British Industrial Photographer, Adolf Morath, Exhibits at George Eastman House," News Release, October 21, 1959. George Eastman House Archives, Rochester, New York.

Aircraft Operating Company. "Aerial Survey and Empire Development" BP Archive, University of Warwick.

Giesler, Rodney. "Memories of Kuwait 1958–1961," File 1/1. Rodney Giesler Collection, Middle East Centre Archive, St Antony's College, Oxford.

Invitation to the Exhibition *Kuwait and Its People* at the Near East Foundation, New York. Adolf Morath Photography Bio File, Museum of Modern Art Archives.

John M. Pattinson's Visit to Kuwait, Abu Dhabi, Persia and Iraq, January 14 to February 6, 1956, Diary No. 1. BP Archive, University of Warwick.

Kuwait Situation in Relation to the Middle East Crisis, Files 3 and 6. BP Archive, University of Warwick.

Kuwait State Development Board, File 101. The National Archives of the UK.

Military Protection of AIOC Interests in Iran. BP Archive, University of Warwick.

Minoprio, Spencely, and P. W. Macfarlane. "Plan for the Town of Kuwait. Report to His Highness Shaikh Abdullah Assalim Assubah, C.I.E., the Amir of Kuwait" November 1951. Center for Research and Studies on Kuwait.

Pattinson, John M. Kuwait: General. BP Archive, University of Warwick.

———. Kuwait: General (Photographs). BP Archive, University of Warwick.

Post Office Accommodation, Part 3. British Postal Agency Kuwait, The Royal Mail Archive, London.

Press and Publications 1957: Broadcasting. BP Archive, University of Warwick.

Press, Broadcasting, Papers. BP Archive, University of Warwick.

Recruitment of Experts for Kuwait Development, File 1052. The National Archives of the UK.

Town Office, 1957. BP Archive, University of Warwick.

Town Office, 1957–1958. BP Archive, University of Warwick.

Transfer of Responsibility for Postal Services, Part 1. British Postal Agency Kuwait, The Royal Mail Archive, London.

Transfer of Responsibility for Postal Services, Part 2. British Postal Agency Kuwait, The Royal Mail Archive, London.

Visit [to the Gulf] by Brigadier K. S. Holmes and Mr. T. U. Meyer, January 1957. British Postal Agencies, Persian Gulf Agency, The Royal Mail Archive, London.

Published Sources and Secondary Literature

"A Portrait of Oil—Unretouched." *Fortune*, September 1948, 102–7. Accessed January 30, 2021. http://fortune.com/1948/09/01/standard-oil-photos-1948/.

A Special Correspondent. "Town Planning in Kuwait: Rebuilding a Middle East Capital." *The Times Review of Industry* 5, no. 57 (October 1951): 91.

Abu-Ayyash, Abdullah. "Urban Development and Planning Strategies in Kuwait." *International Journal of Urban and Regional Research* 4, no. 4 (1980): 549–71.

Abu-Hakima, Ahmad M. *The Modern History of Kuwait: 1750–1965*. London: Luzac, 1983.

Administration of Posts, Telegraphs & Telephones, Post Office Department. *Post Office Guide*. Kuwait: Government Printing Press, 1959.

Aerofilms and Aero Pictorial. *Classified Index to the Library of Aerial Photographs*. Rev. ed. London: A Hunting Group Company Publication, [1954] 1962.

Akcan, Esra. "Global Conflict and Global Glitter: Architecture of West Asia (1960–2010)." In *A Critical History of Contemporary Architecture: 1960–2010*. Edited by Elie Haddad and David Rifkind, 311–37. Farnham: Ashgate, 2014.

Alabdulmughni, Khaled. "60 Years Since Issuing the Shaykh Abdullah Al-Salem Stamp: Boycotting Israel—Postal Service Nationalization." *al-Būsṭa (al-Posta)*, no. 40 (May 2018): 41–50.

Al Kouh, Mohammed. "*Tomorrow's Past*: Artist's Statement (2012)." Artist's website. Accessed February 5, 2021. https://www.mohammedalkouh.com/tomorrowpast.

Al Najdi, Khaled, and Rosalie Smith McCrea. "The History of Advertising Design in Kuwait: Post-Oil Cultural Shifts 1947–1959." *Journal of Design History* 25, no. 1 (2012): 55–87.

Al Qassemi, Sultan S. "Correcting Misconceptions of the Gulf's Modern Art Movement." *Al-Monitor*, November 22, 2013. Accessed January 22, 2021. https://www.al-monitor.com/pulse/originals/2013/11/gulf-visual-arts-modern-indigenous-tradition-misconception.html.

Al-Bahar, Huda. "Traditional Kuwaiti Houses." *Mimar*, no. 13 (1984): 71–78.

Ali, Evangelia S. "Retracing Old Kuwait." In *Kuwait Arts and Architecture: A Collection of Essays*. Edited by Arlene Fullerton and Géza Fehérvári, 173–88. Kuwait: Oriental, 1995.

Ali, Wijdan. *Modern Islamic Art: Development and Continuity*. Gainesville: University Press of Florida, 1997.

"al-ʿImāra bi-l-Kuwayt [Architecture in Kuwait]." *al-ʿArabī*, no. 13 (December 1959): 62–72.

Alissa, Reem. "Building for Oil: Corporate Colonialism, Nationalism and Urban Modernity in Ahmadi, 1946–1992." PhD diss., School of Architecture, University of California, 2012.

"al-Kuwayt fī l-layl [Kuwait at Night]." *al-ʿArabī*, no. 25 (December 1960): 140–49.

"al-Kuwayt fī l-maʿāriḍ al-duwaliyya: Baʿḍa āyām tashtariku fī maʿriḍ mīlānū al-ʿālamī [Kuwait at the International Exhibitions: In a Few Days It Is Participating in Milan's International Exhibition]." *al-ʿArabī*, no. 65 (April 1964): 103–7.

"al-Kuwayt yataṭalaʿu ilā l-mustaqbal fī sabīl ghadd ʾafḍal [Kuwait Is Looking Forward to the Future on the Road to a Better Tomorrow]." *al-ʿArabī*, no. 11 (October 1959): 112–15.

Alloughani, Basem E. *Kuwait in Black and White: A Rare Collection of Pictures of Kuwait Before Oil*. Kuwait: Xlibris, 2008.

Al-Maria, Sophia. "The Way of the Ostrich: Or, How Not to Resist Modernity." *Bidoun*, no. 11 (Summer 2007). Accessed February 5, 2021. https://www.bidoun.org/articles/the-way-of-the-ostrich-or-how-not-to-resist-modernity.

———. “The Gaze of Sci-Fi Wahabi: A Theoretical Pulp Fiction and Serialized Videographic Adventure in the Arabian Gulf.” Artist’s blog. Accessed February 5, 2021. http://scifiwahabi.blogspot.com/.

Al-Nakib, Farah. “Inside a Gulf Port: The Dynamics of Urban Life in Pre-Oil Kuwait.” In *The Persian Gulf in Modern Times: People, Ports, and History*. Edited by Lawrence G. Potter, 199–228. New York: Palgrave Macmillan, 2014.

———. “Revisiting *Ḥaḍar* and *Badū* in Kuwait: Citizenship, Housing, and the Construction of a Dichotomy.” *International Journal of Middle East Studies* 46, no. 1 (2014): 5–30.

———. *Kuwait Transformed: A History of Oil and Urban Life*. Stanford: Stanford University Press, 2016.

Al-Othman, Nasser. *With Their Bare Hands: The Story of the Oil Industry in Qatar.* First published in Arabic in 1980, translated into English and edited by Ken Whittingham. London/New York: Longman, 1984.

Al-Ragam, Asseel. “Towards a Critique of an Architectural *Nahdha*: A Kuwaiti Example.” PhD diss., School of Architecture, University of Pennsylvania, 2008. Accessed September 29, 2019. https://repository.upenn.edu/dissertations/AAI3309387/.

———. “Representation and Ideology in Postcolonial Urban Development: The Arabian Gulf.” *The Journal of Architecture* 16, no. 4 (2011): 455–69. https://doi.org/10.1080/13602365.2011.598702.

al-Ra’īs, ‘Alī G. “al-Muṣṣawir al-futūghrāfī ‘Abd al-Razzāk Badrān rā’id ṣuwar al-biṭāqāt al-barīdiyya fī l-Kuwayt [The Photographer Abdel Razzaq Badran Is the Pioneer of Postage Stamps Images in Kuwait].” *al-Būsṭa (al-Posta)*, no. 28 (April 2013): 6–9.

———. *Kuwait in Postcards*. Kuwait: Center for Research and Studies on Kuwait, 2009.

———. *Ṣuwar min aswāq al-Kuwayt al-qadīma: 1916–1966 milādī* [*Pictures of the Souks of Old Kuwait: The Years 1916–1966*]. al-Kuwayt: Markaz al-Buḥūth wa-l-Dirāsāt al-Kuwaytiyya, 2017.

Al-Rashid, Rashid. *Planning and Urban Development in Kuwait*. Kuwait: Kuwait Municipality, 1980.

Alsager, Noura, ed. *Acquiring Modernity*. Kuwait: National Council for Culture, Arts and Letters, 2014; Exhibition booklet of the Kuwait Pavilion curated by Alia Farid, published for the 14th International Architecture Exhibition of the Venice Biennale.

Alshalfan, Sharifa. *The Right to Housing in Kuwait: An Urban Injustice in a Socially Just System.* Kuwait Programm on Development, Governance and Globalisation in the Gulf States 28. London: London School of Economics, 2013.

———. “The Aftermath of a Masterplan for Kuwait: An Exploration of the Forces that Shape Kuwait City.” In *“Wise Cities” in the Mediterranean? Challenges of Urban Sustainability*. Edited by Eckart Woertz, 211–23. Barcelona: CIDOB edicions, 2018.

AlYaqoub, Aseel. “GCC Narratives: National Nostalgia: The Construction of Kuwaiti Identity.” YouTube video, 19:43 min., uploaded by Abu Dhabi Art, January 4, 2018. Presentation originally delivered at Abu Dhabi Art, November 2017. Accessed February 5, 2021. https://www.youtube.com/watch?v=am2sY-ZLIwg.

Al-Yousifi, Adel. “Kuwait Invasion: The Evidence.” *Evidence*. Accessed February 5, 2021. http://www.evidence.org.kw.

Alzaid, Barrak. “Staging the Nation.” *Ibraaz*, May 6, 2016. Accessed July 8, 2020. https://www.ibraaz.org/essays/149.

Anderson, Benedict. *Imagined Communities: Reflections on the Origin and Spread of Nationalism*. Rev. ed. London: Verso, [1983] 2006.

Anscombe, Frederick F. *The Ottoman Gulf: The Creation of Kuwait, Saudi Arabia, and Qatar*. New York: Columbia University Press, 1997.

Antrim, Zayde. *Mapping the Middle East*. London: Reaktion, 2018.

Appel, Hannah, Arthur Mason, and Michael Watts. "Oil Talk: Introduction." In *Subterranean Estates: Life Worlds of Oil and Gas*. Edited by Hannah Appel, Arthur Mason and Michael Watts, 1–29. Ithaca: Cornell University Press, 2015.

Appel, Hannah C. "Walls and White Elephants: Oil Extraction, Responsibility, and Infrastructural Violence in Equatorial Guinea." *Ethnography* 13, no. 4 (2012): 439–65.

Assaf, Laure, and Clémence Montagne. "Urban Images and Imaginaries: Gulf Cities through Their Representations." *Arabian Humanities*, no. 11 (2019): 1–20. https://doi.org/10.4000/cy.4137.

———, eds. *Urban Images and Imaginaries: Gulf Cities through their Representations*. 2019; special issue, no.11, *Arabian Humanities*.

Auty, Richard M. *Sustaining Development in Mineral Economies: The Resource Curse Thesis*. London: Routledge, 1993.

Badry, Roswitha. "Posta." In *Encyclopaedia of Islam: Second Online Edition*. Edited by Peri J. Bearman et al. Leiden: Brill, 2012. Accessed April 17, 2020. https://doi.org/10.1163/1573-3912_islam_SIM_6138.

Badry, Roswitha, and Johannes Niehoff. *Die ideologische Botschaft von Briefmarken: dargestellt am Beispiel Libyens und des Iran*. Tübingen: Niehoff, 1988.

Baird, Ileana P., and Hülya Yağcıoğlu, eds. *All Things Arabia: Arabian Identity and Material Culture*. Arts and Archaeology of the Islamic World 16. Leiden, Boston: Brill, 2021.

Bamberg, James H. *British Petroleum and Global Oil 1950–1975: The Challenge of Nationalism*. Cambridge, UK: Cambridge University Press, 2000.

Bani Hashim, Alamira R. *Planning Abu Dhabi: An Urban History*. Abingdon: Routledge, 2018.

Banks, R. L. "Notes on a Visit to Kuwait." *Town Planning Review* 26 (April 1955): 46–50.

Barrett, Ross, and Daniel Worden. "Oil Culture: Guest Editors' Introduction." *Journal of American Studies* 46, no. 2 (2012): 269–72.

Barry, Robert. "Remembering the Future: An Interview with Monira Al Qadiri." *The Quietus*, July 22, 2017. Accessed February 5, 2021. https://thequietus.com/articles/22891-monira-al-qadiri-gcc-gasworks-london-interview.

Basar, Shumon, ed. *Cities From Zero*. London: Architectural Association, 2007.

Basar, Shumon, Douglas Coupland, and Hans U. Obrist. *The Age of Earthquakes: A Guide to the Extreme Present*. New York: Blue Rider, 2015.

Bauman, Zygmunt. *Liquid Modernity*. Repr. ed. Cambridge, UK: Polity, [2000] 2006.

Beblawi, Hazem. "The Rentier State in the Arab World." In Beblawi; Luciani, *The Rentier State*, 49–62.

Beblawi, Hazem, and Giacomo Luciani, eds. *The Rentier State*. Vol. 2. London: Croom Helm, 1987.

Behdad, Ali. "The Orientalist Photograph." In *Photography's Orientalism: New Essays on Colonial Representation*. Edited by Ali Behdad and Luke Gartlan, 11–32. Los Angeles: Getty Research Institute, 2013.

Benjamin, Walter. "Briefmarken-Handlungen." In *Walter Benjamin. Werke und Nachlaß, Kritische Gesamtausgabe: Einbahnstraße (1928)*. Edited by Detlev Schöttker and Steffen Haug, 182–90. Vol. 8. Frankfurt: Suhrkamp, 2009.

Berger, Morroe, ed. *The New Metropolis in the Arab World*. New Delhi: Allied Publishers, 1963; papers prepared for an international seminar on City Planning and Urban Social Problems, Cairo, December 17–22, 1960.

Beyme, Klaus von. "Politische Ikonologie der modernen Architektur." In Schwelling, *Politikwissenschaft als Kulturwissenschaft*, 351–72.

———. "Why Is There No Political Science of the Arts?" In *Pictorial Cultures and Political Iconographies: Approaches, Perspectives, Case Studies from Europe and America*. Edited by Udo J. Hebel and Christoph Wagner, 13–32. New York: De Gruyter, 2011.

Biemann, Ursula, and Andrew Pendakis. "This is Not a Pipeline: Thoughts on the Politico-Aesthetics of Oil." *Imaginations: Journal of Cross-Cultural Image Studies* 3, no. 2 (2012): 6–16.

Bilstein, Roger E. *Flight in America: From the Wrights to the Astronauts.* Rev. ed. Baltimore: Johns Hopkins University Press, [1984] 1994.

Blum, Elisabeth, and Peter Neitzke, eds. *Dubai: Stadt aus dem Nichts.* Bauwelt Fundamente 143. Gütersloh, Basel: Bauverlag; Birkhäuser, 2009.

Boetzkes, Amanda. *Plastic Capitalism: Contemporary Art and the Drive to Waste.* Cambridge, MA: MIT Press, 2019.

Bonine, Michael E., and Rainer Cordes. "Oil Urbanization: Zum Entwicklungsprozess eines neuen Typs orientalischer Städte." *Geographische Rundschau* 35, no. 9 (1983): 461–75.

Bowen, Richard L. "The Pearl Fisheries of the Persian Gulf." *Middle East Journal* 5, no. 2 (1951): 161–80.

Boyce, David G. *Decolonisation and the British Empire, 1775–1997.* Basingstoke: Macmillan, 1999.

Boym, Svetlana. *The Future of Nostalgia.* New York: Basic Books, 2001.

Bozdoğan, Sibel. *Modernism and Nation Building: Turkish Architectural Culture in the Early Republic.* Seattle: University of Washington Press, 2001.

Branch, Melville C., Jr. *Aerial Photography in Urban Planning and Research.* Harvard City Planning Studies 14. Cambridge, MA: Harvard University Press, 1948.

Bridge, Gary, and Sophie Watson, eds. *The New Blackwell Companion to the City.* Malden: Wiley-Blackwell, 2013.

Broeze, Frank. "Kuwait Before Oil: The Dynamics and Morphology of an Arab Port City." In *Gateways of Asia: Port Cities of Asia in the 13th–20th Centuries.* Edited by Frank Broeze, 149–190. Comparative Asian Studies Series 2. London: Kegan Paul International, 1997.

Brunn, Stanley D. "Stamps as Messengers of Political Transition." *Geographical Review* 101, no. 1 (2011): 19–36.

Buali, Sheyma. "Anachronistic Ambitions: Imagining the Future, Assembling the Past." *Ibraaz,* May 8, 2014. Accessed June 21, 2019. https://www.ibraaz.org/essays/91#_ftn20.

Buchanan, Colin D., & Partners. "Kuwait." *The Architects' Journal* 159, no. 21 (May 1974): 1131–32.

———. "Lifestyle Contrasts and Need for Planning Reform." *The Architects' Journal* 160, no. 40 (October 1974): 794.

Buell, Frederick. "A Short History of Oil Cultures: Or, the Marriage of Catastrophe and Exuberance." *Journal of American Sudies* 46, no. 2 (2012): 273–93.

Burchardt, Hermann. "Ost-Arabien von Basra bis Maskat auf Grund eigener Reisen." *Zeitschrift der Gesellschaft für Erdkunde zu Berlin,* no. 21 (1906): 305–22; reprinted in Nippa and Herbstreuth, *Along the Gulf,* Berlin 2006, 203–27.

Burns, Ken. "The Painful, Essential Images of War." *The New York Times,* January 27, 1991. Accessed February 5, 2021. https://www.nytimes.com/1991/01/27/arts/the-painful-essential-images-of-war.html.

Burtynsky, Edward, and Michael Mitchell. *Edward Burtynsky: Oil.* Göttingen: Steidl, 2009.

"Camera Captures Industrial Drama: Colour Prints on Show." *Manchester Guardian,* May 28, 1957, n.p; reprint.

Carrington, Damian. "Microplastics revealed in the placentas of unborn babies." *The Guardian,* December 22, 2020. Accessed January 27, 2021. https://www.theguardian.com/environment/2020/dec/22/microplastics-revealed-in-placentas-unborn-babies.

Case, Paul E. "Boom Time in Kuwait." *National Geographic Magazine* 102, no. 6 (December 1952): 783–802; photographs by George Rodger.

Chakrabarty, Dipesh. "The Climate of History: Four Theses." *Critical Inquiry* 35, no. 2 (2009): 197–222.

Chalcraft, John T. *Popular Politics in the Making of the Modern Middle East*. Cambridge, UK: Cambridge University Press, 2016.

"Civil Aviation News." *Flight* 59, no. 2211 (June 1951): 683–85.

"Civil Aviation News: 10,000 Sq Miles Air Survey." *Flight* 52, no. 2035 (December 1947): 726–28.

"Civil Aviation News: Surveying for Oil." *Flight* 56, no. 2129 (October 1949): 499.

Clifford, Mary L. *The Land and People of the Arabian Peninsula*. Philadelphia: J. B. Lippincott, 1977.

Cooke, Miriam. *Tribal Modern: Branding New Nations in the Arab Gulf*. Berkeley: University of California Press, 2014.

Cosgrove, Denis, and William L. Fox. *Photography and Flight*. London: Reaktion, 2010.

Cronin, Marionne. "Northern Visions: Aerial Surveying and the Canadian Mining Industry, 1919–1928." *Technology and Culture* 48, no. 2 (2007): 303–30.

Crush, Jonathan. "Imagining Development: Introduction." In *Power of Development*. Edited by Jonathan Crush, 1–23. London: Routledge, 1995.

Crystal, Jill. *Oil and Politics in the Gulf: Rulers and Merchants in Kuwait and Qatar.* Cambridge Middle East Library 24. Cambridge, UK: Cambridge University Press, 1990.

Damluji, Mona. "Petroleum's Promise: The Neo-Colonial Imaginary of Oil Cities in the Modern Arabian Gulf." PhD diss., University of California, 2013. Accessed January 27, 2021. https://escholarship.org/uc/item/7qk5c7kj.

Darwin, John. *Britain and Decolonisation: The Retreat from Empire in the Post-War World*. Basingstoke: Macmillan, 1988.

David Finnie. "Recruitment and Training of Labor: The Middle East Oil Industry." *Middle East Journal* 12, no. 2 (1958): 127–43.

Davis, Eric, and Nicholas Gavrielides. "Statecraft, Historical Memory, and Popular Culture in Iraq and Kuwait." In *Statecraft in the Middle East: Historical Memory and Popular Culture*. Edited by Eric Davis and Nicholas Gavrielides, 116–48. Miami: Florida International University Press, 1991.

Davis, Heather M. "Life & Death in the Anthropocene: A Short History of Plastic." In *Art in the Anthropocene: Encounters Among Aesthetics, Politics, Environments and Epistemologies*. Edited by Heather Davis and Etienne Turpin, 347–58. London: Open Humanities Press, 2015.

de Haas, W. G. L. "Aerial Survey for Developing Countries." *Build International*, no. 11 (November 1970): 345–48.

Dehaene, Michiel. "Surveying and Comprehensive Planning: The 'Co-Ordination of Knowledge' in the Wartime Plans of Patrick Abercrombie and Max Lock." In Whyte, *Man-Made Future*, 38–58.

"Desert Pioneers: Aviation in Kuwait, the Impetus from Oil." *Kuwaiti Digest*, April 1973, 8–11.

Determann, Jörg M. *Space Science and the Arab World: Astronauts, Observatories and Nationalism in the Middle East*. London: I. B. Tauris, 2018.

———. *Islam, Science Fiction and Extraterrestrial Life: The Culture of Astrobiology in the Muslim World*. London: Bloomsbury, 2020.

Dickson, Harold R. P. *The Arab of the Desert: A Glimpse into Badawin Life in Kuwait and Saudi Arabia*. 4th ed. London: George Allen & Unwin, [1949] 1967.

Domhardt, Konstanze S. *The Heart of the City: Die Stadt in den transatlantischen Debatten der CIAM 1933–1951*. Architektonisches Wissen. Zurich: GTA Verlag, 2012.

Donaldson, Neil. *The History of the Postal Service in Kuwait, 1775–1959*. Bombay: Jal Cooper, 1968.

Drucker, Johanna. "Who's Afraid of Visual Culture?" *Art Journal* 58, no. 4 (1999): 36–47.

Dyce, Matt. "Canada between the Photograph and the Map: Aerial Photography, Geographical Vision and the State." *Journal of Historical Geography* 39 (2013): 69–84.

Easton, John. "The Design and Manufacture of Postage Stamps in the Commonwealth." *Journal of the Royal Society of Arts* 110, no. 5066 (January 1962): 103–18.

Edwards, Elizabeth. "Material Beings: Objecthood and Ethnographic Photographs." *Visual Studies* 17, no. 1 (2002): 67–75.

El-Arifi, Salih A. "The Nature of Urbanization in the Gulf Countries." *GeoJournal* 13, no. 3 (1986): 223–35.

Eleey, Peter, and Ruba Katrib. "Preface and Acknowledgements." In *Theater of Operations: The Gulf Wars 1991–2011*. Edited by Peter Eleey and Ruba Katrib, 9–12. New York: MoMA PS1, 2019.

———, eds. *Theater of Operations: The Gulf Wars 1991–2011*. New York: MoMA PS1, 2019; Exhibition catalog published in conjunction with the exhibition of the same name, shown at MoMA PS1, New York, from November 3, 2019 until March 1, 2020.

Elgenius, Gabriella. *Symbols of Nations and Nationalism: Celebrating Nationhood*. New York: Palgrave Macmillan, 2011.

Elsheshtawy, Yasser, ed. *The Evolving Arab City: Tradition, Modernity and Urban Development*. Planning, History and Environment Series. London: Routledge, 2008.

———. *Dubai: Behind an Urban Spectacle*. Planning, History and Environment Series. London: Routledge, 2010.

———, ed. *Planning Middle Eastern Cities: An Urban Kaleidoscope in a Globalizing World*. Planning, History and the Environment Series. London: Routledge, 2010.

Escobar, Arturo. *Encountering Development: The Making and Unmaking of the Third World*. Princeton: Princeton University Press, 1995.

Exell, Karen, and Trinidad Rico. "'There is no Heritage in Qatar': Orientalism, Colonialism and Other Problematic Histories." *World Archaeology* 45, no. 4 (2013): 670–85.

Fabbri, Roberto, Sara Saragoça, and Ricardo Camacho. *Modern Architecture Kuwait: 1949–1989*. Zurich: Niggli, 2016.

———, eds. *Essays, Arguments & Interviews on Modern Architecture Kuwait*. Zurich: Niggli, 2018.

Facey, William, and Gillian Grant. *Kuwait by the First Photographers*. London: I. B. Tauris, 1999.

Ferrier, Ronald W., and James H. Bamberg. *The History of the British Petroleum Company*. Cambridge, UK: Cambridge University Press, 2009. Vol. 1: The Developing Years 1901–1932; vol. 2: *The Anglo-Iranian Years, 1928–1954*.

Flam, Faye. "A Brighter Forecast from Kuwait." *Science* 253, no. 5015 (1991): 28–29.

Fleckner, Uwe, Martin Warnke, and Hendrik Ziegler, eds. *Handbuch der politischen Ikonographie*. 2 vols. Munich: C. H. Beck, 2011.

Fletcher, Robert S. "'Between the Devil of the Desert and the Deep Blue Sea': Re-orienting Kuwait c. 1900–1940." *Journal of Historical Geography* 50 (2015): 51–65.

Forrest, D. M. *A Hundred Years of Ceylon Tea, 1867–1967*. London: Chatto & Windus, 1967. Photographs by Adolf Morath.

Frohardt-Lane, Sarah. "Promoting a Culture of Driving: Rationing, Car Sharing, and Propaganda in World War II." *Journal of American Studies* 46, no. 2 (special issue: Oil Cultures) (2012): 337–55.

Fuccaro, Nelida. "Visions of the City: Urban Studies on the Gulf." *Middle East Studies Association Bulletin* 35, no. 2 (2001): 175–87.

———. "Visions of the City: Urban Studies on the Gulf." *Middle East Studies Association Bulletin* 35, no. 2 (2001): 175–87.

———. *Histories of City and State in the Persian Gulf: Manama since 1800*. Cambridge Middle East Studies 30. Cambridge, UK: Cambridge University Press, 2009.

———. “Pearl Towns and Early Oil Cities: Migration and Integration in the Arab Coast of the Persian Gulf.” In *The City in the Ottoman Empire: Migration and the Making of Urban Modernity*. Edited by Ulrike Freitag et al., 99–116. SOAS/Routledge Studies on the Middle East 14. London: Routledge, 2011.

———. “Introduction: Histories of Oil and Modernity in the Middle East.” *Comparative Studies of South Asia, Africa and the Middle East* 33, no. 1 (2013): 1–6.

———. “Middle Eastern Oil Towns as Petro-Histories.” Paper presented at the conference “The Global Petroleumscape,” Technical University Delft, May 18, 2017.

Gabriel, Gottfried. “Ästhetik und Politische Ikonographie der Briefmarke.” *Zeitschrift für Ästhetik und Allgemeine Kunstwissenschaft* 54, no. 2 (2009): 183–201.

Gandy, Matthew. “Landscape and Infrastructure in the Late-Modern Metropolis.” In Bridge; Watson, *The New Blackwell Companion to the City*, 57–65.

Gardiner, Stephen. *Kuwait: The Making of a City*. Burnt Mill: Longman, 1983.

Ghosn, Rania. “Territories of Oil: The Trans-Arabian Pipeline.” In *The Arab City: Architecture and Representation*. Edited by Amale Andraos, Nora Akawi and Caitlin Blanchfield, 164–75. New York: Columbia Books on Architecture and the City, 2016.

Ghrawi, Claudia. “A Tamed Urban Revolution: Saudi Arabia’s Oil Conurbation and the 1967 Riots.” In *Violence and the City in the Modern Middle East*. Edited by Nelida Fuccaro, 109–26. Stanford: Stanford University Press, 2016.

Giedion, Sigfried. “CIAM 8: The Heart of the City: A Summing Up.” *Ekistics* 52, no. 314/315 (1985): 475–77.

Gilman, Nils. *Mandarins of the Future: Modernization Theory in Cold War America*. New Studies in American Intellectual and Cultural History. Baltimore: Johns Hopkins University Press, 2003.

Gottschalk, Marie. “Operation Desert Cloud: The Media and the Gulf War.” *World Policy Journal* 9, no. 3 (1992): 449–86.

Government of Kuwait. “Kuwait Vision 2035 *New Kuwait*.” Accessed February 7, 2021. https://www.newkuwait.gov.kw/home.aspx.

Gräf, Bettina and Laura Hindelang, “The Transregional Illustrated Magazine *al-ʿArabi*: Knowledge Production and Cultural Imaginations in the 1950s and 1960s,” *Middle East Journal of Culture and Communication* (forthcoming 2022).

Gronlund, Melissa. “A Tropical-Island, Dream-Land Purgatory Place: Monira Al Qadiri Lands in Abu Dhabi.” *The National*, November 17, 2018. Accessed February 5, 2021. https://www.thenational.ae/arts-culture/art/a-tropical-island-dream-land-purgatory-place-monira-al-qadiri-lands-in-abu-dhabi-1.792771.

Gruber, Christiane J., and Sune Haugbolle. “Introduction: Visual Culture in the Modern Middle East.” In *Visual Culture in the Modern Middle East: Rhetoric of the Image*. Edited by Christiane J. Gruber and Sune Haugbolle, ix–xxvii. Bloomington: Indiana University Press, 2013.

Gugler, Josef, ed. *The Urban Transformation of the Developing World*. Oxford: Oxford University Press, 1996.

Günter, Roland. “Die politische Ikonographie des Ruhrgebietes in der Epoche der Industrialisierung.” In *Architektur als politische Kultur: Philosophia practica*. Edited by Hermann Hipp and Ernst Seidl, 213–24. Berlin: Dietrich Reimer, 1996.

Haarmann, Ulrich W. “Early Sources on Kuwait: Murtaḍā b. ʿAlī b. ʿAlwān and Carsten Niebuhr: An Arab and a German Report from the Eighteenth Century.” *Hadīth al-Dār* 3 (1995): 16–20.

———. “Two 18th-Century Sources on Kuwait: Murtaḍā b. ʿAlī b. ʿAlwān and Carsten Niebuhr.” In Slot, *Kuwait*, 30–48.

Hajithomas, Joana, and Khalil Joreige. “On the Lebanese Rocket Society.” *e-flux journal*, no. 43 (March 2013). Accessed June 24, 2019. https://www.e-flux.com/journal/43/60187/on-the-lebanese-rocket-society/.

Hallett, L. E. “Other London Exhibitions: Henri Cartier Bresson, Adolf Morath (Member).” *The Photographic Journal* 97, no. 4 (1957): 65.

Halpern, Manfred. *The Politics of Social Change in the Middle East and North Africa*. Princeton: Princeton University Press, 1963.

Hammett, Daniel. "Envisaging the Nation: The Philatelic Iconography of Transforming South African National Narratives." *Geopolitics* 17, no. 3 (2012): 526–52.

Hanisch-Wolfram, Alexander. *Postalische Identitätskonstruktionen: Briefmarken als Medien totalitärer Propaganda*. Kommunikationswissenschaft und Publizistik 95. Frankfurt: Peter Lang, 2006.

Haraway, Donna. "Situated Knowledges: The Science Question in Feminism and the Privilege of Partial Perspective." *Feminist Studies* 14, no. 3 (1988): 575–99.

———. "Tentacular Thinking: Anthropocene, Capitalocene, Chthulucene." *e-flux journal*, no. 75 (September 2016). Accessed January 27, 2021. https://www.e-flux.com/journal/75/67125/tentacular-thinking-anthropocene-capitalocene-chthulucene/.

Harper, Douglas A. *Changing Works: Visions of a Lost Agriculture*. Chicago: University of Chicago Press, 2001.

Harrison, B. G. "The Postage Stamp." *Journal of the Royal Society of Arts* 88, no. 4562 (May 1940): 650–62.

Harvey, Penelope, and Hannah Knox, eds. *Roads: An Anthropology of Infrastructure and Expertise*. Ithaca: Cornell University Press, 2015.

Harvey, Penny, and Hannah Knox. "The Enchantments of Infrastructure." *Mobilities* 7, no. 4 (2012): 521–36.

Hazard, Harry W. "Islamic Philately as an Ancillary Discipline." In *The World of Islam: Studies in Honour of Philip K. Hitti*. Edited by James Kritzeck and Richard B. Winder, 199–232. Repr. ed. London: Macmillan, [1959] 1960.

Hein, Carola. "Oil Spaces: The Global Petroleumscape in the Rotterdam/The Hague Area." *Journal of Urban History* 44, no. 5 (2018): 887–929. https://doi.org/10.1177/0096144217752460.

"Here and There: Oil Survey in Iran." *Flight* 54, no. 2084 (December 1948): 652.

Hightower, Victoria. "Pearls and the Southern Persian/Arabian Gulf: A Lesson in Sustainability." *Environmental History* 18, no. 1 (2013): 44–59.

Hinchcliffe, Tanis. "'The Synoptic View': Aerial Photographs and Twentieth-Century Planning." In *Camera Constructs: Photography, Architecture and the Modern City*. Edited by Andrew Higgott and Timothy Wray, 135–46. Farnham: Ashgate, 2012.

Hindelang, Laura. "Photographing Crude in the Desert: Sight and Sense among Oilmen." In *The Life Worlds of Middle Eastern Oil*. Edited by Nelida Fuccaro and Mandana E. Limbert. Edinburgh: University of Edinburgh Press, forthcoming.

———. "Precious Property: Oil and Water in Twentieth-Century Kuwait." In *Oil Spaces: Exploring the Global Petroleumscape*. Edited by Carola Hein, 159–75. New York: Routledge, 2021. https://doi.org/10.4324/9780367816049-12.

———. "Oil Media: Changing Portraits of Petroleum in Visual Culture Between the US, Kuwait, and Switzerland." *Centaurus* 63, no. 4 (2021). doi:10.1111/1600-0498.12418.

Hobbs, Peter V., and Lawrence F. Radke. "Airborne Studies of the Smoke From the Kuwait Oil Fires." *Science* 256, no. 5059 (1992): 987–91.

Homer, William I. "Visual Culture: A New Paradigm." *American Art* 12, no. 1 (1998): 6–9.

"Humanism in Industrial Photography: Colour, and the 'Dynamic Moment.'" *Manchester Guardian*, January 28, 1957, n.p., reprint.

"Hunting Aerosurveys." *Flight* 51, no. 1994 (March 1947): 215–16.

Hurley, F. J. *Industry and the Photographic Image: 153 Great Prints from 1850 to the Present*. Rochester: George Eastman House, 1980. Published in conjunction with an exhibition at George Eastman House, Rochester, in 1976.

Hussain, Muayad H. "Modern Art from Kuwait: Khalifa Qattan and Circulism." PhD diss., University of Birmingham, 2012. Accessed January 21, 2021. https://etheses.bham.ac.uk/id/eprint/3909/1/Hussain_12_PhD_v1.pdf.

"Industry in Colour: An Exhibition by Adolf Morath." *British Journal of Photography*, February 15, 1957, n.p., reprint.

Ingham, Bruce. "Men's Dress in the Arabian Peninsula: Historical and Present Perspectives." In *Languages of Dress in the Middle East*. Edited by Nancy Lindisfarne-Tapper and Bruce Ingham, 40–54. Richmond: Curzon, 1997.

Ismael, Jacqueline S. *Kuwait: Dependency and Class in a Rentier State*. 2nd ed. Gainesville: University Press of Florida, [1982] 1993.

Jamal, Karim. "Kuwait: A Salutary Tale." *The Architects' Journal* 158, no. 50 (December 1973): 1452–57.

———. "Destruction of the Middle East?" *The Architects' Journal* 164, no. 30 (July 1976): 161–62.

Jamal, Mohamad A. H. *The Old Crafts, Trades, and Commercial Activities in Kuwait*. Kuwait: Center for Research and Studies on Kuwait, 2009.

Jeffery, Keith. "Crown, Communication and the Colonial Post: Stamps, the Monarchy and the British Empire." *The Journal of Imperial and Commonwealth History* 34, no. 1 (2006): 45–70. https://doi.org/10.1080/03086530500411290.

Johnson, Bob. *Mineral Rites: An Archaeology of the Fossil Economy*. Energy Humanities. Baltimore: Johns Hopkins University Press, 2019.

Jones, Peter. "Posting the Future: British Stamp Design and the 'White Heat' of a Technological Revolution." *Journal of Design History* 17, no. 2 (2004): 163–76.

Joyce, Miriam. *Kuwait, 1945–1996: An Anglo-American Perspective*. London: Frank Cass, 1998.

Kadoi, Yuka. "Postage Stamps in Islamic Art." *Grove Art Online*, July 2, 2009. Accessed January 31, 2021. https://doi.org/10.1093/gao/9781884446054.article.T2082293.

Kaika, Maria. "Dams as Symbols of Modernization: The Urbanization of Nature between Geographical Imagination and Materiality." *Annals of the Association of American Geographers* 96, no. 2 (2006): 276–301.

Karimi, Ali, and Frederick Kim. "On Protectorates and Consultanates: The Birth and Demise of Modernization in the Gulf States." In *Unsettling Colonial Modernity in Islamicate Contexts*. Edited by Siavash Saffari et al., 88–101. Newcastle-upon-Tyne: Cambridge Scholars, 2017.

Karimi, Pamela. *Domesticity and Consumer Culture in Iran: Interior Revolutions of the Modern Era*. London: Routledge, 2013.

Karl, Terry L. *The Paradox of Plenty: Oil Booms and Petro-States*. Studies in International Political Economy 26. Berkeley: University of California Press, 1997.

Khalaf, Sulayman. "The Evolution of the Gulf City: Type, Oil, and Globalization." In *Globalization and the Gulf*. Edited by John W. Fox, Nada Mourtada-Sabbah and Mohammed A. Mutawa, 244–65. London: Routledge, 2006.

Khalaf, Sulayman, and Hassan Hammoud. "The Emergence of the Oil Welfare State: The Case of Kuwait." *Dialectical Anthropology* 12, no. 3 (1987): 343–57.

Khatib, Lina. *Image Politics in the Middle East: The Role of the Visual in Political Struggle*. London: I. B. Tauris, 2013.

Kheirallah, George. *Arabia Reborn*. Albuquerque: University of New Mexico Press, 1952. Photographs by courtesy of ARAMCO.

Khouri, Kristine. "Mapping Arab Art through the Sultan Gallery." *ArteEast Quarterly*, Spring 2014. Accessed January 22, 2021. http://arteeast.org/quarterly/mapping-arab-art-through-the-sultan-gallery/.

Kingston, Paul W. T. *Britain and the Politics of Modernization in the Middle East: 1945–1958*. Cambridge Middle East Studies 4. Cambridge, UK: Cambridge University Press, 1996.

Kitson, William. "Kuwait's Distillation Plant for Domestic Water." *The Times Review of Industry and Technology*, December 1951, 22–23.

Klare, Michael T. "The Third Carbon Age." *Huffington Post*, August 8, 2013, updated December 6, 2017. Accessed January 27, 2021. https://www.huffingtonpost.com/michael-t-klare/renewable-energy_b_3725777.html.

Knöbl, Wolfgang. *Spielräume der Modernisierung: Das Ende der Eindeutigkeit*. Weilerswist: Velbrück Wissenschaft, 2001.

Köppel, Hans-Jürgen. *Politik auf Briefmarken: 130 Jahre Propaganda auf Postwertzeichen*. Düsseldorf: Droste, 1971.

Krawietz, Birgit. "The Sports Path Not Taken: Pearl Diving Heritage and Cosmopolitanism from Below." *Sport, Ethics and Philosophy* 14, no. 3 (2020): 1–14.

Krebs, Justus. "The Application of Aerial Geology and Aero-Photogrammetry in Petroleum Exploration." *Photogrammetria* 4, no. 2 (1941): 53–84.

Kurgan, Laura. *Close Up at a Distance: Mapping, Technology, and Politics*. New York: Zone Books, 2013.

Küttel, André. "50'300'000'000'000'000'000 Joule." In *Luca Zanier: Power Book*. Edited by Luca Zanier, 5–13. Bern: Benteli, 2012.

"Kuwait." In *The Grove Encyclopedia of Islamic Art and Architecture*. Edited by Jonathan Bloom and Sheila Blair. Vol. 2. Oxford, New York: Oxford University Press, 2009. Accessed February 2, 2021. https://www.oxfordreference.com/view/10.1093/acref/9780195309911.001.0001/acref-9780195309911-e-525?rskey=bSbVLs&result=1.

Kuwait National Council for Culture, Arts and Letters. *Mubarakiya School: 100 Years' History of Education in Kuwait*. Kuwait: Kuwait National Council for Culture, Arts and Letters, 2011.

Kuwait Oil Company. *The Story of Kuwait*. London: Kuwait Oil Company, ca. 1945.

———. *The Story of Kuwait*. London: Kuwait Oil Company, 1955.

———. *The Story of Kuwait*. London: Kuwait Oil Company, 1957.

Lance, Kate. *Alan Villiers: Voyager of the Winds*. London: National Maritime Museum, 2009.

Langford, Michael J. "Photography in Industry and Commerce." *Journal of the Royal Society of Arts* 109, no. 5061 (1961): 665–78.

Larkham, Peter, and Keith Lilley. "Exhibiting the City: Planning Ideas and Public Involvement in Wartime and Early Post-War Britain." *Town Planning Review* 83, no. 6 (2012): 647–68.

Larkham, Peter J. "Selling the Future City: Images in UK Post-War Reconstruction Plans." In Whyte, *Man-Made Future*, 98–120.

Larkham, Peter J., and Keith D. Lilley. "Plans, Planners and City Images: Place Promotion and Civic Boosterism in British Reconstruction Planning." *Urban History* 30, no. 2 (2003): 183–205.

Larkin, Brian. "The Politics and Poetics of Infrastructure." *Annual Review of Anthropology* 42 (2013): 327–43.

Latour, Bruno. *We Have Never Been Modern*. Cambridge, MA: Harvard University Press, 1993.

Lawless, Richard I., and Ian J. Seccombe. "Impact of the Oil Industry on Urbanization in the Persian Gulf Region." In *Urban Development in the Muslim World*. Edited by Hooshang Amirahmadi and Salah S. El-Shakhs, 183–212. New Brunswick: Rutgers University Press, 1993.

LeMenager, Stephanie. *Living Oil: Petroleum Culture in the American Century*. Oxford Studies in American Literary History. New York: Oxford University Press, 2014. https://doi.org/10.1093/acprof:oso/9780199899425.001.0001.

Lenssen, Anneka, Sarah Rogers, and Nada M. Shabout, eds. *Modern Art in the Arab World: Primary Documents*. New York, NY: Museum of Modern Art, 2017.

Lerner, Daniel. *The Passing of Traditional Society: Modernizing the Middle East*. New York: Free Press, 1958.

Leturcq, Jean-Gabriel. “Camera Arabia: An Introduction to the History of Photography in the Arab Peninsula.” Accessed December 4, 2017. https://leturcq.wordpress.com/2015/10/03/camera-arabia-1/#comments.

Levy, Marion J., Jr. “Some Sources of the Vulnerability of the Structures of Relatively Non-Industrialized Societies to Those of Highly Industrialized Societies.” In *The Progress of Underdeveloped Areas*. Edited by Bert F. Hoselitz, 113–25. Chicago: University of Chicago Press, 1952.

Lewcock, Ronald, and Zahra Freeth. *Traditional Architecture in Kuwait and the Northern Gulf*. Art and Archaeology Research Papers. London: United Bank of Kuwait, 1978.

Lienhardt, Peter. *Disorientations: A Society in Flux: Kuwait in the 1950s*. Reading: Ithaca Press, 1993. Edited by Ahmed Al-Shahi.

Lockhart, Laurence. “Outline of the History of Kuwait.” *Journal of the Royal Central Asian Society* 34, 3–4 (1947): 262–74.

Longrigg, Stephen. “The Economics and Politics of Oil in the Middle East.” *Journal of International Affairs* 19, 1 (special issue, The Arab World: Paths to Modernization) (1965): 111–22.

Lord Kinross. “The Richest State in the World.” *The Listener* December 11, 1952: 407–9.

Luciani, Giacomo. “Allocation vs. Production States: A Theoretical Framework.” In Beblawi; Luciani, *The Rentier State*, 63–82.

Macarthur, John. *The Picturesque: Architecture, Disgust and other Irregularities*. Abingdon: Routledge, 2008.

MacDonald, M. “Exhibition of Industrial Photographs: Brilliance of Works.” *The Glasgow Herald*, February 4, 1959, n.p., reprint.

Macfarlane, Peter W. “Planning Problems of Kuwait.” *Town and Country Planning* 19, no. 89 (September 1951): 414–17.

———. “Planning an Arab Town: Kuwait on the Persian Gulf.” *Journal of the Town Planning Institute* 40, no. 5 (April 1954): 110–13.

MacLean, Matthew. “Suburbanization, National Space and Place, and the Geography of Heritage in the UAE.” *Journal of Arabian Studies* 7, no. 2 (2017): 157–78.

Mahdavy, Hossein. “The Pattern and Problems of Economic Development in Rentier States.” In *Studies in the Economic History of the Middle East: From the Rise of Islam to the Present Day*. Edited by Michael A. Cook, 428–67. London: Oxford University Press, 1970.

Mahgoub, Yasser. “The Impact of the War on the Architecture of Kuwait.” *International Journal of Architectural Research* 2, no. 1 (2008): 232–46.

Malm, Andreas. “‘This Is the Hell That I Have Heard of’: Some Dialectical Images in Fossil Fuel Fiction.” *Forum for Modern Language Studies* 53, no. 2 (2017): 121–41. https://doi.org/10.1093/fmls/cqw090.

Maneval, Stefan. *New Islamic Urbanism: The Architecture of Public and Private Space in Jeddah, Saudi Arabia*. London: UCL Press, 2019.

Mansfield, Peter. *Kuwait: Vanguard of the Gulf*. London: Hutchinson, 1990.

Matz, Reinhard. *Industriefotografie: Aus Firmenarchiven des Ruhrgebiets*. Schriftreihe der Kulturstiftung Ruhr 2. Essen: Kulturstiftung Ruhr, 1987.

“Mawlid shāriʿ fī l-Kuwayt [Birth of a Street in Kuwait].” *al-ʿArabī*, no. 21 (August 1960): 79–84.

May, Jenny. “Obituary: Michael Langford.” *The Guardian*, May 25, 2000. Accessed January 30, 2021. https://www.theguardian.com/news/2000/may/25/guardianobituaries1.

McCauley, Elizabeth A. *Industrial Madness: Commercial Photography in Paris, 1848–1871*. Yale Publications in the History of Art. New Haven: Yale University Press, 1994.

Mehos, Donna, and Suzanne Moon. "The Uses of Portability: Circulating Experts in the Technopolitics of Cold War and Decolonization." In *Entangled Geographies: Empire and Technopolitics in the Global Cold War*. Edited by Gabrielle Hecht, 43–74. Cambridge, MA: MIT Press, 2011.

Melman, Billie. "The Middle East/Arabia: 'The Cradle of Islam.'" In *The Cambridge Companion to Travel Writing*. Edited by Peter Hulme and Tim Youngs, 105–21. Cambridge, UK: Cambridge University Press, 2002.

Menoret, Pascal. *Joyriding in Riyadh: Oil, Urbanism, and Road Revolt*. New York: Cambridge University Press, 2014.

Midgley, John. "Kuwait." *The Sphere*, June 16, 1956, 406–411.

Mielche, Hakon. *Lands of Aladdin*. London: William Hodge, 1955. Marginal drawings and colored photographs by the author.

Ministry of Energy, Electricity and Water. *Water and Electricity in the State of Kuwait*. Kuwait: Center for Research and Studies on Kuwait, 2005.

Minoprio, Anthony, Hugh Spencely, and Peter W. Macfarlane. "Planning Problems of Kuwait." *The Architect and Building News* 200, no. 4310 (July 1951): 104.

Minoprio, Charles A., Hugh G. C. Spencely, and Peter W. Macfarlane. "Plan for Kuwait." *Architectural Design* 27, 3 (special issue, Architecture in the Middle East, edited by Raglan Squire) (March 1957): 75.

Mirzoeff, Nicholas. "Visualizing the Anthropocene." *Public Culture* 26, no. 2 (2014): 213–32.

Mitchell, Timothy. "The Stage of Modernity." In *Questions of Modernity*. Edited by Timothy Mitchell, 1–34. Contradictions of Modernity. Minneapolis: University of Minnesota Press, 2000.

Monroe, Elizabeth. "The Shaikhdom of Kuwait." *International Affairs* 30, no. 3 (July 1954): 271–84.

Müller, Marion G. "Politologie und Ikonologie: Visuelle Interpretation als politologisches Verfahren." In Schwelling, *Politikwissenschaft als Kulturwissenschaft*, 335–49.

Nasr, Joe. "Saba Shiber, 'Mr. Arab Planner': Parcours professionnel d'un urbaniste au Moyen-Orient." *Géocarrefour* 80, no. 3 (2005): 197–206. https://doi.org/10.4000/geocarrefour.1175.

Neil Donaldson. "Arabica Bracadabra." *Gibbons Stamp Monthly* 1 (January 1970): 138–41.

Newhall, Beaumont. *Airborne Camera: The World from the Air and Outer Space*. New York: Hastings House, 1969.

Niebuhr, Carsten. *Beschreibung von Arabien: Aus eigenen Beobachtungen und im Lande selbst gesammleten Nachrichten abgefasset*. Copenhagen: Nicolaus Möller, 1772.

Nippa, Annegret, and Peter Herbstreuth. *Along the Gulf: From Basra to Muscat: Photographs by Hermann Burchardt*. Berlin: Hans Schiler, 2006.

Obojski, Robert. "A Philatelic Tour." *Saudi Aramco World* 34, no. 1 (1983). Accessed January 31, 2021. https://archive.aramcoworld.com/issue/198301/a.philatelic.tour.htm.

"Oil Stamps." *Saudi Aramco World* 13, no. 8 (1962). Accessed January 31, 2021. https://archive.aramcoworld.com/issue/196208/oil.stamps.htm.

"One of the Richest Cities in the World, Threatened by Iraqi Claims of Sovereignty: An Aerial View of Kuwait Town which Flourishes on Oil Revenues." *Illustrated London News*, July 8, 1961, 54–55.

Ormrod, Jane. "Response to 'What Is the Glue on the Back of Postage Stamps and Envelopes Made From?'" *The Guardian*, 2011. Accessed January 31, 2021. https://www.theguardian.com/notesandqueries/query/0,-1680,00.html.

Orton, Karen. "The Desert of the Unreal: Conversation with Fatima Al Qadiri and Sophia Al-Maria." *Dazed*, November 9, 2012. Accessed February 5, 2021. https://www.dazeddigital.com/artsandculture/article/15040/1/the-desert-of-the-unreal.

Owen, E. R. "One Hundred Years of Middle Eastern Oil." *Middle East Brief*, no. 24 (2008): 1–8. Accessed January 25, 2021. https://www.brandeis.edu/crown/publications/middle-east-briefs/pdfs/1-100/meb24.pdf.

Paine, Christ, and John Quigley. "Gulf War Oil Disaster." *Counterspill*. Accessed February 5, 2021. https://www.counterspill.org/disaster/gulf-war-oil-disaster#timeline.

Pelly, Lewis. *Report on a Journey to Riyadh in Central Arabia (1865)*. Repr. ed. Cambridge: Oleander, [1866] 1978.

Pelt, Mary C. van. "The Sheikdom of Kuwait." *Middle East Journal* 4, no 1 (January 1950): 12–26.

Pendakis, Andrew. "Being and Oil: Or, How to Run a Pipeline through Heidegger." In Wilson; Carlson; Szeman, *Petrocultures*, 377–88.

Pendakis, Andrew, and Sheena Wilson. "Sight, Site, Cite: Oil in the Field of Vision." *Imaginations: Journal of Cross-Cultural Image Studies* 3, no. 2 (2012): 4–5.

Perry, Clarence A. *The Neighborhood Unit: Neighborhood and Community Planning; Regional Plan of New York and its Environs*. New York: Regional Plan Association, 1929.

Peterson, J. E. "Britain and the Gulf: At the Periphery of Empire." In Potter, *The Persian Gulf in History*, 277–93.

Petroleum Information Bureau. *The Philatelist's Story of Oil*. London: Petroleum Information Bureau, 1960.

"Pictures of Power." *The Birmingham Post & Gazette*, January 29, 1957, 4.

Piper, Karen L. *Cartographic Fictions: Maps, Race, and Identity*. New Brunswick: Rutgers University Press, 2002.

Plattner, Steven W., ed. *The Standard Oil (New Jersey) Photography Project*. Austin: University of Texas Press, 1983; published in conjunction with the exhibition *Roy Stryker: U.S.A, 1943–1950* presented at the International Center of Photography, New York.

Potter, Lawrence G. "Introduction." In Potter, *The Persian Gulf in History*, 1–24.

———, ed. *The Persian Gulf in History*. New York: Palgrave Macmillan, 2009.

Purvis, Stewart. "The Media and the Gulf War." *RSA Journal* 139, no.5423 (1991): 735–44.

Pyla, Panayiota I., ed. *Landscapes of Development: The Impact of Modernization Discourses on the Physical Environment of the Eastern Mediterranean*. Cambridge: The Aga Khan Program at the Harvard University Graduate School of Design, 2013.

Rajab, Tareq S. *Glimpses from the Recent Past, Kuwait 1960–65*. Kuwait: Tareq Rajab Museum, 1999.

———. *Tareq Sayid Rajab and the Development of Fine Art in Kuwait*. Kuwait: Tareq Rajab Museum, 2001.

———. *Glimpses from the Recent Past: Kuwait 1960–1980*. Kuwait: Tareq Rajab Museum, 2005.

———. *Glimpses from Kuwait 60–06*. Kuwait: Tareq Rajab Museum, 2007.

"Ramzi Kayello: Artist's Website, Documents." Accessed January 25, 2021. http://www.ramzikayelloartscapes.com/documents/CentralOfficeInterviewStamps.pdf.

Raulff, Ulrich. "Der aufhaltsame Aufstieg einer Idee: Warburg und die Vernuft der Republik." In *Wilde Energien: Vier Versuche zu Aby Warburg*. Edited by Ulrich Raulff, 72–116. Göttinger Gespräche zur Geschichtswissenschaft 19. Göttingen: Wallstein, 2003.

Raunkiær, Barclay. *Through Wahhabiland on Camelback (1913)*. New York: Frederick A. Praeger, 1969. Introduction by Gerald de Gaury.

Redman, James C. A. "The *Diwaniyya*: Guestroom Sociability and Bureaucratic Brokerage in Kuwait." PhD diss., University of Utah, 2014. Accessed January 31, 2021. https://core.ac.uk/download/pdf/276264928.pdf.

Reid, Donald M. "The Symbolism of Postage Stamps: A Source for the Historian." *Journal of Contemporary History* 19, no. 2 (April 1984): 223–49.

———. "The Postage Stamp: A Window on Saddam Hussein's Iraq." *Middle East Journal* 47, no. 1 (1993): 77–89.

Reißig, Rolf. "Transformation – ein spezifischer Typ sozialen Wandels: Ein analytischer und sozialtheoretischer Entwurf." In *Futuring: Perspektiven der Transformation im Kapitalismus über ihn hinaus*. Edited by Michael Brie, 50–100. Münster: Westfälisches Dampfboot, 2014.

Reyna, Stephen P., and Andrea Behrends. "The Crazy Curse and Crude Domination: Towards an Anthropology of Oil." In *Crude Domination: An Anthropology of Oil*. Edited by Andrea Behrends, Stephen P. Reyna, and Günther Schlee, 3–29. New York: Berghahn, 2011.

Riad, Mohamed. "Some Aspects of Petro-Urbanism in the Arab Gulf States." *Bulletin of the Faculty of Humanities and Social Sciences*, no. 4 (1981): 7–24.

Ritchie, Hannah. "Kuwait: Energy Country Profile." *Our World in Data*. Accessed January 30, 2021. https://ourworldindata.org/energy/country/kuwait?country=~KWT#citation.

Ritter, E. "Nachruf: Krebs, Justus." *Verhandlungen der Schweizerischen Naturforschenden* 193 (1959): 427–32.

Ross, Andrew. "The Ecology of Images." In *Visual Culture: Images and Interpretations*. Edited by Norman Bryson, Michael A. Holly, and Keith P. F. Moxey, 325–346. Hanover: Wesleyan University Press, 1994.

Rostow, Walt W. *The Stages of Economic Growth: A Non-Communist Manifesto*. Cambridge, UK: Cambridge University Press, 1960.

Ryzova, Lucie. "Nostalgia for the Modern: Archive Fever in Egypt in the Age of Post-Photography." In *Photo Archives and the Idea of Nation*. Edited by Costanza Caraffa and Tiziana Serena, 301–18. Berlin: De Gruyter, 2015.

Sadiq, Muhammad, and John C. McCain. *The Gulf War Aftermath: An Environmental Tragedy*. Environment & Assessment 4. Dordrecht: Kluwer Academic, 1993.

Salgado, Sebastião, and Lélia W. Salgado. *Kuwait: A Desert on Fire*. Cologne: Taschen, 2016.

Sanger, Richard H. *The Arabian Peninsula*. Ithaca: Cornell University Press, 1954. Photographs by courtesy of ARAMCO, California Texas Oil and Gulf Oil.

Scarlett, Frank. "The Application of Air Photography to Architecture and Town Planning." *Journal of the Royal Institute of British Architects* 53, no. 8 (1946): 319–23.

"Scenes from Oil Industry in London Exhibition." *The Birmingham Post & Gazette*, January 28, 1957, 7.

Scheiwiller, Staci G., ed. *Performing the Iranian State: Visual Culture and Representations of Iranian Identity*. London: Anthem, 2013.

Schermerhorn, Willem. "Planning in Modern Aerial Survey." *Photogrammetria* 17, no. 1 (1960): 7–17.

Schneider, Laurie. "Leon Battista Alberti: Some Biographical Implications of the Winged Eye." *The Art Bulletin* 72, no. 2 (1990): 261–70.

Schuessler, Raymond. "Petrophilately." *Saudi Aramco World* 39, no. 1 (1988). Accessed January 31, 2021. https://archive.aramcoworld.com/issue/198801/petrophilately.htm.

Schwelling, Birgit, ed. *Politikwissenschaft als Kulturwissenschaft: Theorien, Methoden, Problemstellungen*. Wiesbaden: VS Verlag für Sozialwissenschaften, 2004.

Scott, James C. *Seeing Like a State: How Certain Schemes to Improve the Human Condition Have Failed*. New Haven: Yale University Press, 1998.

Segal, Eran. "Merchants' Networks in Kuwait: The Story of Yusuf al-Marzuk." *Middle Eastern Studies* 45, no. 5 (2009): 709–19.

Sharples, Joseph, ed. *Charles Reilly & the Liverpool School of Architecture 1904–1933*. Liverpool: Liverpool University Press, 1996; exhibition catalog.

———. "Reilly and His Students, on Merseyside and Beyond." In *Charles Reilly & the Liverpool School of Architecture 1904–1933*. Edited by Joseph Sharples, 25–42. Liverpool: Liverpool University Press, 1996.

Shenon, Philip. "A New Divide for Kuwaitis: Who Stayed and Who Fled." *The New York Times*, March 12, 1991, 13. Accessed January 18, 2021. https://www.nytimes.com/1991/03/12/world/after-the-war-kuwaiti-politics-a-new-divide-for-kuwaitis-who-stayed-and-who-fled.html.

Shiber, Saba G. *The Kuwait Urbanization: Being an Urbanistic Case-Study of a Developing Country; Documentation, Analysis, Critique*. Kuwait: Kuwait Government Printing Press, 1964.

———. "Kuwait: A Case Study." In *From Madina to Metropolis: Heritage and Change in the Near Eastern City*. Edited by L. C. Brown, 168–93. Princeton Studies on the Near East. Princeton: Darwin, 1973.

Shouse, Ben. "Kuwait Unveils Plan to Treat Festering Desert Wound." *Science* 293, no. 5534 (2001): 1410.

Shuhaiber, Suhail. "Social and Political Developments in Kuwait Prior to 1961." In Slot, *Kuwait*, 95–110.

Sivan, Emmanuel. "The Arab Nation-State: In Search of a Usable Past." *Middle East Review* 19, no. 3 (1987): 21–30.

Slot, Ben J. *The Origins of Kuwait*. Leiden: Brill, 1991.

———, ed. *Kuwait: The Growth of a Historic Identity*. London: Arabian Publishing, 2003.

———. *Mubarak Al-Sabah: Founder of Modern Kuwait 1896–1915*. London: Arabian Publishing, 2005.

Smith, Simon C. "'A Vulnerable Point in the Sterling Area': Kuwait in the 1950s." *Contemporary British History* 17, no. 4 (2003): 25–42. https://doi.org/10.1080/13619460308565456.

———. "Power Transferred? Britain, the United States, and the Gulf, 1956–1971." *Contemporary British History* 21, no. 1 (2007): 1–23.

———. "Britain's Decision to Withdraw from the Persian Gulf: A Pattern Not a Puzzle." *The Journal of Imperial and Commonwealth History* 44, no. 2 (2016): 328–51.

"Smoke from a Distant Fire." *Nasa Earth Observatory*, July 8, 2011. Accessed January 18, 2021. https://earthobservatory.nasa.gov/features/ShuttleRetrospective/page8.php.

Smolarski, Pierre, René Smolarski, and Silke Vetter-Schultheiss, eds. *Gezähnte Geschichte: Die Briefmarke als historische Quelle*. Post-Wert-Zeichen 1. Göttingen: V&R Unipress, 2019.

Sontag, Susan. "The Image-World." In *On Photography*. Edited by Susan Sontag, 119–41. Repr. ed. New York: Rosetta Books, [1977] 2005.

Southwell, C. A. Philip. "Kuwait." *Journal of the Royal Society of Arts* 102, no. 4914 (1953): 24–41.

"Specialist Princes: New Variants of Percival Feederliner for Survey and Military Training." *Flight* 56, no. 2128 (October 1949): 476–77.

"Stamp News in Brief: British Commonwealth." *Gibbons' Stamp Monthly* 32 (February 1958): 71.

State of Kuwait, Central Statistical Bureau. "Statistical Review 2014." Kuwait, 2014.

Steininger, Benjamin. "Refinery and Catalysis." In *Textures of the Anthropocene: Grain, Vapor, Ray*. Edited by Katrin Klingan et al., 108–18. Cambridge, MA: MIT Press; Berlin: Revolver 2015.

Stocqueler, Joachim H. *Fifteen Months' Pilgrimage Through Untrodden Tracts of Khuzistan and Persia: In a Journey from India to England, through Parts of Turkish Arabia, Persia, Armenia, Russia, and Germany; Performed in the Years 1831 and 1832*. London: Saunders & Otley, 1832.

Stürken, Alfred. "Reisebriefe aus dem Persischen Golf und Persien." *Mitteilungen der Geographischen Gesellschaft in Hamburg* 22 (1907): 69–124.

Sultan, Ghazi. "Kuwait." *The Architects' Journal* 160, no. 40 (October 1974): 792–94.

"Sweet Talk: A Conversation with Thuraya Al-Baqsami and Monira Al Qadiri." *Bidoun*, [2018]. Accessed February 5, 2021. https://www.bidoun.org/articles/sweet-talk.

Symes, Peter. "Gulf Rupees: A History." *Islamic Banknotes*. Accessed January 31, 2021. https://web.archive.org/web/20030630072004/http://www.islamicbanknotes.com/gulfrupees%20(article).htm.

Szeman, Imre. "The Cultural Politics of Oil: On *Lessons of Darkness* and *Black Sea Files*." *Polygraph*, no. 22 (2010): 33–45.

———. "Crude Aesthetics: The Politics of Oil Documentaries." *Journal of American Studies* 46, no. 2 (2012): 423–39.

———. "Introduction to Focus: Petrofictions." *American Book Review* 33, no. 3 (2012): 3.

Szeman, Imre, and Maria Whiteman. "Oil Imaginaries: Critical Realism and the Oil Sands." *Imaginations: Journal of Cross-Cultural Image Studies* 3, no. 2 (2012): 46–67.

Tétreault, Mary A. "Kuwait: The Morning After." *Current History* 91, no. 561 (1992): 6–10.

"The Allure of Oil and the Threat to Independence: Tension in Kuwait." *Illustrated London News*, July 8, 1961, 40–41.

"The Fabulously Rich Oilfield of Kuwait: Aspects New and Old of the Tiny State." *Illustrated London News*, December 22, 1951, 1030–31.

"The Mysterious Land of Kuwait." *Picture Post*, July 13, 1946, 13–15; photographs by N. Tim Gidal.

"The News in Pictures." *The Sphere* July 8, 1961: 43.

"The Philatelist's Story of Oil." *Stamp Collecting*, July 23, 1954, 611–15.

"The Snapshot Schoolboy Is Now a Top Photographer." *The Bulletin*, February 4, 1959, n.p., reprint.

"The Survey Prince." *Flight* 57, no. 2146 (February 1950): 196–97.

"The World's Largest Single Oilfield: Kuwait and Its Fabulously Rich Ruler." *Illustrated London News*, June 30, 1951, 1061–62.

"Threatened by Iraq but Supported by the Other Arab Countries: Oil-Rich Kuwait and Its Ruler." *Illustrated London News*, July 8, 1961, 1.

Trench, Richard, ed. *Arab Gulf Cities: Kuwait City.* Vol. 4. Cambridge, UK: Archive Editions, 1994.

Tucker, Ernest. "Lockhart, Laurence." *Encyclopædia Iranica Online*, May 24, 2013. Accessed January 30, 2021. http://www.iranicaonline.org/articles/lockhart-laurence.

Tyagi, Ila. "Spatial Survey: Mapping Alaskan Oilfield Infrastructures Using Drones." *Synoptique* 8, no. 1 (2018): 32–44.

Vali, Murtaza. *Crude*. Dubai: Art Jameel, 2019. Exhibition catalog published in conjunction with the exhibition of the same name, shown at Jameel Arts Centre, Dubai, from November 11, 2018, until March 30, 2019.

Venturi, Robert, Denise Scott Brown, and Steven Izenour. *Learning from Las Vegas*. Cambridge, MA: MIT Press, 1972.

Vidler, Anthony. "Photourbanism: Planning the City from Above and from Below." In Bridge; Watson, *The New Blackwell Companion to the City*, 656–66.

Villiers, Alan. *Sons of Sindbad: An Account of Sailing with the Arabs in Their Dhows, in the Red Sea, round the Coasts of Arabia, and to Zanzibar and Tanganyika; Pearling in the Persian Gulf; and the Life of the Shipmasters and the Mariners of Kuwait*. Rev. ed. London: Arabian Publishing, [1940] 2006.

———. *Sons of Sindbad: The Photographs*. London: National Maritime Museum, 2006.

Wald, Matthew L. "Sebastiao Salgado: The Eye of The Photojournalist." *The New York Times*, June 9, 1991. Accessed February 5, 2021. https://www.nytimes.com/1991/06/09/magazine/sebastiao-salgado-the-eye-of-the-photojournalist.html.

Walton, Frank. *The De La Rue Collection*. 6 vols. London: The Royal Philatelic Society London, 2014.

Warburg, Aby. "Die Funktion des Briefmarkenbildes im Geistesverkehr der Welt (1927)." In *Aby Warburg: Bilderreihen und Ausstellungen*. Edited by Uwe Fleckner and Isabella Woldt, 150–89. Aby Warburg Gesammelte Schriften 2.2. Berlin: Akademie Verlag, 2011.

Ward, Stephan V. "Transnational Planners in a Postcolonial World." In *Crossing Borders: International Exchange and Planning Practices*. Edited by Patsy Healey and Robert Upton, 47–72. London: Routledge, 2010.

Warnke, Martin. "Politische Ikonographie: Hinweise auf eine sichtbare Politik." In *Wozu Politikwissenschaft? Über das Neue in der Politik*. Edited by Claus Leggewie, 170–78. Darmstadt: Wissenschaftliche Buchgesellschaft, 1994.

Watts, Michael, and Ed Kashi. "Oil City: Petro-Landscapes and Sustainable Futures." In *Ecological Urbanism*. Edited by Mohsen Mostafavi and Gareth Doherty, 420–30. Baden: Lars Müller, 2010.

Wedeen, Lisa. *Ambiguities of Domination: Politics, Rhetoric, and Symbols in Contemporary Syria*. Rev. ed. Chicago: University of Chicago Press, [1999] 2015.

Weizman, Eyal, and Fazal Sheikh. *The Conflict Shoreline: Colonization as Climate Change in the Negev Desert*. Göttingen: Steidl, 2015.

Whittle, Jack. "The Use of Air Photographs: Examination and Interpretation." In *Town and Country Planning Textbook: An Indispensable Book for Town Planners, Architects and Students*. Edited by Association for Planning and Regional Reconstruction, 560–65. London: Architectural Press, 1950.

Whyte, Iain B., ed. *Man-Made Future: Planning, Education and Design in Mid-Twentieth Century Britain*. Milton Park: Routledge, 2007.

Williams, Keith. "Commercial Aviation in Arab States: The Pattern of Control." *Middle East Journal* 11, no. 2 (1957): 123–38.

Wilson, Arnold T. *The Persian Gulf: An Historical Sketch from the Earliest Times to the Beginning of the 20th Century*. Rev. ed. Westport: Hyperion, [1928] 1981.

Wilson, Sheena. "Energy Imaginaries: Feminist and Decolonial Futures." In *Materialism and the Critique of Energy*. Edited by Brent R. Bellamy and Jeff Diamanti, 377–412. Chicago: MCM, 2018.

Wilson, Sheena, Adam Carlson, and Imre Szeman, eds. *Petrocultures: Oil, Politics, Culture*. Montreal: McGill-Queen's University Press, 2017.

Wilson, Sheena, Imre Szeman, and Adam Carlson. "On Petrocultures: Or, Why We Need to Understand Oil to Understand Everything Else." In Wilson; Carlson; Szeman, *Petrocultures*, 3–19.

Wippel, Steffen, Katrin Bromber, Christian Steiner, and Birgit Krawietz, eds. *Under Construction: Logics of Urbanism in the Gulf Region*. Farnham: Ashgate, 2014.

Worden, Daniel. "Fossil-Fuel Futurity: Oil in *Giant*." *Journal of American Studies* 46, no. 2 (2012): 441–60.

Zahlan, Rosemarie S. *The Making of the Modern Gulf States: Kuwait, Bahrain, Qatar, the United Arab Emirates and Oman*. London: Unwin Hyman, 1989.

Zardini, Mirko. "Homage to Asphalt." *Log*, no. 15 (2009): 8–15.

IMAGE CREDITS

Fig. 1.1 Image courtesy of Monira Al Qadiri.

Fig. 2.1 Image courtesy of Barjeel Art Foundation.

Fig. 2.2 Image courtesy of Khaled Alabdulmughni.

Fig 2.3 Image courtesy of Ali AlRais.

Fig. 2.4 Image courtesy of Mathaf: Arab Museum of Modern Art, Doha, MAT.2007.1.2225.

Fig. 3.1 Middle East Centre Archive, St Antony's College, Oxford. GB165-0085, Harold Dickson Collection, album 2, no. 202.

Fig. 3.2 *Flight* magazine, March 7, 1952, cover. Courtesy of Flight Global.

Fig. 3.3 Courtesy of the Municipality of Kuwait.

Fig. 3.4 Courtesy of the Municipality of Kuwait.

Fig. 3.5 *Flight*, June 22, 1944, 30. Courtesy of Flight Global.

Fig. 3.6 *Flight*, October 18, 1945, 26. Courtesy of Flight Global.

Fig. 3.7 *Flight*, December 6, 1945, 30. Courtesy of Flight Global.

Fig. 3.8 British Postal Agency, Kuwait: Post Office accommodation, part 1, POST 122/1061, The Postal Museum. © Royal Mail Group (2021). Courtesy of The Postal Museum.

Fig. 3.9 Stephen Gardiner, *Kuwait: The Making of a City* (Burnt Mill: Longman, 1983), 41.

Fig. 3.10 "The Mysterious Land of Kuwait," *Picture Post*, July 13, 1946, 14. © 2021 Getty Images.

Fig. 3.11 "The World's Largest Single Oilfield: Kuwait and Its Fabulously Rich Ruler," *Illustrated London News*, June 30, 1951, 1061. © Illustrated London News Ltd/Mary Evans.

Fig. 3.12 Peter W. Macfarlane, "Planning Problems of Kuwait," *Town and Country Planning* 19, no. 89 (September 1951): 414–15. Courtesy of *Town and Country Planning.*

Fig. 3.13 Peter W. Macfarlane, "Planning an Arab Town: Kuwait on the Persian Gulf," *Journal of the Town Planning Institute* 40, no. 5 (April 1954): 110–11. Courtesy of *The Planner.*

Fig. 3.14 "The Fabulously Rich Oilfield of Kuwait: Aspects New and Old of the Tiny State," *Illustrated London News*, December 22, 1951, 1030–31. © Illustrated London News Ltd/Mary Evans.

Fig. 3.15 Laura Kurgan, *Close Up at a Distance: Mapping, Technology, and Politics* (New York: Zone Books, 2013), 87.

Fig. 3.16 29°20'58.61" N 47°59'39.98" E, Eye alt 22.53 km. Data SIO, NOAA, U.S. Navy, NGA, GEBCO. Image © 2021 TerraMetrics. Image © 2021 Maxar Technologies.

Fig. 4.1 Kuwait Oil Company, *The Story of Kuwait* (London: Kuwait Oil Company, ca. 1945), title page. BP Archive, University of Warwick, 107800.

Fig. 4.2 "The Mysterious Land of Kuwait," *Picture Post*, July 13, 1946, 14. © 2021 Getty Images.

Fig. 4.3 Hakon Mielche, *Lands of Aladdin* (London: William Hodge, 1955), 188. Collection of the author, photograph by the author.

https://doi.org/10.1515/9783110714739-011

Fig. 4.4 Kuwait Oil Company, *The Story of Kuwait* (London: Kuwait Oil Company, 1955), frontispiece and table of contents. BP Archive, University of Warwick, 106882.

Fig. 4.5 Kuwait Oil Company, *The Story of Kuwait* (London: Kuwait Oil Company, 1955), 46–47. BP Archive, University of Warwick, 106882.

Fig. 4.6 Kuwait Oil Company, *The Story of Kuwait* (London: Kuwait Oil Company, 1955), 58–59. BP Archive, University of Warwick, 106882.

Fig. 4.7 Kuwait Oil Company, *The Story of Kuwait* (London: Kuwait Oil Company, 1957), 58–59. BP Archive, University of Warwick, 30821.

Fig. 4.8 Kuwait Oil Company, *The Story of Kuwait* (London: Kuwait Oil Company, 1957), 68–69. BP Archive, University of Warwick, 30821.

Fig. 4.9 Kuwait Oil Company, *The Story of Kuwait* (London: Kuwait Oil Company, 1957), 76. BP Archive, University of Warwick, 30821.

Fig. 4.10 Kuwait Oil Company Limited: Photographs, March 1958, volume 18 (large), image 7. BP Archive, University of Warwick, 107047.

Fig. 4.11 Kuwait Oil Company Limited: Photographs, April 1956, volume 4 (large), image 8. BP Archive, University of Warwick, 107027.

Fig. 4.12 Kuwait Oil Company Limited: Photographs, April 1956, volume 4 (large), image 4. BP Archive, University of Warwick, 107027.

Fig. 4.13 "Al-ʿImāra bi-l-Kuwayt" [Architecture in Kuwait], *al-ʿArabī*, no. 13 (December 1959): 71–72. Courtesy of *al-ʿArabī* magazine.

Fig. 4.14 "Al-ʿImāra bi-l-Kuwayt" [Architecture in Kuwait], *al-ʿArabī*, no. 13 (December 1959): 67–68. Courtesy of *al-ʿArabī* magazine.

Fig. 4.15 Courtesy of Ziad Rajab.

Fig. 4.16 Kuwait Oil Company Limited: Colour Photographs 1 to 21, April 1956, image 14. BP Archive, University of Warwick, 107049.

Fig. 4.17 Kuwait Oil Company Limited: Photographs, April 1960, volume 23, image 19. BP Archive, University of Warwick, 107058.

Fig. 4.18 "Mawlid shāriʿ fī l-Kuwayt" [Birth of a Street in Kuwait], *al-ʿArabī*, no. 21 (August 1960): 79. Courtesy of *al-ʿArabī* magazine.

Fig. 4.19 Kuwait Oil Company Limited: Photographs, March 1958, volume 15 (large), image 11. BP Archive, University of Warwick, 107042.

Fig. 5.1 Photograph taken by the author, February 2018.

Fig. 5.2 Collection of the author, photograph by the author.

Fig. 5.3 Kuwait Oil Company, Ahmadi. Photographic Archive, image no. PR9330.

Fig. 5.4 Khaled Al Najdi and Rosalie Smith McCrea, "The History of Advertising Design in Kuwait: Post-Oil Cultural Shifts 1947–1959," *Journal of Design History* 25, no. 1 (2012): 63, fig. 6. Collection of Jamal Al-Refaie, Kuwait. Courtesy of Khaled Al Najdi.

Fig. 5.5 Collection of the author, photograph by the author.

Fig. 5.6 Collection of the author, photograph by the author.

Fig. 5.7 Collection of the author, photograph by the author.

Fig. 5.8 Image courtesy of Ali AlRais.

Fig. 5.9 Kuwait Oil Company Limited: Photographs, March 1958, volume 18 (large), image 6. BP Archive, University of Warwick, 107047.

Fig. 5.10 Image courtesy of Khaled Alabdulmughni.

Fig. 5.11 Courtesy of the Kuwait Ministry of Energy, Electricity and Water.

Fig. 5.12 Kuwait Oil Company, Photographic Archive, Ahmadi, image no. PR10194.

Fig. 5.13 Image courtesy of Khaled Alabdulmughni.

Fig. 5.14 Image courtesy of Ali AlRais.

Fig. 5.15 Image courtesy of Farjam Khajehee.

Fig. 5.16 Collection of the author, photograph by the author.

Fig. 5.17 Image courtesy of Farjam Khajehee.

Fig. 5.18 Kuwait Oil Company Limited: Photographs, January 1949, volume 2, image 12. BP Archive, University of Warwick, ARC107069.

Fig. 5.19 Image courtesy of Sanaz Sohrabi.

Fig. 5.20a Collection of the author, photograph by the author.

Fig. 5.20b Collection of the author, photograph by the author.

Fig. 5.21 Elizabeth Monroe, "The Shaikdom of Kuwait," *International Affairs* 30, no. 3 (July 1954): 272. © The Economist Group Limited, London (2021).

Fig. 5.22 Collection of the author, photograph by the author.

Fig. 5.23 Image courtesy of Artprecium, Paris and Millon, Paris.

Fig. 5.24 Collection of the author, photograph by the author.

Fig. 5.25 "Al-Kuwayt fī l-maʿāriḍ al-duwaliyya. Baʿḍa āyām tashtariku fī maʿriḍ mīlānū al-ʿālamī" (Kuwait at the International Exhibitions: In a Few Days It Is Participating in Milan's International Exhibition), *al-ʿArabī*, no. 65 (April 1964): 106–7. Courtesy of *al-ʿArabī* magazine.

Fig. 6.1 STS037-152-091 Oil Well Fires and Smoke, Kuwait, April 1991, photograph taken by NASA, April 7, 1991. Accessed February 7, 2021, https://eol.jsc.nasa.gov/SearchPhotos/photo.pl?mission=STS037&roll=152&frame=91.

Fig. 6.2 FreeKuwait.org, accessed May 25, 2021, http://freekuwait.org.kw/photos.php?page=116904_Hat-and-Mug.

Fig. 6.3 Photograph taken by the author, February 2016.

Fig. 6.4 © Sebastião Salgado.

Fig. 6.5 Photographs of His Highness Sheikh Jabir al Sabah at the Ceremony to Celebrate the First Loading of Oil in Kuwait, 1946, image 4. BP Archive, University of Warwick, ARC108103.

Fig. 6.6 Courtesy of KUNA News Agency, Kuwait.

Fig. 6.7 Collection of the author, photograph by the author.

Fig. 7.1 Madinat al-Hareer, website of Tamdeen Group, Kuwait. Accessed September 9, 2021, https://www.tamdeen.com/portfolio/madinat-al-hareer.

Fig. 7.2 Courtesy of the Aseel AlYaqoub, photo courtesy of Mohamad Chehimi.

Fig. 7.3 Courtesy of the Aseel AlYaqoub, photo courtesy of Mohamad Chehimi.

Fig. 7.4 Image courtesy of Mohammed Al Kouh.

Fig. 7.5 Image courtesy of Mohammed Al Kouh.

Fig. 7.6 Image courtesy of Monira Al Qadiri.

Fig. 7.7 Image courtesy of Monira Al Qadiri.

Fig. 7.8 Photograph taken by the author, January 2016.

Fig. 7.9 Photograph taken by the author, February 2016.